THE POEMS OF
LONGFELLOW

THE POEMS OF

LONGFELLOW

INCLUDING

EVANGELINE

THE SONG OF HIAWATHA

THE COURTSHIP OF
MILES STANDISH

TALES OF A WAYSIDE INN

THE
MODERN LIBRARY
NEW YORK

Random House IS THE PUBLISHER OF

THE MODERN LIBRARY

BENNETT A. CERF · DONALD S. KLOPFER · ROBERT K. HAAS

Manufactured in the United States of America

Printed by Parkway Printing Company   Bound by H. Wolff

CONTENTS

CONTENTS

EVANGELINE

A Tale of Acadie

THIS is the forest primeval. The murmuring pines and the hemlocks,

Bearded with moss, and in garments green, indistinct in the twilight,

Stand like Druids of old,[1] with voices sad and prophetic,

Stand like harpers hoar, with beards that rest on their bosoms.

Loud from its rocky caverns, the deep-voiced neighboring ocean

Speaks, and in accents disconsolate answers the wail of the forest.

This is the forest primeval; but where are the hearts that beneath it

Leaped like the roe, when he hears in the woodland the voice of the huntsman?

Where is the thatch-roofed village, the home of Acadian farmers,—

Men whose lives glided on like rivers that water the woodlands,

Darkened by shadows of earth, but reflecting an image of heaven?

Waste are those pleasant farms, and the farmers forever departed!

Scattered like dust and leaves, when the mighty blasts of October

[1] *Druids.*—An ancient order of priests, chiefly in Great Britain, whose sacred rites were performed mostly in forests. Some of these were also bards.

Seize them, and whirl them aloft, and sprinkle them far o'er
the ocean.
Naught but tradition remains of the beautiful village of
Grand-Pré.

Ye who believe in affection that hopes, and endures, and is
patient,
Ye who believe in the beauty and strength of woman's devotion,
List to the mournful tradition still sung by the pines of the
forest;
List to a Tale of Love in Acadie, home of the happy.

PART THE FIRST

I

IN the Acadian land, on the shores of the Basin of Minas,
Distant, secluded, still, the little village of Grand-Pré
Lay in the fruitful valley.[1] Vast meadows stretched to the
eastward,
Giving the village its name, and pasture to flocks without
number.
Dikes, that the hands of the farmers had raised with labor
incessant,
Shut out the turbulent tides; but at stated seasons the flood-
gates
Opened, and welcomed the sea to wander at will o'er the
meadows.
West and south there were fields of flax, and orchards and
cornfields
Spreading afar and unfenced o'er the plain; and away to the
northward
Blomidon rose, and the forests old, and aloft on the mountains

[1] "Hunting and fishing gave way to agriculture, which had been
established in the marshes and lowlands, by repelling, with dikes, the
sea and rivers which covered these plains. At the same time these
immense meadows were covered with numerous flocks."—*Haliburton.*

Sea-fogs pitched their tents, and mists from the mighty
    Atlantic
Looked on the happy valley, but ne'er from their station
    descended.
There, in the midst of its farms, reposed the Acadian village.
Strongly built were the houses, with frames of oak and of
    chestnut,
Such as the peasants of Normandy built in the reign of the
    Henries.
Thatched were the roofs, with dormer-windows; and gables
    projecting
Over the basement below protected and shaded the door-way.
There in the tranquil evenings of summer, when brightly the
    sunset
Lighted the village street, and gilded the vanes on the
    chimneys,
Matrons and maidens sat in snow-white caps and in kirtles
Scarlet and blue and green, with distaffs spinning the golden
Flax for the gossiping looms, whose noisy shuttles within
    doors
Mingled their sound with the whir of the wheels and the
    songs of the maidens.
Solemnly down the street came the parish priest, and the
    children
Paused in their play to kiss the hand he extended to bless
    them.
Reverend walked he among them; and up rose matrons and
    maidens,
Hailing his slow approach with words of affectionate welcome.
Then came the laborers home from the field, and serenely
    the sun sank
Down to his rest, and twilight prevailed. Anon from the
    belfry
Softly the Angelus [1] sounded, and over the roofs of the village
Columns of pale blue smoke, like clouds of incense ascending,
Rose from a hundred hearths, the homes of peace and con-
    tentment.

[1] *Angelus.*—The ringing of the church bell, calling to prayer. The
celebrated picture of "The Angelus," by J. F. Millet, has given an
added interest to the subject.

Thus dwelt together in love these simple Acadian farmers,—
Dwelt in the love of God and of man. Alike were they free
from
Fear, that reigns with the tyrant, and envy, the vice of re-
publics.
Neither locks had they to their doors, nor bars to their
windows;
But their dwellings were open as day and the hearts of the
owners;
There the richest was poor, and the poorest lived in abundance.[1]

Somewhat apart from the village, and nearer the Basin of
Minas,
Benedict Bellefontaine, the wealthiest farmer of Grand-Pré,
Dwelt on his goodly acres; and with him, directing his house-
hold,
Gentle Evangeline lived, his child, and the pride of the village.
Stalworth and stately in form was the man of seventy
winters;
Hearty and hale was he, an oak that is covered with snow-
flakes;
White as the snow were his locks, and his cheeks as brown as
the oak-leaves.
Fair was she to behold, that maiden of seventeen summers.
Black were her eyes as the berry that grows on the thorn by
the wayside,
Black, yet how softly they gleamed beneath the brown shade
of her tresses!
Sweet was her breath as the breath of kine that feed in the
meadows.
When in the harvest heat she bore to the reapers at noontide
Flagons of home-brewed ale, ah! fair in sooth was the
maiden.
Fairer was she when, on Sunday morn, while the bell from
its turret

---

[1] "Real misery was wholly unknown, and benevolence anticipated
the demands of poverty. Every misfortune was relieved, as it were,
before it could be felt, without ostentation on the one hand, and
without meanness on the other. It was, in short, a society of brethren."
—*Abbé Reynal.*

Sprinkled with holy sounds the air, as the priest with his
    hyssop
Sprinkles the congregation, and scatters blessings upon them.
Down the long street she passed, with her chaplet of beads
    and her missal,
Wearing her Norman cap, and her kirtle of blue, and the
    earrings,
Brought in the olden time from France, and since, as an
    heirloom,
Handed down from mother to child, through long genera-
    tions.
But a celestial brightness—a more ethereal beauty—
Shone on her face and encircled her form, when, after con-
    fession,
Homeward serenely she walked with God's benediction upon
    her.
When she had passed, it seemed like the ceasing of exquisite
    music.

    Firmly builded with rafters of oak, the house of the farmer
Stood on the side of a hill commanding the sea; and a shady
Sycamore grew by the door, with a woodbine wreathing
    around it.
Rudely carved was the porch, with seats beneath; and a
    footpath
Led through an orchard wide, and disappeared in the meadow
Under the Sycamore-tree were hives overhung by a pent-
    house,
Such as the traveller sees in regions remote by the roadside,
Built o'er a box for the poor, or the blessed image of Mary.
Farther down, on the slope of the hill, was the well with its
    moss-grown
Bucket, fastened with iron, and near it a trough for the
    horses.
Shielding the house from storms, on the north, were the
    barns and the farmyard.
There stood the broad-wheeled wains and the antique ploughs
    and the harrows;
There were the folds for the sheep; and there, in his feathered
    seraglio,

Strutted the lordly turkey, and crowed the cock, with the selfsame
Voice that in ages of old had startled the penitent Peter.
Bursting with hay were the barns, themselves a village. In each one
Far o'er the gable projected a roof of thatch; and a staircase,
Under the sheltering eaves, led up to the odorous corn-loft.
There too the dove-cot stood, with its meek and innocent inmates
Murmuring ever of love; while above in the variant breezes
Numberless noisy weathercocks rattled and sang of mutation.

Thus, at peace with God and the world, the farmer of Grand-Pré
Lived on his sunny farm, and Evangeline governed his household.
Many a youth, as he knelt in the church and opened his missal,
Fixed his eyes upon her, as the saint of his deepest devotion;
Happy was he who might touch her hand or the hem of her garment!
Many a suitor came to her door, by the darkness befriended,
And as he knocked and waited to hear the sound of her footsteps,
Knew not which beat the louder, his heart or the knocker of iron;
Or at the joyous feast of the Patron Saint of the village,
Bolder grew, and pressed her hand in the dance as he whispered
Hurried words of love, that seemed a part of the music.
But, among all who came, young Gabriel only was welcome;
Gabriel Lajeunesse, the son of Basil the blacksmith,
Who was a mighty man in the village, and honored of all men;
For since the birth of time, throughout all ages and nations,
Has the craft of the smith been held in repute by the people.
Basil was Benedict's friend. Their children from earliest childhood
Grew up together as brother and sister; and Father Felician,

Priest and pedagogue both in the village, had taught them
  their letters
Out of the selfsame book, with the hymns of the church and
  the plain-song.
But when the hymn was sung, and the daily lesson completed,
Swiftly they hurried away to the forge of Basil the black-
  smith.
There at the door they stood, with wondering eyes to behold
  him
Take in his leathern lap the hoof of the horse as a plaything,
Nailing the shoe in its place; while near him the tire of the
  cartwheel
Lay like a fiery snake, coiled round in a circle of cinders.
Oft on autumnal eves, when without in the gathering dark-
  ness
Bursting with light seemed the smithy, through every cranny
  and crevice,
Warm by the forge within they watched the laboring bellows,
And as its panting ceased, and the sparks expired in the ashes,
Merrily laughed, and said they were nuns going into the
  chapel.
Oft on sledges in winter, as swift as the swoop of the eagle,
Down the hillside bounding, they glided away o'er the
  meadow.
Oft in the barns they climbed to the populous nests on the
  rafters,
Seeking with eager eyes that wondrous stone, which the
  swallow
Brings from the shore of the sea to restore the sight of its
  fledglings;
Lucky was he who found that stone in the nest of the
  swallow!
Thus passed a few swift years, and they no longer were
  children.
He was a valiant youth, and his face, like the face of the
  morning,
Gladdened the earth with its light, and ripened thought into
  action.
She was a woman now, with the heart and hopes of a woman.

"Sunshine of Saint Eulalie" [1] was she called; for that was the sunshine
Which, as the farmers believed, would load their orchards with apples;
She, too, would bring to her husband's house delight and abundance,
Filling it full of love and the ruddy faces of children.

II

Now had the season returned, when the nights grow colder and longer,
And the retreating sun the sign of the Scorpion [2] enters.
Birds of passage sailed through the leaden air from the ice-bound,
Desolate northern bays to the shores of tropical islands.
Harvests were gathered in; and wild with the winds of September
Wrestled the trees of the forest, as Jacob of old with the angel.
All the signs foretold a winter long and inclement.
Bees, with prophetic instinct of want, had hoarded their honey
Till the hives overflowed; and the Indian hunters asserted
Cold would the winter be, for thick was the fur of the foxes.
Such was the advent of autumn. Then followed that beautiful season,
Called by the pious Acadian peasants the Summer of All-Saints!
Filled was the air with a dreamy and magical light; and the landscape
Lay as if new-created in all the freshness of childhood.
Peace seemed to reign upon earth, and the restless heart of the ocean
Was for a moment consoled. All sounds were in harmony blended.

---

[1] *Eulalie*—The name is derived from the Greek and means "Fair Speech."

[2] *Sign of the Scorpion.*—The eighth sign of the zodiac. The sun enters this the latter part of October.

Voices of children at play, the crowing of cocks in the farm-
    yards,
Whir of wings in the drowsy air, and the cooing of pigeons,
All were subdued and low as the murmurs of love, and the
    great sun
Looked with the eye of love through the golden vapors around
    him;
While arrayed in its robes of russet and scarlet and yellow,
Bright with the sheen of the dew, each glittering tree of the
    forest
Flashed like the plane-tree the Persian adorned with mantles
    and jewels.[1]

Now recommenced the reign of rest and affection and
    stillness.
Day with its burden and heat had departed, and twilight
    descending
Brought back the evening star to the sky, and the herds to
    the homestead.
Pawing the ground they came, and resting their necks on each
    other,
And with their nostrils distended inhaling the freshness of
    evening.
Foremost, bearing the bell, Evangeline's beautiful heifer,
Proud of her snow-white hide, and the ribbon that waved
    from her collar,
Quietly paced and slow, as if conscious of human affection.
Then came the shepherd back with his bleating flock from
    the seaside,
Where was their favorite pasture. Behind them followed the
    watch-dog,
Patient, full of importance, and grand in the pride of his
    instinct,
Walking from side to side with a lordly air, and superbly
Waving his bushy tail, and urging forward the stragglers;
Regent of flocks was he when the shepherd slept; their pro-
    tector

[1] Xerxes saw in Asia Minor a plane-tree, and was so impressed
with its beauty that he decorated it with jewels.

When from the forest at night, through the starry silence the
    wolves howled.
Late, with the rising moon, returned the wains from the
    marshes,
Laden with briny hay, that filled the air with its odor.
Cheerily neighed the steeds, with dew on their manes and
    their fetlocks,
While aloft on their shoulders the wooden and ponderous
    saddles,
Painted with brilliant dyes, and adorned with tassels of
    crimson,
Nodded in bright array, like hollyhocks heavy with blossoms.
Patiently stood the cows meanwhile, and yielded their udders
Unto the milkmaid's hand; whilst loud and in regular ca-
    dence
Into the sounding pails the foaming streamlets descended.
Lowing of cattle and peals of laughter were heard in the farm-
    yard,
Echoed back by the barns. Anon they sank into stillness;
Heavily closed, with a jarring sound, the valves of the barn-
    doors,
Rattled the wooden bars, and all for a season was silent.

    Indoors, warm by the wide-mouthed fireplace, idly the
    farmer
Sat in his elbow-chair, and watched how the flames and the
    smoke-wreaths
Struggled together like foes in a burning city. Behind him,
Nodding and mocking along the wall, with gestures fantastic,
Darted his own huge shadow, and vanished away into dark-
    ness.
Faces, clumsily carved in oak, on the back of his arm-chair
Laughed in the flickering light, and the pewter plates on the
    dresser
Caught and reflected the flame, as shields of armies the
    sunshine.
Fragments of song the old man sang, and carols of Christmas,
Such as at home, in the olden time, his fathers before him
Sang in their Norman orchards and bright Burgundian vine-
    yards.

Close at her father's side was the gentle Evangeline seated,
Spinning flax for the loom, that stood in the corner behind
her.
Silent awhile were its treadles, at rest was its diligent shuttle,
While the monotonous drone of the wheel, like the drone of a
bagpipe,
Followed the old man's song, and united the fragments to-
gether.
As in a church, when the chant of the choir at intervals
ceases,
Footfalls are heard in the aisles, or words of the priest at
the altar,
So, in each pause of the song, with measured motion the clock
clicked.

Thus as they sat, there were footsteps heard, and, suddenly
lifted,
Sounded the wooden latch, and the door swung back on its
hinges.
Benedict knew by the hob-nailed shoes it was Basil the black-
smith,
And by her beating heart Evangeline knew who was with him.
"Welcome!" the farmer exclaimed, as their footsteps paused
on the threshold,
"Welcome, Basil, my friend! Come, take thy place on the
settle
Close by the chimney-side, which is always empty without
thee;
Take from the shelf overhead thy pipe and the box of
tobacco;
Never so much thyself art thou as when through the curling
Smoke of the pipe or the forge thy friendly and jovial face
gleams
Round and red as the harvest moon through the mist of the
marshes."
Then, with a smile of content, thus answered Basil the black-
smith,
Taking with easy air the accustomed seat by the fireside:—
"Benedict Bellefontaine, thou hast ever thy jest and thy
ballad!

Ever in cheerfullest mood art thou, when others are filled
with
Gloomy forebodings of ill, and see only ruin before them.
Happy art thou, as if every day thou hadst picked up a horse-
shoe."

Pausing a moment, to take the pipe that Evangeline brought
him,
And with a coal from the embers had lighted, he slowly
continued:—

"Four days now are passed since the English ships at their
anchors
Ride in the Gaspereau's mouth, with their cannon pointed
against us.
What their design may be is unknown; but all are com-
manded
On the morrow to meet in the church, where his Majesty's
mandate
Will be proclaimed as law in the land. Alas! in the mean time
Many surmises of evil alarm the hearts of the people."

Then made answer the farmer:—"Perhaps some friendlier
purpose
Brings these ships to our shores. Perhaps the harvests in
England
By the untimely rains or untimelier heat have been blighted,
And from our bursting barns they would feed their cattle and
children."

"Not so thinketh the folk in the village," said, warmly, the
blacksmith,
Shaking his head, as in doubt; then, heaving a sigh, he continued:—

"Louisburg [1] is not forgotten, nor Beau Séjour, nor Port
Royal. [2]

Many already have fled to the forest, and lurk on its outskirts,

[1] *Louisburg.*—A village on Cape Breton which was, in 1758, cap-
tured by the British and utterly destroyed.

[2] *Port Royal.*—An abbey of the Jansenists situated near Paris—Port
Royal des Champs. In 1709 the nuns refused to subscribe to the papal
decree against Jansen and were scattered and imprisoned, and the
buildings were entirely destroyed.

Waiting with anxious hearts the dubious fate of to-morrow.
Arms have been taken from us, and warlike weapons of all
    kinds;
Nothing is left but the blacksmith's sledge and the scythe of
    the mower."
Then with a pleasant smile made answer the jovial farmer:—
"Safer are we unarmed, in the midst of our flocks and our
    cornfields,
Safer within these peaceful dikes, besieged by the ocean,
Than were our fathers in forts, besieged by the enemy's
    cannon.
Fear no evil, my friend, and to-night may no shadow of
    sorrow
Fall on this house and hearth; for this is the night of the
    contract.
Built are the house and the barn.[1] The merry lads of the
    village
Strongly have built them and well; and, breaking the glebe
    round about them,
Filled the barn with hay, and the house with food for a
    twelvemonth.
René Leblanc [2] will be here anon, with his papers and ink-
    horn.
Shall we not then be glad, and rejoice in the joy of our
    children?"
As apart by the window she stood, with her hand in her
    lover's,
Blushing Evangeline heard the words that her father had
    spoken,
And as they died on his lips the worthy notary entered.

[1] "As soon as a young man arrived at the proper age, the commu-
nity built him a house, broke up the land about it, and supplied him
with all the necessaries of life for a twelvemonth. There he received
the partner whom he had chosen, and who brought him her portion
in flocks."—*Abbé Reynal.*

[2] "René Leblanc (our public notary) was taken prisoner by the
Indians when actually traveleing in your Majesty's service, his house
pillaged, and himself carried to the Frence fort, from whence he did
not recover his liberty, but with great difficulty, after four years'
captivity."—*Petition of the Acadians to the King.*

III

Bent like a laboring oar, that toils in the surf of the ocean,
Bent, but not broken, by age was the form of the notary
    public;
Shocks of yellow hair, like the silken floss of the maize, hung
Over his shoulders; his forehead was high; and glasses with
    horn-bows
Sat astride on his nose, with a look of wisdom supernal.
Father of twenty children was he, and more than a hundred
Children's children rode on his knee, and heard his great
    watch tick.
Four long years in the times of the war had he languished a
    captive,
Suffering much in an old French fort as the friend of the
    English.
Now, though warier grown, without all guile or suspicion,
Ripe in wisdom was he, but patient, and simple, and child-
    like.
He was beloved by all, and most of all by the children;
For he told them tales of the Loup-garou [1] in the forest,
And of the goblin that came in the night to water the horses,
And of the white Létiche, the ghost of a child who un-
    christened
Died, and was doomed to haunt unseen the chambers of
    children;
And how on Christmas eve the oxen talked in the stable.
And how the fever was cured by a spider shut up in a nut-
    shell,
And of the marvellous powers of four-leaved clover and horse
    shoes,
With whatsoever else was writ in the lore of the village.
Then up rose from his seat by the fireside Basil the black-
    smith,
Knocked from his pipe the ashes, and slowly extending his
    right hand,
"Father Leblanc," he exclaimed, "thou hast heard the talk in
    the village,

---

[1] *Loup-garoo.*—The were-wolf, a human being transformed into a
wolf.

And, perchance, canst tell us some news of these ships and
    their errand."
Then with modest demeanor made answer the notary pub-
    lic,—
"Gossip enough have I heard, in sooth, yet am never the
    wiser;
And what their errand may be I know not better than others,
Yet I am not of those who imagine some evil intention
Brings them here, for we are at peace; and why then molest
    us!"
"God's name!" shouted the hasty and somewhat irascible
    blacksmith;
"Must we in all things look for the how, and the why, and the
    wherefore?
Daily injustice is done, and might is the right of the
    strongest!"
But, without heeding his warmth, continued the notary
    public,—
"Man is unjust, but God is just; and finally justice
Triumphs; and well I remember a story, that often consoled
    me,
When as a captive I lay in the old French Fort at Port
    Royal."
This was the old man's favorite tale, and he loved to repeat it
When his neighbors complained that any injustice was done
    them.
"Once in an ancient city, whose name I no longer remember,
Raised aloft on a column, a brazen statue of justice
Stood in the public square, upholding the scales in its left
    hand,
And in its right a sword, as an emblem that justice presided
Over the laws of the land, and the hearts and homes of the
    people.
Even the birds had built their nests in the scales of the
    balance,
Having no fear of the sword that flashed in the sunshine
    above them.
But in the course of time the laws of the land were corrupted;
Might took the place of right, and the weak were oppressed,
    and the mighty

Ruled with an iron rod. Then it chanced in a nobleman's
    palace
That a necklace of pearls was lost, and ere long a suspicion
Fell on an orphan girl who lived as maid in the household.
She, after form of trial condemned to die on the scaffold,
Patiently met her doom at the foot of the statue of Justice.
As to her Father in heaven her innocent spirit ascended,
Lo! o'er the city a tempest rose; and the bolts of the
    thunder
Smote the statue of bronze, and hurled in wrath from its left
    hand
Down on the pavement below the clattering scales of the
    balance,
And in the hollow thereof was found the nest of a magpie,
Into whose clay-built walls the necklace of pearls was in-
    woven."
Silenced, but not convinced, when the story was ended, the
    blacksmith
Stood like a man who fain would speak, but findeth no
    language;
All his thoughts were congealed into lines on his face, as the
    vapors
Freeze in fantastic shapes on the window-panes in the winter.

Then Evangeline lighted the brazen lamp on the table,
Filled, till it overflowed, the pewter tankard with home-
    brewed
Nut-brown ale, that was famed for its strength in the village
    of Grand-Pré;
While from his pocket the notary drew his papers and ink-
    horn,
Wrote with a steady hand the date and the age of the parties,
Naming the dower of the bride in flocks of sheep and in
    cattle.
Orderly all things proceeded, and duly and well were com-
    pleted,
And the great seal of the law was set like a sun on the margin.
Then from his leathern pouch the farmer threw on the table
Three times the old man's fee in solid pieces of silver;

And the notary rising, and blessing the bride and the bride-
groom,
Lifted aloft the tankard of ale and drank to their welfare.
Wiping the foam from his lip, he solemnly bowed and de-
parted,
While in silence the others sat and mused by the fireside,
Till Evangeline brought the draught-board out of its corner.
Soon was the game begun. In friendly contention the old men
Laughed at each lucky hit, or unsuccessful manœuvre,
Laughed when a man was crowned, or a breach was made
in the king-row.
Meanwhile apart, in the twilight gloom of a window's em-
brasure,
Sat the lovers, and whispered together, beholding the moon
rise
Over the pallid sea and the silvery mist of the meadows.
Silently, one by one, in the infinite meadows of heaven,
Blossomed the lovely stars, the forget-me-nots of the angels.

Thus passed the evening away. Anon the bell from the
belfry
Rang out the hour of nine, the village curfew,[1] and straight-
way
Rose the guests and departed; and silence reigned in the
household.
Many a farewell word and sweet good-night on the door-step
Lingered long in Evangeline's heart, and filled it with glad-
ness.
Carefully then were covered the embers that glowed on the
hearth-stone,
And on the oaken stairs resounded the tread of the farmer.
Soon with a soundless step the foot of Evangeline followed.
Up the staircase moved a luminous space in the darkness,
Lighted less by the lamp than the shining face of the maiden.
Silent she passed through the hall, and entered the door of
her chamber.
Simple that chamber was, with its curtains of white, and its
clothes-press

[1] *The Curfew.*—The signal to extinguish all lights and retire.

Ample and high, on whose spacious shelves were carefully
folded
Linen and woollen stuffs, by the hand of Evangeline woven.
This was the precious dower she would bring to her husband
in marriage,
Better than flocks and herds, being proofs of her skill as a
housewife.
Soon she extinguished her lamp, for the mellow and radiant
moonlight
Streamed through the windows and lighted the room, till the
heart of the maiden
Swelled and obeyed its power, like the tremulous tides of
the ocean.
Ah! she was fair, exceeding fair to behold, as she stood with
Naked snow-white feet on the gleaming floor of her chamber!
Little she dreamed that below, among the trees of the
orchard,
Waited her lover and watched for the gleam of her lamp and
her shadow.
Yet were her thoughts of him, and at times a feeling of
sadness
Passed o'er her soul, as the sailing shade of clouds in the
moonlight
Flitted across the floor and darkened the room for a moment.
And as she gazed from the window she saw serenely the moon
pass
Forth from the folds of a cloud, and one star follow her
footsteps,
As out of Abraham's tent young Ishmael wandered with
Hagar!

IV

Pleasantly rose next morn the sun on the village of Grand-
Pré.
Pleasantly gleamed in the soft, sweet air the Basin of Minas,
Where the ships, with their wavering shadows, were riding at
anchor.
Life had long been astir in the village, and clamorous labor
Knocked with its hundred hands at the golden gates of the
morning.

Now from the country around, from the farms and the neigh-
    boring hamlets,
Came in their holiday dresses the blithe Acadian peasants.
Many a glad good-morrow and jocund laugh from the young
    folk
Made the bright air brighter, as up from the numerous
    meadows,
Where no path could be seen but the track of wheels in the
    greensward,
Group after group appeared, and joined, or passed on the
    highway.
Long ere noon, in the village all sounds of labor were silenced.
Thronged were the streets with people; and noisy groups at
    the house-doors
Sat in the cheerful sun, and rejoiced and gossiped together.
Every house was an inn, where all were welcomed and
    feasted;
For with this simple people, who lived like brothers together,
All things were held in common, and what one had was an-
    other's.
Yet under Benedict's roof hospitality seemed more abundant:
For Evangeline stood among the guests of her father;
Bright was her face with smiles, and words of welcome and
    gladness
Fell from her beautiful lips, and blessed the cup as she
    gave it.

    Under the open sky, in the odorous air of the orchard,
Bending with golden fruit, was spread the feast of betrothal.
There in the shade of the porch were the priest and the
    notary seated;
There good Benedict sat, and sturdy Basil the blacksmith.
Not far withdrawn from these, by the cider-press and the
    bee-hives,
Michael the fiddler was placed, with the gayest of hearts and
    of waistcoats.
Shadow and light from the leaves alternately played on his
    snow-white
Hair, as it waved in the wind, and the jolly face of the fiddler

Glowed like a living coal when the ashes are blown from the
      embers.
Gayly the old man sang to the vibrant sound of his fiddle,
Tous les Bourgeois de Chartres, and *Le Carillon de Dun-
      kerque,*[1]
And anon with his wooden shoes beat time to the music.
Merrily, merrily whirled the wheels of the dizzying dances
Under the orchard-trees and down the path to the meadows;
Old folk and young together, and children mingled among
      them.
Fairest of all the maids was Evangeline, Benedict's daughter!
Noblest of all the youths was Gabriel, son of the blacksmith!

So passed the morning away. And lo! with a summons
      sonorous
Sounded the bell from its tower, and over the meadows a
      drum beat.
Thronged ere long was the church with men. Without, in the
      churchyard,
Waited the women. They stood by the graves, and hung on
      the headstones
Garlands of autumn leaves and evergreens fresh from the
      forest.
Then came the guard from the ships, and marching proudly
      among them
Entered the sacred portal. With loud and dissonant clangor
Echoed the sound of their brazen drums from ceiling and
      casement,—
Echoed a moment only, and slowly the ponderous portal
Closed, and in silence the crowd awaited the will of the
      soldiers.
Then up rose their commander, and spake from the steps of
      the altar,
Holding aloft in his hands, with its seals, the royal com-
      mission,
"You are convened this day," he said, "by his Majesty's
      orders.

[1] Translated: "All citizens of Chartres," and "The Chimes of
Dunkerque." The latter is the French spelling for Dunkirk.

"Down with the tyrants of England! we never have sworn
        them allegiance!
Death to these foreign soldiers, who seize on our homes and
        our harvests!"
More he fain would have said, but the merciless hand of a
        soldier
Smote him upon the mouth, and dragged him down to the
        pavement.

In the midst of the strife and tumult of angry contention,
Lo! the door of the chancel opened, and Father Felician
Entered, with serious mien, and ascended the steps of the
        altar.
Raising his reverend hand, with a gesture he awed into
        silence
All that clamorous throng; and thus he spake to his people;
Deep were his tones and solemn; in accents measured and
        mournful
Spake he, as, after the tocsin's alarum, distinctly the clock
        strikes.
"What is this that ye do, my children? what madness has
        seized you?
Forty years of my life have I labored among you, and taught
        you,
Not in word alone, but in deed, to love one another!
Is this the fruits of my toils, of my vigils and prayers and
        privations?
Have you so soon forgotten all lessons of love and forgive-
        ness?
This is the house of the Prince of Peace, and would you pro-
        fane it
Thus with violent deeds and hearts overflowing with hatred?
Lo! where the crucified Christ from his cross is gazing upon
        you!
See! in those sorrowful eyes what meekness and holy com-
        passion!
Hark! how those lips still repeat the prayer, 'O Father, for-
        give them!'
Let us repeat that prayer in the hour when the wicked assail
        us,

Clement and kind has he been; but how you have answe
    his kindness,
Let your own hearts reply! To my natural make and n
    temper
Painful the task is I do, which to you I know must b
    grievous.
Yet must I bow and obey, and deliver the will of our
    monarch;
Namely, that all your lands, and dwellings, and cattle of all
    kinds
Forfeited be to the crown; and that you yourselves from
    this province
Be transported to other lands. God grant you may dwell there
Ever as faithful subjects, a happy and peaceable people!
Prisoners now I declare you; for such is his Majesty's
    pleasure!"
As, when the air is serene in the sultry solstice of summer,
Suddenly gathers a storm, and the deadly sling of the hail-
    stones
Beats down the farmer's corn in the field and shatters his
    windows,
Hiding the sun, and strewing the ground with thatch from the
    house-roofs,
Bellowing fly the herds, and seek to break their inclosures,
So on the hearts of the people descended the words of the
    speaker.
Silent a moment they stood in speechless wonder, and then
    rose
Louder and ever louder a wail of sorrow and anger,
And, by one impulse moved, they madly rushed to the door-
    way.
Vain was the hope of escape; and cries and fierce impreca-
    tions
Rang through the house of prayer; and high o'er the heads
    of the others
Rose, with his arms uplifted, the figure of Basil the black-
    smith,
As, on a stormy sea, a spar is tossed by billows.
Flushed was his face and distorted with passion; and wildly
    he shouted,—

Let us repeat it now, and say, 'O Father, forgive them!' "
Few were his words of rebuke, but deep in the hearts of his
    people
Sank they, and sobs of contrition succeeded that passionate
    outbreak;
And they repeated his prayer, and said, "O Father, forgive
    them!"

Then came the evening service. The tapers gleamed from
    the altar.
Fervent and deep was the voice of the priest, and the people
    responded,
Not with their lips alone, but their hearts; and the Ave Maria
Sang they, and fell on their knees, and their souls, with devo-
    tion translated,
Rose on the ardor of prayer, like Elijah ascending to heaven.

Meanwhile had spread in the village the tidings of ill, and
    on all sides
Wandered, wailing, from house to house the women and
    children.
Long at her father's door Evangeline stood, with her right
    hand
Shielding her eyes from the level rays of the sun, that, de-
    scending,
Lighted the village street with mysterious splendor, and
    roofed each
Peasant's cottage with golden thatch, and emblazoned its
    windows.
Long within had been spread the snow-white cloth on the
    table;
There stood the wheaten loaf, and the honey fragrant with
    wild flowers;
There stood the tankard of ale, and the cheese fresh brought
    from the dairy,
And at the head of the board the great armchair of the
    farmer.
Thus did Evangeline wait at her father's door, as the sunset
Threw the long shadows of trees o'er the broad ambrosial
    meadows,

And on her spirit within a deeper shadow had fallen,
And from the fields of her soul a fragrance celestial ascended,—
Charity, meekness, love, and hope, and forgiveness, and patience!
Then, all-forgetful of self, she wandered into the village,
Cheering with looks and words the disconsolate hearts of the women
As o'er the darkening fields with lingering steps they departed,
Urged by their household cares, and the weary feet of their children.
Down sank the great red sun, and in golden, glimmering vapor
Veiled the light of his face, like the Prophet descending from Sinai.
Sweetly over the village the bell of the Angelus sounded.

Meanwhile, amid the gloom, by the church Evangeline lingered.
All was silent within; and in vain at the door and the windows
Stood she, and listened and looked, until, overcome by emotion
"Gabriel!" cried she aloud with tremulous voice; but no answer
Came from the graves of the dead, nor the gloomier grave of the living.
Slowly at length she returned to the tenantless house of her father.
Smouldered the fire on the hearth, on the board stood the supper untasted,
Empty and drear was each room, and haunted with phantoms of terror,
Sadly echoed her step on the stair and the floor of her chamber.
In the dead of the night she heard the whispering rain fall
Loud on the withered leaves of the Sycamore-tree by the window.

Keenly the lightning flashed; and the voice of the echoing
    thunder
Told her that God was in heaven, and governed the world he
    created!
Then she remembered the tale she had heard of the justice of
    heaven;
Soothed was her troubled soul, and she peacefully slumbered
    till morning.

V

Four times the sun had risen and set; and now on the fifth
    day
Cheerily called the cock to the sleeping maids of the farm-
    house.
Soon o'er the yellow fields, in silent and mournful procession,
Came from the neighboring hamlets and farms the Acadian
    women,
Driving in ponderous wains their household goods to the
    seashore,
Pausing and looking back to gaze once more on their
    dwellings,
Ere they were shut from sight by the winding road and the
    woodland.
Close at their sides their children ran, and urged on the oxen,
While in their little hands they clasped some fragments of
    playthings.

Thus to the Gaspereau's mouth they hurried; there on the
    sea-beach
Piled in confusion lay the household goods of the peasants.
All day long between the shore and the ships did the boats
    ply;
All day long the wains came laboring down from the village.
Late in the afternoon, when the sun was near to his setting,
Echoing far o'er the fields came the roll of drums from the
    churchyard.
Thither the women and children thronged. On a sudden the
    church-doors

Opened, and forth came the guard, and marching in gloomy
    procession
Followed the long-prisoned, but patient Acadian farmers.
Even as pilgrims, who journey afar from their homes and
    their country,
Sing as they go, and in singing forget they are weary and
    wayworn,
So with songs on their lips the Acadian peasants descended
Down from the church to the shore, amid their wives and
    their daughters.
Foremost the young men came; and, raising together their
    voices,
Sang they with tremulous lips a chant of the Catholic Mis-
    sions:—
"Sacred heart of the Saviour! O inexhaustible fountain!
Fill our hearts this day with strength and submission and
    patience!"
Then the old men, as they marched, and the women that
    stood by the wayside
Joined in the sacred psalm, and the birds in the sunshine
    above them
Mingled their notes therewith, like voices of spirits departed.

Half-way down to the shore Evangeline waited in silence,
Not overcome with grief, but strong in the hour of afflic-
    tion,—
Calmly and sadly waited, until the procession approached
    her,
And she beheld the face of Gabriel pale with emotion.
Tears then filled her eyes, and eagerly running to meet him,
Clasped she his hands, and laid her head on his shoulder, and
    whispered,—
"Gabriel! be of good cheer! for if we love one another,
Nothing, in truth, can harm us, whatever mischances may
    happen!"
Smiling she spake these words; then suddenly paused, for her
    father
Saw she slowly advancing. Alas! how changed was his aspect!
Gone was the glow from his cheek, and the fire from his eye,
    and his footstep

Heavier seemed with the weight of the weary heart in his
    bosom.
But with a smile and a sigh, she clasped his neck and em-
    braced him,
Speaking words of endearment where words of comfort
    availed not.
Thus to the Gaspereau's mouth moved on that mournful
    procession.

  There disorder prevailed, and the tumult and stir of
    embarking.
Busily plied the freighted boats; and in the confusion
Wives were torn from their husbands, and mothers, too late,
    saw their children [1]
Left on the land, extending their arms, with wildest en-
    treaties.
So unto separate ships were Basil and Gabriel carried,
While in despair on the shore Evangeline stood with her
    father.
Half the task was not done when the sun went down, and
    the twilight
Deepened and darkened around; and in haste the refluent
    ocean
Fled away from the shore, and left the line of the sand-beach
Covered with waifs of the tide, with kelp and the slippery
    sea-weed.
Farther back in the midst of the household goods and the
    wagons,
Like a gypsy camp, or a leaguer after a battle,
All escape cut off by the sea, and the sentinels near them,
Lay encamped for the night the houseless Acadian farmers.
Back to its nethermost caves retreated the bellowing ocean,
Dragging adown the beach the rattling pebbles, and leaving

[1] "Parents were separated from children, and husbands from wives,
some of whom have not to this day met again; and we were so
crowded in the transport vessels, that we had not room even for all
our bodies to lay down at once, and consequently, were prevented
from carrying with us proper necessaries, especially for the support
and comfort of the aged and weak, many of whom quickly
ended their misery with their lives."—*Petition of the Acadians to
the King.*

Inland and far up the shore the stranded boats of the sailors.
Then, as the night descended, the herds returned from their
　　pastures;
Sweet was the moist still air with the odor of milk from their
　　udders;
Lowing they waited, and long, at the well-known bars of the
　　farmyard,—
Waited and looked in vain for the voice and the hand of the
　　milkmaid.
Silence reigned in the streets; from the church no Angelus
　　sounded,
Rose no smoke from the roofs, and gleamed no lights from
　　the windows.

But on the shores meanwhile the evening fires had been
　　kindled,
Built of the drift-wood thrown on the sands from wrecks in
　　the tempest.
Round them shapes of gloom and sorrowful faces were
　　gathered,
Voices of women were heard, and of men, and the crying of
　　children.
Onward from fire to fire, as from hearth to hearth in his
　　parish,
Wandered the faithful priest, consoling and blessing and
　　cheering,
Like unto shipwrecked Paul on Melita's desolate seashore.
Thus he approached the place where Evangeline sat with
　　her father,
And in the flickering light beheld the face of the old man,
Haggard and hollow and wan, and without either thought or
　　emotion,
E'en as the face of a clock from which the hands have been
　　taken,
Vainly Evangeline strove with words and caresses to cheer
　　him,
Vainly offered him food; yet he moved not, he looked not,
　　he spake not,
But, with a vacant stare, ever gazed at the flickering fire-light.

"Benedicite!" [1] murmured the priest, in tones of compassion.
More he fain would have said, but his heart was full, and
    his accents
Faltered and paused on his lips, as the feet of a child on a
    threshold,
Hushed by the scene he beholds, and the awful presence of
    sorrow.
Silently, therefore, he laid his hand on the head of the
    maiden,
Raising his eyes, full of tears, to the silent stars that above
    them
Moved on their way, unperturbed by the wrongs and sorrows
    of mortals,
Then sat he down at her side, and they wept together in
    silence.

Suddenly rose from the south a light, as in autumn the
    blood-red
Moon climbs the crystal walls of heaven, and o'er the horizon
Titan-like [2] stretches its hundred hands upon mountain and
    meadow,
Seizing the rocks and the rivers, and piling huge shadows
    together.
Broader and ever broader it gleamed on the roofs of the
    village,
Gleamed on the sky and the sea, and the ships that lay in the
    roadstead.
Columns of shining smoke uprose, and flashes of flame were
Thrust through their folds and withdrawn, like the quivering
    hands of a martyr.
Then as the wind seized the gleeds and the burning thatch
    and, uplifting,
Whirled them aloft through the air, at once from a hundred
    house-tops
Started the sheeted smoke with flashes of flame intermingled

These things beheld in dismay the crowd on the shore and
    on shipboard.

[1] *Benedicite.*—The priest's greeting. It is a Latin word meaning
"Bless you!"
[2] The Titans were the ancient giants of mythology.

Speechless at first they stood, then cried aloud in their
      anguish,
"We shall behold no more our homes in the village of Grand-
      Pré!"
Loud on a sudden the cocks began to crow in the farmyards,
Thinking the day had dawned; and anon the lowing of cattle
Came on the evening breeze, by the barking of dogs inter-
      rupted.
Then rose a sound of dread, such as startles the sleeping en-
      campments
Far in the western prairies or forests that skirt the Nebraska,
When the wild horses affrighted sweep by with the speed of
      the whirlwind,
Or the loud bellowing herds of buffaloes rush to the river.
Such was the sound that arose on the night, as the herds and
      the horses
Broke through their folds and fences, and madly rushed o'er
      the meadows.

   Overwhelmed with the sight, yet speechless, the priest and
      the maiden
Gazed on the scene of terror that reddened and widened
      before them;
And as they turned at length to speak to their silent com-
      panion,
Lo! from his seat he had fallen, and stretched abroad on the
      seashore
Motionless lay his form, from which the soul had departed.
Slowly the priest uplifted the lifeless head, and the maiden
Knelt at her father's side, and wailed aloud in her terror.
Then in a swoon she sank, and lay with her head on his
      bosom.
Through the long night she lay in deep, oblivious slumber;
And when she woke from the trance, she beheld a multitude
      near her.
Faces of friends she beheld, that were mournfully gazing
      upon her,
Pallid, with tearful eyes, and looks of saddest compassion.
Still the blaze of the burning village illumined the landscape,
Reddened the sky overhead, and gleamed on the faces around
      her,

And like the day of doom it seemed to her wavering senses.
Then a familiar voice she heard, as it said to the people,—
"Let us bury him here by the sea. When a happier season
Brings us again to our homes from the unknown land of our
    exile,
Then shall his sacred dust be piously laid in the churchyard."
Such were the words of the priest. And there in haste by the
    seaside,
Having the glare of the burning village for funeral torches,
But without bell or book,[1] they buried the farmer of Grand-
    Pré.
And as the voice of the priest repeated the service of sorrow,
Lo! with a mournful sound, like the voice of a vast congre-
    gation,
Solemnly answered the sea, and mingled its roar with the
    dirge,
'T was the returning tide, that afar from the waste of the
    ocean,
With the first dawn of the day, came heaving and hurrying
    landward.
Then recommenced once more the stir and noise of embark-
    ing;
And with the ebb of that tide the ships sailed out of the
    harbor,
Leaving behind them the dead on the shore, and the village
    in ruins.

PART THE SECOND

I

Many a weary year has passed since the burning of Grand-
    Pré
When on the falling tide the freighted vessels departed,
Bearing a nation, with all its household gods, into exile,
Exile without an end, and without an example in story.
Far asunder, on separate coasts, the Acadians landed;
Scattered were they, like flakes of snow, when the wind from
    the northeast

---

[1] That is, without religious service.

Strikes through the fogs that darken the Banks of Newfoundland.

Friendless, homeless, hopeless, they wandered from city to
city,

From the cold lakes of the North to the sultry Southern
savannas,— [1]

From the bleak shores of the sea to the lands where the
Father of Waters

Seizes the hills in his hands, and drags them down to the
ocean,

Deep in their sands to bury the scattered bones of the mam-
moth.

Friends they sought and homes; and many, despairing, heart-
broken,

Asked of the earth but a grave, and no longer a friend nor a
fireside.

Written their history stands on tablets of stone in the churchyards.[2]

Long among them was seen a maiden who waited and wandered,

Lowly and meek in spirit, and patiently suffering all things.

Fair was she and young; but, alas! before her extended,

Dreary and vast and silent, the desert of life, with its pathway

Marked by the graves of those who had sorrowed and suffered
before her,

Passions long extinguished, and hopes long dead and abandoned,

As the emigrant's way o'er the Western desert is marked by

Camp-fires long consumed, and bones that bleach in the sunshine.

Something there was in her life incomplete, imperfect, unfinished;

As if a morning of June, with all its music and sunshine,

[1] Describing the extent of their wanderings, which included the
entire length and breadth of the United States.

[2] "We have already seen, in this province of Pennsylvania, two
hundred and fifty of our people, which is more than half the number
that were landed here, perish through misery and various diseases."—
Petition of the Acadians to the King.

Suddenly paused in the sky, and, fading, slowly descended
Into the east again, from whence it late had arisen.
Sometimes she lingered in towns, till, urged by the fever
    within her,
Urged by a restless longing, the hunger and thirst of the
    spirit,
She would commence again her endless search and endeavor;
Sometimes in churchyards strayed, and gazed on the crosses
    and tombstones,
Sat by some nameless grave, and thought that perhaps in its
    bosom
He was already at rest, and she longed to slumber beside him.
Sometimes a rumor, a hearsay, an inarticulate whisper,
Came with its airy hand to point and beckon her forward.
Sometimes she spake with those who had seen her beloved
    and known him,
But it was long ago, in some far-off place or forgotten.
"Gabriel Lajeunesse!" said they; "O, yes! we have seen him.
He was with Basil the blacksmith, and both have gone to
    the prairies;
Coureurs-des-Bois [1] are they, and famous hunters and trap-
    pers."
"Gabriel Lajeunesse!" said others; "O, yes! we have seen
    him.
He is a *Voyageur* [1] in the lowlands of Louisiana."
Then would they say,—"Dear child! why dream and wait
    for him longer?
Are there not other youths as fair as Gabriel? others
Who have hearts as tender and true, and spirits as loyal?
Here is Baptiste Leblanc, the notary's son, who has loved
    thee
Many a tedious year; come, give him thy hand and be
    happy!
Thou art too fair to be left to braid St. Catherine's tresses."

[1] *Coureur-des-Bois. Voyageur.*—The words have practically the
same meaning, the latter replacing the former, which had fallen into
disrepute. They designate the employés of the Hudson Bay Company, whose business it was to transport men and supplies between
trading posts. They were skilful woodsmen, travelling with marvellous ease and accuracy through forests afoot, and navigating rivers
and lakes in canoes.

Then would Evangeline answer, serenely but sadly,—"I cannot!

Whither my heart has gone, there follows my hand, and not elsewhere.

For when the heart goes before, like a lamp, and illumines the pathway,

Many things are made clear, that else lie hidden in darkness."

And thereupon the priest, her friend and father-confessor,

Said, with a smile,—"O daughter! thy God thus speaketh within thee!

Talk not of wasted affection, affection never was wasted;

If it enrich not the heart of another, its waters, returning

Back to their springs, like the rain, shall fill them full of refreshment;

That which the fountain sends forth returns again to the fountain.

Patience; accomplish thy labor; accomplish thy work of affection!

Sorrow and silence are strong, and patient endurance is godlike.

Therefore accomplish thy labor of love, till the heart is made godlike,

Purified, strengthened, perfected, and rendered more worthy of heaven!"

Cheered by the good man's words, Evangeline labored and waited.

Still in her heart she heard the funeral dirge of the ocean,

But with its sound there was mingled a voice that whispered, "Despair not!"

Thus did that poor soul wander in want and cheerless discomfort,

Bleeding, barefooted, over the shards and thorns of existence.

Let me essay, O Muse! to follow the wanderer's footsteps;—

Not through each devious path, each changeful year of existence;

But as a traveller follows a streamlet's course through the valley;

Far from its margin at times, and seeing the gleam of its water

Here and there, in some open space, and at intervals only;

Then drawing nearer its banks, through sylvan glooms that
    conceal it,
Though he behold it not, he can hear its continuous murmur;
Happy, at length, if we find the spot where it reaches an
    outlet.

II

It was the month of May. Far down the Beautiful River,[1]
Past the Ohio shore and past the mouth of the Wabash,
Into the golden stream of the broad and swift Mississippi,
Floated a cumbrous boat, that was rowed by Acadian boat-
    men.
It was a band of exiles: a raft, as it were, from the ship-
    wrecked
Nation, scattered along the coast, now floating together,
Bound by the bonds of a common belief and a common mis-
    fortune;
Men and women and children, who, guided by hope or by
    hearsay,
Sought for their kith and their kin among the few-acred
    farmers
On the Acadian coast, and the prairies of fair Opelousas.
With them Evangeline went, and her guide, the Father
    Felician.
Onward o'er sunken sands, through a wilderness sombre with
    forests,
Day after day they glided adown the turbulent river;
Night after night, by their blazing fires, encamped on its
    borders.
Now through rushing chutes, among green islands, where
    plumelike
Cotton-trees nodded their shadowy crests, they swept with
    the current,
Then emerged into broad lagoons, where silvery sand-bars
Lay in the stream, and along the wimpling waves of their
    margin,

[1] *Beautiful River.*—This is the meaning of the word Ohio, which
the Iroquois Indians applied to the river. The name was definitely
fixed by La Salle.

Shining with snow-white plumes, large flocks of pelicans
　　　waded.

Level the landscape grew, and along the shores of the river,
Shaded by china-trees, in the midst of luxuriant gardens,
Stood the houses of planters, with negro-cabins and dove-
　　　cots.

They were approaching the region where reigns perpetual
　　　summer,

Where through the Golden Coast,[1] and groves of orange and
　　　citron,

Sweeps with majestic curve the river away to the eastward.

They, too, swerved from their course; and, entering the
　　　Bayou of Plaquemine,[2]

Soon were lost in a maze of sluggish and devious waters,

Which, like a network of steel, extended in every direction.

Over their heads the towering and tenebrous boughs of the
　　　cypress

Met in a dusky arch, and trailing mosses in mid-air

Waved like banners that hang on the walls of ancient ca-
　　　thedrals.

Deathlike the silence seemed, and unbroken, save by the
　　　herons

Home to their roosts in the cedar-trees returning at sunset,

Or by the owl, as he greeted the moon with demoniac
　　　laughter.

Lovely the moonlight was as it glanced and gleamed on the
　　　water,

Gleamed on the columns of cypress and cedar sustaining the
　　　arches,

Down through whose broken vaults it fell as through chinks
　　　in a ruin.

Dreamlike, and indistinct, and strange were all things around
　　　them;

And o'er their spirits there came a feeling of wonder and
　　　sadness,—

[1] *Golden Coast.*—A name applied to the Louisiana shore, on
account of the yellow color of the tropical fruit growing there.

[2] Plaquemine, at the delta which is formed by the mouths of the
Mississippi river.

Strange forebodings of ill, unseen and that cannot be com-
    passed.
As, at the tramp of a horse's hoof on the turf of the prairies,
Far in advance are closed the leaves of the shrinking mimosa,
So, at the hoof-beats of fate, with sad forebodings of evil,
Shrinks and closes the heart, ere the stroke of doom has
    attained it.
But Evangeline's heart was sustained by a vision, that faintly
Floated before her eyes, and beckoned her on through the
    moonlight.
It was the thought of her brain that assumed the shape of a
    phantom.
Through those shadowy aisles had Gabriel wandered before
    her,
And every stroke of the oar now brought him nearer and
    nearer.

Then, in his place, at the prow of the boat, rose one of the
    oarsmen,
And, as a signal sound, if others like them peradventure
Sailed on those gloomy and midnight streams, blew a blast
    on his bugle.
Wild through the dark colonnades and corridors leafy the
    blast rang,
Breaking the seal of silence, and giving tongues to the forest.
Soundless above them the banners of moss just stirred to the
    music.
Multitudinous echoes awoke and died in the distance,
Over the watery floor, and beneath the reverberant branches;
But not a voice replied; no answer came from the darkness;
And when the echoes had ceased, like a sense of pain was the
    silence.
Then Evangeline slept; but the boatmen rowed through the
    midnight,
Silent at times, then singing familiar Canadian boat-songs,
Such as they sang of old on their own Acadian rivers.
And through the night were heard the mysterious sounds of
    the desert,
Far off, indistinct, as of wave or wind in the forest,

Mixed with the whoop of the crane and the roar of the grim
alligator.

Thus ere another noon they emerged from those shades;
and before them
Lay, in the golden sun, the lakes of the Atchafalaya.
Water-lilies in myriads rocked on the slight undulations
Made by the passing oars, and, resplendent in beauty, the
lotus
Lifted her golden crown above the heads of the boatmen.
Faint was the air with the odorous breath of magnolia blos-
soms,
And with the heat of noon; and numberless sylvan islands,
Fragrant and thickly embowered with blossoming hedges of
roses,
Near to whose shores they glided along, invited to slumber.
Soon by the fairest of these their weary oars were suspended.
Under the boughs of Wachita willows, that grew by the
margin,
Safely their boat was moored; and scattered about on the
greensward,
Tired with their midnight toil, the weary travellers slum-
bered.
Over them vast and high extended the cope of a cedar.
Swinging from its great arms, the trumpet-flower and the
grapevine
Hung their ladder of ropes aloft like the ladder of Jacob,
On whose pendulous stairs the angels ascending, descending,
Were the swift humming-birds, that flitted from blossom to
blossom.
Such was the vision Evangeline saw as she slumbered beneath
it.
Filled was her heart with love, and the dawn of an opening
heaven
Lighted her soul in sleep with the glory of regions celestial.

Nearer and ever nearer, among the numberless islands,
Darted a light, swift boat, that sped away o'er the water,
Urged on its course by the sinewy arms of hunters and
trappers.

Northward its prow was turned, to the land of the bison and
    beaver.

At the helm sat a youth, with countenance thoughtful and
    careworn.

Dark and neglected locks overshadowed his brow, and a
    sadness

Somewhat beyond his years on his face was legibly written.

Gabriel was it, who, weary with waiting, unhappy and restless

Sought in the Western wilds oblivion of self and of sorrow.

Swiftly they glided along, close under the lee of the island,

But by the opposite bank, and behind a screen of palmettos,

So that they saw not the boat, where it lay concealed in the
    willows,

And undisturbed by the dash of their oars, and unseen, were
    the sleepers;

Angel of God was there none to awaken the slumbering
    maiden?

Swiftly they glided away, like the shade of a cloud on the
    prairie.

After the sound of their oars on the tholes had died in the
    distance,

As from a magic trance the sleepers awoke, and the maiden

Said with a sigh to the friendly priest,—"O Father Felician!

Something says in my heart that near me Gabriel wanders.

Is it a foolish dream, an idle and vague superstition?

Or has an angel passed, and revealed the truth to my spirit?"

Then, with a blush, she added,—"Alas for my credulous
    fancy!

Unto ears like thine such words as these have no meaning."

But made answer the reverend man, and he smiled as he
    answered,—

"Daughter, thy words are not idle; nor are they to me with-
    out meaning.

Feeling is deep and still; and the word that floats on the
    surface

Is as the tossing buoy, that betrays where the anchor is
    hidden.

Therefore trust to thy heart, and to what the world calls
    illusions.

Gabriel truly is near thee; for not far away to the southward,

On the banks of the Têche,[1] are the towns of St. Maur and
St. Martin.

There the long-wandering bride shall be given again to her
bridegroom,

There the long-absent pastor regain his flock and his sheepfold.

Beautiful is the land, with its prairies and forests of fruittrees;

Under the feet a garden of flowers, and the bluest of heavens

Bending above, and resting its dome on the walls of the
forest.

They who dwell there have named it the Eden of Louisiana."

And with these words of cheer they arose and continued
their journey.

Softly the evening came. The sun from the western horizon

Like a magician extended his golden wand o'er the landscape;

Twinkling vapors arose; and sky and water and forest

Seemed all on fire at the touch, and melted and mingled
together.

Hanging between two skies, a cloud with edges of silver,

Floated the boat, with its dripping oars, on the motionless
water.

Filled was Evangeline's heart with inexpressible sweetness.

Touched by the magic spell, the sacred fountains of feeling

Glowed with the light of love, as the skies and waters around
her.

Then from a neighboring thicket the mocking-bird, wildest
of singers,

Swinging aloft on a willow spray that hung o'er the water,

Shook from his little throat such floods of delirious music,

That the whole air and the woods and the waves seemed
silent to listen.

Plaintive at first were the tones and sad; then soaring to
madness

[1] *Têche.*—A bayou west of the Mississippi River and near the
Gulf. It is 180 miles long and is navigable by steamboats.

Seemed they to follow or guide the revel of frenzied Bac-
    chantes.[1]
Single notes were then heard, in sorrowful, low lamentation;
Till, having gathered them all, he flung them abroad in de-
    rision,
As when, after a storm, a gust of wind through the tree-tops
Shakes down the rattling rain in a crystal shower on the
    branches.
With such a prelude as this, hearts that throbbed with emo-
    tion,
Slowly they entered the Têche, where it flows through the
    green Opelousas,
And through the amber air, above the crest of the woodland,
Saw the column of smoke that arose from a neighboring
    dwelling;—
Sounds of a horn they heard, and the distant lowing of
    cattle.

III

Near to the bank of the river, o'ershadowed by oaks, from
    whose branches
Garlands of Spanish moss and of mystic mistletoe [2] flaunted,
Such as the Druids cut down with golden hatchets at Yule-
    tide,
Stood secluded and still, the house of the herdsman. A garden
Girded it round about with a belt of luxuriant blossoms,
Filling the air with fragrance. The house itself was of timbers
Hewn from the cypress-tree, and carefully fitted together.
Large and low was the roof; and on slender columns sup-
    ported,
Rose-wreathed, vine-encircled, a broad and spacious veranda
Haunt of the humming-bird and the bee, extended around it
At each end of the house, amid the flowers of the garden,
Stationed the dove-cots were, as love's perpetual symbol,

---

[1] *Bacchantes.*—Priestesses of Bacchus, the god of wine, whose rites
were celebrated with dancing and revelry.

[2] *Mystic Mistletoe.*—The custom of using mistletoe at Yule-tide
or Christmas celebrations has come from the time whereof the
memory of man runneth not to the contrary, and is here ascribed
to the Druids.

Scenes of endless wooing, and endless contentions of rivals.
Silence reigned o'er the place. The line of shadow and sun-
      shine
Ran near the tops of the trees; but the house itself was in
      shadow,
And from its chimney-top, ascending and slowly expanding
Into the evening air, a thin blue column of smoke rose.
In the rear of the house, from the garden gate, ran a pathway
Through the great groves of oak to the skirts of the limitless
      prairie,
Into whose sea of flowers the sun was slowly descending.
Full in his track of light, like ships with shadowy canvas
Hanging loose from their spars in a motionless calm in the
      tropics,
Stood a cluster of trees, with tangled cordage of grape-vines.

    Just where the woodlands met the flowery surf of the
      prairie,
Mounted upon his horse, with Spanish saddle and stirrups,
Sat a herdsman, arrayed in gaiters and doublet of deerskin.
Broad and brown was the face that from under the Spanish
      sombrero
Gazed on the peaceful scene, with the lordly look of its
      master.
Round about him were numberless herds of kine, that were
      grazing
Quietly in the meadows, and breathing the vapory freshness
That uprose from the river, and spread itself over the land-
      scape.
Slowly lifting the horn that hung at his side, and expanding
Fully his broad, deep chest, he blew a blast, that resounded
Wildly and sweet and far, through the still damp air of the
      evening.
Suddenly out of the grass the long white horns of the cattle
Rose like flakes of foam on the adverse currents of ocean.
Silent a moment they gazed, then bellowing rushed o'er the
      prairie,
And the whole mass became a cloud, a shade in the distance.
Then, as the herdsman turned to the house, through the gate
      of the garden

Saw he the forms of the priest and the maiden advancing
    to meet him.
Suddenly down from his horse he sprang in amazement, and
    forward
Rushed with extended arms and exclamations of wonder;
When they beheld his face, they recognized Basil the black-
    smith.
Hearty his welcome was, as he led his guests to the garden.
There in an arbor of roses with endless question and answer
Gave they vent to their hearts, and renewed their friendly
    embraces,
Laughing and weeping by turns, or sitting silent and thought-
    ful.
Thoughtful, for Gabriel came not; and now dark doubts
    and misgivings
Stole o'er the maiden's heart; and Basil, somewhat embar-
    rassed,
Broke the silence and said,—"If you came by the Atcha-
    falaya,
How have you nowhere encountered my Gabriel's boat on the
    bayous?"
Over Evangeline's face at the words of Basil a shade passed.
Tears came into her eyes, and she said, with a tremulous
    accent,—
"Gone? is Gabriel gone?" and, concealing her face on his
    shoulder,
All her o'erburdened heart gave way and she wept and
    lamented.
Then the good Basil said,—and his voice grew blithe as he
    said it,—
"Be of good cheer, my child; it is only to-day he departed.
Foolish boy! he has left me alone with my herds and my
    horses.
Moody and restless grown, and, tried and troubled, his
    spirit
Could no longer endure the calm of this quiet existence.
Thinking ever of thee, uncertain and sorrowful ever,
Ever silent, or speaking only of thee and his troubles,
He at length had become so tedious to men and to maidens,

Tedious even to me, that at length I bethought me, and sent
    him
Unto the town of Adayes to trade for mules with the Span-
    iards.
Thence he will follow the Indian trails to the Ozark Moun-
    tains,[1]
Hunting for furs in the forests, on rivers trapping the beaver.
Therefore be of good cheer; we will follow the fugitive lover;
He is not far on his way, and the Fates and the streams are
    against him.
Up and away to-morrow, and through the red dew of the
    morning
We will follow him fast, and bring him back to his prison."

Then glad voices were heard, and up from the banks of
    the river,
Borne aloft on his comrades' arms, came Michael the fiddler.
Long under Basil's roof had he lived like a god on Olympus,
Having no other care than dispensing music to mortals.
Far renowned was he for his silver locks and his fiddle.
"Long live Michael," they cried, "our brave Acadian min-
    strel!"
As they bore him aloft in triumphal procession; and straight-
    way
Father Felician advanced with Evangeline, greeting the old
    man
Kindly and oft, and recalling the past, while Basil, enrap-
    tured,
Hailed with hilarious joy his old companions and gossips,
Laughing loud and long, and embracing mothers and
    daughters.
Much they marvelled to see the wealth of the ci-devant black-
    smith,
All his domains and his herds, and his patriarchal demeanor;
Much they marvelled to hear his tales of the soil and the
    climate,
And of the prairies, whose numberless herds were his who
    would take them;

[1] *Ozark Mountains.*—A group of hills in Missouri and Arkansas.

Each one thought in his heart, that he, too, would go and
    do likewise.
Thus they ascended the steps, and, crossing the airy veranda,
Entered the hall of the house, where already the supper of
    Basil
Waited his late return; and they rested and feasted together.

    Over the joyous feast the sudden darkness descended.
All was silent without, and, illuming the landscape with
    silver,
Fair rose the dewy moon and the myriad stars; but within
    doors,
Brighter than these, shone the faces of friends in the glim-
    mering lamplight.
Then from his station aloft, at the head of the table, the
    herdsman
Poured forth his heart and his wine together in endless
    profusion.
Lighting his pipe, that was filled with sweet Natchitoches
    tobacco,
Thus he spake to his guests, who listened, and smiled as
    they listened:—
"Welcome once more, my friends, who so long have been
    friendless and homeless,
Welcome once more to a home, that is better perchance than
    the old one!
Here no hungry winter congeals our blood like the rivers!
Here no stony ground provokes the wrath of the farmer;
Smoothly the ploughshare runs through the soil as a keel
    through the water.
All the year round the orange-groves are in blossom; and
    grass grows
More in a single night than a whole Canadian summer.
Here, too, numberless herds run wild and unclaimed in the
    prairies;
Here, too, lands may be had for the asking, and forests of
    timber
With a few blows of the axe are hewn and framed into
    houses.

After your houses are built, and your fields are yellow with
    harvests,
No King George of England shall drive you away from your
    homesteads,
Burning your dwellings and barns, and stealing your farms
    and your cattle."
Speaking these words, he blew a wrathful cloud from his
    nostrils,
And his huge, brawny hand came thundering down on the
    table,
So that the guests all started; and Father Felician, aston-
    ished,
Suddenly paused, with a pinch of snuff half-way to his
    nostrils.
But the brave Basil resumed, and his words were milder and
    gayer:—
"Only beware of the fever, my friends, beware of the fever!
For it is not like that of our cold Acadian climate,
Cured by wearing a spider hung round one's neck in a nut-
    shell!"
Then there were voices heard at the door, and footsteps
    approaching
Sounded upon the stairs and floor of the breezy veranda.
It was the neighboring Creole and small Acadian planters,
Who had been summoned all to the house of Basil the
    Herdsman.
Merry the meeting was of ancient comrades and neighbors:
Friend clasped friend in his arms; and they who before were
    as strangers,
Meeting in exile, became straightway as friends to each
    other,
Drawn by the gentle bond of a common country together.
But in the neighboring hall a strain of music, proceeding
From the accordant strings of Michael's melodious fiddle,
Broke up all further speech. Away, like children delighted,
All things forgotten beside, they gave themselves to the
    maddening
Whirl of the dizzy dance, as it swept and swayed to the
    music,

Dreamlike, with beaming eyes and the rush of fluttering
  garments.

  Meanwhile, apart, at the head of the hall, the priest and
    the herdsman
Sat, conversing together of past and present and future;
While Evangeline stood like one entranced, for within her
Olden memories rose, and loud in the midst of the music
Heard she the sound of the sea, and an irrepressible sadness
Came o'er her heart, and unseen she stole forth into the
  garden.
Beautiful was the night. Behind the black wall [1] of the
  forest,
Tipping its summit with silver, arose the moon. On the river
Fell here and there through the branches a tremulous gleam
    of the moonlight,
Like the sweet thoughts of love on a darkened and devious
    spirit,
Nearer and round about her, the manifold flowers of the
  garden
Poured out their souls in odors, that were their prayers and
  confessions
Unto the night, as it went its way, like a silent Carthusian. [2]
Fuller of fragrance than they, and as heavy with shadows
    and night-dews,
Hung the heart of the maiden. The calm and the magical
    moonlight
Seemed to inundate her soul with indefinable longings,

[1] *Behind the black wall, etc.*—In observing the beauty of this
passage, one may quote appropriately from Gilfillan's Second Gallery
of Literary Portraits: "The light of the Golden Age—itself joy,
music and poetry—is shining above. There are evenings of summer
or autumntide so exquisitely beautiful, so complete in their own
charms, that the entrance of the moon is felt almost as a painful
and superfluous addition. It is like a candle dispelling the weird
darkness of a twilight room. . . . But even as the moon by-and-by
vindicates her intrusion and creates her own 'holier day,' so with the
delicate and lovely heroine of this simple story: she becomes the
centre of the entire scene."

[2] *Carthusian.*—An austere religious establishment at Chartreuse,
France.

As, through the garden gate, beneath the brown shade of the
    oak-trees,
Passed she along the path to the edge of the measureless
    prairie.
Silent it lay, with a silvery haze upon it, and fire-flies
Gleaming and floating away in mingled and infinite numbers.
Over her head the stars, the thoughts of God in the heavens,
Shone on the eyes of man, who had ceased to marvel and
    worship,
Save when a blazing comet was seen on the walls of that
    temple,
As if a hand had appeared and written upon them, "Uphar-
    sin." [1]
And the soul of the maiden, between the stars and the fire-
    flies,
Wandered alone, and she cried,—"O Gabriel! O my beloved!
Art thou so near unto me, and yet I cannot behold thee?
Art thou so near unto me, and yet thy voice does not reach
    me?
Ah! how often thy feet have trod this path to the prairie!
Ah! often thine eyes have looked on the woodlands around
    me!
Ah! how often beneath this oak, returning from labor,
Thou hast lain down to rest, and to dream of me in thy
    slumbers.
When shall these eyes behold, these arms be folded about
    thee?"
Loud and sudden and near the note of a whippoorwill
    sounded
Like a flute in the woods; and anon, through the neighboring
    thickets,
Farther and farther away it floated and dropped into silence.
"Patience!" whispered the oaks from oracular caverns of
    darkness;
And, from the moonlit meadow, a sigh responded, "To-mor-
    row!"

[1] *Upharsin.*—The writing by the mysterious hand upon the palace
wall at Belshazzar's feast. The word is translated, "Thy kingdom is
divided." See the Book of Daniel, v. 28.

Bright rose the sun next day; and all the flowers of the
    garden
Bathed his shining feet with their tears, and anointed his
    tresses
With the delicious balm that they bore in their vases of
    crystal.
"Farewell!" said the priest, as he stood at the shadowy
    threshold;
"See that you bring us the Prodigal Son from his fasting and
    famine,
And, too, the Foolish Virgin, who slept when the bridegroom
    was coming."
"Farewell!" answered the maiden, and, smiling, with Basil
    descended
Down to the river's brink, where the boatmen already were
    waiting,
Thus beginning their journey with morning, and sunshine,
    and gladness,
Swiftly they followed the flight of him who was speeding
    before them,
Blown by the blast of fate like a dead leaf over the desert.
Not that day, nor the next, nor yet the day that succeeded,
Found they trace of his course, in lake or forest or river,
Nor, after many days, had they found him; but vague and
    uncertain
Rumors alone were their guides through a wild and desolate
    country;
Till, at the little inn of the Spanish town of Adayes,
Weary and worn, they alighted, and learned from the gar-
    rulous landlord
That on the day before, with horses and guides and com-
    panions,
Gabriel left the village, and took the road to the prairies.

IV

Far in the West there lies a desert land, where the mountains
Lift, through perpetual snows, their lofty and luminous
    summits.

Down from their jagged, deep ravines, where the gorge, like
    a gateway,
Opens a passage rude to the wheels of the emigrant's wagon,
Westward the Oregon flows and the Walleway and Owyhee.
Eastward, with devious course, among the Wind-river
    Mountains,
Through the Sweet-water Valley precipitate leaps the Ne-
    braska;
And to the south, from Fontaine-qui-bout and the Spanish
    sierras,
Fretted with sands and rocks, and swept by the wind of the
    desert,
Numberless torrents, with ceaseless sound, descend to the
    ocean,
Like the great chords of a harp, in loud and solemn vibra-
    tions.
Spreading between these streams are the wondrous, beautiful
    prairies,
Billowy bays of grass ever rolling in shadow and sunshine,
Bright with luxuriant clusters of roses and purple amorphas.
Over them wander the buffalo herds, and the elk and the
    roebuck;
Over them wander the wolves, and herds of riderless horses;
Fires that blast and blight, and winds that are weary with
    travel;
Over them wander the scattered tribes of Ishmael's children,
Staining the desert with blood; and above their terrible
    war-trails
Circles and sails aloft, on pinions majestic, the vulture,
Like the implacable soul of a chieftain slaughtered in battle,
By invisible stairs ascending and scaling the heavens.
Here and there rise smokes from the camps of these savage
    marauders;
Here and there rise groves from the margins of swift-running
    rivers;
And the grim, taciturn bear, the anchorite monk of the
    desert,
Climbs down their dark ravines to dig for roots by the
    brookside,
And over all is the sky, the clear and crystalline heaven,

Like the protecting hand of God inverted above them.

Into this wonderful land, at the base of the Ozark Moun-
    tains,
Gabriel far had entered, with hunters and trappers behind
    him.
Day after day, with their Indian guides, the maiden and
    Basil
Followed his flying steps, and thought each day to o'ertake
    him.
Sometimes they saw, or thought they saw, the smoke of his
    camp-fire
Rise in the morning air from the distant plain; but at night-
    fall,
When they had reached the place, they found only embers
    and ashes.
And, though their hearts were sad at times and their bodies
    were weary,
Hope still guided them on, as the magic Fata Morgana
Showed them her lakes of light, that retreated and vanished
    before them.

Once, as they sat by their evening fire, there silently en-
    tered
Into the little camp an Indian woman, whose features
Wore deep traces of sorrow, and patience as great as her
    sorrow.
She was a Shawnee woman returning home to her people,
From the far-off hunting-grounds of the cruel Camanches,
Where her Canadian husband, a Coureur-des-Bois, had been
    murdered.
Touched were their hearts at her story, and warmest and
    friendliest welcome
Gave they, with words of cheer, and she sat and feasted
    among them
On the buffalo-meat and the venison cooked on the embers,
But when their meal was done, and Basil and all his com-
    panions,
Worn with the long day's march and the chase of the deer
    and the bison,

Stretched themselves on the ground, and slept where the
    quivering firelight
Flashed on their swarthy cheeks, and their forms wrapped
    up in their blankets,
Then at the door of Evangeline's tent she sat and repeated
Slowly, with soft, low voice, and the charm of her Indian
    accent,
Ail the tale of her love, with its pleasures, and pains, and
    reverses.
Much Evangeline wept at the tale, and to know that another
Hapless heart like her own had loved and had been disap-
    pointed.
Moved to the depths of her soul by pity and woman's com-
    passion,
Yet in her sorrow pleased that one who had suffered was
    near her,
She in turn related her love and all its disasters.
Mute with wonder the Shawnee sat, and when she had ended
Still was mute; but at length, as if a mysterious horror
Passed through her brain, she spake, and repeated the tale
    of the Mowis;
Mowis, the bridegroom of snow, who won and wedded a
    maiden,
But, when the morning came, arose and passed from the
    wigwam,
Fading and melting away and dissolving into the sunshine,
Till she beheld him no more, though she followed far into the
    forest.
Then, in those sweet, low tones, that seemed like a weird
    incantation,
Told she the tale of the fair Lilinau, who was wooed by a
    phantom,
That, through the pines o'er her father's lodge, in the hush
    of the twilight,
Breathed like the evening wind, and whispered love to the
    maiden,
Till she followed his green and waving plume through the
    forest,
And never more returned, nor was seen again by her people.
Silent with wonder and strange surprise, Evangeline listened

To the soft flow of her magical words, till the region around
  her
Seemed like enchanted ground, and her swarthy guest the
  enchantress.
Slowly over the tops of the Ozark Mountains the moon rose,
Lighting the little tent, and with a mysterious splendor
Touching the sombre leaves, and embracing and filling the
  woodland.
With a delicious sound the brook rushed by, and the branches
Swayed and sighed overhead in scarcely audible whispers.
Filled with the thoughts of love was Evangeline's heart, but
  a secret,
Subtile sense crept in of pain and indefinite terror,
As the cold, poisonous snake creeps into the nest of the
  swallow.
It was no earthly fear. A breath from the region of spirits
Seemed to float in the air of night; and she felt for a moment
That, like the Indian maid, she, too, was pursuing a phantom.
And with this thought she slept, and the fear and the phan-
  tom had vanished.

  Early upon the morrow the march was resumed; and the
  Shawnee
Said, as they journeyed along,—"On the western slope of
  these mountains
Dwells in his little village the Black Robe chief of the
  Mission.
Much he teaches the people, and tells them of Mary and
  Jesus;
Loud laugh their hearts with joy, and weep with pain, as
  they hear him."
Then, with a sudden and secret emotion, Evangeline an·
  swered,—
"Let us go to the Mission, for there good tidings await us!"
Thither they turned their steeds; and behind a spur of the
  mountains,
Just as the sun went down, they heard a murmur of voices,
And in a meadow green and broad, by the bank of a river,
Saw the tents of the Christians, the tents of the Jesuit
  Mission.

Under a towering oak, that stood in the midst of the village,
Knelt the Black Robe chief with his children. A crucifix
fastened
High on the trunk of the tree, and overshadowed by grape-
vines,
Looked with its agonized face on the multitude kneeling
beneath it.
This was their rural chapel. Aloft, through the intricate
arches
Of its aërial roof, arose the chant of their vespers,
Mingling its notes with the soft susurrus and sighs of the
branches.
Silent, with heads uncovered, the travellers, nearer approach-
ing,
Knelt on the swarded floor, and joined in the evening devo-
tions.
But when the service was done, and the benediction had
fallen
Forth from the hands of the priest, like seed from the hands
of the sower,
Slowly the reverend man advanced to the strangers, and
bade them
Welcome; and when they replied, he smiled with benignant
expression,
Hearing the homelike sounds of his mother-tongue in the
forest,
And with words of kindness conducted them into his wigwam.
There upon mats and skins they reposed, and on cakes of the
maize-ear
Feasted, and slaked their thirst from the water-gourd of
the teacher.
Soon was their story told; and the priest with solemnity
answered:—
"Not six suns have risen and set since Gabriel, seated
On this mat by my side, where now the maiden reposes,
Told me this same sad tale; then arose and continued his
journey!"
Soft was the voice of the priest, and he spake with an accent
of kindness;

But on Evangeline's heart fell his words as in winter the
    snow-flakes
Fall into some lone nest from which the birds have departed.
"Far to the north he has gone," continued the priest; "but
    in autumn,
When the chase is done, will return again to the Mission."
Then Evangeline said, and her voice was meek and submis-
    sive,—
"Let me remain with thee, for my soul is sad and afflicted."
So seemed it wise and well unto all; and betimes on the
    morrow,
Mounting his Mexican steed, with his Indian guides and
    companions,
Homeward Basil returned, and Evangeline stayed at the
    Mission.

Slowly, slowly, slowly the days succeeded each other,—
Days and weeks and months; and the fields of maize that
    were springing
Green from the ground when a stranger she came, now
    waving above her,
Lifted their slender shafts, with leaves interlacing, and
    forming
Cloisters for mendicant crows and granaries pillaged by
    squirrels.
Then in the golden weather the maize was husked, and the
    maidens
Blushed at each blood-red ear, for that betokened a lover,
But at the crooked laughed, and called it a thief in the
    corn-field.
Even the blood-red ear to Evangeline brought not her lover.
"Patience!" the priest would say; "have faith, and thy
    prayer will be answered!
Look at this delicate plant that lifts its head from the
    meadow,
See how its leaves all point to the north, as true as the
    magnet;
It is the compass-flower, that the finger of God has suspended
Here on its fragile stalk, to direct the traveller's journey
Over the sea-like, pathless, limitless waste of the desert.

Such in the soul of man is faith. The blossoms of passion,
Gay and luxuriant flowers, are brighter and fuller of fra-
    grance,
But they beguile us, and lead us astray, and their odor is
    deadly.
Only this humble plant can guide us here, and hereafter
Crown us with asphodel flowers, that are wet with the dews
    of nepenthe."

    So came the autumn, and passed, and the winter,—yet
        Gabriel came not;
Blossomed the opening spring and the notes of the robin
    and blue-bird
Sounded sweet upon wold and in wood, yet Gabriel came not.
But on the breath of the summer winds a rumor was wafted
Sweeter than song of bird, or hue or odor of blossom.
Far to the north and east, it said, in the Michigan forests,
Gabriel had his lodge by the banks of the Saginaw river.
And, with returning guides, that sought the lakes of St.
    Lawrence,
Saying a sad farewell, Evangeline went from the Mission.
When over weary ways, by long and perilous marches,
She had attained at length the depths of the Michigan forests,
Found she the hunter's lodge deserted and fallen to ruin!

    Thus did the long sad years glide on, and in seasons and
    places
Divers and distant far was seen the wandering maiden;—
Now in the tents of grace of the meek Moravian Missions,
Now in the noisy camps and the battle-fields of the army,
Now in secluded hamlets, in towns and populous cities.
Like a phantom she came, and passed away unremembered.
Fair was she and young, when in hope began the long jour-
    ney;
Faded was she and old, when in disappointment it ended.
Each succeeding year stole something away from her beauty,
Leaving behind it, broader and deeper, the gloom and the
    shadow.
Then there appeared and spread faint streaks of gray o'er
    her forehead,

Dawn of another life, that broke o'er her earthly horizon,
As in the eastern sky the first faint streaks of the morning.

V

In that delightful land which is washed by the Delaware's
     waters
Guarding in sylvan shades the name of Penn the apostle,
Stands on the banks of its beautiful stream the city he
     founded.
There all the air is balm, and the peach is the emblem of
     beauty
And the streets still re-echo the names of the trees of the
     forest,
As if they fain would appease the Dryads whose haunts they
     molested.
There from the troubled sea had Evangeline landed, an exile,
Finding among the children of Penn a home and a country.
There old René Leblanc had died; and when he departed,
Saw at his side only one of all his hundred descendants.
Something at least there was in the friendly streets of the
     city,
Something that spake to her heart, and made her no longer
     a stranger;
And her ear was pleased with the Thee and Thou of the
     Quakers,
For it recalled the past, the old Acadian country,
Where all men were equal, and all were brothers and sisters.
So, when the fruitless search, the disappointed endeavor,
Ended, to recommence no more upon earth, uncomplaining,
Thither, as leaves to the light, were turned her thoughts and
     her footsteps.
As from mountain's top the rainy mists of the morning
Roll away, and afar we behold the landscape below us,
Sun-illumined, with shining rivers and cities and hamlets,
So fell the mists from her mind, and she saw the world far
     below her,
Dark no longer, but all illumined with love; and the pathway
Which she had climbed so far, lying smooth and fair in the
     distance.

Gabriel was not forgotten. Within her heart was his image,
Clothed in the beauty of love and youth, as last she beheld
    him,
Only more beautiful made by his deathlike silence and ab-
    sence.
Into her thoughts of him time entered not, for it was not.
Over him years had no power; he was not changed, but
    transfigured;
He had become to her heart as one who is dead, and not
    absent;
Patience and abnegation of self, and devotion to others,
This was the lesson a life of trial and sorrow had taught her.
So was her love diffused, but, like to some odorous spices,
Suffered no waste nor loss, though filling the air with aroma.
Other hope had she none, nor wish in life, but to follow
Meekly, with reverent steps, the sacred feet of her Saviour.
Thus many years she lived as a Sister of Mercy; frequenting
Lonely and wretched roofs in the crowded lanes of the city,
Where distress and want concealed themselves from the sun-
    light,
Where disease and sorrow in garrets languished neglected.
Night after night, when the world was asleep, as the watch-
    man repeated
Loud, through the gusty streets, that all was well in the city,
High at some lonely window he saw the light of her taper.
Day after day, in the gray of the dawn, as slow through the
    suburbs
Plodded the German farmer, with flowers and fruits for the
    market,
Met he that meek, pale face, returning home from its watch-
    ings.

Then it came to pass that a pestilence fell on the city,
Presaged by wondrous signs, and mostly by flocks of wild
    pigeons,
Darkening the sun in their flight, with naught in their craws
    but an acorn.
And, as the tides of the sea arise in the month of September,
Flooding some silver stream, till it spreads to a lake in the
    meadow,

So death flooded life, and, o'erflowing its natural margin,
Spread to a brackish lake, the silver stream of existence.
Wealth had no power to bribe, nor beauty to charm, the
   oppressor;
But all perished alike beneath the scourge of his anger;—
Only, alas! the poor, who had neither friends nor attendants,
Crept away to die in the almshouse, home of the homeless.
Then in the suburbs it stood, in the midst of meadows and
   woodlands;—
Now the city surrounds it; but still, with its gateway and
   wicket
Meek, in the midst of splendor, its humble walls seem to
   echo
Softly the words of the Lord:—"The poor ye always have
   with you."
Thither, by night and by day, came the Sister of Mercy.
   The dying
Looked up into her face, and thought, indeed, to behold there
Gleams of celestial light encircle her forehead with splendor,
Such as the artist paints o'er the brows of saints and apostles,
Or such as hangs by night o'er a city seen at a distance.
Unto their eyes it seemed the lamps of the city celestial,
Into whose shining gates ere long their spirits would enter.

   Thus, on a Sabbath morn, through the streets, deserted
      and silent,
Wending her quiet way, she entered the door of the alms-
   house.
Sweet on the summer air was the odor of flowers in the
   garden;
And she paused on her way to gather the fairest among them,
That the dying once more might rejoice in their fragrance
   and beauty.
Then, as she mounted the stairs to the corridors, cooled by
   the east wind,
Distant and soft on her ear fell the chimes from the belfry
   of Christ Church,
While, intermingled with these, across the meadows were
   wafted

Sounds of psalms, that were sung by the Swedes in the
    church at Wicaco.
Soft as descending wings fell the calm of the hour on her
    spirit;
Something within her said,—"At length thy trials are
    ended;"
And, with light in her looks, she entered the chambers of
    sickness.
Noiselessly moved about the assiduous, careful attendants,
Moistening the feverish lip, and the aching brow, and in
    silence
Closing the sightless eyes of the dead, and concealing their
    faces,
Where on their pallets they lay, like drifts of snow by the
    road side.
Many a languid head, upraised as Evangeline entered,
Turned on its pillow of pain to gaze while she passed, for
    her presence
Fell on their hearts like a ray of the sun on the walls of a
    prison.
And, as she looked around, she saw how Death, the consoler,
Laying his hand upon many a heart, had healed it forever.
Many familiar forms had disappeared in the night-time;
Vacant their places were, or filled already by strangers.

Suddenly, as if arrested by fear or a feeling of wonder,
Still she stood, with her colorless lips apart, while a shudder
Ran through her frame, and forgotten, the flowerets dropped
    from her fingers,
And from her eyes and cheeks the light and bloom of the
    morning.
Then there escaped from her lips a cry of such terrible
    anguish,
That the dying heard it, and started up from their pillows.
On the pallet before her was stretched the form of an old
    man.
Long, and thin, and gray were the locks that shaded his
    temples;
But, as he lay in the morning light, his face for a moment

Seemed to assume once more the forms of its earlier man-
    hood;
So are wont to be changed the faces of those who are dying.
Hot and red on his lips still burned the flush of the fever,
As if life, like the Hebrew, with blood had besprinkled its
    portals,
That the Angel of Death might see the sign, and pass over.
Motionless, senseless, dying, he lay, and his spirit exhausted
Seemed to be sinking down through infinite depths in the
    darkness,
Darkness of slumber and death, forever sinking and sinking.
Then through those realms of shade, in multiplied reverbera-
    tions,
Heard he that cry of pain, and through the hush that suc-
    ceeded
Whispered a gentle voice, in accents tender and saint like,
"Gabriel! O my beloved!" and died away into silence.
Then he beheld, in a dream, once more the home of his child-
    hood;
Green Acadian meadows, with sylvan rivers among them,
Village, and mountain, and woodlands; and, walking under
    their shadow,
As in the days of her youth, Evangeline rose in his vision.
Tears came into his eyes; and as slowly he lifted his eyelids,
Vanished the vision away, but Evangeline knelt by his bed-
    side.
Vainly he strove to whisper her name, for the accents unut-
    tered
Died on his lips, and their motion revealed what his tongue
    would have spoken.
Vainly he strove to rise; and Evangeline, kneeling beside
    him,
Kissed his dying lips, and laid his head on her bosom.
Sweet was the light of his eyes; but it suddenly sank into
    darkness,
As when a lamp is blown out by a gust of wind at a casement.

All was ended now, the hope, and the fear, and the sorrow,
All the aching of heart, the restless, unsatisfied longing,
All the dull, deep pain, and constant anguish of patience!

And, as she pressed once more the lifeless head to her bosom,
Meekly she bowed her own, and murmured, "Father, I thank
thee!"

Still stands the forest primeval; but far away from its
shadow,
Side by side, in their nameless graves, the lovers are sleeping.
Under the humble walls of the little Catholic churchyard,
In the heart of the city, they lie, unknown and unnoticed.
Daily the tides of life go ebbing and flowing beside them,
Thousands of throbbing hearts, where theirs are at rest and
forever,
Thousands of aching brains, where theirs no longer are busy,
Thousands of toiling hands, where theirs have ceased from
their labors,
Thousands of weary feet, where theirs have completed their
journey!

Still stands the forest primeval; but under the hade of its
branches
Dwells another race, with other customs and language.
Only along the shores of the mournful and misty Atlantic
Linger a few Acadian peasants whose fathers from exile
Wandered back to their native land to die in its bosom.
In the fisherman's cot the wheel and the loom are still busy;
Maidens still wear their Norman caps and their kirtles of
homespun,
And by the evening fire repeat Evangeline's story,
While from its rocky caverns the deep-voiced, neighboring
ocean
Speaks, and in accents disconsolate answers the wail of the
forest.

THE COURTSHIP OF MILES STANDISH

I

MILES STANDISH

IN the Old Colony days, in Plymouth the land of the Pilgrims,
To and fro in a room of his simple and primitive dwelling,
Clad in doublet and hose, and boots of Cordovan leather,
Strode, with a martial air, Miles Standish the Puritan Captain.
Buried in thought he seemed, with his hands behind him, and pausing
Ever and anon to behold his glittering weapons of warfare,
Hanging in shining array along the walls of the chamber,—
Cutlass and corselet of steel, and his trusty sword of Damascus,
Curved at the point and inscribed with its mystical Arabic sentence,
While underneath, in a corner, were fowling-piece, musket, and matchlock.
Short of stature he was, but strongly built and athletic,
Broad in the shoulders, deep-chested, with muscles and sinews of iron;
Brown as a nut was his face, but his russet beard was already
Flaked with patches of snow, as hedges sometimes in November.
Near him was seated John Alden, his friend, and household companion,
Writing with diligent speed at a table of pine by the window;
Fair-haired, azure-eyed, with delicate Saxon complexion,
Having the dew of his youth, and the beauty thereof, as the captives
Whom Saint Gregory saw, and exclaimed, "Not Angles but Angels."
Youngest of all was he of the men who came in the May Flower.

Suddenly breaking the silence, the diligent scribe inter-
rupting,
Spake, in the pride of his heart, Miles Standish the Captain
of Plymouth.
"Look at these arms," he said, "the warlike weapons that
hang here
Burnished and bright and clean, as if for parade or inspec-
tion!
This is the sword of Damascus I fought with in Flanders;
this breastplate,
Well I remember the day! once saved my life in a skirmish;
Here in front you can see the very dint of the bullet
Fired point-blank at my heart by a Spanish arcabucero.
Had it not been of sheer steel, the forgotten bones of Miles
Standish
Would at this moment be mould, in their grave in the Flemish
morasses."
Thereupon answered John Alden, but looked not up from his
writing:
"Truly the breath of the Lord hath slackened the speed of
the bullet;
He in his mercy preserved you, to be our shield and our
weapon!"
Still the Captain continued, unheeding the words of the strip-
ling:
"See, how bright they are burnished, as if in an arsenal
hanging;
That is because I have done it myself, and not left it to
others.
Serve yourself, would you be well served, is an excellent
adage;
So I take care of my arms, as you of your pens and your ink-
horn.
Then, too, there are my soldiers, my great, invincible army,
Twelve men, all equipped, having each his rest and his match-
lock,
Eighteen shillings a month, together with diet and pillage,
And, like Cæsar, I know the name of each of my soldiers!"
This he said with a smile, that danced in his eyes, as the sun-
beams

Dance on the waves of the sea, and vanish again in a moment.
Alden laughed as he wrote, and still the Captain continued:
"Look! you can see from this window my brazen howitzer
    planted
High on the roof of the church, a preacher who speaks to the
    purpose,
Steady, straight-forward, and strong, with irresistible logic,
Orthodox, flashing conviction right into the hearts of the
    heathen.
Now we are ready, I think, for any assault of the Indians;
Let them come, if they like, and the sooner they try it the
    better,—
Let them come if they like, be it sagamore, sachem, or pow-
    wow,
Aspinet, Samoset, Corbitant, Squanto, or Tokamahamon!"

Long at the window he stood, and wistfully gazed on the
    landscape,
Washed with a cold gray mist, the vapory breath of the east
    wind,
Forest and meadow and hill, and the steel-blue rim of the
    ocean,
Lying silent and sad, in the afternoon shadows and sunshine.
Over his countenance flitted a shadow like those on the land-
    scape,
Gloom intermingled with light; and his voice subdued with
    emotion,
Tenderness, pity, regret, as after a pause he proceeded:
"Yonder there, on the hill by the sea, lies buried Rose
    Standish;
Beautiful rose of love, that bloomed for me by the wayside!
She was the first to die of all who came in the May Flower!
Green above her is growing the field of wheat we have sown
    there,
Better to hide from the Indian scouts the graves of our
    people,
Lest they should count them and see how many already
    have perished!"
Sadly his face he averted, and strode up and down, and was
    thoughtful.

Fixed to the opposite wall was a shelf of books, and among them
Prominent three, distinguished alike for bulk and for binding;
Bariffe's Artillery Guide, and the Commentaries of Cæsar,
Out of the Latin translated by Arthur Goldinge of London,
And, as if guarded by these, between them was standing the Bible.
Musing a moment before them, Miles Standish paused, as if doubtful
Which of the three he should choose for his consolation and comfort,
Whether the wars of the Hebrews, the famous campaigns of the Romans,
Or the Artillery practice, designed for belligerent Christians.
Finally down from its shelf he dragged the ponderous Roman,
Seated himself at the window, and opened the book, and in silence
Turned o'er the well-worn leaves, where thumb-marks thick on the margin,
Like the trample of feet, proclaimed the battle was hottest.
Nothing was heard in the room but the hurrying pen of the stripling,
Busily writing epistles important, to go by the May Flower,
Ready to sail on the morrow, or next day at latest, God willing!
Homeward bound with the tidings of all that terrible winter,
Letters written by Alden, and full of the name of Priscilla.
Full of the name and the fame of the Puritan maiden Priscilla!

II

LOVE AND FRIENDSHIP

Nothing was heard in the room but the hurrying pen of the stripling,
Or an occasional sigh from the laboring heart of the Captain,
Reading the marvellous words and achievements of Julius Cæsar.

After a while he exclaimed, as he smote with his hand, palm
    downwards,
Heavily on the page: "A wonderful man was this Cæsar!
You are a writer, and I am a fighter, but here is a fellow
Who could both write and fight, and in both was equally
    skilful!"
Straightway answered and spake John Alden, the comely, the
    youthful:
"Yes, he was equally skilled, as you say, with his pen and
    his weapons.
Somewhere have I read, but where I forget, he could dictate
Seven letters at once, at the same time writing his memoirs."
"Truly," continued the Captain, not heeding or hearing the
    other,
"Truly a wonderful man was Caius Julius Cæsar!
Better be first, he said, in a little Iberian village,
Than be second in Rome, and I think he was right when he
    said it.
Twice was he married before he was twenty, and many times
    after;
Battles five hundred he fought, and a thousand cities he con-
    quered;
He, too, fought in Flanders, as he himself has recorded;
Finally he was stabbed by his friend, the orator Brutus!
Now, do you know what he did on a certain occasion in Flan-
    ders,
When the rear-guard of his army retreated, the front giving
    way too,
And the immortal Twelfth Legion was crowded so closely to-
    gether
There was no room for their swords? Why, he seized a shield
    from a soldier,
Put himself straight at the head of his troops, and com-
    manded the captains,
Calling on each by his name, to order forward the ensigns;
Then to widen the ranks, and give more room for their
    weapons;
So he won the day, the battle of something-or-other.
That's what I always say; if you wish a thing to be well done,
You must do it yourself, you must not leave it to others!"

All was silent again; the Captain continued his reading.
Nothing was heard in the room but the hurrying pen of the
    stripling
Writing epistles important to go next day by the May Flower,
Filled with the name and the fame of the Puritan maiden
    Priscilla;
Every sentence began or closed with the name of Priscilla,
Till the treacherous pen, to which he confided the secret,
Strove to betray it by singing and shouting the name of
    Priscilla!
Finally closing his book, with a bang of the ponderous cover,
Sudden and loud as the sound of a soldier grounding his
    musket,
Thus to the young man spake Miles Standish the Captain of
    Plymouth:
"When you have finished your work, I have something im-
    portant to tell you.
Be not, however, in haste; I can wait; I shall not be im-
    patient!"
Straightway Alden replied, as he folded the last of his letters,
Pushing his papers aside, and giving respectful attention:
"Speak; for whenever you speak, I am always ready to listen,
Always ready to hear whatever pertains to Miles Standish."
Thereupon answered the Captain, embarrassed, and culling
    his phrases:
" 'Tis not good for a man to be alone, say the Scriptures.
This I have said before, and again and again I repeat it:
Every hour in the day, I think it, and feel it, and say it.
Since Rose Standish died, my life has been weary and dreary;
Sick at heart have I been, beyond the healing of friendship.
Oft in my lonely hours have I thought of the maiden Priscilla.
She is alone in the world; her father and mother and brother
Died in the winter together; I saw her going and coming,
Now to the grave of the dead, and now to the bed of the
    dying,
Patient, courageous, and strong, and said to myself, that if
    ever
There were angels on earth, as there are angels in heaven,
Two have I seen and known: and the angel whose name is
    Priscilla

Holds in my desolate life the place which the other aban-
doned.
Long have I cherished the thought, but never have dared to
reveal it,
Being a coward in this, though valiant enough for the most
part.
Go to the damsel Priscilla, the loveliest maiden of Plymouth,
Say that a blunt old Captain, a man not of words but of
actions,
Offers his hand and his heart, the hand and heart of a soldier.
Not in these words, you know, but this in short is my
meaning;
I am a maker of war, and not a maker of phrases.
You, who are bred as a scholar, can say it in elegant language,
Such as you read in your books of the pleadings and wooings
of lovers,
Such as you think best adapted to win the heart of a maiden."

When he had spoken, John Alden, the fairhaired, taciturn
stripling,
All aghast at his words, surprised, embarrassed, bewildered,
Trying to mask his dismay by treating the subject with light-
ness,
Trying to smile, and yet feeling his heart stand still in his
bosom,
Just as a timepiece stops in a house that is stricken by light-
ning,
Thus made answer and spake, or rather stammered than
answered:
"Such a message as that, I am sure I should mangle and
mar it;
If you would have it well done,—I am only repeating your
maxim,—
You must do it yourself, you must not leave it to others!"
But with the air of a man whom nothing can turn from his
purpose,
Gravely shaking his head, made answer the Captain of Plym-
outh,
"Truly the maxim is good, and I do not mean to gainsay it;

But we must use it discreetly, and not waste powder for
　　　　nothing.
Now, as I said before, I was never a maker of phrases.
I can march up to a fortress and summon the place to sur-
　　　　render,
But march up to a woman with such a proposal, I dare not.
I'm not afraid of bullets, nor shot from the mouth of a
　　　　cannon,
But of a thundering "No!" point-blank from the mouth of a
　　　　woman,
That I confess I'm afraid of, nor am I ashamed to confess it!
So you must grant my request, for you are an elegant scholar,
Having the graces of speech, and skill in the turning of
　　　　phrases."
Taking the hand of his friend, who still was reluctant and
　　　　doubtful,
Holding it long in his own, and pressing it kindly, he added:
"Though I have spoken thus lightly, yet deep is the feeling
　　　　that prompts me;
Surely you cannot refuse what I ask in the name of our
　　　　friendship!"
Then made answer John•Alden: "The name of friendship is
　　　　sacred;
What you demand in that name, I have not the power to
　　　　deny you!"
So the strong will prevailed, subduing and moulding the
　　　　gentler,
Friendship prevailed over love, and Alden went on his errand.

III

The Lover's Errand

So the strong will prevailed, and Alden went on his errand,
Out of the street of the village, and into the paths of the
　　　　forest,
Into the tranquil woods, where blue-birds and robins were
　　　　building
Towns in the populous trees, with hanging gardens of
　　　　verdure,

Peaceful, aerial cities of joy and affection and freedom.
All around him was calm, but within him commotion and con-
    flict,
Love contending with friendship, and self with each generous
    impulse.
To and fro in his breast his thoughts were heaving and
    dashing,
As in a foundering ship, with every roll of the vessel,
Washes the bitter sea, the merciless surge of the ocean!
"Must I relinquish it all," he cried with a wild lamentation,
"Must I relinquish it all, the joy, the hope, the illusion?
Was it for this I have loved, and waited, and worshipped in
    silence?
Was it for this I have followed the flying feet and the shadow
Over the wintry sea, to the desolate shores of New England?
Truly the heart is deceitful, and out of its depths of corrup-
    tion
Rise, like an exhalation, the misty phantoms of passion;
Angels of light they seem, but are only delusions of Satan.[1]
All is clear to me now; I feel it, I see distinctly!
This is the hand of the Lord; it is laid upon me in anger,
For I have followed too much the heart's desires and devices,
Worshipping Astaroth [2] blindly, and impious idols of Baal.[2]
This is the cross I must bear; the sin and the swift retribution."

So through the Plymouth woods John Alden went on his
    errand;
Crossing the brook at the ford, where it brawled over pebble
    and shallow,
Gathering still, as he went, the May-flowers [3] blooming
    around him,
Fragrant, filling the air with a strange and wonderful sweet-
    ness,

[1] The reference is to 2 Cor. xi. 14.
[2] Baal and Ashtaroth, the supreme male and female divinities of
the Phœnicians and Canaanites.
[3] The English May-flower, for which the vessel was named is the
hawthorn blossom. The New England May-flower is the trailing
arbutus.

Children lost in the woods, and covered with leaves [1] in their
    slumber.
"Puritan flowers," he said, "and the type of Puritan maidens,
Modest and simple and sweet, the very type of Priscilla!
So I will take them to her; to Priscilla the May-flower of
    Plymouth,
Modest and simple and sweet, as a parting gift will I take
    them;
Breathing their silent farewells, as they fade and wither and
    perish,
Soon to be thrown away as is the heart of the giver."
So through the Plymouth woods John Alden went on his
    errand;
Came to an open space, and saw the disk of the ocean,
Sailless, sombre and cold with the comfortless breath of the
    east-wind;
Saw the new-built house, and people at work in a meadow;
Heard, as he drew near the door, the musical voice of
    Priscilla
Singing the hundreth Psalm, the grand old Puritan anthem,
Music that Luther sang to the sacred words of the Psalmist,
Full of the breath of the Lord, consoling and comforting
    many.
Then, as he opened the door, he beheld the form of the
    maiden
Seated beside her wheel, and the carded wool like a snow-
    drift
Piled at her knee, her white hands feeding the ravenous
    spindle,
While with her foot on the treadle she guided the wheel in its
    motions.
Open wide on her lap lay the well-worn psalm-book of Ains-
    worth,
Printed in Amsterdam, the words and the music together,
Rougs-hewn, angular notes, [2] like stones in the wall of a
    churchyard,

---

[1] The trailing arbutus blooms underneath the dead leaves. The
reference is to the nursery story of the Babes in the Wood.
[2] A spirited description of the musical notation of that day.

Darkened and overhung by the running vine of the verses.
Such was the book from whose pages she sang the old Puritan
    anthem,
She, the Puritan girl, in the solitude of the forest,
Making the humble house and the modest apparel of home-
    spun
Beautiful with her beauty, and rich with the wealth of her
    being!
Over him rushed, like a wind that is keen and cold and re-
    lentless,
Thoughts of what might have been, and the weight and woe
    of his errand;
All the dreams that had faded, and all the hopes that had
    vanished,
All his life henceforth a dreary and tenantless mansion,
Haunted by vain regrets, and pallid, sorrowful faces.
Still he said to himself, and almost fiercely he said it,
"Let not him that putteth his hand to the plough look back-
    wards; [1]
Though the ploughshare cut through the flowers of life to its
    fountains,
Though it pass o'er the graves of the dead and the hearths of
    the living,
It is the will of the Lord; and his mercy endureth for ever!"

So he entered the house: and the hum of the wheel and the
    singing
Suddenly ceased; for Priscilla, aroused by his step on the
    threshold,
Rose as he entered, and gave him her hand, in signal of
    welcome,
Saying, "I knew it was you, when I heard your step in the
    passage;
For I was thinking of you, as I sat there singing and spin-
    ning."
Awkward and dumb with delight, that a thought of him had
    been mingled

---

[1] Luke ix. 62. "No man, having put his hand to the plough and
looking back, is fit for the kingdom of God."

Thus in the sacred psalm, that came from the heart of the
maiden,
Silent before her he stood, and gave her the flowers for an
answer,
Finding no words for his thought. He remembered that day
in the winter,
After the first great snow, when he broke a path from the
village,
Reeling and plunging along through the drifts that encum-
bered the doorway,
Stamping the snow from his feet as he entered the house, and
Priscilla
Laughed at his snowy locks, and gave him a seat by the fire-
side,
Grateful and pleased to know he had thought of her in the
snow-storm.
Had he but spoken then! perhaps not in vain had he spoken;
Now it was all too late; the golden moment had vanished!
So he stood there abashed, and gave her the flowers for an
answer.

Then they sat down and talked of the birds and the beau-
tiful Spring-time,
Talked of their friends at home, and the May Flower that
sailed on the morrow.
"I have been thinking all day," said gently the Puritan
maiden,
"Dreaming all night, and thinking all day, of the hedgerows
of England,—
They are in blossom now, and the country is all like a garden;
Thinking of lanes and fields, and the song of the lark [1] and
the linnet,
Seeing the village street, and familiar faces of neighbors
Going about as of old, and stopping to gossip together,
And, at the end of the street, the village church, with the ivy
Climbing the old gray tower, and the quiet graves in the
churchyard.
Kind are the people I live with, and dear to me my religion;

[1] These birds are practically identified with England.

Still my heart is so sad, that I wish myself back in Old
    England.
You will say it is wrong, but I cannot help it: I almost
Wish myself back in Old England, I feel so lonely and
    wretched."

Thereupon answered the youth:—"Indeed I do not con-
    demn you;
Stouter hearts than a woman's have quailed in this terrible
    winter.
Yours is tender and trusting, and needs a stronger to lean on;
So I have come to you now, with an offer and proffer of mar-
    riage
Made by a good man and true, Miles Standish the Captain
    of Plymouth!"

Thus he delivered his message, the dexterous writer of
    letters,—
Did not embellish the theme, nor array it in beautiful phrases,
But came straight to the point, and blurted it out like a
    schoolboy;
Even the Captain himself could hardly have said it more
    bluntly.
Mute with amazement and sorrow, Priscilla the Puritan
    maiden
Looked into Alden's face, her eyes dilated with wonder,
Feeling his words like a blow, that stunned her and rendered
    her speechless;
Till at length she exclaimed, interrupting the ominous si-
    lence:
"If the great Captain of Plymouth is so very eager to wed me,
Why does he not come himself, and take the trouble to woo
    me?
If I am not worth the wooing, I surely am not worth the
    winning!"
Then John Alden began explaining and smoothing the matter,
Making it worse as he went, by saying the Captain was
    busy,—
Had no time for such things;—such things! the words
    grating harshly

Fell on the ear of Priscilla; and swift as a flash she made
>   answer:
"Has he no time for such things, as you call it, before he is
>   married,
Would he be likely to find it, or make it, after the wedding?
That is the way with you men; you don't understand us, you
>   cannot.
When you have made up your minds, after thinking of this
>   one and that one,
Choosing, selecting, rejecting, comparing one with another,
Then you make known your desire, with abrupt and sudden
>   avowal,
And are offended and hurt, and indignant perhaps, that a
>   woman
Does not respond at once to a love that she never suspected,
Does not attain at a bound the height to which you have
>   been climbing.
This is not right nor just: for surely a woman's affection
Is not a thing to be asked for, and had for only the asking.
When one is truly in love, one not only says it, but shows it.
Had he but waited awhile, had he only showed that he loved
>   me,
Even this Captain of yours—who knows?—at last might have
>   won me,
Old and rough as he is; but now it never can happen."

Still John Alden went on, unheeding the words of Priscilla,
Urging the suit of his friend, explaining, persuading, ex-
>   panding;
Spoke of his courage and skill, and of all his battles in
>   Flanders,
How with the people of God he had chosen to suffer affliction,
How, in return for his zeal, they had made him Captain of
>   Plymouth;
He was a gentleman born, could trace his pedigree plainly
Back to Hugh Standish of Duxbury Hall, in Lancashire, Eng-
>   land,
Who was the son of Ralph, and the grandson of Thurston de
>   Standish;
Heir unto vast estates, of which he was basely defrauded.

Still bore the family arms, and had for his crest [1] a cock
    argent
Combed and wattled gules, and all the rest of the blazon.
He was a man of honor, of noble and generous nature;
Though he was rough, he was kindly; she knew how during
    the winter
He had attended the sick, with a hand as gentle as woman's;
Somewhat hasty and hot, he could not deny it, and head-
    strong,
Stern as a soldier might be, but hearty, and placable always,
Not to be laughed at and scorned, because he was little of
    stature;
For he was great of heart, magnanimous, courtly, coura-
    geous;
Any woman in Plymouth, nay, any woman in England,
Might be happy and proud to be called the wife of Miles
    Standish!

But as he warmed and glowed, in his simple and eloquent
    language,
Quite forgetful of self, and full of the praise of his rival,
Archly the maiden smiled, and, with eyes overrunning with
    laughter,
Said, in a tremulous voice, "Why don't you speak for your-
    self, John?"

IV

JOHN ALDEN

Into the open air John Alden, perplexed and bewildered,
Rushed like a man insane, and wandered alone by the sea-
    side;
Paced up and down the sands, and bared his head to the east-
    wind,
Cooling his heated brow, and the fire and fever within him.
Slowly as out of the heavens, with apocalyptical splendors,
Sank the City of God,[2] in the vision of John the Apostle,
So, with its cloudy walls of chrysolite, jasper, and sapphire,

---

[1] Crest, argent, gules, and blazon, are terms of heraldry.
[2] Rev. xxi. 2.10. ff.

Sank the broad red sun, and over its turrets uplifted
Glimmered the golden reed of the angel who measured the
city.

"Welcome, O wind of the East!" he exclaimed in his wild
exultation,
"Welcome, O wind of the East, from the caves of the misty
Atlantic!
Blowing o'er fields of dulse,[1] and measureless meadows of sea-
grass,
Blowing o'er rocky wastes, and the grottos and gardens of
ocean!
Lay thy cold, moist hand on my burning forehead, and wrap
me
Close in thy garments of mist, to allay the fever within me!"

Like an awakened conscience, the sea was moaning and
tossing,
Beating remorseful and loud the mutable sands of the sea-
shore.
Fierce in his soul was the struggle and tumult of passions
contending;
Love triumphant and crowned, and friendship wounded and
bleeding,
Passionate cries of desire, and importunate pleadings of duty!
"Is it my fault," he said, "that the maiden has chosen be-
tween us?
Is it my fault that he failed,—my fault that I am the victor?"
Then within him there thundered a voice, like the voice of
the Prophet:
"It hath displeased the Lord!"—and he thought of David's
transgression,[2]
Bathsheba's beautiful face, and his friend in the front of the
battle!
Shame and confusion of guilt, and abasement and self-con-
demnation,
Overwhelmed him at once; and he cried in the deepest con-
trition:
"It hath displeased the Lord! It is the temptation of Satan!"

[1] Dulse, a sea weed.   [2] 2 Samuel xi.

Then, uplifting his head, he looked at the sea, and beheld
there
Dimly the shadowy form of the May Flower riding at anchor,
Rocked on the rising tide, and ready to sail on the morrow;
Heard the voices of men through the mist, the rattle of
cordage
Thrown on the deck, the shouts of the mate, and the sailors'
"Ay, ay, Sir!"
Clear and distinct, but not loud, in the dripping air of the
twilight.
Still for a moment he stood, and listened, and stared at the
vessel,
Then went hurriedly on, as one who, seeing a phantom,
Stops, then quickens his pace, and follows the beckoning
shadow.
"Yes, it is plain to me now," he murmured; "the hand of the
Lord is
Leading me out of the land of darkness, the bondage of error,
Through the sea, that shall lift the walls of its waters around
me,
Hiding me, cutting me off, from the cruel thoughts that pur-
sue me.
Back will I go o'er the ocean, this dreary land will abandon,
Her whom I may not love, and him whom my heart has
offended.
Better to be in my grave in the green old churchyard in Eng-
land,
Close by my mother's side, and among the dust of my
kindred;
Better be dead and forgotten, than living in shame and dis-
honor!
Sacred and safe and unseen, in the dark of the narrow
chamber
With me my secret shall lie, like a buried jewel that glimmers
Bright on the hand that is dust, in the chambers of silence
and darkness,—
Yes, as the marriage ring of the great espousal hereafter!"

Thus as he spake, he turned, in the strength of his strong
resolution,

Leaving behind him the shore, and hurried along in the twi-
    light,
Through the congenial gloom of the forest silent and sombre,
Till he beheld the lights in the seven houses of Plymouth,
Shining like seven stars in the dusk and mist of the evening.
Soon he entered his door, and found the redoubtable Captain
Sitting alone, and absorbed in the martial pages of Cæsar,
Fighting some great campaign in Hainault or Brabant or
    Flanders.
"Long have you been on your errand," he said with a cheery
    demeanor,
Even as one who is waiting an answer, and fears not the
    issue.
"Not far off is the house, although the woods are between us;
But you have lingered so long, that while you were going and
    coming
I have fought ten battles and sacked and demolished a city.
Come, sit down, and in order relate to me all that has hap-
    pened."

    Then John Alden spake, and related the wondrous adven-
    ture,
From beginning to end, minutely, just as it happened;
How he had seen Priscilla, and how he had sped in his court-
    ship,
Only smoothing a little, and softening down her refusal.
But when he came at length to the words Priscilla had
    spoken,
Words so tender and cruel: "Why don't you speak for your-
    self, John?"
Up leaped the Captain of Plymouth, and stamped on the
    floor, till his armor
Clanged on the wall, where it hung, with a sound of sinister
    omen.
All his pent-up wrath burst forth in a sudden explosion,
Even as a hand-grenade, that scatters destruction around it.
Wildly he shouted, and loud: "John Alden! you have be-
    trayed me!
Me, Miles Standish, your friend! have supplanted, defrauded,
    betrayed me!

One of my ancestors ran his sword through the heart of Wat
    Tyler;
Who shall prevent me from running my own through the
    heart of a traitor?
Yours is the greater treason, for yours is a treason to friend-
    ship!
You, who lived under my roof, whom I cherished and loved
    as a brother;
You, who have fed at my board, and drunk at my cup, to
    whose keeping
I have intrusted my honor, my thoughts the most sacred and
    secret,—
You too, Brutus! [1] ah woe to the name of friendship here-
    after!
Brutus was Cæsar's friend, and you were mine, but hence-
    forward
Let there be nothing between us save war, and implacable
    hatred!"

So spake the Captain of Plymouth, and strode about in the
    chamber,
Chafing and choking with rage; like cords were the veins on
    his temples.
But in the midst of his anger a man appeared at the doorway,
Bringing in uttermost haste a message of urgent importance,
Rumors of danger and war and hostile incursions of Indians!
Straightway the Captain paused, and, without further ques-
    tion or parley,
Took from the nail on the wall his sword with its scabbard
    of iron,
Buckled the belt round his waist, and, frowning fiercely,
    departed.
Alden was left alone. He heard the clank of the scabbard
Growing fainter and fainter, and dying away in the distance.
Then he arose from his seat, and looked forth into the dark-
    ness,

[1] Dying words of Cæsar, quoted by Shakespeare: "Et tu, Brute!"
Julius Cæsar, III. 1.

Felt the cool air blow on his cheek, that was hot with the
    insult,
Lifted his eyes to the heavens, and, folding his hands as in
    childhood,
Prayed in the silence of night to the Father who seeth in
    secret.

  Meanwhile the choleric Captain strode wrathful away to
    the council,
Found it already assembled, impatiently waiting his coming;
Men in the middle of life, austere and grave in deportment,
Only one of them old, the hill that was nearest to heaven,
Covered with snow, but erect, the excellent Elder [1] of Plym-
    outh.
God had sifted three kingdoms to find the wheat for this
    planting,
Then had sifted the wheat, as the living seed of a nation;
So say the chronicles old, and such is the faith of the people!
Near them was standing an Indian, in attitude stern and
    defiant,
Naked down to the waist, and grim and ferocious in aspect;
While on the table before them was lying unopened a Bible,
Ponderous, bound in leather, brass-studded, printed in Hol-
    land,
And beside it outstretched the skin of a rattlesnake glittered,
Filled, like a quiver, with arrows; a signal and challenge of
    warfare,
Brought by the Indian, and speaking with arrowy tongues of
    defiance.
This Miles Standish beheld, as he entered, and heard them
    debating
What were an answer befitting the hostile message and
    menace,
Talking of this and of that, contriving, suggesting, objecting;
One voice only for peace, and that the voice of the Elder,
Judging it wise and well that some at least were converted,
Rather than any were slain, for this was but Christian be-
    havior! [2]

  [1] William Brewster.
  [2] This was the remark of John Robinson, who wrote them from
Leyden.

Then outspake Miles Standish, the stalwart Captain of
    Plymouth,
Muttering deep in his throat, for his voice was husky with
    anger,
"What! do you mean to make war with milk and the water
    of roses?
Is it to shoot red squirrels you have your howitzer planted
There on the roof of the church, or is it to shoot red devils?
Truly the only tongue that is understood by a savage
Must be the tongue of fire that speaks from the mouth of
    the cannon!"
Thereupon answered and said the excellent Elder of Plym-
    outh,
Somewhat amazed and alarmed at this irreverent language:
"Not so thought Saint Paul, nor yet the other Apostles;
Not from the cannon's mouth were the tongues of fire [1] they
    spake with!"
But unheeded fell this mild rebuke on the Captain,
Who had advanced to the table, and thus continued dis-
    coursing:
"Leave this matter to me, for to me by right it pertaineth.
War is a terrible trade; but in the cause that is righteous,
Sweet is the smell of powder; and thus I answer the chal-
    lenge!"

    Then from the rattlesnake's skin, with a sudden, con-
        temptuous gesture,
Jerking the Indian arrows, he filled it with powder and bullets
Full to the very jaws,[2] and handed it back to the savage,
Saying, in thundering tones: "Here, take it! this is your
    answer!"
Silently out of the room then glided the glistening savage,
Bearing the serpent's skin, and seeming himself like a serpent.
Winding his sinuous way in the dark to the depths of the
    forest.

[1] See Acts ii. 1-4.
[2] This act is usually attributed to Governor Bradford.

V

THE SAILING OF THE MAY FLOWER

Just in the gray of the dawn, as the mists up-rose from the
    meadows,
There was a stir and a sound in the slumbering village of
    Plymouth;
Clanging and clicking of arms, and the order imperative,
    "Forward!"
Given in tone suppressed, a tramp of feet, and then silence.
Figures ten, in the mist, marched slowly out of the village.
Standish the stalwart it was, with eight of his valorous army,
Led by their Indian guide, by Hobomok, friend of the white
    men,
Northward marching to quell the sudden revolt of the savage.
Giants they seemed in the mist, or the mighty men of King
    David; [1]
Giants in heart they were, who believed in God and the
    Bible,—
Ay, who believed in the smiting of Midianites and Philistines.
Over them gleamed far off the crimson banners of morning;
Under them loud on the sands, the serried billows, advancing,
Fired along the line, and in regular order retreated.

Many a mile had they marched, when at length the village
    of Plymouth
Woke from its sleep, and arose, intent on its manifold labors.
Sweet was the air and soft; and slowly the smoke from the
    chimneys
Rose over the roofs of thatch, and pointed steadily eastward;
Men came forth from the doors, and paused and talked of the
    weather,
Said that the wind had changed, and was blowing fair for the
    May Flower;
Talked of their Captain's departure, and all the dangers that
    menaced,
He being gone, the town, and what should be done in his
    absence.

[1] See 2 Samuel xxiii. 8 ff.

Merrily sang the birds, and the tender voices of women
Consecrated with hymns the common cares of the household.
Out of the sea rose the sun, and the billows rejoiced at his
    coming;
Beautiful were his feet on the purple tops of the mountains;
Beautiful on the sails of the May Flower riding at anchor,
Battered and blackened and worn by all the storms of the
    winter.
Loosely against her masts was hanging and flapping her
    canvas,
Rent by so many gales, and patched by the hands of the
    sailors.
Suddenly from her side, as the sun rose over the ocean,
Darted a puff of smoke, and floated seaward; anon rang
Loud over field and forest the cannon's roar, and the echoes
Heard and repeated the sound, the signal-gun of departure!
Ah! but with louder echoes replied the hearts of the people!
Meekly, in voices subdued, the chapter was read from the
    Bible,
Meekly the prayer was begun, but ended in fervent entreaty!
Then from their houses in haste came forth the Pilgrims of
    Plymouth,
Men and women and children, all hurrying down to the sea-
    shore,
Eager, with tearful eyes, to say farewell to the May Flower,
Homeward bound o'er the sea, and leaving them here in the
    desert.

    Foremost among them was Alden. All night he had lain
    without slumber,
Turning and tossing about in the heat and unrest of his fever.
He had beheld Miles Standish, who came back late from the
    council,
Stalking into the room, and heard him mutter and murmur,
Sometimes it seemed a prayer, and sometimes it sounded like
    swearing.
Once he had come to the bed, and stood there a moment in
    silence;
Then he had turned away, and said "I will not awake him;

Let him sleep on, it is best; for what is the use of more
talking!"
Then he extinguished the light, and threw himself down on
his pallet,
Dressed as he was, and ready to start at the break of the
morning,—
Covered himself with the cloak he had worn in his campaigns
in Flanders,—
Slept as a soldier sleeps in his bivouac, ready for action.
But with the dawn he arose; in the twilight Alden beheld him
Put on his corselet of steel, and all the rest of his armor,
Buckle about his waist his trusty blade of Damascus,
Take from the corner his musket, and so stride out of the
chamber.
Often the heart of the youth had burned and yearned to em-
brace him,
Often his lips had essayed to speak, imploring for pardon;
All the old friendship came back, with its tender and grateful
emotions;
But his pride overmastered the nobler nature within him,—
Pride, and the sense of his wrong, and the burning fire of the
insult.
So he beheld his friend departing in anger, but spake not,
Saw him go forth to danger, perhaps to death, and he spake
not!
Then he arose from his bed, and heard what the people were
saying,
Joined in the talk at the door, with Stephen and Richard and
Gilbert,
Joined in the morning prayer, and in the reading of Scripture,
And, with the others, in haste went hurrying down to the sea-
shore,
Down to the Plymouth Rock, that had been to their feet as
a door-step
Into a world unknown,—the corner-stone of a nation!

There with his boat was the Master, already a little impatient
Lest he should lose the tide, or the wind might shift to the
eastward,

Square-built, hearty, and strong, with an odor of ocean about
  him,
Speaking with this one and that, and cramming letters and
  parcels
Into his pockets capacious, and messages mingled together
Into his narrow brain, till at last he was wholly bewildered.
Nearer the boat stood Alden, with one foot placed on the
  gunwale,
One still firm on the rock, and talking at times with the
  sailors.
Seated erect on the thwarts,[1] all ready and eager for starting.
He too was eager to go, and thus put an end to his anguish,
Thinking to fly from despair, that swifter than keel is or
  canvas,
Thinking to drown in the sea the ghost that would rise and
  pursue him.
But as he gazed on the crowd, he beheld the form of Priscilla
Standing dejected among them, unconscious of all that was
  passing.
Fixed were her eyes upon his, as if she divined his intention,
Fixed with a look so sad, so reproachful, imploring, and
  patient,
That with a sudden revulsion his heart recoiled from its pur-
  pose,
As from the verge of a crag, where one step more is destruc-
  tion.
Strange is the heart of man, with its quick, mysterious
  instincts!
Strange is the life of man, and fatal or fated are moments,
Whereupon turn, as on hinges, the gates of the wall adaman-
  tine!
"Here I remain!" he exclaimed, as he looked at the heavens
  above him,
Thanking the Lord whose breath had scattered the mist and
  the madness,
Wherein, blind and lost, to death he was staggering headlong.
"Yonder snow-white cloud, that floats in the ether above me,
Seems like a hand that is pointing and beckoning over the
  ocean.

[1] Thwarts, seats for the oarsmen.

There is another hand, that is not so spectral and ghost-
   like,
Holding me, drawing me back, and clasping mine for pro-
   tection.
Float, O hand of cloud, and vanish away in the ether!
Roll thyself up like a fist, to threaten and daunt me; I heed
   not
Either your warning or menace, or any omen of evil!
There is no land so sacred, no air so pure and so wholesome,
As is the air she breathes, and the soil that is pressed by her
   footsteps.
Here for her sake will I stay, and like an invisible presence
Hover around her for ever, protecting, supporting her weak-
   ·   ness;
Yes! as my foot was the first that stepped on this rock at the
   landing,
So, with the blessing of God, shall it be the last at the
   leaving!"

Meanwhile the Master alert, but with dignified air and
   important,
Scanning with watchful eye the tide and the wind and the
   weather,
Walked about on the sands; and the people crowded around
   him
Saying a few last words, and enforcing his careful remem-
   brance.
Then, taking each by the hand, as if he were grasping a tiller,
Into the boat he sprang, and in haste shoved off to his vessel,
Glad in his heart to get rid of all this worry and flurry,
Glad to be gone from a land of sand and sickness and sorrow,
Short allowance of victual, and plenty of nothing but Gospel!
Lost in the sound of the oars was the last farewell of the Pil-
   grims.
O strong hearts and true! not one went back in the May
   Flower!
No, not one looked back, who had set his hand to this
   ploughing! [1]

[1] See note, p. 73.

Soon were heard on board the shouts and songs of the
    sailors
Heaving the windlass round, and hoisting the ponderous
    anchor.
Then the yards were braced, and all sails set to the west-
    wind.
Blowing steady and strong; and the May Flower sailed from
    the harbor,
Rounded the point of the Gurnet,[1] and leaving far to the
    southward
Island and cape of sand, and the Field of the First En-
    counter,
Took the wind on her quarter, and stood for the open At-
    lantic,
Born on the send [2] of the sea, and the swelling hearts of the
    Pilgrims.

Long in silence they watched the receding sail of the vessel,
Much endeared to them all, as something living and human;
Then, as if filled with the spirit, and wrapt in a vision pro-
    phetic,
Baring his hoary head, the excellent Elder of Plymouth
Said, "Let us pray!" and they prayed, and thanked the Lord
    and took courage.
Mournfully sobbed the waves at the base of the rock, and
    above them
Bowed and whispered the wheat on the hill of death, and
    their kindred
Seemed to awake in their graves, and to join in the prayer
    that they uttered.
Sun-illumined and white, on the eastern verge of the ocean
Gleamed the departing sail, like a marble slab in a grave-
    yard;
Buried beneath it lay for ever all hope of escaping.
Lo! as they turned to depart, they saw the form of an Indian,
Watching them from the hill; but while they spake with each
    other,

[1] At the North side of the entrance to Plymouth Harbor. There
are now two lighthouses there.
[2] The pushing motion of the wave.

Pointing with outstretched hands, and saying, "Look!" he
　　　had vanished.
So they returned to their homes; but Alden lingered a little,
Musing alone on the shore, and watching the wash of the
　　　billows
Round the base of the rock, and the sparkle and flash of the
　　　sunshine,
Like the spirit of God, moving visibly over the waters.

VI

PRISCILLA

Thus for a while he stood, and mused by the shore of the
　　　ocean,
Thinking of many things, and most of all Priscilla;
And as if thought had the power [1] to draw to itself, like the
　　　load-stone,
Whatsoever it touches, by subtile laws of its nature,
Lo! as he turned to depart, Priscilla was standing beside him.

"Are you so much offended, you will not speak to me?" said
　　　she.
"Am I so much to blame, that yesterday, when you were
　　　pleading
Warmly the cause of another, my heart, impulsive and way-
　　　ward,
Pleaded your own, and spake out, forgetful perhaps of
　　　decorum?
Certainly you can forgive me for speaking so frankly, for
　　　saying*
What I ought not to have said, yet now I can never unsay it;
For there are moments in life, when the heart is so full of
　　　emotion,
That if by chance it be shaken, or into its depths like a pebble
Drops some careless word, it overflows, and its secret,
Spilt on the ground like water, can never be gathered to-
　　　gether.

　　[1] This phenomenon is to-day recognized under the name of
telepathy.

Yesterday I was shocked, when I heard you speak of Miles
    Standish,
Praising his virtues, transforming his very defects into vir-
    tues,
Praising his courage and strength, and even his fighting in
    Flanders,
As if by fighting alone you could win the heart of a woman,
Quite overlooking yourself and the rest, in exalting your hero.
Therefore I spake as I did, by an irresistible impulse.
You will forgive me, I hope, for the sake of the friendship
    between us,
Which is too true and too sacred to be so easily broken!"
Thereupon answered John Alden, the scholar, the friend of
    Miles Standish:
"I was not angry with you, with myself alone I was angry,
Seeing how badly I managed the matter I had in my keeping."
"No!" interrupted the maiden, with answer prompt and de-
    cisive;
"No; you were angry with me, for speaking so frankly and
    freely.
It was wrong, I acknowledge; for it is the fate of a woman
Long to be patient and silent, to wait like a ghost that is
    speechless,
Till some questioning voice dissolves the spell of its silence.
Hence is the inner life of so many suffering women
Sunless and silent and deep, like subterranean rivers
Running through caverns of darkness, unheard, unseen, and
    unfruitful,
Chafing their channels of stone, with endless and profitless
    murmurs."
Thereupon answered John Alden, the young man, the lover
    of women:
"Heaven forbid it, Priscilla; and truly they seem to me
    always
More like the beautiful rivers that watered the garden of
    Eden,
More like the river Euphrates, through deserts of Havilah [1]
    flowing,

[1] See Gen. ii. 11, 12. "The land of Havilah where there is gold;
and the gold of that land is good: there is bdellium and the onyx
stone."

Filling the land with delight, and memories sweet of the
 garden!"
"Ah, by these words, I can see," again interrupted the
 maiden,
"How very little you prize me, or care for what I am saying.
When from the depths of my heart, in pain and with secret
 misgiving,
Frankly I speak to you, asking for sympathy only and kind-
 ness,
Straightway you take up my words, that are plain and direct
 and in earnest,
Turn them away from their meaning, and answer with flat-
 tering phrases.
This is not right, is not just, is not true to the best that is
 in you;
For I know and esteem you, and feel that your nature is
 noble,
Lifting mine up to a higher, a more ethereal level.
Therefore I value your friendship, and feel it perhaps the
 more keenly
If you say aught that implies I am only as one among many,
If you make use of those common and complimentary
 phrases
Most men think so fine, in dealing and speaking with women,
But which women reject as insipid, if not as insulting."

Mute and amazed was Alden; and listened and looked at
 Priscilla,
Thinking he never had seen her more fair, more divine in
 her beauty.
He who but yesterday pleaded so glibly the cause of another,
Stood there embarrassed and silent, and seeking in vain for
 an answer.
So the maiden went on, and little divined or imagined
What was at work in his heart, that made him so awkward
 and speechless.
"Let us, then, be what we are, and speak what we think, and
 in all things
Keep ourselves loyal to truth, and the sacred professions of
 friendship.

It is no secret I tell you, nor am I ashamed to declare:
I have liked to be with you, to see you, to speak with you
    always.
So I was hurt at your words, and a little affronted to hear you
Urge me to marry your friend, though he were the Captain
    Miles Standish.
For I must tell you the truth: much more to me is your
    friendship
Than all the love he could give, were he twice the hero you
    think him."
Then she extended her hand, and Alden, who eagerly grasped
    it,
Felt all the wounds in his heart, that were aching and bleed-
    ing so sorely,
Healed by the touch of that hand, and he said, with a voice
    full of feeling:
"Yes, we must ever be friends, and of all who offer you
    friendship
Let me be ever the first, the truest, the nearest and dearest!"

Casting a farewell look at the glimmering sail of the May
    Flower,
Distant, but still in sight, and sinking below the horizon,
Homeward together they walked, with a strange, indefinite
    feeling,
That all the rest had departed and left them alone in the
    desert.
But, as they went through the fields in the blessing and smile
    of the sunshine,
Lighter grew their hearts, and Priscilla said very archly:
"Now that our terrible Captain has gone in pursuit of the
    Indians,
Where he is happier far than he would be commanding a
    household,
You may speak boldly, and tell me of all that happened
    between you,
When you returned last night, and said how ungrateful you
    found me."
Thereupon answered John Alden, and told her the whole of
    the story,—

Told her his own despair, and the direful wrath of Miles
    Standish.
Whereat the maiden smiled, and said between laughing and
    earnest,
"He is a little chimney, and heated hot in a moment!"
But as he gently rebuked her, and told her how much he had
    suffered,—
How he had even determined to sail that day in the May
    Flower,
And had remained for her sake, on hearing the dangers that
    threatened,—
All her manner was changed, and she said with a faltering
    accent,
"Truly I thank you for this: how good you have been to
    me always!"

    Thus, as a pilgrim devout, who toward Jerusalem journeys,
Taking three steps in advance, and one reluctantly backward,
Urged by importunate zeal, and withheld by pangs of con-
    trition;
Slowly but steadily onward, receding yet ever advancing,
Journeyed this Puritan youth to the Holy Land of his long-
    ings
Urged by the fervor of love, and withheld by remorseful mis-
    givings.

VII

THE MARCH OF MILES STANDISH

Meanwhile the stalwart Miles Standish was marching
    steadily northward,
Winding through forest and swamp, and along the trend of
    the sea-shore;
All day long, with hardly a halt, the fire of his anger
Burning and crackling within, and the sulphurous odor of
    powder
Seeming more sweet to his nostrils than all the scents of the
    forest.
Silent and moody he went, and much he revolved his discom-
    fort;

He who was used to success, and to easy victories always,
Thus to be flouted, rejected, and laughed to scorn by a
    maiden,
Thus to be mocked and betrayed by the friend whom most
    he had trusted!
Ah! 't was too much to be borne, and he fretted and chafed in
    his armor!

"I alone am to blame," he muttered, "for mine was the
    folly.
What has a rough old soldier, grown grim and gray in the
    harness,
Used to the camp and its ways, to do with the wooing of
    maidens?
'T was but a dream,—let it pass,—let it vanish like so many
    others!
What I thought was a flower, is only a weed, and is worth-
    less;
Out of my heart will I pluck it, and throw it away, and hence-
    forward
Be but a fighter of battles, a lover and wooer of dangers!"
Thus he revolved in his mind his sorry defeat and discom-
    fort,
While he was marching by day or lying at night in the forest,
Looking up at the trees, and the constellations beyond them.

After a three days' march he came to an Indian encamp-
    ment
Pitched on the edge of a meadow, between the sea and the
    forest;
Women at work by the tents, and the warriors, horrid with
    war paint,
Seated about a fire, and smoking and talking together;
Who, when they saw from afar the sudden approach of the
    white men,
Saw the flash of the sun on breastplate and sabre and musket,
Straightway leaped to their feet, and two, from among them
    advancing,
Came to parley with Standish, and offer him furs as a present;
Friendship was in their looks, but in their hearts there was
    hatred.

Braves of the tribe were these, and brothers gigantic in
    stature,
Huge as Goliath of Gath, or the terrible Og, king of Bashan;
One was Pecksuot named, and the other was called Watta-
    wamat.
Round their necks were suspended their knives in scabbards
    of wampum,
Two-edged, trenchant knives, with points as sharp as a
    needle.
Other arms had they none, for they were cunning and crafty.
"Welcome, English!" they said,—these words they had
    learned from the traders
Touching at times on the coast, to barter and chaffer for
    peltries.
Then in their native tongue they began to parley with
    Standish,
Through his guide and interpreter, Hobomok, friend of the
    white man,
Begging for blankets and knives, but mostly for muskets and
    powder,
Kept by the white man, they said, concealed, with the plague,
    in his cellars,
Ready to be let loose, and destroy his brother the red man!
But when Standish refused, and said he would give them the
    Bible,
Suddenly changing their tone, they began to boast and to
    bluster,
Then Wattawamat advanced with a stride in front of the
    other,
And, with a lofty demeanor, thus vauntingly spake to the
    Captain:
"Now Wattawamat can see, by the fiery eyes of the Captain,
Angry is he in his heart; but the heart of the brave Watta-
    wamat
Is not afraid at the sight. He was not born of a woman,
But on a mountain, at night, from an oak-tree riven by light-
    ning,
Forth he sprang at a bound, with all his weapons about him,
Shouting, 'Who is there here to fight with the brave Watta-
    wamat?'"

Then he unsheathed his knife, and, whetting the blade on his
    left hand,
Held it aloft and displayed a woman's face on the handle,
Saying, with bitter expression and look of sinister meaning:
"I have another at home, with the face of a man on the
    handle;
By and by they shall marry; and there will be plenty of
    children!"

    Then stood Pecksuot forth, self-vaunting, insulting Miles
    Standish:
While with his fingers he patted the knife that hung at his
    bosom,
Drawing it half from its sheath, and plunging it back, as he
    muttered,
"By and by it shall see; it shall eat; ah, ah! but shall speak
    not!
This is the mighty Captain the white men have sent to
    destroy us!
He is a little man; let him go and work with the women!"

    Meanwhile Standish had noted the faces and figures of
    Indians
Peeping and creeping about from bush to tree in the forest,
Feigning to look for game, with arrows set on their bow-
    strings,
Drawing about him still closer and closer the net of their
    ambush.
But undaunted he stood, and dissembled and treated them
    smoothly;
So the old chronicles say, that were writ in the days of the
    fathers.
But when he heard their defiance, the boast, the taunt, and
    the insult,
All the hot blood of his race, of Sir Hugh and of Thurston
    de Standish,
Boiled and beat in his heart, and swelled in the veins of his
    temples.
Headlong he leaped on the boaster, and, snatching his knife
    from its scabbard,
Plunged it into his heart, and, reeling backward, the savage

Fell with his face to the sky, and a fiendlike fierceness upon it.
Straight there arose from the forest the awful sound of the
  war whoop,
And, like a flurry of snow on the whistling wind of De-
  cember,
Swift and sudden and keen came a flight of feathery arrows.
Then came a cloud of smoke, and out of the cloud came the
  lightning,
Out of the lightning thunder; and death unseen ran before it.
Frightened the savages fled for shelter in swamp and in
  thicket,
Hotly pursued and beset; but their sachem, the brave Watta-
  wamat,
Fled not; he was dead. Unswerving and swift had a bullet
Passed through his brain, and he fell with both hands clutch-
  ing the greensward,
Seeming in death to hold back from his foe the land of his
  fathers.

There on the flowers of the meadow the warriors lay, and
  above them,
Silent, with folded arms, stood Hobomok, friend of the white
  man.
Smiling at length he exclaimed to the stalwart Captain of
  Plymouth:
"Pecksuot bragged very loud, of his courage, his strength,
  and his stature,—
Mocked the great Captain, and called him a little man; but I
  see now
Big enough have you been to lay him speechless before you!"

Thus the first battle was fought and won by the stalwart
  Miles Standish.
When the· tidings thereof were brought to the village of
  Plymouth,
And as a trophy of war the head of the brave Wattawamat
Scowled from the roof of the fort, which at once was a church
  and a fortress,[1]

[1] In Plymouth Colony the house of worship was fortified and
men habitually carried their muskets as they attended church on
Lord's Day.

All who beheld it rejoiced, and praised the Lord, and took
    courage.
Only Priscilla averted her face from this spectre of terror,
Thanking God in her heart that she had not married Miles
    Standish;
Shrinking, fearing almost, lest, coming home from his battles,
He should lay claim to her hand, as the prize and reward of
    his valor.

VIII

THE SPINNING-WHEEL

Month after month passed away, and in Autumn the ships
    of the merchants
Came with kindred and friends, with cattle and corn for the
    Pilgrims.
All in the village was peace; the men were intent on their
    labors,
Busy with hewing and building, with garden-plot and with
    merestead,[1]
Busy with breaking the glebe,[2] and mowing the grass in the
    meadows,
Searching the sea for its fish, and hunting the deer in the
    forest.
All in the village was peace; but at times the rumor of war-
    fare
Filled the air with alarm, and the apprehension of danger.
Bravely the stalwart Miles Standish was scouring the land
    with his forces,
Waxing valiant in fight and defeating the alien armies,
Till his name had become a sound of fear to the nations.
Anger was still in his heart, but at times the remorse and
    contrition
Which in all noble natures succeed the passionate outbreak,
Came like a rising tide, that encounters the rush of a river,
Staying its current awhile, but making it bitter and brackish.

[1] Farmstead.
[2] The word here means simply the turf.

Meanwhile Alden at home had built him a new habitation,
Solid, substantial, of timber rough-hewn from the firs of the
    forest.
Wooden-barred was the door, and the roof was covered with
    rushes;
Latticed the windows were, and the window-panes were of
    paper,
Oiled to admit the light, while wind and rain were excluded.
There too he dug a well, and around it planted an orchard:
Still may be seen to this day some trace of the well and the
    orchard.
Close to the house was the stall, where, safe and secure from
    annoyance,
Raghorn, the snow-white steer, that had fallen to Alden's
    allotment
In the division of cattle, might ruminate in the night-time
Over the pastures he cropped, made fragrant by sweet penny
    royal.

Oft when his labor was finished, with eager feet would the
    dreamer
Follow the pathway that ran through the woods to the house
    of Priscilla,
Led by illusions romantic and subtile deceptions of fancy,
Pleasure disguised as duty, and love in the semblance of
    friendship.
Ever of her he thought, when he fashioned the walls of his
    dwelling;
Ever of her he thought, when he delved in the soil of his
    garden;
Ever of her he thought, when he read in his Bible on Sunday
Praise of the virtuous woman, as she is described in the
    Proverbs,[1]—
How the heart of her husband doth safely trust in her always,
How all the days of her life she will do him good, and not evil,
How she seeketh the wool and the flax and worketh with
    gladness,
How she layeth her hand to the spindle and holdeth the
    distaff,

[1] Proverbs xxxi. 10-31.

How she is not afraid of the snow for herself or her household,
Knowing her household are clothed with the scarlet cloth of
  her weaving!

  So as she sat at her wheel one afternoon in the Autumn,
Alden, who opposite sat, and was watching her dexterous
  fingers,
As if the thread she was spinning were that of his life and
  his fortune,
After a pause in their talk, thus spake to the sound of the
  spindle.
"Truly, Priscilla," he said, "when I see you spinning and
  spinning,
Never idle a moment, but thrifty and thoughtful of others,
Suddenly you are transformed, are visibly changed in a mo-
  ment.
You are no longer Priscilla, but Bertha [1] the Beautiful
  Spinner."
Here the light foot on the treadle grew swifter and swifter;
  the spindle
Uttered an angry snarl, and the thread snapped short in
  her fingers;
While the impetuous speaker, not heeding the mischief, con-
  tinued:
"You are the beautiful Bertha, the spinner, the queen of
  Helvetia;
She whose story I read at a stall in the streets of South-
  ampton,
Who, as she rode on her palfrey, o'er valley and meadow and
  mountain,
Ever was spinning her thread from a distaff fixed to her
  saddle.
She was so thrifty and good, that her name passed into a
  proverb.
So shall it be with your own, when the spinning-wheel shall
  no longer

---

[1] Bertha, mother of Charlemagne, and known as Bertha of the
Great Feet. She died in 783, and during the Middle Ages many poems
and legends were written of her. Longfellow refers to her in his
volume entitled Driftwood.

Hum in the house of the farmer, and fill its chambers with
  music.
Then shall the mothers, reproving, relate how it was in their
  childhood,
Praising the good old times, and the days of Priscilla the
  spinner!"
Straight uprose from her wheel the beautiful Puritan maiden,
Pleased with the praise of her thrift from him whose praise
  was the sweetest,
Drew from the reel on the table a snowy skein of her spin-
  ning,
Thus making answer, meanwhile, to the flattering phrases of
  Alden:
"Come, you must not be idle; if I am a pattern for house-
  wives,
Show yourself equally worthy of being the model of hus-
  bands.
Hold this skein on your hands, while I wind it, ready for
  knitting;
Then who knows but hereafter, when fashions have changed
  and the manners,
Fathers may talk to their sons of the good old times of John
  Alden!"
Thus, with a jest and a laugh, the skein on his hands she
  adjusted,
He sitting awkwardly there, with his arms extended before
  him,
She standing graceful, erect, and winding the thread from
  his fingers,
Sometimes chiding a little his clumsy manner of holding,
Sometimes touching his hands, as she disentangled expertly
Twist or knot in the yarn, unawares—for how could she
  help it?—
Sending electrical thrills through every nerve in his body.

  Lo! in the midst of this scene, a breathless messenger
    entered,
Bringing in hurry and heat the terrible news from the village.
Yes; Miles Standish was dead!—an Indian had brought them
  the tidings,—

Slain by a poisoned arrow, shot down in the front of the
    battle,
Into an ambush beguiled, cut off with the whole of his forces;
All the town would be burned, and all the people be mur-
    dered!
Such were the tidings of evil that burst on the hearts of the
    hearers.
Silent and statue-like stood Priscilla, her face looking back-
    ward
Still at the face of the speaker, her arms uplifted in horror;
But John Alden, upstarting, as if the barb of the arrow
Piercing the heart of his friend had struck his own, and had
    sundered
Once and for ever the bonds that held him bound as a cap-
    tive,
Wild with excess of sensation, the awful delight of his free-
    dom,
Mingled with pain and regret, unconscious of what he was
    doing,
Clasped, almost with a groan, the motionless form of Priscilla,
Pressing her close to his heart, as for ever his own, and ex-
    claiming:
"Those whom the Lord hath united, let no man put them
    asunder!"

Even as rivulets twain, from distant and separate sources,
Seeing each other afar, as they leap from the rocks, and pur-
    suing
Each one its devious path, but drawing nearer and nearer,
Rush together at last, at their trysting-place in the forest;
So these lives that had run thus far in separate channels,
Coming in sight of each other, then swerving and flowing
    asunder,
Parted by barriers strong, but drawing nearer and nearer,
Rushed together at last, and one was lost in the other.

IX

THE WEDDING-DAY

Forth from the curtain of clouds, from the tent of purple and scarlet,
Issued the sun, the great High-Priest,[1] in his garments resplendent,
Holiness unto the Lord, in letters of light, on his forehead,
Round the hem of his robe the golden bells and pomegranates,
Blessing the world he came, and the bars of vapor beneath him
Gleamed like a grate of brass, and the sea at his feet was a laver.

This was the wedding morn of Priscilla the Puritan maiden.
Friends were assembled together; the Elder and Magistrate also
Graced the scene with their presence, and stood like the Law and the Gospel,
One with the sanction of earth and one with the blessing of heaven.
Simple and brief was the wedding, as that of Ruth and of Boaz.
Softly the youth and the maiden repeated the words of betrothal,
Taking each other for husband and wife in the Magistrate's presence,
After the Puritan way, and the laudable custom of Holland.
Fervently then, and devoutly, the excellent Elder of Plymouth
Prayed for the hearth and the home, that were founded that day in affection,
Speaking of life and of death, and imploring divine benedictions.

Lo! when the service was ended, a form appeared on the threshold,

[1] The dress of the High-Priest is fully described in Exodus xxxix. 1-31.

Clad in armor of steel, a sombre and sorrowful figure!
Why does the bridegroom start and stare at the strange apparition?
Why does the bride turn pale, and hide her face on his shoulder?
Is it a phantom of air,—a bodiless, spectral illusion?
Is it a ghost from the grave, that has come to forbid the betrothal?
Long had it stood there unseen, a guest uninvited, unwelcomed;
Over its clouded eyes there had passed at times an expression
Softening the gloom and revealing the warm heart hidden beneath them,
As when across the sky the driving rack of the rain-cloud
Grows for a moment thin, and betrays the sun by its brightness.
Once it had lifted its hand, and moved its lips, but was silent,
As if an iron will had mastered the fleeting intention.
But when were ended the troth and the prayer and the last benediction,
Into the room it strode, and the people beheld with amazement
Bodily there in his armor Miles Standish, the Captain of Plymouth!
Grasping the bridegroom's hand, he said with emotion, "Forgive me!
I have been angry and hurt,—too long have I cherished the feeling;
I have been cruel and hard, but now, thank God! it is ended.
Mine is the same hot blood that leaped in the veins of Hugh Standish,
Sensitive, swift to resent, but as swift in atoning for error.
Never so much as now was Miles Standish the friend of John Alden."
Thereupon answered the bridegroom: "Let all be forgotten between us.—
All save the dear old friendship, and that shall grow older and dearer!"
Then the Captain advanced, and, bowing, saluted Priscilla,

Gravely, and after the manner of old-fashioned gentry in
England,
Something of camp and of court, of town and of country,
commingled,
Wishing her joy of her wedding, and loudly lauding her
husband.
Then he said with a smile: "I should have remembered the
adage,—
If you would be well served, you must serve yourself; and
moreover,
No man can gather cherries in Kent at the season of Christ-
mas."

Great was the people's amazement, and greater yet their
rejoicing,
Thus to behold once more the sun-burnt face of their captain,
Whom they had mourned as dead; and they gathered and
crowded about him,
Eager to see him and hear him, forgetful of bride and of
bridegroom,
Questioning, answering, laughing, and each interrupting the
other,
Till the good Captain declared, being quite overpowered and
bewildered,
He had rather by far break into an Indian encampment,
Than come again to a wedding to which he had not been
invited.

Meanwhile the bridegroom went forth and stood with the
bride at the doorway,
Breathing the perfumed air of that warm and beautiful
morning.
Touched with autumnal tints, but lonely and sad in the sun-
shine,
Lay extended before them the land of toil and privation;
There were the graves of the dead, and the barren waste of
the sea-shore,
There the familiar fields, the groves of pine, and the
meadows;
But to their eyes transfigured, it seemed as the Garden of
Eden,

Filled with the presence of God, whose voice was the sound
of the ocean.

Soon was their vision disturbed by the noise and stir of
departure,
Friends coming forth from the house, and impatient of
longer delaying,
Each with his plan for the day, and the work that was left
uncompleted.
Then from a stall near at hand, amid exclamations of wonder,
Alden the thoughtful, the careful, so happy, so proud of
Priscilla,
Brought out his snow-white steer, obeying the hand of its
master,
Led by a cord that was tied to an iron ring in its nostrils,
Covered with crimson cloth, and a cushion placed for a
saddle.
She should not walk, he said, through the dust and heat of
the noonday;
Nay, she should ride like a queen, not plod along like a
peasant.
Somewhat alarmed at first, but reassured by the others,
Placing her hand on the cushion, her foot in the hand of her
husband,
Gayly, with joyous laugh, Priscilla mounted her palfrey.
"Nothing is wanting now," he said with a smile, "but the
distaff;
Then you would be in truth my queen, my beautiful Bertha!"

Onward the bridal procession now moved to their new
habitation,
Happy husband and wife, and friends conversing together.
Pleasantly murmured the brook, as they crossed the ford in
the forest,
Pleased with the image that passed, like a dream of love
through its bosom,
Tremulous, floating in air, o'er the depths of the azure
abysses.
Down through the golden leaves the sun was pouring his
splendors,

Gleaming on purple grapes, that, from branches above them
    suspended,
Mingled their odorous breath with the balm of the pine and
    the fir-tree,
Wild and sweet as the clusters that grew in the valley of
    Eshcol.[1]
Like a picture it seemed of the primitive, pastoral ages,
Fresh with the youth of the world, and recalling Rebecca and
    Isaac,
Old and yet ever new, and simple and beautiful always,
Love immortal and young in the endless succession of lovers.
So through the Plymouth woods passed onward the bridal
    procession.

[1] See Num. xiii. 23. "And they came unto the valley of Eshcol, and
cut down from thence a branch with one cluster of grapes, and
they bare it upon a staff between two."

THE SONG OF HIAWATHA

INTRODUCTION

SHOULD you ask me, whence these stories?
Whence these legends and traditions,
With the odors of the forest,
With the dew and damp of meadows,
With the curling smoke of wigwams,
With the rushing of great rivers,
With their frequent repetitions,
And their wild reverberations,
As of thunder in the mountains?
　　I should answer, I should tell you,
"From the forests and the prairies,
From the great lakes [1] of the Northland,
From the land of the Ojibways,
From the land of the Dacotahs,
From the mountains, moors, and fen-lands,
Where the heron, and Shuh-shuh-gah,
Feeds among the reeds and rushes.
I repeat them as I heard them
From the lips of Nawadaha,
The musician, the sweet singer."
　　Should you ask where Nawadaha
Found these songs, so wild and wayward,
Found these legends and traditions,
I should answer, I should tell you,
"In the bird's-nests of the forest,
In the lodges of the beaver,
In the hoof-prints of the bison,
In the eyrie of the eagle!
　　"All the wild-fowl sang them to him,
In the moorlands and the fen-lands,
In the melancholy marshes;
Chetowaik, the plover, sang them,

---

[1] The chain of lakes from Superior to Ontario.

Mahng, the loon, the wild-goose, Wawa,
The blue heron, the Shuh-shuh-gah,
And the grouse, the Mushkodasa!"
      If still further you should ask me,
Saying, "Who was Nawadaha?
Tell us of this Nawadaha,"
I should answer your inquiries
Straightway in such words as follow
      In the Vale of Tawasentha,[1]
In the green and silent valley,
By the pleasant watercourses,
Dwelt the singer Nawadaha.
Round about the Indian village
Spread the meadows and the cornfields,
And beyond them stood the forest,
Stood the groves of singing pinetrees;
Green in Summer, white in Winter,
Ever sighing, ever singing.
      "And the pleasant watercourses,
You could trace them through the valley,
By the rushing in the Spring-time,
By the alders in the Summer,
By the white fog in the Autumn,
By the black line in the Winter;
And beside them dwelt the singer,
In the vale of Tawasentha,
In the green and silent valley.
      "There he sang of Hiawatha,
Sang the Song of Hiawatha,
Sang his wondrous birth and being,
How he prayed and how he fasted,
How he lived, and toiled, and suffered,
That the tribes of men might prosper,
That he might advance his people!"
      Ye who love the haunts of Nature,
Love the sunshine of the meadow,
Love the shadow of the forest,
Love the wind among the branches,

[1] A creek now called Norman's Kill, running into the Hudson
River, four miles below Albany, N. Y.

And the rain-shower and the snowstorm,
And the rushing of great rivers
Through their palisades of pinetrees,
And the thunder in the mountains,
Whose innumerable echoes
Flap like eagles in their eyries;—
Listen to these wild traditions,
To this Song of Hiawatha!

Ye who love a nation's legends,
Love the ballads of a people,
That like voices from afar off
Waving like a hand that beckons,
Call to us to pause and listen,
Speak in tones so plain and childlike,
Scarcely can the ear distinguish
Whether they are sung or spoken;—
Listen to this Indian Legend,
To this Song of Hiawatha!

Ye whose hearts are fresh and simple,
Who have faith in God and Nature,
Who believe, that in all ages
Every human heart is human,
That in even savage bosoms
There are longings, yearnings, strivings
For the good they comprehend not,
That the feeble hands and helpless,
Groping blindly in the darkness, ·
Touch God's right hand in that darkness
And are lifted up and strengthened;—
Listen to this simple story,
To this Song of Hiawatha!

Ye, who sometimes in your rambles
Through the green lanes of the country,
Where the tangled barberry-bushes
Hang their tufts of crimson berries
Over stone walls gray with mosses,
Pause by some neglected graveyard,
For a while to muse, and ponder
On a half-effaced inscription,
Written with little skill of song-craft,

Homely phrases, but each letter
Full of hope, and yet of heart-break,
Full of all the tender pathos
Of the Here and the Hereafter;—
Stay and read this rude inscription,
Read this Song of Hiawatha!

I

THE PEACE-PIPE

On the Mountains of the Prairie,[1]
On the great Red Pipe-stone Quarry,
Gitche Manito, the mighty,
He the Master of Life, descending,
On the red crags of the quarry
Stood erect, and called the nations,
Called the tribes of men together.

[1] Mr. Catlin, in his *Letters and Notes on the Manners, Customs, and Conditions of the North American Indians,* Vol. II, p. 160, gives an interesting account of the *Coteau des Prairies,* and the Red Pipe-stone Quarry. He says:—

"Here (according to their traditions) happened the mysterious birth of the red pipe, which has blown its fumes of peace and war to the remotest corners of the continent: which has visited every warrior and passed through its reddened stem the irrevocable oath of war and desolation. And here also the peace-breathing calumet was born, and fringed with the eagle's quills, which has shed its thrilling fumes over the land, and soothed the fury of the relentless savage.

"The Great Spirit at an ancient period here called the Indian nations together, and standing on the precipice of the red pipe-stone rock, broke from its wall a piece, and made a huge pipe by turning it in his hand, which he smoked over them, and to the North, the South, the East, and the West, and told them that this stone was red,—that it was their flesh,—that they must use it for their pipes of peace,—that it belonged to them all, and that the war-club and scalping-knife must not be raised on its ground. At the last whiff of his pipe his head went into a great cloud, and the whole surface of the rock for several miles was melted and glazed; two great ovens were opened beneath, and two women (guardian spirits of the place) entered them in a blaze of fire; and they are heard there yet (Tso-mec-cos-tee and Tso-me-cos-te-won-dee), answering to the invocations of the high-priests or medicine-men, who consult them when they are visitors to this sacred place."

From his footprints flowed a river,
Leaped into the light of morning,
O'er the precipice plunging downward
Gleamed like Ishkoodah, the comet,
And the Spirit, stooping earthward,
With his finger on the meadow
Traced a winding pathway for it,
Saying to it, "Run in this way!"
From the red stone of the quarry
With his hand he broke a fragment,
Moulded it into a pipe-head,
Shaped and fashioned it with figures;
From the margin of the river
Took a long reed for a pipe-stem,
With its dark green leaves upon it;
Filled the pipe with bark of willow,
With the bark of the red willow;
Breathed upon the neighboring forest,
Made its great boughs chafe together,
Till in flame they burst and kindled;
And erect upon the mountains,
Gitche Manito, the mighty,
Smoked the calumet, the Peace-Pipe,
As a signal to the nations.

And the smoke rose slowly, slowly,
Through the tranquil air of morning,
First a single line of darkness,
Then a denser, bluer vapor,
Then a snow-white cloud unfolding,
Like the tree-tops of the forest,
Ever rising, rising, rising,
Till it touched the top of heaven,
Till it broke against the heaven,
And rolled outward all around it.

From the Vale of Tawasentha,
From the Valley of Wyoming,
From the groves of Tuscaloosa,
From the far-off Rocky Mountains,
From the Northern lakes and rivers
All the tribes beheld the signal,

Saw the distant smoke ascending,
The Pukwana [1] of the Peace-Pipe.
    And the Prophets of the nations
Said: "Behold it, the Pukwana,
By this signal from afar off,
Bending like a wand of willow,
Gitche Manito, the mighty,
Calls the tribes of men together,
Calls the warriors to his council!"
    Down the rivers o'er the prairies,
Came the warriors of the nations,
Came the Delawares and Mohawks,
Came the Choctaws and Camanches,
Came the Shoshonies and Blackfeet,
Came the Pawnees and Omawhas,[2]
Came the Mandans and Dacotahs,
Came the Hurons and Ojibways,
All the warriors drawn together
By the signal of the Peace-Pipe,
To the Mountains of the Prairie,
To the Great Red Pipe-stone Quarry.
    And they stood there on the meadow,
With their weapons and their war-gear,
Painted like the leaves of Autumn,
Painted like the sky of morning,
Wildly glaring at each other;
In their faces stern defiance,
In their hearts the feuds of ages,
The hereditary hatred,
The ancestral thirst of vengeance.
    Gitche Manito, the mighty,
The creator of the nations,
Looked upon them with compassion,
With paternal love and pity;
Looked upon their wrath and wrangling

[1] Smoke.
[2] Note the pronunciation, the accent being on the second syllable which makes the word euphonious,—very different from the pronunciation of the present day. A similar remark may be made of the Indian words Ida'ho, Otta'wa, and others.

But as quarrels among children,
But as feuds and fights of children!
  Over them he stretched his right hand,
To subdue their stubborn natures,
To allay their thirst and fever,
By the shadow of his right hand;
Spake to them with voice majestic
As the sound of far-off waters,
Falling into deep abysses,
Warning, chiding, spake in this wise:—
  "O my children! my poor children!
Listen to the words of wisdom,
Listen to the words of warning,
From the lips of the Great Spirit,
From the Master of Life, who made you:
  "I have given you lands to hunt in,
I have given you streams to fish in,
I have given you bear and bison,
I have given you roe and reindeer,
I have given you brant and beaver,
Filled the marshes full of wild fowl,
Filled the rivers full of fishes;
Why then are you not contented?
Why then will you hunt each other?
  "I am weary of your quarrels,
Weary of your wars and bloodshed,
Weary of your prayers for vengeance,
Of your wranglings and dissensions;
All your strength is in your union,
All your danger is in discord;
Therefore be at peace henceforward,
And as brothers live together.
  "I will send a Prophet to you,
A Deliverer of the nations,
Who shall guide you and shall teach you,
Who shall toil and suffer with you.
If you listen to his counsels,
You will multiply and prosper;
If his warnings pass unheeded,
You will fade away and perish!

"Bathe now in the stream before you,
Wash the war-paint from your faces,
Wash the blood-stains from your fingers,
Bury your war-clubs and your weapons,
Break the red stone from this quarry,
Mould and make it into Peace-Pipes,
Take the reeds that grow beside you,
Deck them with your brightest feathers,
Smoke the calumet [1] together,
And as brothers live henceforward!"

Then upon the ground the warriors
Threw their cloaks and shirts of deerskin,
Threw their weapons and their war-gear,
Leaped into the rushing river,
Washed the war-paint from their faces.
Clear above them flowed the water,
Clear and limpid from the footprints
Of the Master of Life descending;
Dark below them flowed the water,
Soiled and stained with streaks of crimson,
As if blood were mingled with it!

From the river came the warriors,
Clean and washed from all their war-paint;
On the banks their clubs they buried,
Buried all their warlike weapons.
Gitche Manito, the mighty,
The Great Spirit, the creator,
Smiled upon his helpless children

And in silence all the warriors
Broke the red stone of the quarry.
Smoothed and formed it into Peace-Pipes,
Broke the long reeds by the river,
Decked them with their brightest feathers,
And departed each one homeward,
While the Master of Life, ascending,
Through the opening of cloud-curtains,
Through the doorway of the heaven,
Vanished from before their faces,

[1] The pipe of peace.

In the smoke that rolled around him,
The Pukwana of the Peace-Pipe!

II

THE FOUR WINDS

"Honor be to Mudjekeewis!" [1]
Cried the warriors, cried the old men,
When he came in triumph homeward
With the sacred Belt of Wampum,
From the regions of the North-Wind,
From the kingdom of Wabasso, [2]
From the land of the White Rabbit
  He had stolen the Belt of Wampum
From the neck of Mishe-Mokwa,
From the Great Bear of the mountains,
From the terror of the nations,
As he lay asleep and cumbrous
On the summit of the mountains,
Like a rock with mosses on it.
Spotted brown and gray with mosses.
  Silently he stole upon him,
Till the red nails of the monster
Almost touched him, almost scared him,
Till the hot breath of his nostrils
Warmed the hands of Mudjekeewis,
As he drew the Belt of Wampum
Over the round ears, that heard not,
Over the small eyes, that saw not,
Over the long nose and nostrils,
The black muffle of the nostrils,
Out of which the heavy breathing
Warmed the hands of Mudjekeewis.
  Then he swung aloft his war-club,
Shouted loud and long his war-cry,
Smote the mighty Mishe-Mokwa

[1] The father of Hiawatha, the Wind, afterwards Kabeyun the
West Wind.
[2] This word means both the North and the white rabbit.

In the middle of the forehead,
Right between the eyes he smote him.
  With the heavy blow bewildered,
Rose the Great Bear of the mountains;
But his knees beneath him trembled,
And he whimpered like a woman,
As he reeled and staggered forward,
As he sat upon his haunches;
And the mighty Mudjekeewis,
Standing fearlessly before him,
Taunted him in loud derision,
Spake disdainfully in this wise:—

  "Hark you, Bear! you are a coward,[1]
And no Brave, as you pretended;
Else you would not cry and whimper
Like a miserable woman!
Bear! you know our tribes are hostile,
Long have been at war together;
Now you find that we are strongest,
You go sneaking in the forest,
You go hiding in the mountains!
Had you conquered me in battle
Not a groan would I have uttered;
But you, Bear! sit here and whimper,
And disgrace your tribe by crying,
Like a wretched Shaugodaya,
Like a cowardly old woman!"

  Then again he raised his war-club,
Smote again the Mishe-Mokwa
In the middle of his forehead,
Broke his skull, as ice is broken
When one goes to fish in Winter.

---

[1] This anecdote is from Heckewelder, in his account of the *Indian Nations,* he describes an Indian hunter as addressing a bear in nearly these words. "I was present," he says, "at the delivery of this curious invective; when the hunter had despatched the bear, I asked him how he thought that poor animal could understand what he said to it? 'O,' said he in answer, 'the bear understood me very well; did you not observe how *ashamed* he looked while I was upbraiding him?'"—*Transactions of the American Philosophical Society,* Vol. I, p. 240.

Thus was slain the Mishe-Mokwa,
He the Great Bear of the mountains,
He the terror of the nations.
  "Honor be to Mudjekeewis!"
With a shout exclaimed the people,
"Honor be to Mudjekeewis!
Henceforth he shall be the West-Wind,
And hereafter and forever
Shall he hold supreme dominion
Over all the winds of heaven.
Call him no more Mudjekeewis,
Call him Kabeyun, the West-Wind!"
  Thus was Mudjekeewis chosen
Father of the Winds of Heaven.
For himself he kept the West-Wind,
Gave the others to his children;
Unto Wabun gave East-Wind,
Gave the South to Shawondasee,
And the North-Wind, wild and cruel,
To the fierce Kabibonokka.
  Young and beautiful was Wabun;
He it was who brought the morning,
He it was whose silver arrows
Chased the dark o'er hill and valley;
He it was whose cheeks were painted
With the brightest streaks of crimson,
And whose voice awoke the village,
Called the deer, and called the hunter.
  Lonely in the sky was Wabun;
Though the birds sang gayly to him,
Though the wild-flowers of the meadow
Filled the air with odors for him,
Though the forests and the rivers
Sang and shouted at his coming.
Still his heart was sad within him,
For he was alone in heaven.
  But one morning, gazing earthward,
While the village still was sleeping,
And the fog lay on the river,
Like a ghost, that goes at sunrise,

He beheld a maiden walking
All alone upon a meadow,
Gathering water-flags and rushes
By a river in the meadow.

Every morning, gazing earthward,
Still the first thing he beheld there
Was her blue eyes looking at him,
Two blue lakes among the rushes.
And he loved the lonely maiden,
Who thus waited for his coming;
For they both were solitary,
She on earth and he in heaven.

And he wooed her with caresses,
Wooed her with his smile of sunshine,
With his flattering words he wooed her,
With his sighing and his singing,
Gentlest whispers in the branches,
Softest music, sweetest odors,
Till he drew her to his bosom,
Folded in his robes of crimson,
Till into a star he changed her,
Trembling still upon his bosom;
And forever in the heavens
They are seen together walking,
Wabun and the Wabun-Annung,
Wabun and the Star of Morning.

But the fierce Kabibonokka
Had his dwelling among icebergs,
In the everlasting snowdrifts,
In the kingdom of Wabasso,
In the land of the White Rabbit.
He it was whose hand in Autumn
Painted all the trees with scarlet,
Stained the leaves with red and yellow;
He it was who sent the snowflakes,
Sifting, hissing through the forest,
Froze the ponds, the lakes, the rivers,
Drove the loon and sea-gull southward,
Drove the cormorant and curfew

To their nests of sedge and sea-tang
In the realms of Shawondasee.
　　Once the fierce Kabibonokka
Issued from his lodge of snowdrifts,
From his home among the icebergs,
And his hair, with snow besprinkled,
Streamed behind him like a river,
Like a black and wintry river,
As he howled and hurried southward,
Over frozen lakes and moorlands.
　　There among the reeds and rushes
Found he Shingebis, the diver,
Trailing strings of fish behind him,
O'er the frozen fens and moorlands,
Lingering still among the moorlands,
Though his tribe had long departed
To the land of Shawondasee.
　　Cried the fierce Kabibonokka,
"Who is this that dares to brave me?
Dares to stay in my dominions,
When the Wawa has departed,
When the wild-goose has gone southward,
And the heron, the Shuh-shuh-gah,
Long ago departed southward?
I will go into his wigwam,
I will put his smouldering fire out!"
　　And at night Kabibonokka
To the lodge came wild and wailing,
Heaped the snow in drifts about it,
Shouted down into the smoke-flue,
Shook the lodge-poles in his fury,
Flapped the curtain of the doorway
Shingebis, the diver, feared not,
Shingebis, the diver, cared not;
Four great logs had he for firewood,
One for each moon of the winter,
And for food the fishes served him.
By his blazing fire he sat there,
Warm and merry, eating, laughing,
Singing "O Kabibonokka,

You are but my fellow-mortal!"
    Then Kabibonokka entered,
And though Shingebis, the diver,
Felt his presence by the coldness,
Felt his icy breath upon him,
Still he did not cease his singing,
Still he did not leave his laughing,
Only turned the log a little,
Only made the fire burn brighter,
Made the sparks fly up the smoke flue.
    From Kabibonokka's forehead,
From his snow-besprinkled tresses,
Drops of sweat fell fast and heavy,
Making dints upon the ashes,
As along the eaves of lodges,
As from drooping boughs of hemlock,
Drips the melting snow in springtime,
Making hollows in the snowdrifts.
    Till at last he rose defeated,
Could not bear the heat and laughter,
Could not bear the merry singing,
But rushed headlong through the doorway,
Stamped upon the crusted snowdrifts,
Stamped upon the lakes and rivers,
Made the snow upon them harder,
Made the ice upon them thicker,
Challenged Shingebis, the diver,
To come forth and wrestle with him,
To come forth and wrestle naked
On the frozen fens and moorlands.
    Forth went Shingebis, the diver,
Wrestled all night with the North-Wind,
    Wrestled naked on the moorlands
With the fierce Kabibonokka,
Till his panting breath grew fainter,
Till his frozen grasp grew feebler,
Till he reeled and staggered backward,
And retreated, baffled, beaten,
To the kingdom of Wabasso,
To the land of the White Rabbit,

Hearing still the gusty laughter,
Hearing Shingebis, the diver,
Singing, "O Kabibonokka,
You are but my fellow-mortal!"
    Shawondasee, fat and lazy,
Had his dwelling far to southward,
In the drowsy, dreamy sunshine,
In the never-ending Summer.
He it was who sent the wood-birds,
Sent the Opechee, the robin,
Sent the blue-bird, the Owaissa,
Sent the Shawshaw, sent the swallow,
Sent the wild-goose, Wawa, northward,
Sent the melons and tobacco,
And the grapes in purple clusters.
    From his pipe the smoke ascending
Filled the sky with haze and vapor,
Filled the air with dreamy softness,
Gave a twinkle to the water,
Touched the rugged hills with smoothness,
Brought the tender Indian Summer
To the melancholy North-land,
In the dreary Moon of Snow-shoes.
    Listless, careless, Shawondasee!
In his life he had one shadow,
In his heart one sorrow had he.
Once, as he was gazing northward,
Far away upon a prairie
He beheld a maiden standing,
Saw a tall and slender maiden
All alone upon a prairie;
Brightest green were all her garments
And her hair was like the sunshine.
    Day by day he gazed upon her,
Day by day he sighed with passion,
Day by day his heart within him
Grew more hot with love and longing
For the maid with yellow tresses.
But he was too fat and lazy
To bestir himself and woo her;

Yes, too indolent and easy
To pursue her and persuade her.
So he only gazed upon her,
Only sat and sighed with passion
For the maiden of the prairie.

Till one morning, looking northward,
He beheld her yellow tresses
Changed and covered o'er with whiteness,
Covered as with whitest snowflakes.
"Ah! my brother from the North-land,
From the kingdom of Wabasso,
From the land of the White Rabbit!
You have stolen the maiden from me,
You have laid your hand upon her,
You have wooed and won my maiden,
With your stories of the North-land!"

Thus the wretched Shawondasee
Breathed into the air his sorrow;
And the South-Wind o'er the prairie
Wandered warm with sighs of passion
With the sighs of Shawondasee,
Till the air seemed full of snowflakes,
Full of thistle-down the prairie,
And the maid with hair like sunshine
Vanished from his sight forever;
Nevermore did Shawondasee
See the maid with yellow tresses!

Poor, deluded Shawondasee!
'T was no woman that you gazed at,
'T was no maiden that you sighed for,
'T was the prairie dandelion
That through all the dreamy Summer
You had gazed at with such longing,
You had sighed for with such passion
And had puffed away forever,
Blown into the air with sighing.
Ah! deluded Shawondasee!

Thus the Four Winds were divided;
Thus the sons of Mudjekeewis
Had their stations in the heavens,

At the corners of the heavens;
For himself the West-Wind only
Kept the mighty Mudjekeewis.

III

HIAWATHA'S CHILDHOOD

Downward through the evening twilight,
In the days that are forgotten,
In the unremembered ages,
From the full moon fell Nokomis,
Fell the beautiful Nokomis,
She a wife, but not a mother.
   She was sporting with her women
Swinging in a swing of grapevines,
When her rival, the rejected,
Full of jealousy and hatred,
Cut the leafy swing asunder,
Cut in twain the twisted grapevines,
And Nokomis fell affrighted
Downward through the evening twilight,
On the Muskoday, the meadow,
On the prairie full of blossoms.
"See! a star falls!" said the people;
"From the sky a star is falling!"
There among the ferns and mosses,
There among the prairie lilies,
On the Muskoday the meadow,
In the moonlight and the starlight,
Fair Nokomis bore a daughter.
And she called her name Wenonah,[1]
As the first-born of her daughters.
And the daughter of Nokomis
Grew up like the prairie lilies,
Grew a tall and slender maiden,
With the beauty of the moonlight,
With the beauty of the starlight.

[1] Now spelled Winona, but should be pronounced as above.

And Nokomis warned her often,
Saying oft, and oft repeating,
"O, beware of Mudjekeewis,
Of the West-Wind, Mudjekeewis;
Listen not to what he tells you;
Lie not down upon the meadow,
Stoop not down among the lilies,
Lest the West-Wind come and harm you!"
But she heeded not the warning,
Heeded not those words of wisdom,
And the West-Wind came at evening,
Walking lightly o'er the prairie,
Whispering to the leaves and blossoms,
Bending low the flowers and grasses,
Found the beautiful Wenonah,
Lying there among the lilies,
Wooed her with his words of sweetness,
Wooed her with his soft caresses,
Till she bore a son in sorrow,
Bore a son of love and sorrow.
Thus was born my Hiawatha,
Thus was born the child of wonder;
But the daughter of Nokomis,
Hiawatha's gentle mother,
In her anguish died deserted
By the West-Wind, false and faithless,
By the heartless Mudjekeewis.
For her daughter, long and loudly
Wailed and wept the sad Nokomis;
"O that I were dead!" she murmured,
"O that I were dead, as thou art
No more work, and no more weeping,
Wahonowin! Wahonowin!" [1]
By the shores of Gitche Gumee. [2]
By the shining Big-Sea-Water,
Stood the wigwam of Nokomis.
Daughter of the Moon, Nokomis,
Dark behind it rose the forest,
Rose the black and gloomy pine-trees,

---

[1] A cry of lamentation.   [2] Lake Superior.

Rose the firs with cones upon them;
Bright before it beat the water,
Beat the clear and sunny water,
Beat the shining Big-Sea-Water.

There the wrinkled, old Nokomis
Nursed the little Hiawatha,
Rocked him in his linden cradle,
Bedded soft in moss and rushes,
Safely bound with reindeer sinews;
Stilled his fretful wail by saying,
"Hush! the Naked Bear [1] will get thee!"
Lulled him into slumber, singing,
"Ewa-yea! my little owlet!
Who is this, that lights the wigwam?
With his great eyes lights the wigwam?
Ewa-yea! [2] my little owlet!"

Many things Nokomis taught him
Of the stars that shine in heaven;
Showed him Ishkoodah, the comet,
Ishkoodah, with fiery tresses;
Showed the Death-Dance of the spirits,
Warriors with their plumes and war-clubs,
Flaring far away to Northward
In the frosty nights of Winter;
Showed the broad, white road in heaven,
Pathway of the ghosts, the shadows,
Running straight across the heavens,
Crowded with the ghosts, the shadows.

[1] Heckewelder, in a letter published in the *Transactions of the American Philosophical Society*, Vol. IV., p. 260, speaks of this tradition as prevalent among the Mohicans and Delawares.

"Their reports," he says, "run thus: that among all animals had been formerly in this country, this was the most ferocious; that it was much larger than the largest of the common bears, and remarkably long-bodied; all over (except a spot of hair on its back of a white color) naked. . . .

"The history of this animal used to be a subject of conversation among the Indians, especially when in the woods a-hunting. I have also heard them say to their children when crying: 'Hush! the naked bear will hear you, be upon you, and devour you.'"

[2] Lullaby.

At the door on Summer evenings
Sat the little Hiawatha;
Heard the whispering of the pine-trees,
Heard the lapping of the water,
Sounds of music, words of wonder:
"Minne-wawa!" said the pine-trees,
"Mudway-aushka!" said the water.

Saw the fire-fly, Wah-wah-taysee,
Flitting through the dusk of evening,
With the twinkle of its candle
Lighting up the brakes and bushes,
And he sang the song of children,
Sang the song Nokomis taught him:
"Wah-wah-taysee, little firefly,
Little, flitting, white-fire insect,
Little, dancing, white-fire creature,
Light me with your little candle,
Ere upon my bed I lay me,
Ere in sleep I close my eyelids!"

Saw the moon rise from the water
Rippling, rounding from the water,
Saw the flecks and shadows on it,
Whispered, "What is that, Nokomis?"
And the good Nokomis answered:
"Once a warrior, very angry,
Seized his grandmother, and threw her
Up into the sky at midnight;
Right against the moon he threw her;
'T is her body that you see there."

Saw the rainbow in the heaven,
In the eastern sky, the rainbow
Whispered, "What is that, Nokomis?"
And the good Nokomis answered:
" 'T is the heaven of flowers you see there;
All the wild-flowers of the forest,
All the lilies of the prairie,
When on earth they fade and perish,
Blossom in that heaven above us."

When he heard the owls at midnight,
Hooting, laughing in the forest,

"What is that?" he cried in terror:
"What is that?" he said, "Nokomis?"
And the good Nokomis answered:
"That is but the owl and owlet,
Talking in their native language,
Talking, scolding at each other."
    Then the little Hiawatha,
Learned of every bird its language,
Learned their names and all their secrets,
How they built their nests in Summer,
Where they hid themselves in Winter,
Talked with them whene'er he met them,
Called them "Hiawatha's Chickens."
    Of all beasts he learned the language,
Learned their names and all their secrets,
How the beavers built their lodges,
Where the squirrels hid their acorns,
How the reindeer ran so swiftly,
Why the rabbit was so timid,
Talked with them whene'er he met them,
Called them "Hiawatha's Brothers."
    Then Iagoo, the great boaster,
He the marvellous story-teller,
He the traveller and the talker,
He the friend of old Nokomis,
Made a bow for Hiawatha:
From a branch of ash he made it,
From an oak-bough made the arrows,
Tipped with flint, and winged with feathers,
And the cord he made of deer-skin.
    Then he said to Hiawatha:
"Go, my son, into the forest,
Where the red deer herd together,
Kill for us a famous roebuck,
Kill for us a deer with antlers!"
    Forth into the forest straightway
All alone walked Hiawatha
Proudly, with his bow and arrows;
And the birds sang round him, o'er him,
"Do not shoot us, Hiawatha!"

Sang the Opechee, the robin,
Sang the bluebird, the Owaissa,
"Do not shoot us, Hiawatha!"
    Up the oak-tree, close beside him,
Sprang the squirrel, Adjidaumo,
In and out among the branches,
Coughed and chattered from the oak-tree,
Laughed, and said between his laughing,
"Do not shoot me, Hiawatha!"
    And the rabbit from his pathway
Leaped aside, and at a distance
Sat erect upon his haunches,
Half in fear and half in frolic,
Saying to the little hunter,
"Do not shoot me, Hiawatha!"
    But he heeded not, nor heard them,
For his thoughts were with the red deer;
On their tracks his eyes were fastened,
Leading downward to the river,
To the ford across the river,
And as one in slumber walked he.
Hidden in the alder bushes,
There he waited till the deer came,
Till he saw two antlers lifted,
Saw two eyes look from the thicket,
Saw two nostrils point to windward,
And a deer came down the pathway,
Flecked with leafy light and shadow.
And his heart within him fluttered,
Trembled like the leaves above him,
Like the birch-leaf palpitated,
As the deer came down the pathway.
    Then upon one knee uprising,
Hiawatha aimed an arrow;
Scarce a twig moved with his motion,
Scarce a leaf was stirred or rustled,
But the wary roebuck started,
Stamped with all his hoofs together,
Listened with one foot uplifted,
Leaped as if to meet the arrow;

Ah! the singing, fatal arrow,
Like a wasp it buzzed and stung him!
  Dead he lay there in the forest,
By the ford across the river;
Beat his timid heart no longer,
But the heart of Hiawatha
Throbbed and shouted and exulted,
As he bore the red deer homeward
And Iagoo and Nokomis
Hailed his coming with applauses.
From the red deer's hide Nokomis
Made a cloak for Hiawatha,
From the red deer's flesh Nokomis
Made a banquet in his honor.
All the village came and feasted,
All the guests praised Hiawatha,
Called him Strong-Heart, Soan-getaha!
Called him Loon-Heart, Mahn-go-taysee!

IV

HIAWATHA AND MUDJEKEEWIS

Out of childhood into manhood
Now had grown my Hiawatha,
Skilled in all the craft of hunters,
Learned in all the lore of old men,
In all youthful sports and pastimes,
In all manly arts and labors.
  Swift of foot was Hiawatha;
He could shoot an arrow from him,
And run forward with such fleetness,
That the arrow fell behind him!
Strong of arm was Hiawatha;
He could shoot ten arrows upward,
Shoot them with such strength and swiftness,
That the tenth had left the bowstring
Ere the first to earth had fallen!
  He had mittens, Minjekahwun,
Magic mittens made of deer-skin;

When upon his hands he wore them,
He could smite the rocks asunder,
He could grind them into powder,
He had moccasins enchanted,
Magic moccasins of deer-skin;
When he bound them round his ankles,
When upon his feet he tied them,
At each stride a mile he measured!

Much he questioned old Nokomis
Of his father Mudjekeewis;
Learned from her the fatal secret
Of the beauty of his mother,
Of the falsehood of his father;
And his heart was hot within him,
Like a living coal his heart was.

Then he said to old Nokomis,
"I will go to Mudjekeewis,
See how fares it with my father,
At the doorways of the West-Wind,
At the portals of the Sunset!"

From his lodge went Hiawatha,
Dressed for travel, armed for hunting;
Dressed in deer-skin shirt and leggings,
Richly wrought with quills and wampum;
On his head his eagle feathers,
Round his waist his belt of wampum,
In his hand his bow of ash-wood,
Strung with sinews of the reindeer;
In his quiver oaken arrows,
Tipped with jasper, winged with feathers;
With his mittens, Minjekahwun,
With his moccasins enchanted.

Warning said the old Nokomis,
"Go not forth, O Hiawatha!
To the kingdom of the West-Wind,
To the realms of Mudjekeewis,
Lest he harm you with his magic
Lest he kill you with his cunning!"

But the fearless Hiawatha
Heeded not her woman's warning;

Forth he strode into the forest,
At each stride a mile he measured;
Lurid seemed the sky above him,
Lurid seemed the earth beneath him,
Hot and close the air around him,
Filled with smoke and fiery vapors,
As of burning woods and prairies,
For his heart was hot within him,
Like a living coal his heart was.

So he journeyed westward, westward,
Left the fleetest deer behind him,
Left the antelope and bison;
Crossed the rushing Esconawbaw,[1]
Crossed the mighty Mississippi,
Passed the Mountains of the Prairie,
Passed the land of Crows and Foxes,
Passed the dwellings of the Blackfeet
Came unto the Rocky Mountains,
To the kingdom of the West-Wind,
Where upon the gusty summits
Sat the ancient Mudjekeewis,
Ruler of the winds of heaven.

Filled with awe was Hiawatha
At the aspect of his father.
On the air about him wildly
Tossed and streamed his cloudy tresses,
Gleamed like drifting snow his tresses,
Glared like Ishkoodah, the comet,
Like the star with fiery tresses.

Filled with joy was Mudjekeewis
When he looked on Hiawatha,
Saw his youth rise up before him
In the face of Hiawatha,
Saw the beauty of Wenonah
From the grave rise up before him.

"Welcome!" said he, "Hiawatha,
To the kingdom of the West-Wind!
Long have I been waiting for you!

[1] The Escanoba is on the upper Peninsula of Michigan and empties into Green Bay of Lake Michigan.

Youth is lovely, age is lonely,
Youth is fiery, age is frosty;
You bring back the days departed,
You bring back my youth of passion,
And the beautiful Wenonah!"

Many days they talked together,
Questioned, listened, waited, answered;
Much the mighty Mudjekeewis
Boasted of his ancient prowess,
Of his perilous adventures,
His indomitable courage,
His invulnerable body.

Patiently sat Hiawatha,
Listening to his father's boasting;
With a smile he sat and listened,
Uttered neither threat nor menace,
Neither word nor look betrayed him,
But his heart was hot within him,
Like a living coal his heart was.

Then he said, "O Mudjekeewis,
Is there nothing that can harm you?
Nothing that you are afraid of?"
And the mighty Mudjekeewis,
Grand and gracious in his boasting,
Answered, saying, "There is nothing,
Nothing but the black rock yonder,
Nothing but the fatal Wawbeek!"

And he looked at Hiawatha
With a wise look and benignant,
With a countenance paternal,
Looked with pride upon the beauty
Of his tall and graceful figure,
Saying, "O my Hiawatha!
Is there anything can harm you?
Anything you are afraid of?"

But the wary Hiawatha
Paused awhile, as if uncertain,
Held his peace, as if resolving,
And then answered, "There is nothing,

Nothing but the bulrush yonder,
Nothing but the great Apukwa!"
    And as Mudjekeewis, rising,
Stretched his hand to pluck the bulrush,
Hiawatha cried in terror,
Cried in well-dissembled terror,
"Kago! kago! [1] do not touch it!"
"Ah, kaween!" [2] said Mudjekeewis.
"No, indeed, I will not touch it!"
    Then they talked of other matters;
First of Hiawatha's brothers,
First of Wabun, of the East-Wind,
Of the South Wind, Shawondasee,
Of the North, Kabibonokka;
Then of Hiawatha's mother,
Of the beautiful Wenonah,
Of her birth upon the meadow,
Of her death, as old Nokomis
Had remembered and related.
    And he cried, "O Mudjekeewis,
It was you who killed Wenonah,
Took her young life and her beauty,
Broke the Lily of the Prairie,
Trampled it beneath your footsteps;
You confess it! you confess it!"
And the mighty Mudjekeewis
Tossed his gray hairs to the west wind,
Bowed his hoary head in anguish.
With a silent nod assented.
    Then up started Hiawatha,
And with threatening look and gesture
Laid his hand upon the black rock,
On the fatal Wawbeek [3] laid it.
With his mittens, Minjekahwun,
Rent the jutting crag asunder,
Smote and crushed it into fragments,
Hurled them madly at his father,
The remorseful Mudjekeewis,

[1] Do not.   [2] No, indeed.   [3] Black rock.

For his heart was hot within him,
Like a living coal his heart was.
  But the ruler of the West-Wind
Blew the fragments backwards from him,
With the breathing of his nostrils,
With the tempest of his anger,
Blew them back at his assailant;
Seized the bulrush, the Apukwa,
Dragged it with its roots and fibres
From the margin of the meadow,
From its ooze, the giant bulrush;
Long and loud laughed Hiawatha!
  Then began the deadly conflict,
Hand to hand among the mountains;
From his eyrie screamed the eagle,
The Keneu, the great war-eagle,
Set upon the crags around them,
Wheeling flapped his wings above them.
  Like a tall tree in the tempest
Bent and lashed the giant bulrush;
And in masses huge and heavy
Crashing fell the fatal Wawbeek;
Till the earth shook with the tumult
And confusion of the battle,
And the air was full of shoutings,
And the thunder of the mountains,
Starting, answered, "Baim-wawa!" [1]
  Back retreated Mudjekeewis,
Rushing westward o'er the mountains,
Stumbling westward down the mountains
Three whole days retreated fighting,
Still pursued by Hiawatha
To the doorways of the West-Wind,
To the portals of the Sunset,
To the earth's remotest border,
Where into the empty spaces
Sinks the sun, as a flamingo
Drops into her nest at nightfall,
In the melancholy marshes.

[1] The sound of thunder.

"Hold!" at length cried Mudjekeewis,
"Hold, my son, my Hiawatha!
'Tis impossible to kill me,
For you cannot kill the immortal.
I have put you to this trial,
But to know and prove your courage;
Now receive the prize of valor!

"Go back to your home and people,
Live among them, toil among them,
Cleanse the earth from all that harms it,
Clear the fishing-grounds and rivers,
Slay all monsters and magicians,
All the Wendigoes, the giants,
All the serpents, the Kenabeeks,
As I slew the Mishe-Mokwa,
Slew the Great Bear of the mountains,

"And at last when Death draws near you,
When the awful eyes of Pauguk [1]
Glare upon you in the darkness,
I shall share my kingdom with you.
Ruler shall you be thenceforward
Of the Northwest-Wind, Keewaydin,
Of the home-wind, the Keewaydin."

Thus was fought that famous battle
In the dreadful days of Shah-shah, [2]
In the days long since departed,
In the kingdom of the West-Wind.
Still the hunter sees its traces
Scattered far o'er hill and valley;
Sees the giant bulrush growing
By the ponds and watercourses,
Sees the masses of the Wawbeek
Lying still in every valley.

Homeward now went Hiawatha;
Pleasant was the landscape round him,
Pleasant was the air above him,
For the bitterness of anger
Had departed wholly from him,

[1] Death.   [2] Long ago.

From his brain the thought of vengeance,
From his heart the burning fever.
Only once his pace he slackened,
Only once he paused or halted,
Paused to purchase heads of arrows
Of the ancient Arrow-maker,
In the land of the Dacotahs,
Where the Falls of Minnehaha [1]
Flash and gleam among the oak trees,
Laugh and leap into the valley.
There the ancient Arrow-maker
Made his arrow-heads of sandstone,
Arrow-heads of chalcedony,
Arrow-heads of flint and jasper,
Smoothed and sharpened at the edges,
Hard and polished, keen and costly.
With him dwelt his dark-eyed daughter,
Wayward as the Minnehaha,
With her moods of shade and sunshine,
Eyes that smiled and frowned alternate,
Feet as rapid as the river,
Tresses flowing like the water,
And as musical a laughter;
And he named her from the river,
From the waterfall he named her,
Minnehaha, Laughing Water.
Was it then for heads of arrows,
Arrow-heads of chalcedony,
Arrow-heads of flint and jasper,
That my Hiawatha halted
In the land of the Dacotahs?
Was it not to see the maiden,
See the face of Laughing Water,
Peeping from behind the curtain,

[1] In a park now included in the city of Minneapolis.
"The scenery about Fort Snelling is rich in beauty. The Falls of
St. Anthony are familiar to travellers, and to readers of Indian
sketches. Between the fort and these falls are the 'Little Falls,' forty
feet in height, on a stream that empties into the Mississippi. The
Indians call them Mine-hah-hah, or 'laughing waters.'"—Mrs. East-
man's *Dacotah, or Legends of the Sioux*, Introduction, p. ii.

Hear the rustling of her garments
From behind the waving curtain,
As one sees the Minnehaha
Gleaming, glancing through the branches,
As one hears the Laughing Water
From behind its screen of branches?
  Who shall say what thoughts and visions
Fill the fiery brains of young men?
Who shall say what dreams of beauty
Filled the heart of Hiawatha?
All he told to old Nokomis,
When he reached the lodge at sunset,
Was the meeting with his father,
Was his fight with Mudjekeewis;
Not a word he said of arrows,
Not a word of Laughing Water.

V

HIAWATHA'S FASTING

You shall hear how Hiawatha
Prayed and fasted in the forest,
Not for greater skill in hunting,
Not for greater craft in fishing,
Not for triumphs in the battle,
And renown among the warriors,
But for profit of the people,
For advantage of the nations.
  First he built a lodge for fasting,
Built a wigwam in the forest,
By the shining Big-Sea-Water,
In the blithe and pleasant Springtime,
In the moon of Leaves he built it
And, with dreams and visions many,
Seven whole days and nights he fasted.
  On the first day of his fasting
Through the leafy woods he wandered;
Saw the deer start from the thicket,
Saw the rabbit in his burrow,

Heard the pheasant, Bena, drumming,
Heard the squirrel, Adjidaumo,
Rattling in his hoard of acorns,
Saw the pigeon, the Omeme,
Building nests among the pine-trees,
And in flocks the wild goose, Wawa,
Flying to the fenlands northward,
Whirring, wailing, far above him.
"Master of Life!" he cried, desponding,
"Must our lives depend on these things?"

On the next day of his fasting
By the river's bank he wandered,
Through the Muskoday, the meadow,
Saw the wild rice, Mahnomonee,[1]
Saw the blueberry, Meenahga,
And the strawberry, Odahmin,
And the gooseberry, Shahbomin,
And the grape-vine, the Bemahgut
Trailing o'er the alder-branches,
Filling all the air with fragrance!
"Master of Life!" he cried, desponding,
"Must our lives depend on these things?"

On the third day of his fasting
By the lake he sat and pondered,
By the still, transparent water;
Saw the sturgeon, Nahma, leaping,
Scattering drops like beads of wampum,
Saw the yellow perch, the Sahwa,
Like a sunbeam in the water,
Saw the pike, the Maskenozha,
And the herring, Okahahwis,
And the Shawgashee, the crawfish!
"Master of Life!" he cried, desponding,
"Must our lives depend on these things?"

On the fourth day of his fasting
In his lodge he lay exhausted;
From his couch of leaves and branches

[1] The word is preserved in Menom'onie, Wis., and Menom'inee, Mich. The pronunciation of the present day is not that of the Indian tongue.

Gazing with half-open eyelids,
Full of shadowy dreams and visions,
On the dizzy, swimming landscape,
On the gleaming of the water,
On the splendor of the sunset.

And he saw a youth approaching,
Dressed in garments green and yellow
Coming through the purple twilight,
Through the splendor of the sunset;
Plumes of green bent o'er his forehead,
And his hair was soft and golden.

Standing at the open doorway,
Long he looked at Hiawatha,
Looked with pity and compassion
On his wasted form and features,
And, in accents like the sighing
Of the South-Wind in the tree-tops,
Said he, "O my Hiawatha!
All your prayers are heard in heaven,
For you pray not like the others;
Not for greater skill in hunting,
Not for greater craft in fishing,
Not for triumph in the battle,
Nor renown among the warriors,
But for profit of the people,
For advantage of the nations.

"From the Master of Life descending,
I, the friend of man, Mondamin,
Come to warn you and instruct you,
How by struggle and by labor
You shall gain what you have prayed for.
Rise up from your bed of branches,
Rise, O youth, and wrestle with me!"

Faint with famine, Hiawatha
Started from his bed of branches,
From the twilight of his wigwam
Forth into the flush of sunset
Came, and wrestled with Mondamin;
At his touch he felt new courage
Throbbing in his brain and bosom,

Felt new life and hope and vigor
Run through every nerve and fibre.
    So they wrestled there together
In the glory of the sunset,
And the more they strove and struggled,
Stronger still grew Hiawatha;
Till the darkness fell around them,
And the heron, the Shuh-shuh-gah,
From her haunts among the fenlands,
Gave a cry of lamentation,
Gave a scream of pain and famine.
    " 'Tis enough!" then said Mondamin,
Smiling upon Hiawatha,
"But to-morrow, when the sun sets
I will come again to try you."
And he vanished, and was seen not
Whether sinking as the rain sinks,
Whether rising as the mists rise,
Hiawatha saw not, knew not,
Only saw that he had vanished,
Leaving him alone and fainting,
With the misty lake below him,
And the reeling stars above him.
On the morrow and the next day,
When the sun through heaven descending,
Like a red and burning cinder
From the hearth of the Great Spirit
Fell into the western waters,
Came Mondamin for the trial,
For the strife with Hiawatha;
Came as silent as the dew comes,
From the empty air appearing,
Into empty air returning,
Taking shape when earth it touches,
But invisible to all men
In its coming and its going.
    Thrice they wrestled there together
In the glory of the sunset,
Till the darkness fell around them,
Till the heron, the Shuh-shuh-gah,

From her haunts among the fenlands,
Uttered her loud cry of famine,
And Mondamin paused to listen.

Tall and beautiful he stood there,
In his garments green and yellow;
To and fro his plumes above him
Waved and nodded with his breathing,
And the sweat of the encounter
Stood like drops of dew upon him.

And he cried, "O Hiawatha!
Bravely have you wrestled with me,
Thrice have wrestled stoutly with me,
And the Master of Life, who sees us,
He will give to you the triumph!"

Then he smiled, and said: "To-morrow
Is the last day of your conflict,
Is the last day of your fasting.
You will conquer and o'ercome me:
Make a bed for me to lie in,
Where the rain may fall upon me,
Where the sun may come and warm me;
Strip these garments, green and yellow,
Strip this nodding plumage from me,
Lay me in the earth, and make it
Soft and loose and light above me.

"Let no hand disturb my slumber,
Let no weed nor worm molest me,
Let not Kahgahgee, the raven,
Come to haunt me and molest me,
Only come yourself to watch me,
Till I wake, and start, and quicken,
Till I leap into the sunshine."

And thus saying, he departed.
Peacefully slept Hiawatha,
But he heard the Wawonaissa,
Heard the whip-poor-will complaining,
Perched upon his lonely wigwam;
Heard the rushing Sebowisha,
Heard the rivulet rippling near him,
Talking to the darksome forest;

Heard the sighing of the branches,
As they lifted and subsided
At the passing of the night-wind,
Heard them, as one hears in slumber
Far-off murmurs, dreamy whispers:
Peacefully slept Hiawatha.

On the morrow came Nokomis,
On the seventh day of his fasting,
Came with food for Hiawatha,
Came imploring and bewailing,
Lest his hunger should o'ercome him,
Lest his fasting should be fatal.

But he tasted not, and touched not,
Only said to her, "Nokomis,
Wait until the sun is setting,
Till the darkness falls around us,
Till the heron, the Shuh-shuh-gah,
Crying from the desolate marshes,
Tells us that the day is ended."

Homeward weeping went Nokomis,
Sorrowing for her Hiawatha,
Fearing lest his strength should fail him,
Lest his fasting should be fatal.
He meanwhile sat weary waiting
For the coming of Mondamin,[1]
Till the shadows, pointing eastward,
Lengthened over field and forest,
Till the sun dropped from the heaven,
Floating on the waters westward,
As a red leaf in the Autumn
Falls and floats upon the water,
Falls and sinks into its bosom.

And behold! the young Mondamin,
With his soft and shining tresses,
With his garments green and yellow,
With his long and glossy plumage,
Stood and beckoned at the doorway.
And as one in slumber walking,
Pale and haggard, but undaunted,

[1] Indian Corn. See detailed description below.

From the wigwam Hiawatha
Came and wrestled with Mondamin.

Round about him spun the landscape,
Sky and forest reeled together,
And his strong heart leaped within him,
As the sturgeon leaps and struggles
In a net to break its meshes.
Like a ring of fire around him
Blazed and flared the red horizon,
And a hundred suns seemed looking
At the combat of the wrestlers.

Suddenly upon the greensward
All alone stood Hiawatha,
Panting with his wild exertion,
Palpitating with the struggle;
And before him, breathless, lifeless,
Lay the youth, with hair dishevelled,
Plumage torn, and garments tattered,
Dead he lay there in the sunset.

And victorious Hiawatha
Made the grave as he commanded,
Stripped the garments from Mondamin,
Stripped his tattered plumage from him,
Laid him in the earth, and made it
Soft and loose and light above him;
And the heron, the Shuh-shuh-gah,
From the melancholy moorlands,
Gave a cry of lamentation,
Gave a cry of pain and anguish!

Homeward then went Hiawatha
To the lodge of old Nokomis,
And the seven days of his fasting
Were accomplished and completed.
But the place was not forgotten
Where he wrestled with Mondamin;
Nor forgotten nor neglected
Was the grave where lay Mondamin,
Sleeping in the rain and sunshine,
Where his scattered plumes and garments
Faded in the rain and sunshine.

Day by day did Hiawatha
Go to wait and watch beside it;
Kept the dark mould soft above it,
Kept it clean from weeds and insects,
Drove away, with scoffs and shoutings,
Kahgahgee, the king of ravens.

Till at length a small green feather
From the earth shot slowly upward,
Then another and another,
And before the Summer ended
Stood the maize in all its beauty,
With its shining robes about it,
And its long, soft, yellow tresses;
And in rapture Hiawatha
Cried aloud, "It is Mondamin!
Yes, the friend of man, Mondamin!"

Then he called to old Nokomis
And Iagoo, the great boaster,
Showed them where the maize was growing,
Told them of his wondrous vision,
Of his wrestling and his triumph,
Of this new gift to the nations,
Which should be their food forever.

And still later, when the Autumn
Changed the long, green leaves to yellow,
And the soft and juicy kernels
Grew like wampum hard and yellow,
Then the ripened ears he gathered,
Stripped the withered husks from off them,
As he once had stripped the wrestler,
Gave the first Feast of Mondamin,
And made known unto the people
This new gift of the Great Spirit.

VI

HIAWATHA'S FRIENDS

Two good friends had Hiawatha,
Singled out from all the others,

Bound to him in closest union,
And to whom he gave the right hand
Of his heart, in joy and sorrow;
Chibiabos, the musician,
And the very strong man, Kwasind.

Straight between them ran the pathway,
Never grew the grass upon it;
Singing birds, that utter falsehoods,
Story-tellers, mischief-makers,
Found no eager ear to listen,
Could not breed ill-will between them,
For they kept each other's counsel,
Spake with naked hearts together,
Pondering much and much contriving
How the tribes of men might prosper.

Most beloved by Hiawatha
Was the gentle Chibiabos,
He the best of all musicians,
He the sweetest of all singers.
Beautiful and childlike was he,
Brave as man is, soft as woman,
Pliant as a wand of willow,
Stately as a deer with antlers.

When he sang, the village listened.
All the warriors gathered round him,
All the women came to hear him;
Now he stirred their souls to passion,
Now he melted them to pity.

From the hollow reeds he fashioned
Flutes so musical and mellow,
That the brook, the Sebowisha,
Ceased to murmur in the woodland,
That the wood-birds ceased from singing,
And the squirrel, Adjidaumo,
Ceased his chatter in the oak-tree,
And the rabbit, the Wabasso,
Sat upright to look and listen.

Yes, the brook, the Sebowisha,
Pausing, said, "O Chibiabos,

Teach my waves to flow in music,
Softly as your words in singing!"

Yes, the bluebird, the Owaissa,
Envious, said, "O Chibiabos,
Teach me tones as wild and wayward,
Teach me songs as full of frenzy!"

Yes, the Opechee, the robin,
Joyous, said, "O Chibiabos,
Teach me tones as sweet and tender,
Teach me songs as full of gladness!"

And the whippoorwill, Wawonaissa,
Sobbing, said, "O Chibiabos,
Teach me tones as melancholy,
Teach me songs as full of sadness!"

All the many sounds of nature
Borrowed sweetness from his singing;
All the hearts of men were softened
By the pathos of his music;
For he sang of peace and freedom,
Sang of beauty, love, and longing;
Sang of death, and life undying
In the Islands of the Blessed,
In the kingdom of Ponemah,
In the land of the Hereafter.

Very dear to Hiawatha
Was the gentle Chibiabos,
He the best of all musicians,
He the sweetest of all singers;
For his gentleness he loved him,
And the magic of his singing.

Dear, too, unto Hiawatha
Was the very strong man, Kwasind,
He the strongest of all mortals,
He the mightiest among many;
For his very strength he loved him,
For his strength allied to goodness.

Idle in his youth was Kwasind,
Very listless, dull, and dreamy,
Never played with other children,
Never fished and never hunted,

Not like other children was he;
But they saw that much he fasted,
Much his Manito entreated,
Much besought his Guardian Spirit.

"Lazy Kwasind!" said his mother,
"In my work you never help me!
In the Summer you are roaming
Idly in the fields and forests;
In the Winter you are cowering
O'er the firebrands in the wigwam!
In the coldest days of Winter
I must break the ice for fishing;
With my nets you never help me;
At the door my nets are hanging,
Dripping, freezing with the water;
Go and wring them, Yenadizze! [1]
Go and dry them in the sunshine!"

Slowly, from the ashes, Kwasind
Rose, but made no angry answer;
From the lodge went forth in silence,
Took the nets, that hung together,
Dripping, freezing at the doorway,
Like a wisp of straw he wrung them,
Like a wisp of straw he broke them,
Could not wring them without breaking,
Such the strength was in his fingers.

"Lazy Kwasind!" said his father,
"In the hunt you never help me;
Every bow you touch is broken,
Snapped asunder every arrow;
Yet come with me to the forest,
You shall bring the hunting homeward."

Down a narrow pass they wandered,
Where a brooklet led them onward,
Where the trail of deer and bison
Marked the soft mud on the margin,
Till they found all further passage
Shut against them, barred securely
By the trunks of trees uprooted,

[1] Indian dude.

Lying lengthwise, lying crosswise,
And forbidding further passage.
  "We must go back," said the old man,
"O'er these logs we cannot clamber;
Not a woodchuck could get through them,
Not a squirrel clamber o'er them!"
And straightway his pipe he lighted,
And sat down to smoke and ponder.
But before his pipe was finished,
Lo! the path was cleared before him;
All the trunks had Kwasind lifted,
To the right hand, to the left hand,
Shot the pine-trees swift as arrows,
Hurled the cedars light as lances.

  "Lazy Kwasind!" said the young men,
As they sported in the meadow:
"Why stand idly looking at us,
Leaning on the rock behind you?
Come and wrestle with the others,
Let us pitch the quoit together!"

  Lazy Kwasind made no answer,
To their challenge made no answer,
Only rose, and, slowly turning,
Seized the huge rock in his fingers,
Tore it from its deep foundation,
Poised it in the air a moment,
Pitched it sheer into the river,
Sheer into the swift Pauwating,
Where it still is seen in Summer.

  Once as down that foaming river,
Down the rapids of Pauwating,
Kwasind sailed with his companions,
In the stream he saw a beaver,
Saw Ahmeek, the King of Beavers,
Struggling with the rushing currents,
Rising, sinking in the water.

  Without speaking, without pausing,
Kwasind leaped into the river,
Plunged beneath the bubbling surface,
Through the whirlpools chased the beaver,

Followed him among the islands,
Stayed so long beneath the water,
That his terrified companions
Cried, "Alas! good-by to Kwasind!
We shall never more see Kwasind!"
But he reappeared triumphant,
And upon his shining shoulders
Brought the beaver, dead and dripping,
Brought the King of all the Beavers.

And these two, as I have told you,
Were the friends of Hiawatha,
Chibiabos, the musician,
And the very strong man, Kwasind.
Long they lived in peace together,
Spake with naked hearts together,
Pondering much and much contriving
How the tribes of men might prosper.

VII

HIAWATHA'S SAILING [1]

"Give me of your bark, O Birch-Tree!
Of your yellow bark, O Birch-Tree!
Growing by the rushing river,
Tall and stately in the valley!
I a light canoe will build me,
Build a swift Cheemaun for sailing,
That shall float upon the river,
Like a yellow leaf in Autumn,
Like a yellow water-lily!

"Lay aside your cloak, O Birch-Tree!
Lay aside your white-skin wrapper,
For the Summer-time is coming,
And the sun is warm in heaven,
And you need no white-skin wrapper!"
Thus aloud cried Hiawatha
In the solitary forest,

[1] This beautiful description of the building of the canoe reminds
one of Longfellow's more elaborate poem "The Building of the Ship."

By the rushing Taquamenaw,
When the birds were singing gayly,
In the Moon of Leaves were singing,
And the sun, from sleep awaking,
Started up and said, "Behold me!
Gheezis, the great Sun, behold me!"
    And the tree with all its branches
Rustled in the breeze of morning,
Saying, with a sigh of patience,
"Take my cloak, O Hiawatha!"
    With his knife the tree he girdled;
Just beneath its lowest branches,
Just above the roots he cut it,
Till the sap came oozing outward;
Down the trunk, from top to bottom,
Sheer he cleft the bark asunder,
With a wooden wedge he raised it,
Stripped it from the trunk unbroken.
    "Give me of your boughs, O Cedar!
Of your strong and pliant branches,
My canoe to make more steady,
Make more strong and firm beneath me!"
    Through the summit of the cedar
Went a sound, a cry of horror,
Went a murmur of resistance;
But it whispered, bending downward,
"Take my boughs, O Hiawatha!"
    Down he hewed the boughs of cedar,
Shaped them straightway to a framework,
Like two bows he formed and shaped them,
Like two bended bows together.
    "Give me of your roots, O Tamarack!
Of your fibrous roots, O Larch-Tree!
My canoe to bind together,
So to bind the ends together
That the water may not enter,
That the river may not wet me!"
    And the larch, with all its fibres,
Shivered in the air of morning,
Touched his forehead with its tassels,

Said, with one long sigh of sorrow,
"Take them all, O Hiawatha!"
    From the earth he tore the fibres,
Tore the tough roots of the Larch-Tree,
Closely sewed the bark together,
Bound it closely to the framework.
    "Give me of your balm, O Fir-Tree!
Of your balsam and your resin,
So to close the seams together
That the water may not enter,
That the river may not wet me!"
    And the Fir-Tree, tall and sombre,
Sobbed through all its robes of darkness,
Rattled like a shore with pebbles,
Answered wailing, answered weeping,
"Take my balm, O Hiawatha!"
    And he took the tears of balsam,
Took the resin of the Fir-Tree,
Smeared therewith each seam and fissure,
Made each crevice safe from water.
    "Give me of your quills, O Hedgehog!
All your quills, O Kagh, the Hedgehog!
I will make a necklace of them,
Make a girdle for my beauty,
And two stars to deck her bosom!"
    From a hollow tree the Hedgehog
With his sleepy eyes looked at him,
Shot his shining quills, like arrows,
Saying, with a drowsy murmur,
Through the tangle of his whiskers,
"Take my quills, O Hiawatha!"
    From the ground the quills he gathered,
All the little shining arrows,
Stained them red and blue and yellow,
With the juice of roots and berries;
Into his canoe he wrought them,
Round its waist a shining girdle,
Round its bows a gleaming necklace,
On its breast two stars resplendent.
    Thus the Birch Canoe was builded

In the valley, by the river,
In the bosom of the forest;
And the forest's life was it,
All its mystery and its magic,
All the lightness of the birch-tree,
All the toughness of the cedar,
All the larch's supple sinews;
And it floated on the river
Like a yellow leaf in Autumn,
Like a yellow water-lily.

Paddles none had Hiawatha,
Paddles none he had or needed,
For his thoughts as paddles served him,
And his wishes served to guide him.
Swift or slow at will he glided,
Veered to right or left at pleasure.

Then he called aloud to Kwasind,
To his friend, the strong man Kwasind,
Saying, "Help me clear this river
Of its sunken logs and sand-bars."

Straight into the river Kwasind
Plunged as if he were an otter,
Dived as if he were a beaver,
Stood up to his waist in water,
To his armpits in the river,
Swam and shouted in the river,
Tugged at sunken logs and branches,
With his hands he scooped the sand-bars,
With his feet the ooze and tangle.

And thus sailed my Hiawatha
Down the rushing Taquamenaw,
Sailed through all its bends and windings,
Sailed through all its deeps and shallows,
While his friend, the strong man, Kwasind,
Swam the deeps, the shallows waded.

Up and down the river went they,
In and out among its islands,
Cleared its bed of root and sand-bar,
Dragged the dead trees from its channel,
Made its passage safe and certain,

Made a pathway for the people,
From its springs among the mountains,
To the water of Pauwating,
To the bay of Taquamenaw.

VIII

HIAWATHA'S FISHING

Forth upon the Gitche Gumee,
On the shining Big-Sea-Water,
With his fishing-line of cedar,
Of the twisted bark of cedar,
Forth to catch the sturgeon Nahma,
Mishe-Nahma, King of Fishes,
In his birch canoe exulting
All alone went Hiawatha.

Through the clear, transparent water
He could see the fishes swimming
Far down in the depths below him;
See the yellow perch, the Sahwa,
Like a sunbeam in the water,
See the Shawgashee, the crawfish,
Like a spider on the bottom,
On the white and sandy bottom.

At the stern sat Hiawatha,
With his fishing-line of cedar;
In his plumes the breeze of morning
Played as in the hemlock branches;
On the bows, with tail erected,
Sat the squirrel, Adjidaumo;
In his fur the breeze of morning
Played as in the prairie grasses.

On the white sand of the bottom
Lay the monster Mishe-Nahma,
Lay the sturgeon, King of Fishes;
Through his gills he breathed the water,
With his fins he fanned and winnowed,
With his tail he swept the sand-floor.

There he lay in all his armor;
On each side a shield to guard him,
Plates of bone upon his forehead,
Down his sides and back and shoulders
Plates of bone with spines projecting!
Painted was he with his war-paints,
Stripes of yellow, red, and azure,
Spots of brown and spots of sable;
And he lay there on the bottom,
Fanning with his fins of purple,
As above him Hiawatha
In his birch canoe came sailing,
With his fishing-line of cedar.

"Take my bait," cried Hiawatha,
Down into the depths beneath him,
   "Take my bait, O Sturgeon, Nahma!
Come up from below the water,
Let us see which is the stronger!"
And he dropped his line of cedar
Through the clear, transparent water,
Waited vainly for an answer,
Long sat waiting for an answer,
And repeating loud and louder,
"Take my bait, O King of Fishes!"

Quiet lay the sturgeon, Nahma,
Fanning slowly in the water,
Looking up at Hiawatha,
Listening to his call and clamor,
His unnecessary tumult,
Till he wearied of the shouting;
And he said to the Kenozha,
To the pike, the Maskenozha,
"Take the bait of this rude fellow,
Break the line of Hiawatha!"
In his fingers Hiawatha
Felt the loose line jerk and tighten;
As he drew it in, it tugged so
That the birch canoe stood endwise,
Like a birch log in the water,
With the squirrel, Adjidaumo,

Perched and frisking on the summit.
    Full of scorn was Hiawatha
When he saw the fish rise upward,
Saw the pike, the Maskenozha,
Coming nearer, nearer to him,
And he shouted through the water,
"Esa! esa! shame upon you!
You are but the pike, Kenozha,
You are not the fish I wanted,
You are not the King of Fishes!"
    Reeling downward to the bottom
Sank the pike in great confusion,
And the mighty sturgeon, Nahma,
Said to Ugudwash, the sun-fish,
"Take the bait of this great boaster,
Break the line of Hiawatha!"
    Slowly upward, wavering, gleaming,
Like a white moon in the water,
Rose the Ugudwash, the sun-fish,
Seizęd the line of Hiawatha,
Swung with all his weight upon it,
Made a whirlpool in the water,
Whirled the birch canoe in circles,
Round and round in gurgling eddies,
Till the circles in the water
Reached the far-off sandy beaches,
Till the water-flags and rushes
Nodded on the distant margins.
    But when Hiawatha saw him
Slowly rising through the water,
Lifting his great disk of whiteness,
Loud he shouted in derision,
"Esa! esa! shame upon you!
You are Ugudwash, the sun-fish,
You are not the fish I wanted,
You are not the King of Fishes!"
Wavering downward, white and ghastly,
Sank the Ugudwash, the sun-fish,
And again the sturgeon, Nahma,
Heard the shout of Hiawatha,

Heard his challenge of defiance,
The unnecessary tumult,
Ringing far across the water.

From the white sand of the bottom
Up he rose with angry gesture,
Quivering in each nerve and fibre,
Clashing all his plates of armor,
Gleaming bright with all his war-paint;
In his wrath he darted upward,
Flashing leaped into the sunshine,
Opened his great jaws, and swallowed
Both canoe and Hiawatha.

Down into that darksome cavern
Plunged the headlong Hiawatha,
As a log on some black river
Shoots and plunges down the rapids,
Found himself in utter darkness,
Groped about in helpless wonder,
Till he felt a great heart beating,
Throbbing in that utter darkness.

And he smote it in his anger,
With his fist, the heart of Nahma,
Felt the mighty King of Fishes
Shudder through each nerve and fibre,
Heard the water gurgle round him
As he leaped and staggered through it,
Sick at heart, and faint and weary.

Crosswise then did Hiawatha
Drag his birch-canoe for safety,
Lest from out the jaws of Nahma,
In the turmoil and confusion,
Forth he might be hurled and perish.
And the squirrel, Adjidaumo,
Frisked and chattered very gayly,
Toiled and tugged with Hiawatha
Till the labor was completed.

Then said Hiawatha to him,
"O my little friend, the squirrel,
Bravely have you toiled to help me;
Take the thanks of Hiawatha,

And the name which now he gives you;
For hereafter and forever
Boys shall call you Adjidaumo,
Tail-in-air the boys shall call you!"
     And again the sturgeon, Nahma,
Gasped and quivered in the water,
Then was still, and drifted landward,
Till he grated on the pebbles,
Till the listening Hiawatha
Heard him grate upon the margin,
Felt him strand upon the pebbles,
Knew that Nahma, King of Fishes,
Lay there dead upon the margin.
     Then he heard a clang and flapping
As of many wings assembling,
Heard a screaming and confusion,
As of birds of prey contending,
Saw a gleam of light above him,
Shining through the ribs of Nahma,
Saw the glittering eyes of sea-gulls,
Of Kayoshk, the sea-gulls, peering,
Gazing at him through the opening,
Heard them saying to each other,
" 'Tis our brother, Hiawatha!"
     And he shouted from below them,
Cried exulting from the caverns:
"O ye sea-gulls! O my brothers!
I have slain the sturgeon, Nahma;
Make the rifts a little larger,
With your claws the openings widen,
Set me free from this dark prison,
And henceforward and forever
Men shall speak of your achievements.
Calling you Kayoshk, the sea-gulls,
Yes, Kayoshk, the Noble Scratchers!"
     And the wild and clamorous sea-gulls
Toiled with beak and claws together,
Made the rifts and openings wider
In the mighty ribs of Nahma,
And from peril and from prison,

From the body of the sturgeon,
From the peril of the water,
Was released my Hiawatha.

He was standing near his wigwam,
On the margin of the water,
And he called to old Nokomis,
Called and beckoned to Nokomis,
Pointed to the sturgeon, Nahma,
Lying lifeless on the pebbles,
With the sea-gulls feeding on him.

"I have slain the Mishe-Nahma,
Slain the King of Fishes!" said he;
"Look! the sea-gulls feed upon him,
Yes, my friends Kayoshk, the sea-gulls;
Drive them not away, Nokomis,
They have saved me from great peril
In the body of the sturgeon,
Wait until their meal is ended,
Till their craws are full with feasting,
Till they homeward fly, at sunset,
To their nests among the marshes;
Then bring all your pots and kettles
And make oil for us in Winter."

And she waited till the sun set,
Till the pallid moon, the Night-sun,
Rose above the tranquil water,
Till Kayoshk, the sated sea-gulls,
From their banquet rose with clamor,
And across the fiery sunset
Winged their way to far-off islands
To their nests among the rushes.

To his sleep went Hiawatha,
And Nokomis to her labor,
Toiling patient in the moonlight
Till the sun and moon changed places,
Till the sky was red with sunrise,
And Kayoshk, the hungry sea-gulls,
Came back from the reedy islands,
Clamorous for their morning banquet.

Three whole days and nights alternate

Old Nokomis and the sea-gulls
Stripped the oily flesh of Nahma,
Till the waves washed through the rib-bones,
Till the sea-gulls came no longer,
And upon the sands lay nothing
But the skeleton of Nahma.

IX

HIAWATHA AND THE PEARL-FEATHER

On the shores of Gitche Gumee,
Of the shining Big-Sea-Water,
Stood Nokomis, the old woman,
Pointing with her finger westward,
O'er the water pointing westward
To the purple clouds of sunset.

Fiercely the red sun descending,
Burned his way along the heavens,
Set the sky on fire behind him,
As war-parties, when retreating,
Burn the prairies on their war-trail
And the moon, the Night-sun, eastward,
Suddenly starting from his ambush,
Followed fast those bloody footprints,
Followed in that fiery war-trail,
With its glare upon his features.

And Nokomis, the old woman,
Pointing with her finger westward,
Spake these words to Hiawatha:
"Yonder dwells the great Pearl-Feather,
Megissogwon, the Magician,
Manito of Wealth and Wampum,
Guarded by his fiery serpents,
Guarded by the black pitch-water.
You can see his fiery serpents,
The Kenabeek, the great serpents,
Coiling, playing in the water;
You can see the black pitch-water
Stretching far away beyond them,

To the purple clouds of sunset!
"He it was who slew my father,
By his wicked wiles and cunning,
When he from the moon descended,
When he came on earth to seek me.
He, the mightiest of Magicians,
Sends the fever from the marshes,
Sends the pestilential vapors,
Sends the poisonous exhalations,
Sends the white fog from the fenlands,
Sends disease and death among us!

　"Take your bow, O Hiawatha,
Take your arrows, jasper-headed,
Take your war-club, Puggawaugun,
And your mittens, Minjekahwun,
And your birch-canoe for sailing,
And the oil of Mishe-Nahma,
So to smear its sides, that swiftly
You may pass the black pitch-water;
Slay this merciless magician,
Save the people from the fever
That he breathes across the fenlands,
And avenge my father's murder!"

　Straightway then my Hiawatha
Armed himself with all his war-gear,
Launched his birch-canoe for sailing;
With his palm its sides he patted,
Said with glee, "Cheemaun, my darling,
O my Birch-Canoe! leap forward,
Where you see the fiery serpents,
Where you see the black pitch-water!"

　Forward leaped Cheemaun exulting,
And the noble Hiawatha
Sang his war-song wild and woeful
And above him the war-eagle,
The Keneu, the great war-eagle,
Master of all fowls with feathers,
Screamed and hurtled through the heavens.

　Soon he reached the fiery serpents,
The Kenabeek, the great serpents,

Lying huge upon the water,
Sparkling, rippling in the water,
Lying coiled across the passage,
With their blazing crests uplifted,
Breathing fiery fogs and vapors,
So that none could pass beyond them.

But the fearless Hiawatha
Cried aloud, and spake in this wise,
"Let me pass my way, Kenabeek,
Let me go upon my journey!"
And they answered, hissing fiercely,
With their fiery breath made answer:
"Back, go back! O Shaugodaya! [1]
Back to old Nokomis, Faint-heart!"

Then the angry Hiawatha
Raised his mighty bow of ash-tree,
Seized his arrows, jasper-headed,
Shot them fast among the serpents;
Every twanging of the bowstring
Was a war-cry and a death-cry,
Every whizzing of an arrow
Was a death-song of Kenabeek.

Weltering in the bloody water,
Dead lay all the fiery serpents,
And among them Hiawatha
Harmless sailed, and cried exulting:
"Onward, O Cheemaun, [2] my darling!
Onward to the black pitch-water!"

Then he took the oil of Nahma,
And the bows and sides anointed,
Smeared them well with oil, that swiftly
He might pass the black pitch-water.

All night long he sailed upon it,
Sailed upon that sluggish water,
Covered with its mould of ages,
Black with rotting water-rushes,
Rank with flags and leaves of lilies,
Stagnant, lifeless, dreary, dismal,
Lighted by the shimmering moonlight,

[1] Coward.   [2] Canoe.

And by will-o'-the-wisps illumined,
Fires by ghosts of dead men kindled,
In their weary night-encampments.

All the air was white with moonlight,
All the water black with shadow,
And around him the Suggema,
The mosquito, sang his war-song,
And the fireflies, Wah-wah-taysee,
Waved their torches to mislead him;
And the bullfrog, the Dahinda,
Thrust his head into the moonlight,
Fixed his yellow eyes upon him,
Sobbed and sank beneath the surface;
And anon a thousand whistles,
Answered over all the fenlands,
And the heron, the Shuh-shuh-gah,
Far off on the reedy margin,
Heralded the hero's coming.

Westward thus fared Hiawatha,
Toward the realm of Megissogwon,
Toward the land of the Pearl-Feather,
Till the level moon stared at him,
In his face stared pale and haggard,
Till the sun was hot behind him,
Till it burned upon his shoulders,
And before him on the upland
He could see the Shining Wigwam
Of the Manito of Wampum,
Of the mightiest of Magicians.

Then once more Cheemaun he patted,
To his birch-canoe said, "Onward!"
And it stirred in all its fibres,
And with one great bound of triumph
Leaped across the water-lilies,
Leaped through tangled flags and rushes,
And upon the beach beyond them
Dry-shod landed Hiawatha.

Straight he took his bow of ash-tree,
One end on the sand he rested,
With his knee he pressed the middle,

Stretched the faithful bowstring tighter,
Took an arrow, jasper-headed,
Shot it at the Shining Wigwam,
Sent it singing as a herald,
As a bearer of his message,
Of his challenge loud and lofty:
"Come forth from your lodge, Pearl-Feather!
Hiawatha waits your coming!"
　　Straightway from the Shining Wigwam
Came the mighty Megissogwon,
Tall of stature, broad of shoulder,
Dark and terrible in aspect,
Clad from head to foot in wampum,
Armed with all his warlike weapons,
Painted like the sky of morning,
Streaked with crimson, blue, and yellow,
Crested with great eagle-feathers,
Streaming upward, streaming outward.
　　"Well I know you, Hiawatha!"
Cried he in a voice of thunder,
In a tone of loud derision.
"Hasten back, O Shaugodaya!
Hasten back among the women,
Back to old Nokomis, Faint-heart,
I will slay you as you stand there,
As of old I slew her father!"
　　But my Hiawatha answered,
Nothing daunted, fearing nothing:
"Big words do not smite like war-clubs,
Boastful breath is not a bowstring,
Taunts are not so sharp as arrows,
Deeds are better things than words are,
Actions mightier than boastings!"
　　Then began the greatest battle
That the sun had ever looked on,
That the war-birds ever witnessed.
All a Summer's day it lasted,
From the sunrise to the sunset;
For the shafts of Hiawatha
Harmless hit the shirt of wampum,

Harmless fell the blows he dealt it
With his mittens, Minjekahwun,
Harmless fell the heavy war-club;
It could dash the rocks asunder,
But it could not break the meshes
Of that magic shirt of wampum.

Till at sunset Hiawatha,
Leaning on his bow of ash-tree,
Wounded, weary, and desponding,
With his mighty war-club broken,
With his mittens torn and tattered,
And three useless arrows only,
Paused to rest beneath a pine-tree,
From whose branches trailed the mosses,
And whose trunk was coated over
With the Dead-man's Moccasin-leather,
With the fungus white and yellow.

Suddenly from the boughs above him
Sang the Mama, the woodpecker:
"Aim your arrows, Hiawatha,
At the head of Megissogwon,
Strike the tuft of hair upon it,
At their roots the long black tresses;
There alone can he be wounded!"

Winged with feathers, tipped with jasper,
Swift flew Hiawatha's arrow,
Just as Megissogwon, stooping,
Raised a heavy stone to throw it.
Full upon the crown it struck him,
At the roots of his long tresses,
And he reeled and staggered forward,
Plunging like a wounded bison,
Yes, like Pezhekee, the bison,
When the snow is on the prairie.

Swifter flew the second arrow,
In the pathway of the other,
Piercing deeper than the other,
Wounding sorer than the other,
And the knees of Megissogwon
Shook like windy reeds beneath him,

Bent and trembled like the rushes.
But the third and latest arrow
Swiftest flew, and wounded sorest,
And the mighty Megissogwon
Saw the fiery eyes of Pauguk,
Saw the eyes of Death glare at him,
Heard his voice call in the darkness;
At the feet of Hiawatha
Lifeless lay the great Pearl-Feather,
Lay the mightiest of Magicians.

Then the grateful Hiawatha
Called the Mama, the woodpecker,
From his perch among the branches
Of the melancholy pine-tree,
And in honor of his service,
Stained with blood the tuft of feathers
On the little head of Mama;
Even to this day he wears it,
Wears the tuft of crimson feathers,
As a symbol of his service.

Then he stripped the shirt of wampum
From the back of Megissogwon,
As a trophy of the battle,
As a signal of his conquest.
On the shore he left the body,
Half on land and half in water,
In the sand his feet were buried,
And his face was in the water.
And above him, wheeled and clamored
The Keneu, the great war-eagle,
Sailing round in narrower circles
Hovering nearer, nearer, nearer.

From the wigwam Hiawatha
Bore the wealth of Megissogwon,
All his wealth of skins and wampum,
Furs of bison and of beaver,
Furs of sable and of ermine,
Wampum belts and strings and pouches,
Quivers wrought with beads of wampum,
Filled with arrows, silver-headed.

Homeward then he sailed exulting,
Homeward through the black pitch-water
Homeward through the weltering serpent'
With the trophies of the battle,
With a shout and song of triumph.
On the shore stood old Nokomis,
On the shore stood Chibiabos,
And the very strong man, Kwasind,
Waiting for the hero's coming,
Listening to his song of triumph.
And the people of the village
Welcomed him with songs and dances,
Made a joyous feast, and shouted!
"Honor be to Hiawatha!
He has slain the great Pearl-Feather,
Slain the mightiest of Magicians,
Him, who sent the fiery fever,
Sent the white fog from the fenlands,
Sent disease and death among us!"
Ever dear to Hiawatha
Was the memory of Mama!
And in token of his friendship,
As a mark of his remembrance,
He adorned and decked his pipe-stem
With the crimson tuft of feathers,
With the blood-red crest of Mama.
But the wealth of Megissogwon,
All the trophies of the battle,
He divided with his people,
Shared it equally among them.

X

Hiawatha's Wooing

"As unto the bow the cord is,
So unto the man is woman,
Though she bends him, she obeys him,
Though she draws him, yet she follows,
Useless each without the other!"

Thus the youthful Hiawatha
Said within himself and pondered,
Much perplexed by various feelings,
Listless, longing, hoping, fearing,
Dreaming still of Minnehaha,
Of the lovely Laughing Water,
In the land of the Dacotahs.
"Wed a maiden of your people,"
Warning said the old Nokomis;
"Go not eastward, go not westward,
For a stranger, whom we know not!
Like a fire upon the hearthstone
Is a neighbor's homely daughter,
Like the starlight or the moonlight
Is the handsomest of strangers!"
    Thus dissuading spake Nokomis,
And my Hiawatha answered
Only this: "Dear old Nokomis,
Very pleasant is the firelight,
But I like the starlight better,
Better do I like the moonlight!"
    Gravely then said old Nokomis:
"Bring not here an idle maiden,
Bring not here a useless woman,
Hands unskilful, feet unwilling;
Bring a wife with nimble fingers,
Heart and hand that move together,
Feet that run on willing errands!"
    Smiling answered Hiawatha;
"In the land of the Dacotahs
Lives the Arrow-maker's daughter,
Minnehaha, Laughing Water,
Handsomest of all the women.
I will bring her to your wigwam,
She shall run upon your errands,
Be your starlight, moonlight, firelight,
Be the sunlight of my people!"
    Still dissuading said Nokomis:
"Bring not to my lodge a stranger
From the land of the Dacotahs!

Very fierce are the Dacotahs,
Often is there war between us,
There are feuds yet unforgotten,
Wounds that ache and still may open!"
  Laughing answered Hiawatha:
"For that reason, if no other,
Would I wed the fair Dacotah,
That our tribes might be united,
That old feuds might be forgotten,
And old wounds be healed forever!"
  Thus departed Hiawatha
To the land of the Dacotahs,
To the land of handsome women;
Striding over moor and meadow,
Through interminable forests,
Through uninterrupted silence.
  With his moccasins of magic,
At each stride a mile he measured;
Yet the way seemed long before him,
And his heart outran his footsteps;
And he journeyed without resting,
Till he heard the cataract's thunder,
Heard the Falls of Minnehaha,
Calling to him through the silence.
"Pleasant is the sound!" he murmured,
"Pleasant is the voice that calls me!"
  On the outskirts of the forest,
'Twixt the shadow and the sunshine,
Herds of fallow deer were feeding,
But they saw not Hiawatha;
To his bow he whispered, "Fail not!"
To his arrow whispered, "Swerve not!"
Sent it singing on its errand,
To the red heart of the roebuck;
Threw the deer across his shoulder,
And sped forward without pausing.
  At the doorway of his wigwam
Sat the ancient Arrow-maker,
In the land of the Dacotahs,
Making arrow-heads of jasper

Arrow-heads of chalcedony.
At his side, in all her beauty,
Sat the lovely Minnehaha,
Sat his daughter, Laughing Water,
Plaiting mats of flags and rushes;
Of the past the old man's thoughts were,
And the maiden's of the future.

He was thinking, as he sat there,
Of the days when with such arrows
He had struck the deer and bison,
On the Muskoday, the meadow;
Shot the wild goose, flying southward,
On the wing, the clamorous Wawa;
Thinking of the great war-parties,
How they came to buy his arrows,
Could not fight without his arrows.
Ah, no more such noble warriors
Could be found on earth as they were!
Now the men were all like women,
Only used their tongues for weapons!

She was thinking of a hunter,
From another tribe and country,
Young and tall and very handsome,
Who one morning, in the Spring-time,
Came to buy her father's arrows,
Sat and rested in the wigwam,
Lingered long about the doorway,
Looking back as he departed.
She had heard her father praise him,
Praise his courage and his wisdom;
Would he come again for arrows
To the Falls of Minnehaha?
On the mat her hands lay idle,
And her eyes were very dreamy.

Through their thoughts they heard a footstep,
Heard a rustling in the branches,
And with glowing cheek and forehead,
With the deer upon his shoulders,
Suddenly from out the woodlands
Hiawatha stood before them.

Straight the ancient Arrow-maker
Looked up gravely from his labor,
Laid aside the unfinished arrow,
Bade him enter at the doorway,
Saying, as he rose to meet him,
"Hiawatha, you are welcome!"
At the feet of Laughing Water
Hiawatha laid his burden,
Threw the red deer from his shoulders;
And the maiden looked up at him,
Looked up from her mat of rushes,
Said with gentle look and accent,
"You are welcome, Hiawatha!"
Very spacious was the wigwam,
Made of deerskin dressed and whitened,[1]
With the Gods of the Dacotahs
Drawn and painted on its curtains,
And so tall the doorway, hardly
Hiawatha stooped to enter,
Hardly touched his eagle-feathers
As he entered at the doorway.
Then uprose the Laughing Water,
From the ground fair Minnehaha,
Laid aside her mat unfinished,
Brought forth food and set before them,
Water brought them from the brooklet,
Gave them food in earthen vessels,
Gave them drink in bowls of basswood,
Listened while the guest was speaking,
Listened while her father answered,
But not once her lips she opened,
Not a single word she uttered.
Yes, as in a dream she listened
To the words of Hiawatha,
As he talked of old Nokomis,
Who had nursed him in his childhood,
As he told of his companions,
Chibiabos, the musician,
And the very strong man, Kwasind,

[1] Whitened with white clay. (Parkman.)

And of happiness and plenty
In the land of the Ojibways,
In the pleasant land and peaceful.
"After many years of warfare,
Many years of strife and bloodshed,
There is peace between the Ojibways
And the tribe of the Dacotahs."
Thus continued Hiawatha,
And then added, speaking slowly,
"That this peace may last forever,
And on our hands be clasped more closely,
And our hearts be more united,
Give me as my wife this maiden,
Minnehaha, Laughing Water,
Loveliest of Dacotah women!"
    And the ancient Arrow-maker
Paused a moment ere he answered,
Smoked a little while in silence,
Looked at Hiawatha proudly,
Fondly looked at Laughing Water,
And made answer very gravely:
"Yes, if Minnehaha wishes;
Let your heart speak, Minnehaha!"
    And the lovely Laughing Water
Seemed more lovely, as she stood there,
Neither willing nor reluctant,
As she went to Hiawatha,
Softly took the seat beside him,
While she said, and blushed to say it,
"I will follow you, my husband!"
    This was Hiawatha's wooing!
Thus it was he won the daughter
Of the ancient Arrow-maker,
In the land of the Dacotahs!
    From the wigwam he departed,
Leading with him Laughing Water;
Hand in hand they went together,
Through the woodland and the meadow,
Left the old man standing lonely
At the doorway of his wigwam,

Heard the Falls of Minnehaha
Calling to them from the distance,
Crying to them from afar off,
"Fare thee well, O Minnehaha!"
And the ancient Arrow-maker
Turned again unto his labor,
Sat down by his sunny doorway,
Murmuring to himself, and saying:
"Thus it is our daughters leave us,
Those we love, and those who love us!
Just when they have learned to help us,
When we are old and lean upon them,
Comes a youth with flaunting feathers,
With his flute of reeds, a stranger
Wanders piping through the village,
Beckons to the fairest maiden,
And she follows where he leads her,
Leaving all things for the stranger!"
Pleasant was the journey homeward,
Through interminable forests,
Over meadow, over mountain,
Over river, hill, and hollow.
Short it seemed to Hiawatha,
Though they journeyed very slowly,
Though his pace he checked and slackened
To the steps of Laughing Water.
Over wide and rushing rivers
In his arms he bore the maiden;
Light he thought her as a feather,
As the plume upon his headgear;
Cleared the tangled pathway for her,
Bent aside the swaying branches,
Made at night a lodge of branches,
And a bed with boughs of hemlock,
And a fire before the doorway
With the dry cones of the pine tree.
All the travelling winds went with them,
O'er the meadow, through the forest;
All the stars of night looked at them,
Watched with sleepless eyes their slumber;

From his ambush in the oak tree
Peeped the squirrel, Adjidaumo,
Watched with eager eyes the lovers;
And the rabbit, the Wabasso,
Scampered from the path before them,
Peering, peeping from his burrow,
Sat erect upon his haunches,
Watched with curious eyes the lovers.

Pleasant was the journey homeward!
All the birds sang loud and sweetly
Songs of happiness and heart's-ease;
Sang the bluebird, the Owaissa,
"Happy are you, Hiawatha,
Having such a wife to love you!"
Sang the Opechee, the robin,
"Happy are you, Laughing Water,
Having such a noble husband!"

From the sky the sun benignant
Looked upon them through the branches,
Saying to them, "O my children,
Love is sunshine, hate is shadow,
Life is checkered shade and sunshine,
Rule by love, O Hiawatha!"

From the sky the moon looked at them,
Filled the lodge with mystic splendors,
Whispered to them, "O my children,
Day is restless, night is quiet,
Man imperious, woman feeble;
Half is mine, although I follow;
Rule by patience, Laughing Water!"

Thus it was they journeyed homeward;
Thus it was that Hiawatha
To the lodge of old Nokomis
Brought the moonlight, starlight, firelight
Brought the sunshine of his people,
Minnehaha, Laughing Water,
Handsomest of all the women
In the land of the Dacotahs,
In the land of handsome women.

XI

HIAWATHA'S WEDDING-FEAST

You shall hear how Pau-Puk-Keewis,[1]
How the handsome Yenadizze
Danced at Hiawatha's wedding;
How the gentle Chibiabos,
He the sweetest of musicians,
Sang his songs of love and longing;
How Iagoo, the great boaster,
He the marvellous story-teller,
Told his tales of strange adventure,
That the feast might be more joyous,
That the time might pass more gayly,
And the guests be more contented.

Sumptuous was the feast Nokomis
Made at Hiawatha's wedding;
All the bowls were made of basswood,
White and polished very smoothly,
All the spoons of horn and bison,
Black and polished very smoothly.

She had sent through all the village
Messengers with wands of willow,
As a sign of invitation,
As a token of the feasting;
And the wedding guests assembled,
Clad in all their richest raiment,
Robes of fur and belts of wampum,
Splendid with their paint and plumage,
Beautiful with beads and tassels.

First they ate the sturgeon, Nahma,
And the pike, the Maskenozha,
Caught and cooked by old Nokomis;
Then on pemican they feasted,
Pemican and buffalo marrow,
Haunch of deer and hump of bison,
Yellow cakes of the Mondamin,
And the wild rice of the river.

[1] The Storm Fool. (See below.)

But the gracious Hiawatha,
And the lovely Laughing Water,
And the careful old Nokomis,
Tasted not the food before them,
Only waited on the others,
Only served their guests in silence.

And when all the guests had finished,
Old Nokomis, brisk and busy,
From an ample pouch of otter,
Filled the redstone pipes for smoking
With tobacco from the South-land,
Mixed with bark of the red willow,
And with herbs and leaves of fragrance.

Then she said, "O Pau-Puk-Keewis,
Dance for us your merry dances,
Dance the Beggar's Dance to please us,
That the feast may be more joyous,
That the time may pass more gayly,
And our guests be more contented!"

Then the handsome Pau-Puk-Keewis,
He the idle Yenadizze,
He the merry mischief-maker,
Whom the people called the Storm-Fool,
Rose among the guests assembled.
Skilled was he in sports and pastimes,
In the merry dance of snow shoes,
In the play of quoits and ball-play;
Skilled was he in games of hazard,
In all games of skill and hazard,
Pugasaing, the Bowl and Counters,
Kuntassoo, the Game of Plum-stones.

Though the warriors called him Faint-Heart,
Called him coward, Shaugodaya,
Idler, gambler, Yenadizze,
Little heeded he their jesting,
Little cared he for their insults,
For the women and the maidens
Loved the handsome Pau-Puk-Keewis.

He was dressed in shirt of doeskin,
White and soft, and fringed with ermine,

All inwrought with beads of wampum;
He was dressed in deerskin leggings,
Fringed with hedgehog quills and ermine,
And in moccasins of buckskin,
Thick with quills and beads embroidered.
On his head were plumes of swan's down,
On his heels were tails of foxes,
In one hand a fan of feathers,
And a pipe was in the other.

Barred with streaks of red and yellow,
Streaks of blue and bright vermilion,
Shone the face of Pau-Puk-Keewis.
From his forehead fell his tresses,
Smooth, and parted like a woman's,
Shining bright with oil, and plaited,
Hung with braids of scented grasses,
As among the guests assembled,
To the sound of flutes and singing,
To the sound of drums and voices,
Rose the handsome Pau-Puk-Keewis,
And began his mystic dances.

First he danced a solemn measure,
Very slow in step and gesture,
In and out among the pine trees,
Through the shadows and the sunshine,
Treading softly like a panther,
Then more swiftly and still swifter,
Whirling, spinning round in circles,
Leaping o'er the guests assembled,
Eddying round and round the wigwam,
Till the leaves went whirling with him,
Till the dust and wind together
Swept in eddies round about him.

Then along the sandy margin
Of the lake, the Big-Sea-Water,
On he sped with frenzied gestures,
Stamped upon the sand, and tossed it
Wildly in the air around him;
Till the wind became a whirlwind,
Till the sand was blown and sifted

Like great snowdrifts o'er the landscape,
Heaping all the shores with Sand Dunes,
Sand Hills of the Nagow Wudjoo! [1]
  Thus the merry Pau-Puk-Keewis
Danced his Beggar's Dance to please them,
And, returning, sat down laughing
There among the guests assembled,
Sat and fanned himself serenely
With his fan of turkey-feathers.
  Then they said to Chibiabos,
To the friend of Hiawatha,
To the sweetest of all singers,
To the best of all musicians,
"Sing to us, O Chibiabos!
Songs of love and songs of longing,
That the feast may be more joyous,
That the time may pass more gayly,
And our guests be more contented!"
  And the gentle Chibiabos
Sang in accents sweet and tender,
Sang in tones of deep emotion,
Songs of love and songs of longing;
Looking still at Hiawatha,
Looking at fair Laughing Water,
Sang he softly, sang in this wise.
  "Onaway! Awake, beloved! [2]
Thou the wild flower of the forest!

[1] A description of the *Grand Sable,* or great sand dunes of Lake Superior, is given in Foster and Whitney's *Report on the Geology of the Lake Superior Land District,* Part II, p. 131.
"The Grand Sable possesses a scenic interest little inferior to that of the Pictured Rocks. The explorer passes abruptly from a coast of consolidated sand to one of loose materials; and although in the one case the cliffs are less precipitous, yet in the other they attain a higher altitude. He sees before him a long reach of coast, resembling a vast sand-bank, more than three hundred and fifty feet in height, without a trace of vegetation. Ascending to the top, rounded hillocks of blown sand are observed, with occasional clumps of trees, standing out like oases in the desert."
[2] The original of this song may be found in *Littell's Living Age,* Vol. XXV, p. 45.

Thou the wild bird of the prairie!
Thou with eyes so soft and fawn-like!
　"If thou only lookest on me,
I am happy, I am happy,
As the lilies of the prairie,
When they feel the dew upon them!
　"Sweet thy breath is as the fragrance
Of the wild flowers in the morning,
As their fragrance is at evening,
In the Moon when leaves are falling.
　"Does not all the blood within me,
Leap to meet thee, leap to meet thee,
As the springs to meet the sunshine,
In the Moon when nights are brightest?
　"Onaway! my heart sings to thee,
Sings with joy when thou art near me,
As the sighing, singing branches
In the pleasant Moon of Strawberries!
　"When thou art not pleased, beloved,
Then my heart is sad and darkened,
As the shining river darkens
When the clouds drop shadows on it!
　"When thou smilest, my beloved,
Then my troubled heart is brightened,
As in sunshine gleam the ripples
That the cold wind makes in rivers.
　"Smiles the earth, and smile the waters,
Smile the cloudless skies above us,
But I lose the way of smiling
When thou art no longer near me!
　"I myself, myself! behold me!
Blood of my beating heart, behold me!
O awake, awake, beloved!
Onaway! awake, beloved!"
　Thus the gentle Chibiabos
Sang his song of love and longing;
And Iagoo, the great boaster,
He the marvellous story-teller,
He the friend of old Nokomis,
Jealous of the sweet musician,

Jealous of the applause they gave him,
Saw in all the eyes around him,
Saw in all their looks and gestures,
That the wedding guests assembled
Longed to hear his pleasant stories,
His immeasurable falsehoods.

Very boastful was Iagoo;
Never heard he an adventure
But himself had met a greater;
Never any deed of daring
But himself had done a bolder;
Never any marvellous story
But himself could tell a stranger.

Would you listen to his boasting,
Would you only give him credence,
No one ever shot an arrow
Half so far and high as he had;
Ever caught so many fishes,
Ever killed so many reindeer,
Ever trapped so many beaver!

None could run so fast as he could,
None could dive so deep as he could,
None could swim so far as he could;
None had made so many journeys,
None had seen so many wonders,
As this wonderful Iagoo,
As this marvellous-story-teller!

Thus his name became a byword
And a jest among the people;
And whene'er a boastful hunter
Praised his own address too highly,
Or a warrior, home returning,
Talked too much of his achievements,
All his hearers cried, "Iagoo!
Here's Iagoo come among us!"

He it was who carved the cradle
Of the little Hiawatha,
Carved its framework out of linden,
Bound it strong with reindeer sinews;
He it was who taught him later

How to make his bows and arrows,
How to make the bows of ash tree,
And the arrows of the oak tree,
So among the guests assembled
At my Hiawatha's wedding
Sat Iagoo, old and ugly,
Sat the marvellous story-teller.

  And they said, "O good Iagoo,
Tell us now a tale of wonder,
Tell us of some strange adventure,
That the feast may be more joyous,
That the time may pass more gayly,
And our guests be more contented!"

  And Iagoo answered straightway,
"You shall hear a tale of wonder.
You shall hear the strange adventures
Of Osseo, the Magician,
From the Evening Star descended."

XII

THE SON OF THE EVENING STAR

Can it be the sun descending,
O'er the level plain of water?
Or the Red Swan floating, flying,[1]
Wounded by the magic arrow,

---

[1] The fanciful tradition of the Red Swan may be found in School-craft's *Algic Researches,* Vol. II., p. 9. Three brothers were hunting on a wager to see who would bring home the first game.

"They were to shoot no other animal," so the legend says, "but such as each was in the habit of killing. They set out different ways; Odjibwa, the youngest, had not gone far before he saw a bear, an animal he was not to kill, by the agreement. He followed him close, and drove an arrow through him, which brought him to the ground. Although contrary to the bet, he immediately commenced skinning him, when suddenly something red tinged all the air around him. He rubbed his eyes, thinking he was perhaps deceived, but without effect, for the red hue continued. At length he heard a strange noise at a distance. It first appeared like a human voice; but after following the sound for some distance, he reached the shores of a lake, and soon saw the object he was looking for. At a

Staining all the waves with crimson,
With the crimson of its life-blood,
Filling all the air with splendor,
With the splendor of its plumage?
 Yes; it is the sun descending,
Sinking down into the water;
All the sky is stained with purple,
All the water flushed with crimson;
No; it is the Red Swan floating,
Diving down beneath the water;
To the sky its wings are lifted,
With its blood the waves are reddened!
 Over it the Star of Evening
Melts and trembles through the purple,
Hangs suspended in the twilight.
No; it is a bead of wampum
On the robes of the Great Spirit,
As he passes through the twilight,
Walks in silence through the heavens.
 This with joy beheld Iagoo
And he said in haste: "Behold it!

distance out in the lake sat a most beautiful Red Swan whose
plumage glittered in the sun, and who would now and then make
the same noise he had heard. He was within long bow-shot, and
pulling the arrow from the bow-string up to his ear, took deliberate
aim and shot. The arrow took no effect; and he shot and shot
again till his quiver was empty. Still the swan remained, moving
round and round, stretching its long neck and dipping its bill into
the water, as if heedless of the arrows shot at it. Odjibwa ran
home, and got all his own and his brother's arrows, and shot them
all away. He then stood and gazed at the beautiful bird. While
standing, he remembered his brother's saying that in their deceased
father's medicine-sack were three magic arrows. Off he started, his
anxiety to kill the swan overcoming all scruples. At any other time
he would have deemed it sacrilege to open his father's medicine-
sack; but now he hastily seized the three arrows and ran back,
leaving the other contents of the sack scattered over the lodge. The
swan was still there. He shot the first arrow with great precision,
and came very near to it. The second came still closer; as he took
the last arrow, he felt his arm firmer, and drawing it up with vigor,
saw it pass through the neck of the swan a little above the breast.
Still it did not prevent the bird from flying off, which it did, however, at first slowly, flapping its wings and rising gradually into the
air, and then flying off toward the sinking of the sun."—Pp. 10-12.

See the Sacred Star of Evening!
You shall hear a tale of wonder,
Hear the story of Osseo,
Son of the Evening Star, Osseo!

"Once, in days no more remembered,
Ages nearer the beginning,
When the heavens were closer to us,
And the Gods were more familiar,
In the North-land lived a hunter,
With ten young and comely daughters,
Tall and lithe as wands of willow;
Only Oweenee, the youngest,
She the wilful and the wayward,
She the silent, dreamy maiden,
Was the fairest of the sisters.

"All these women married warriors,
Married brave and haughty husbands;
Only Oweenee, the youngest,
Laughed and flouted all her lovers,
All her young and handsome suitors,
And then married old Osseo,
Old Osseo, poor and ugly,
Broken with age and weak from coughing,
Always coughing like a squirrel.

"Ah, but beautiful within him
Was the spirit of Osseo,
From the Evening Star descended,
Star of Evening, Star of Woman,
Star of tenderness and passion!
All its fire was in his bosom,
All its beauty in his spirit,
All its mystery in his being,
All its splendor in his language!

"And her lovers, the rejected,
Handsome men with belts of wampum,
Handsome men with paint and feathers,
Pointed at her in derision,
Followed her with jest and laughter.
But she said: 'I care not for you,
Care not for your belts of wampum,

Care not for your paint and feathers,
Care not for your jests and laughter;
I am happy with Osseo!'
   "Once to some great feast invited,
Through the damp and dusk of evening
Walked together the ten sisters,
Walked together with their husbands;
Slowly followed old Osseo,
With fair Oweenee beside him;
All the others chatted gayly,
These two only walked in silence.
   "At the western sky Osseo
Gazed intent, as if imploring,
Often stopped and gazed imploring
At the trembling Star of Evening,
At the tender Star of Woman;
And they heard him murmur softly,
'Ah, showain nemeshin, Nosa! [1]
Pity, pity me, my father!'
   " 'Listen!' said the eldest sister,
'He is praying to his father!
What a pity that the old man
Does not stumble in the pathway,
Does not break his neck by falling!'
And they laughed till all the forest
Rang with their unseemly laughter.
   "On their pathway through the woodlands
Lay an oak, by storms uprooted,
Lay the great trunk of an oak tree,
Buried half in leaves and mosses,
Mouldering, crumbling, huge and hollow
And Osseo, when he saw it,
Gave a shout, a cry of anguish,
Leaped into its yawning cavern,
At one end went in an old man,
Wasted, wrinkled, old and ugly;
From the other came a young man,
Tall and straight and strong and handsome.
   "Thus Osseo was transfigured,

[1] The following line is the translation of this.

Thus restored to youth and beauty;
But alas for good Osseo,
And for Oweenee, the faithful!
Strangely, too, was she transfigured,
Changed into a weak old woman,
With a staff she tottered onward,
Wasted, wrinkled, old, and ugly!
And the sisters and their husbands
Laughed until the echoing forest
Rang with their unseemly laughter.

"But Osseo turned not from her,
Walked with slower step beside her,
Took her hand, as brown and withered
As an oak-leaf is in Winter,
Called her sweetheart, Nenomoosha,
Soothed her with soft words of kindness,
Till they reached the lodge of feasting,
Till they sat down in the wigwam,
Sacred to the Star of Evening,
To the tender Star of Woman.

"Wrapt in visions, lost in dreaming,
At the banquet sat Osseo;
All were merry, all were happy,
All were joyous but Osseo,
Neither food nor drink he tasted,
Neither did he speak nor listen,
But as one bewildered sat he,
Looking dreamily and sadly,
First at Oweenee, then upward
At the gleaming sky above them.

"Then a voice was heard, a whisper,
Coming from the starry distance.
Coming from the empty vastness,
Low, and musical, and tender;
And the voice said: 'O Osseo!
O my son, my best beloved!
Broken are the spells that bound you,
All the charms of the magicians,
All the magic powers of evil;
Come to me; ascend, Osseo!

" 'Taste the food that stands before you;
It is blessed and enchanted,
It has magic virtues in it,
It will change you to a spirit.
All your bowls and all your kettles
Shall be wood and clay no longer;
But the bowls be changed to wampum,
And the kettles shall be silver;
They shall sh'ne like shells of scarlet,
Like the fire shall gleam and glimmer.

" 'And the women shall no longer
Bear the dreary doom of labor,
But be changed to birds, and glisten
With the beauty of the starlight,
Painted with the dusky splendors
Of the skies and clouds of evening!'

"What Osseo heard as whispers,
What as words he comprehended,
Was but music to the others,
Music as of birds afar off,
Of the whip-poor-will afar off,
Of the lonely Wawonaissa
Singing in the darksome forest.

"Then the lodge began to tremble,
Straight began to shake and tremble,
And they felt it rising, rising,
Slowly through the air ascending,
From the darkness of the treetops
Forth into the dewy starlight,
Till it passed the topmost branches;
And behold! the wooden dishes
All were changed to shells of scarlet!
And behold! the earthen kettles
All were changed to bowls of silver!
And the roof-poles of the wigwam
Were as glittering rods of silver,
And the roof of bark upon them
As the shining shards of beetles.

"Then Osseo gazed around him,
And he saw the nine fair sisters,

All the sisters and their husbands,
Changed to birds of various plumage.
Some were jays and some were magpies,
Others thrushes, others blackbirds;
And they hopped, and sang, and twittered,
Pecked and fluttered all their feathers,
Strutted in their shining plumage,
And their tails like fans unfolded,

    "Only Oweenee, the youngest,
Was not changed, but sat in silence,
Wasted, wrinkled, old, and ugly,
Lookly sadly at the others;
Till Osseo, gazing upward,
Gave another cry of anguish,
Such a cry as he had uttered
By the oak tree in the forest.

    "Then returned her youth and beauty
And her soiled and tattered garments
Were transformed to robes of ermine.
And her staff became a feather,
Yes, a shining silver feather!

    "And again the wigwam trembled,
Swayed and rushed through airy currents,
Through transparent cloud and vapor
And amid celestial splendors
On the Evening Star alighted,
As a snowflake falls on snowflake,
As a leaf drops on a river,
As the thistledown on water.

    "Forth with cheerful words of welcome
Came the father of Osseo,
He with radiant locks of silver,
He with eyes serene and tender,
And he said: 'My son, Osseo,
Hang the cage of birds you bring there,
Hang the cage with rods of silver,
And the birds with glistening feathers,
At the doorway of my wigwam.'

    "At the door he hung the bird cage,
And they entered in and gladly

Listened to Osseo's father,
Ruler of the Star of Evening,
As he said: 'O my Osseo!
I have had compassion on you,
Given you back your youth and beauty,
Into birds of various plumage
Changed your sisters and their husbands;
Changed them thus because they mocked you
In the figure of the old man,
In that aspect sad and wrinkled,
Could not see your heart of passion,
Could not see your youth immortal;
Only Oweenee, the faithful,
Saw your naked heart and loved you.

    " 'In the lodge that glimmers yonder,
In the little star that twinkles
Through the vapors, on the left hand,
Lives the envious Evil Spirit,
The Wabeno, the magician,
Who transformed you to an old man.
Take heed lest his beams fall on you,
For the rays he darts around him
Are the power of his enchantment,
Are the arrows that he uses.'

    "Many years, in peace and quiet,
On the peaceful Star of Evening
Dwelt Osseo with his father;
Many years, in song and flutter,
At the doorway of the wigwam,
Hung the cage with rods of silver,
And fair Oweenee, the faithful,
Bore a son unto Osseo,
With the beauty of his mother,
With the courage of his father.

    "And the boy grew up and prospered,
And Osseo, to delight him,
Made him little bows and arrows,
Opened the great cage of silver,
And let loose his aunts and uncles,
All those birds with glossy feathers,

For his little son to shoot at.

"Round and round they wheeled and darted,
Filled the Evening Star with music,
With their songs of joy and freedom;
Filled the Evening Star with splendor,
With the fluttering of their plumage;
Till the boy, the little hunter,
Bent his bow and shot an arrow,
Shot a swift and fatal arrow,
And a bird, with shining feathers,
At his feet fell wounded sorely.

"But, O wondrous transformation!
'T was no bird he saw before him,
'T was a beautiful young woman,
With the arrow in her bosom!

"When her blood fell on the planet,
On the sacred Star of Evening,
Broken was the spell of magic
Powerless was the strange enchantment,
And the youth, the fearless bowman,
Suddenly felt himself descending,
Held by unseen hands, but sinking
Downward through the empty spaces,
Downward through the clouds and vapors,
Till he rested on an island,
On an island, green and grassy,
Yonder in the Big-Sea-Water.

"After him he saw descending
All the birds with shining feathers,
Fluttering, falling, wafted downward,
Like the painted leaves of Autumn;
And the lodge with poles of silver,
With its roof like wings of beetles,
Like the shining shards of beetles,
By the winds of heaven uplifted,
Slowly sank upon the island,
Bringing back the good Osseo,
Bringing Oweenee, the faithful.

"Then the birds again transfigured,
Reassumed the shape of mortals,

Took their shape but not their stature;
They remained as Little People,
Like the pygmies, the Puk-Wudjies,
And on pleasant nights of Summer,
When the Evening Star was shining,
Hand in hand they danced together
On the island's craggy headlands,
On the sandbeach low and level.

   "Still their glittering lodge is seen there,
On the tranquil Summer evenings,
And upon the shore the fisher,
Sometimes hears their happy voices,
Sees them dancing in the starlight!"

   When the story was completed,
When the wondrous tale was ended,
Looking round upon his listeners,
Solemnly Iagoo added:
"There are great men, I have known such,
Whom their people understand not,
Whom they even make a jest of,
Scoff and jeer at in derision.
From the story of Osseo
Let them learn the fate of jesters!"

   All the wedding guests delighted
Listened to the marvellous story,
Listened, laughing and applauding,
And they whispered to each other:
"Does he mean himself, I wonder?
And are we the aunts and uncles?"

   Then again sang Chibiabos,
Sang a song of love and longing,
In those accents sweet and tender,
In those tones of pensive sadness,
Sang a maiden's lamentation
For her lover her Algonquin.

   "When I think of my beloved,[1]
Ah me! think of my beloved,
When my heart is thinking of him,
O my sweetheart, my Algonquin!

[1] The original of this song may be found in *Oneóta*, p. 15.

"Ah me! when I parted from him,
Round my neck he hung the wampum,
As a pledge, the snow-white wampum,
O my sweetheart, my Algonquin!

"I will go with you, he whispered,
Ah me! to your native country;
Let me go with you, he whispered,
O my sweetheart, my Algonquin!

"Far away, away, I answered,
Very far away, I answered,
Ah me! is my native country,
O my sweetheart, my Algonquin!

"When I looked back to behold him,
Where we parted, to behold him,
After me he still was gazing,
O my sweetheart, my Algonquin!

"By the tree he still was standing,
By the fallen tree was standing,
That had dropped into the water,
O my sweetheart, my Algonquin!

"When I think of my beloved,
Ah me! think of my beloved,
When my heart is thinking of him
O my sweetheart, my Algonquin!"

Such was Hiawatha's Wedding,
Such the dance of Pau-Puk-Keewis,
Such the story of Iagoo,
Such the songs of Chibiabos;
Thus the wedding banquet ended,
And the wedding guests departed,
Leaving Hiawatha happy
With the night and Minnehaha.

XIII

BLESSING THE CORNFIELDS

Sing, O Song of Hiawatha,
Of the happy days that followed,
In the land of the Ojibways,

In the pleasant land and peaceful!
Sing the mysteries of Mondamin,[1]
Sing the Blessing of the Cornfields!
  Buried was the bloody hatchet,
Buried was the dreadful warclub,
Buried were all warlike weapons,
And the warcry was forgotten.
There was peace among the nations;
Unmolested roved the hunters,
Built the birch canoe for sailing,
Caught the fish in lake and river,
Shot the deer and trapped the beaver;
Unmolested worked the women,
Made their sugar from the maple,
Gathered wild rice in the meadows,
Dressed the skins of deer and beaver.
  All around the happy village,
Stood the maize fields, green and shining,
Waved the green plumes of Mondamin,
Waved his soft and sunny tresses,
Filling all the land with plenty.
'T was the women who in Springtime
Planted the broad fields and fruitful,

---

[1] The Indians hold the maize, or Indian corn, in great veneration. "They esteem it so important and divine a grain," says Schoolcraft, "that their story-tellers invented various tales, in which this idea is symbolized under the form of a special gift from the Great Spirit. The Odjibwa-Algonquins, who call it Mon-dà-min, that is, the Spirit's grain or berry, have a pretty story of this kind, in which the stalk in full tassel is represented as descending from the sky, under the guise of a handsome youth, in answer to the prayers of a young man at his fast of virility, or coming to manhood.

"It is well known that corn-planting and corn-gathering, at least among all the still *uncolonized* tribes, are left entirely to the females and children, and a few superannuated old men. It is not generally known, perhaps, that this labor is not compulsory, and that it is assumed by the females as a just equivalent, in their view, for the onerous and continuous labor of the other sex, in providing meats and skins for clothing by the chase, and in defending their villages against their enemies, and keeping intruders off their territories. A good Indian housewife deems this a part of her prerogative, and prides herself to have a store of corn to exercise her hospitality, or duly honor her husband's hospitality, in the entertainment of the lodge guests."—*Oneóta*, p. 82.

Buried in the earth Mondamin;
'T was the women who in Autumn
Stripped the yellow husks of harvest,
Stripped the garments from Mondamin,
Even as Hiawatha taught them.

Once, when all the maize was planted,
Hiawatha, wise and thoughtful,
Spake and said to Minnehaha,
To his wife, the Laughing Water:
You shall bless to-night the cornfields,
Draw a magic circle round them,
To protect them from destruction,
Blast of mildew, blight of insect,
Wagemin, the thief of cornfields,
Paimosaid, who steals the maize-ear!
In the night, when all is silence,
In the night, when all is darkness,
When the Spirit of Sleep, Nepahwin,
Shuts the doors of all the wigwams,
So that not an ear can hear you,
So that not an eye can see you,
Rise up from your bed in silence,
Lay aside your garments wholly,
Walk around the fields you planted,
Round the borders of the cornfields,
Covered by your tresses only,
Robed with darkness as a garment.
"Thus the fields shall be more fruitful,[1]
And the passing of your footsteps

[1] "A singular proof of this belief, in both sexes, of the mysterious influence of the steps of a woman on the vegetable and insect creation, is found in an ancient custom, which was related to me, respecting corn-planting. It was the practice of the hunter's wife, when the field of corn had been planted, to choose the first dark or over-clouded evening to perform a secret circuit, *sans habillement*, around the field. For this purpose she slipped out of the lodge in the evening, unobserved, to some obscure nook, where she completely disrobed. Then, taking her matchecota, or principal garment, in one hand, she dragged it around the field. This was thought to insure a prolific crop, and to prevent the assaults of insects and worms upon the grain. It was supposed they could not creep over the charmed line."—*Oneóta,* p. 83.

Draw a magic circle round them,
So that neither blight nor mildew,
Neither burrowing worm nor insect
Shall pass o'er the magic circle;
Not the dragon fly, Kwo-ne-she,
Nor the spider, Subbekashe,
Nor the grasshopper, Paw-Puk-keena,
Nor the mighty caterpillar,
Way-muk-kwana, with the bearskin,
King of all the caterpillars!"

   On the treetops near the cornfields
Sat the hungry crows and ravens,
Kahgahgee, the King of Ravens,
With his band of black marauders.
And they laughed at Hiawatha,
Till the treetops shook with laughter,
With their melancholy laughter,
At the words of Hiawatha.
"Hear him!" said they; "hear the Wise Man,
Hear the plots of Hiawatha!"

   When the noiseless night descended
Broad and dark o'er field and forest,
When the mournful Wawonaissa,
Sorrowing sang among the hemlocks,
And the Spirit of Sleep, Nepahwin,
Shut the doors of all the wigwams,
From her bed rose Laughing Water,
Laid aside her garments wholly,
And with darkness clothed and guarded,
Unashamed and unaffrighted,
Walked securely round the cornfields,
Drew the sacred, magic circle
Of her footprints round the cornfields.

   No one but the Midnight only
Saw her beauty in the darkness,
No one but the Wawonaissa
Heard the panting of her bosom;
Guskewau, the darkness, wrapped her
Closely in his sacred mantle,
So that none might see her beauty,

So that none might boast, "I saw her!"
    On the morrow, as the day dawned,
Kahgahgee, the King of Ravens,
Gathered all his black marauders,
Crows and blackbirds, jays, and ravens,
Clamorous on the dusky treetops,
And descended, fast and fearless,
On the fields of Hiawatha,
On the grave of the Mondamin.
    "We will drag Mondamin," said they,
"From the grave where he is buried,
Spite of all the magic circles
Laughing Water draws around it,
Spite of all the sacred footprints
Minnehaha stamps upon it!"
    But the wary Hiawatha,
Ever thoughtful, careful, watchful,
Had o'erheard the scornful laughter
When they mocked him from the treetops.
"Kaw!" he said, "my friends the ravens!
Kahgahgee, my King of Ravens!
I will teach you all a lesson
That shall not be soon forgotten!"
    He had risen before the daybreak,
He had spread o'er all the cornfields
Snares to catch the black marauders,
And was lying now in ambush
In the neighboring grove of pine-trees,
Waiting for the crows and blackbirds,
Waiting for the jays and ravens.
    Soon they came with caw and clamor,
Rush of wings and cry of voices,
To their work of devastation,
Settling down upon the cornfields,
Delving deep with beak and talon,
For the body of Mondamin.
And with all their craft and cunning,
All their skill in wiles of warfare,
They perceived no danger near them,
Till their claws became entangled,

Till they found themselves imprisoned
In the snares of Hiawatha.
From his place of ambush came he,
Striding terrible among them,
And so awful was his aspect
That the bravest quailed with terror.
Without mercy he destroyed them
Right and left, by tens and twenties,
And their wretched, lifeless bodies
Hung aloft on poles for scarecrows
Round the consecrated cornfields,
As a signal of his vengeance,
As a warning to marauders.

Only Kahgahgee, the leader,
Kahgahgee, the King of Ravens,
He alone was spared among them
As a hostage for his people.
With his prisoner-string he bound him,[1]
Let him captive to his wigwam,
Tied him fast with cords of elm bark
To the ridgepole of his wigwam.

"Kahgahgee, my raven!" said he,
"You the leader of the robbers,
You the plotter of this mischief,
The contriver of this outrage,
I will keep you, I will hold you,
As a hostage for your people,
As a pledge of good behavior!"

And he left him, grim and sulky,
Sitting in the morning sunshine
On the summit of the wigwam,
Croaking fiercely his displeasure,
Flapping his great sable pinions,

---

[1] "These cords," says Mr. Tanner, "are made of the bark of the elm-tree, by boiling and then immersing it in cold water. . . . The leader of a war party commonly carries several fastened about his waist; and if, in the course of the fight, any one of his young men takes a prisoner, it is his duty to bring him immediately to the chief, to be tied, and the latter is responsible for his safekeeping."—*Narrative of Captivity and Adventures*, p. 412.

Vainly struggling for his freedom,
Vainly calling on his people!
    Summer passed, and Shawondasee
Breathed his sighs o'er all the landscape,
From the Southland sent his ardors,
Wafted kisses warm and tender;
And the maize field grew and ripened.
Till it stood in all the splendor,
Of its garments green and yellow,
Of its tassels and its plumage,
And the maize ears full and shining
Gleamed from bursting sheaths of verdure.
    Then Nokomis, the old woman,
Spake, and said to Minnehaha:
" 'Tis the Moon when leaves are falling;
And the wild rice has been gathered,
And the maize is ripe and ready;
Let us gather in the harvest,
Let us wrestle with Mondamin,
Strip him of his plumes and tassels,
Of his garments green and yellow!"
    And the merry Laughing Water
Went rejoicing from the wigwam,
With Nokomis old and wrinkled,
And they called the women round them,
Called the young men and the maidens,
To the harvest of the cornfields,
To the husking of the maize ear.
    On the border of the forest,
Underneath the fragrant pine trees,
Sat the old men and the warriors
Smoking in the pleasant shadow.
In uninterrupted silence
Looked they at the gamesome labor
Of the young men and the women;
Listened to their noisy talking,
To their laughter and their singing,
Heard them chattering like the magpies,
Heard them laughing like the bluejays,
Heard them singing like the robins.

And whene'er some lucky maiden
Found a red ear in the husking,
Found a maize ear red as blood is,
"Nushka!" [1] cried they all together.
"Nushka! you shall have a sweetheart,
You shall have a handsome husband!"
"Ugh!" the old men all responded
From their seats beneath the pine-trees.

And whene'er a youth or maiden
Found a crooked ear in husking,
Found a maize ear in the husking
Blighted, mildewed, or misshapen,
Then they laughed and sang together,
Crept and limped about the cornfields,
Mimicked in their gait and gestures
Some old man bent almost double,
Singing singly or together:
"Wagemin, the thief of cornfields! [2]
Paimosaid, the skulking robber!"

[1] Look!

[2] "If one of the young female huskers find a *red* ear of corn, it is typical of a brave admirer, and is regarded as a fitting present to some young warrior. But if the ear be *crooked,* and tapering to a point, no matter what color, the whole circle is set in a roar, and *wa-ge-min* is the word shouted aloud. It is the symbol of a thief in the cornfield. It is considered as the image of an old man stooping as he enters the lot. Had the chisel of Praxiteles been employed to produce this image, it could not more vividly bring to the minds of the merry group the idea of a pilferer of their favorite mondà-min. . . .

"The literal meaning of the term is a mass, or crooked ear of grain; but the ear of corn so called is a conventional type of a little old man pilfering ears of corn in a cornfield. It is in this manner that a single word or term, in these curious languages, becomes the fruitful parent of many ideas. And we can thus perceive why it is that the word *wagemin* is alone competent to excite merriment in the husking circle.

"This term is taken as the basis of the cereal chorus, or corn song, as sung by the Northern Algonquin tribes. It is coupled with the prase *Paimosaid,*—a permutative form of the Indian substantive, made from the verb *pim-o-sa,* to walk. Its literal meaning is, *he who walks,* or *the walker;* but the ideas conveyed by it are, he who walks by night to pilfer corn. It offers, therefore. a kind of parallelism in expression to the preceding term."—*Oneóta,* p. 254.

Till the cornfields rang with laughter,
Till from Hiawatha's wigwam
Kahgahgee, the King of Ravens,
Screamed and quivered in his anger,
And from all the neighboring treetops
Cawed and croaked the black marauders.
"Ugh!" the old men all responded,
From their seats beneath the pine-trees!

XIV

PICTURE-WRITING

In those days said Hiawatha,
"Lo! how all things fade and perish!
From the memory of the old men
Fade away the great traditions,
The achievements of the warriors,
The adventures of the hunters,
All the wisdom of the Medas,
All the craft of the Wabenos,
All the marvellous dreams and visions
Of the Jossakeeds, the Prophets!

"Great men die and are forgotten,
Wise men speak; their words of wisdom
Perish in the ears that hear them,
Do not reach the generations
That, as yet unborn, are waiting
In the great, mysterious darkness
Of the speechless days that shall be!

"On the grave-posts of our fathers
Are no signs, no figures painted;
Who are in those graves we know not,
Only know they are our fathers.
Of what kith they are and kindred,
From what old, ancestral Totem,
Be it Eagle, Bear, or Beaver,
They descended, this we know not,
Only know they are our fathers.

"Face to face we speak together,
But we cannot speak when absent,
Cannot send our voices from us
To the friends that dwell afar off;
Cannot send a secret message,
But the bearer learns our secret,
May pervert it, may betray it,
May reveal it unto others."
Thus said Hiawatha, walking
In the solitary forest,
Pondering, musing in the forest,
On the welfare of his people.

From his pouch he took his colors,
Took his paints of different colors,
On the smooth bark of a birch tree
Painted many shapes and figures,
Wonderful and mystic figures,
And each figure had a meaning,
Each some word or thought suggested.
Gitche Manito the Mighty,
He, the Master of Life, was painted
As an egg, with points projecting
To the four winds of the heavens.
Everywhere is the Great Spirit,
Was the meaning of this symbol.

Mitche Manito the Mighty,
He the dreadful Spirit of Evil,
As a serpent was depicted,
As Kenabeek, the great serpent.
Very crafty, very cunning,
Is the creeping Spirit of Evil,
Was the meaning of this symbol.

Life and Death he drew as circle,
Life was white, but Death was darkness;
Sun and moon and stars he painted,
Man and beast, and fish and reptile,
Forests, mountains, lakes, and rivers.

For the earth he drew a straight line,
For the sky a bow above it;
White the space between for daytime,

Filled with little stars for night-time;
On the left a point for sunrise,
On the right a point for sunset,
On the top a point for noontide,
And for rain and cloudy weather
Waving lines descending from it.

Footprints pointing toward a wigwam
Were a sign of invitation,
Were a sign of guests assembling;
Bloody hands with palms uplifted
Were a symbol of destruction,
Were a hostile sign and symbol.

All these things did Hiawatha
Show unto his wondering people,
And interpreted their meaning,
And he said: "Behold, your grave posts
Have no mark, no sign, nor symbol.
Go and paint them all with figures;
Each one with its household symbol,
With its own ancestral Totem;
So that those who follow after
May distinguish them and know them."

And they painted on the grave posts
Of the graves yet unforgotten,
Each his own ancestral Totem,
Each the symbol of his household;
Figures of the Bear and Reindeer,
Of the Turtle, Crane, and Beaver,
Each inverted as a token
That the owner was departed,
That the chief who bore the symbol
Lay beneath in dust and ashes.

And the Jossakeeds, the Prophets,
The Wabenos, the Magicians,
And the Medicine-men, the Medas,
Painted upon bark and deerskin
Figures for the songs they chanted,
For each song a separate symbol,
Figures mystical and awful,
Figures strange and brightly colored;

And each figure had its meaning,
Each some magic song suggested.

The Great Spirit, the Creator,
Flashing light through all the heaven;
The Great Serpent, the Kenabeek,
With his bloody crest erected,
Creeping, looking into heaven;
In the sky the sun, that listens,
And the moon eclipsed and dying;
Owl and eagle, crane and henhawk,
And the cormorant, bird of magic;
Headless men, that walk the heavens,
Bodies lying pierced with arrows,
Bloody hands of death uplifted,
Flags on graves, and great war-captains
Grasping both the earth and heaven!

Such as these the shapes they painted
On the birchbark and the deerskin;
Songs of war and songs of hunting,
Songs of medicine and of magic,
All were written in these figures,
For each figure had its meaning,
Each its separate song recorded.

Nor forgotten was the Love-Song,
The most subtle of all medicines,
The most potent spell of magic,
Dangerous more than war or hunting!
Thus the Love-Song was recorded,
Symbol and interpretation.

First a human figure standing,
Painted, in the brightest scarlet;
'T is the lover, the musician,
And the meaning is, "My painting
Makes me powerful over others."

Then the figure seated, singing,
Playing on a drum of magic,
And the interpretation, "Listen!
'T is my voice you hear, my singing!"

Then the same red figure seated
In the shelter of a wigwam,

And the meaning of the symbol,
  "I will come and sit beside you
In the mystery of my passion!"
   Then two figures, man and woman
Standing hand in hand together
With their hands so clasped together
That they seem in one united,
And the words thus represented
Are, "I see your heart within you,
And your cheeks are red with blushes!"
   Next the maiden on an island,
In the centre of an island;
And the song this shape suggested
Was, "Though you were at a distance,
Were upon some far-off island,
Such the spell I cast upon you,
Such the magic power of passion,
I could straightway draw you to me!"
   Then the figure of the maiden
Sleeping, and the lover near her,
Whispering to her in her slumbers;
Saying, "Though you were far from me
In the land of Sleep and Silence,
Still the voice of love would reach you!"
   And the last of all the figures
Was a heart within a circle,
Drawn within a magic circle,
And the image had this meaning:
"Naked lies your heart before me,
To your naked heart I whisper!"
   Thus it was that Hiawatha,
In his wisdom, taught the people
All the mysteries of painting,
All the art of Picture-Writing,
On the smooth bark of the birch tree,
On the white skin of the reindeer,
On the grave posts of the village.

XV

HIAWATHA'S LAMENTATION

In those days the Evil Spirits,
All the Manitos of mischief,
Fearing Hiawatha's wisdom,
And his love for Chibiabos,
Jealous of their faithful friendship,
And their noble words and actions,
Made at length a league against them,
To molest them and destroy them.

Hiawatha, wise and wary,
Often said to Chibiabos,
"O my brother! do not leave me,
Lest the Evil Spirits harm you!"
Chibiabos, young and heedless,
Laughing shook his coal-black tresses,
Answered ever sweet and childlike,
"Do not fear for me, O brother!
Harm and evil come not near me!"

Once when Peboan, the Winter,
Roofed with ice the Big-Sea-Water,
When the snowflakes whirling downward,
Hissed among the withered oak leaves,
Changed the pine trees into wigwams,
Covered all the earth with silence,—
Armed with arrows, shod with snowshoes,
Heeding not his brother's warning,
Fearing not the Evil Spirits,
Forth to hunt the deer with antlers
All alone went Chibiabos.

Right across the Big-Sea-Water
Sprang with speed the deer before him,
With the wind and snow he followed,
O'er the treacherous ice he followed,
Wild with all the fierce commotion
And the rapture of the hunting.

But beneath, the Evil Spirits
Lay in ambush, waiting for him,

Broke the treacherous ice beneath him,
Dragged him downward to the bottom,
Buried in the sand his body,
Unktahee, the god of water,
He the god of the Dacotahs,
Drowned him in the deep abysses
Of the lake of Gitche Gumee.

From the headlands Hiawatha
Sent forth such a wail of anguish,
Such a fearful lamentation,
That the bison paused to listen,
And the wolves howled from the prairies,
And the thunder in the distance
Woke and answered "Baim-wawa!"

Then his face with black he painted,
With his robe his head he covered,
In his wigwam sat lamenting,
Seven long weeks he sat lamenting,
Uttering still this moan of sorrow:

"He is dead, the sweet musician!
He the sweetest of all singers!
He has gone from us forever,
He has moved a little nearer
To the Master of all music,
To the Master of all singing!
O my brother, Chibiabos!"

And the melancholy fir trees
Waved their dark-green fans above him,
Waved their purple cones above him,
Sighing with him to console him,
Mingling with his lamentation
Their complaining, their lamenting.

Came the Spring, and all the forest
Looked in vain for Chibiabos;
Sighed the rivulet Sebowisha,
Sighed the rushes in the meadow.

From the treetops sang the bluebird,
Sang the bluebird, the Owaissa,
"Chibiabos! Chibiabos!
He is dead, the sweet musician!"

From the wigwam sang the robin,
Sang the Opechee, the robin,
"Chibiabos! Chibiabos!
He is dead, the sweetest singer!"
And at night through all the forest
Went the whip-poor-will complaining
Wailing went the Wawonaissa,
"Chibiabos! Chibiabos!
He is dead, the sweet musician!
He the sweetest of all singers!"
Then the Medicine-men, the Medas,
The magicians, the Wabenos,
And the Jossakeeds, the prophets,
Came to visit Hiawatha;
Built a Sacred Lodge beside him,
To appease him, to console him,
Walked in silent, grave procession,
Bearing each a pouch of healing,
Skin of beaver, lynx, or otter,
Filled with magic roots and simples,
Filled with very potent medicines.
When he heard their steps approaching,
Hiawatha ceased lamenting,
Called no more on Chibiabos;
Naught he questioned, naught he answered
But his mournful head uncovered,
From his face the mourning colors
Washed he slowly and in silence,
Slowly and in silence followed
Onward to the Sacred Wigwam.
There a magic drink they gave him,
Made of Nahma-wusk, the spearmint,
And Wabeno-wusk, the yarrow,
Roots of power, and herbs of healing;
Beat their drums, and shook their rattles;
Chanted singly and in chorus,
Mystic songs like these, they chanted.
"I myself, myself! behold me!
'T is the great Gray Eagle talking;
Come, ye white crows, come and hear him!

The loud-speaking thunder help me;
All the unseen spirits help me;
I can hear their voices calling,
All around the sky I hear them;
I can blow you strong, my brother,
I can heal you, Hiawatha!"

    "Hi-au-ha!" [1] replied the chorus,
"Way-ha-way!" the mystic chorus,

    "Friends of mine are all the serpents!
Hear me shake my skin of henhawk!
Mahng, the white loon, I can kill him;
I can shoot your heart and kill it!
I can blow you strong, my brother,
I can heal you, Hiawatha!"

    "Hi-au-ha!" replied the chorus,
"Way-ha-way!" the mystic chorus.

    "I myself, myself! the prophet!
When I speak the wigwam trembles,
Shakes the Sacred Lodge with terror,
Hands unseen begin to shake it!
When I walk, the sky I tread on
Bends and makes a noise beneath me!
I can blow you strong, my brother!
Rise and speak, O Hiawatha!"

    "Hi-au-ha!" replied the chorus,
"Way-ha-way!" the mystic chorus.

Then they shook their medicine-pouches
O'er the head of Hiawatha,
Danced their medicine-dance around him;
And upstarting wild and haggard,
Like a man from dreams awakened,
He was healed of all his madness.
As the clouds are swept from heaven,
Straightway from his brain departed
All his moody melancholy;

---

[1] These words appear to be "the unmeaning ejaculations heard so often at Indian dances, feasts and carousals. They accompany their tunes and are sometimes sung in long strains along with words or without words. They may be either spoken or sung, but always are they uttered with a deep guttural voice."—A. S. G.

As the ice is swept from rivers,
Straightway from his heart departed
All his sorrow and affliction.

Then they summoned Chibiabos
From his grave beneath the waters,
From the sands of Gitche Gumee
Summoned Hiawatha's brother.
And so mighty was the magic
Of that cry and invocation,
That he heard it as he lay there
Underneath the Big-Sea-Water;
From the sand he rose and listened,
Heard the music and the singing,
Came, obedient to the summons,
To the doorway of the wigwam,
But to enter they forbade him.
Through a chink a coal they gave him,
Through the door a burning firebrand;
Ruler in the Land of Spirits,
Ruler o'er the dead, they made him,
Telling him a fire to kindle
For all those that died thereafter,
Camp-fires for their night encampments
On their solitary journey
To the kingdom of Ponemah,
To the land of the Hereafter.

From the village of his childhood,
From the homes of those who knew him,
Passing silent through the forest,
Like a smoke-wreath wafted sideways,
Slowly vanished Chibiabos!
Where he passed, the branches moved out,
Where he trod the grasses bent not,
And the fallen leaves of last year
Made no sound beneath his footsteps.

Four whole days he journeyed onward
Down the pathway of the dead men;
On the dead man's strawberry feasted,
Crossed the melancholy river,
On the swinging log he crossed it,

Came unto the Lake of Silver,
In the Stone Canoe was carried
To the Islands of the Blessed,
To the land of ghosts and shadows.

On that journey, moving slowly,
Many weary spirits saw he,
Panting under heavy burdens,
Laden with war-clubs, bows and arrows,
Robes of fur and pots and kettles,
And with food that friends had given
For that solitary journey.

"Ay! why do the living," said they,
"Lay such heavy burdens on us!
Better were it to go naked,
Better were it to go fasting,
Than to bear such heavy burdens
On our long and weary journey!"

Forth then issued Hiawatha,
Wandered eastward, wandered westward,
Teaching men the use of simples
And the antidotes for poisons,
And the cure of all diseases.
Thus was first made known to mortals
All the mystery of Medamin,
All the sacred art of healing.

XVI

PAU-PUK-KEEWIS

You shall hear how Pau-Puk-Keewis
He, the handsome Yenadizze,
Whom the people called the Storm Fool,
Vexed the village with disturbance;
You shall hear of all his mischief,
And his flight from Hiawatha,
And his wondrous transmigrations,
At the end of his adventures.

On the shores of Gitche Gumee,
On the dunes of Nagow Wudjoo,

By the shining Big-Sea-Water,
Stood the lodge of Pau-Puk-Keewis.
It was he who in his frenzy
Whirled these drifting sands together,
On the dunes of Nagow Wudjoo,
When, among the guests assembled,
He so merrily and madly
Danced at Hiawatha's wedding,
Danced the Beggar's Dance to please them.

Now, in search of new adventures,
From his lodge went Pau-Puk-Keewis,
Came with speed into the village,
Found the young men all assembled
In the lodge of old Iagoo,
Listening to his monstrous stories,
To his wonderful adventures.

He was telling them the story
Of Ojeeg, the Summer-Maker,
How he made a hole in heaven,
How he climbed up into heaven,
And let out the summer weather,
The perpetual, pleasant Summer;
How the Otter first essayed it;
How the Beaver, Lynx, and Badger,
Tried in turn the great achievement,
From the summit of the mountain
Smote their fists against the heavens,
Smote against the sky their foreheads,
Cracked the sky, but could not break it,
How the Wolverine, uprising,
Made him ready for the encounter,
Bent his knees down, like a squirrel,
Drew his arms back, like a cricket.

"Once he leaped," said Old Iagoo,
"Once he leaped, and lo! above him
Bent the sky, as ice in rivers
When the waters rise beneath it;
Twice he leaped, and lo! above him
Cracked the sky, as ice in rivers
When the freshet is at highest!

Thrice he leaped, and lo! above him
Broke the shattered sky asunder,
And he disappeared within it,
And Ojeeg, the Fisher Weasel,
With a bound went in behind him!"
"Hark you!" shouted Pau-Puk-Keewis
As he entered at the doorway:
"I am tired of all this talking,
Tired of old Iagoo's stories,
Tired of Hiawatha's wisdom.
Here is something to amuse you,
Better than this endless talking."

Then from out his pouch of wolf-skin
Forth he drew, with solemn manner,
All the game of Bowl and Counters,
Pugasaing, with thirteen pieces.[1]
White on one side were they painted,
And vermilion on the other;
Two Kenabeeks or great serpents,
Two Ininewug or wedge-men,
One great war-club, Pugamaugun,

---

[1] This Game of the Bowl is the principal game of hazard among the Northern tribes of Indians. Mr. Schoolcraft gives a particular account of it in *Oneóta*, p. 85. "This game," he says, "is very fascinating to some portions of the Indians. They stake at it their ornaments, weapons, clothing, canoes, horses, everything in fact they possess; and have been known, it is said, to set up their wives and children, and even to forfeit their own liberty. Of such desperate stakes I have seen no examples, nor do I think the game itself in common use. It is rather confined to certain persons who hold the relative rank of gamblers in Indian society,—men who are not noted as hunters or warriors, or steady providers for their families. Among these are persons who bear the term of *ienadizzewug*, that is, wanderers about the country, braggadocios, or fops. It can hardly be classed with the popular games of amusement, by which skill and dexterity are acquired. I have generally found the chiefs and graver men of the tribes, who encouraged the young men to play ball, and are sure to be present at the customary sports, to witness and sanction and applaud them, speak lightly and disparagingly of this game of hazard. Yet it cannot be denied that some of the chiefs, distinguished in war and the chase at the West, can be referred to as lending their examples to its fascinating power."

See also his *History, Condition, and Prospects of the Indian Tribes*, Part II, p. 72.

And one slender fish, the Keego,
Four round pieces, Ozawabeeks,
And three Sheshebwug or ducklings,
All were made of bone and painted,
All except the Ozawabeeks;
These were brass, on one side burnished,
And were black upon the other.

In a wooden bowl he placed them,
Shook and jostled them together,
Threw them on the ground before him.
Thus exclaiming and explaining:
"Red side up are all the pieces,
And one great Kenabeek standing
On the bright side of a brass piece,
On a burnished Ozawabeek;
Thirteen tens and eight are counted."

Then again he shook the pieces,
Shook and jostled them together,
Threw them on the ground 'before him,
Still exclaiming and explaining:
"White are both the great Kenabeeks,
White the Ininewug, the wedge-men,
Red are all the other pieces;
Five tens and an eight are counted."

Thus he taught the game of hazard,
Thus displayed it and explained it,
Running through its various chances,
Various changes, various meanings;
Twenty curious eyes stared at him,
Full of eagerness stared at him.

"Many games," said old Iagoo,
"Many games of skill and hazard
Have I seen in different nations,
Have I played in different countries.
He who plays with old Iagoo
Must have very nimble fingers;
Though you think yourself so skilful
I can beat you, Pau-Puk-Keewis,
I can even give you lessons
In your game of Bowl and Counters!"

So they sat and played together,
All the old men and the young men,
Played for dresses, weapons, wampum,
Played till midnight, played till morning,
Played until the Yenadizze,
Till the cunning Pau-Puk-Keewis,
Of their treasures had despoiled them,
Of the best of all their dresses,
Shirts of deerskin, robes of ermine,
Belts of wampum, crests of feathers,
Warlike weapons, pipes and pouches.
Twenty eyes glared wildly at him,
Like the eyes of wolves glared at him.

Said the lucky Pau-Puk-Keewis:
"In my wigwam I am lonely,
In my wanderings and adventures
I have need of a companion,
Fain would have a Meshinauwa,
An attendant and pipe-bearer.
I will venture all these winnings,
All these garments heaped about me.
All this wampum, all these feathers,
On a single throw will venture
All against the young man yonder!"
'T was a youth of sixteen summers.
'T was a nephew of Iagoo;
Face-in-a-Mist the people called him.

As the fire burns in a pipe-head
Dusky red beneath the ashes,
So beneath his shaggy eyebrows
Glowed the eyes of old Iagoo.
"Ugh!" he answered very fiercely.
"Ugh!" they answered all and each one.

Seized the wooden bowl the old man,
Closely in his bony fingers
Clutched the fatal bowl, Onagon,
Shook it fiercely and with fury,
Made the pieces ring together
As he threw them down before him,
Red were both the great Kenabeeks,

Red the Ininewug, the wedge-men,
Red the Sheshewug, the ducklings,
Black the four brass Ozawabeeks,
White alone the fish, the Keego;
Only five the pieces counted!

Then the smiling Pau-Puk-Keewis
Shook the bowl and threw the pieces;
Lightly in the air he tossed them,
And they fell about him scattered;
Dark and bright the Ozawabeeks,
Red and white the other pieces,
And upright among the others
One Ininewug was standing,
Even as crafty Pau-Puk-Keewis
Stood alone among the players,
Saying, "Five tens! mine the game is!"

Twenty eyes glared at him fiercely,
Like the eyes of wolves glared at him,
As he turned and left the wigwam,
Followed by his Meshinauwa,
By the nephew of Iagoo,
By the tall and graceful stripling,
Bearing in his arms the winnings,
Shirts of deer-skin, robes of ermine,
Belts of wampum, pipes and weapons.

"Carry them," said Pau-Puk-Keewis,
Pointing with his fan of feathers,
"To my wigwam far to eastward,
On the dumes of Nagow Wudjoo!"

Hot and red with smoke and gambling
Were the eyes of Pau-Puk-Keewis
As he came forth to the freshness
Of the pleasant summer morning.
All the birds were singing gayly,
All the streamlets flowing swiftly,
And the heart of Pau-Puk-Keewis
Sang with pleasure as the birds sing,
Beat with triumph like the streamlets,
As he wandered through the village,
In the early gray of morning,

With his fan of turkey-feathers,
With his plumes and tufts of swan's down,
Till he reached the farthest wigwam,
Reached the lodge of Hiawatha.

Silent was it and deserted;
No one met him at the doorway,
No one came to bid him welcome;
But the birds were singing round it,
In and out and round the doorway,
Hopping, singing, fluttering, feeding,
And aloft upon the ridge-pole
Kahgahgee, the King of Ravens,
Sat with fiery eyes, and screaming,
Flapped his wings at Pau-Puk-Keewis.

"All are gone! the lodge is empty!"
Thus it was spake Pau-Puk-Keewis,
In his heart resolving mischief;—
"Gone is wary Hiawatha,
Gone the silly Laughing Water,
Gone Nokomis, the old woman,
And the lodge is left unguarded!"

By the neck he seized the raven,
Whirled it round him like a rattle,
Like a medicine-pouch he shook it,
Strangled Kahgahgee, the raven,
From the ridge-pole of the wigwam
Left its lifeless body hanging,
As an insult to its master,
As a taunt to Hiawatha.

With a stealthy step he entered,
Round the lodge in wild disorder
Threw the household things about him,
Piled together in confusion
Bowls of wood and earthen kettles,
Robes of buffalo and beaver,
Skins of otter, lynx, and ermine,
As an insult to Nokomis,
As a taunt to Minnehaha.

Then departed Pau-Puk-Keewis,
Whistling, singing through the forest,

Whistling gayly to the squirrels,
Who from hollow boughs above him
Dropped their acorn-shells upon him,
Singing gayly to the wood birds,
Who from out the leafy darkness
Answered with a song as merry.

Then he climbed the rocky head lands,
Looking o'er the Gitche Gumee,
Perched himself upon the summit,
Waiting full of mirth and mischief
The return of Hiawatha.

Stretched upon his back he lay there;
Far below him plashed the waters,
Plashed and washed the dreamy waters;
Far above him swam the heavens,
Swam the dizzy, dreamy heavens;
Round him hovered, fluttered, rustled,
Hiawatha's mountain chickens,
Flock-wise swept and wheeled about him,
Almost brushed him with their pinions,

And he killed them as he lay there,
Slaughtered them by tens and twenties,
Threw their bodies down the headland,
Threw them on the beach below him,
Till at length Kayoshk, the sea gull
Perched upon a crag above them,
Shouted: "It is Pau-Puk-Keewis!
He is slaying us by hundreds!
Send a message to our brother,
Tidings send to Hiawatha!"

XVII

THE HUNTING OF PAU-PUK-KEEWIS

Full of wrath was Hiawatha,
When he came into the village,
Found the people in confusion,
Heard of all the misdemeanors,
All the malice and the mischief

Of the cunning Pau-Puk-Keewis.
   Hard his breath came through his nostrils,
Through his teeth he buzzed and muttered
Words of anger and resentment,
Hot and humming like a hornet.
"I will slay this Pau-Puk-Keewis,
Slay this mischief-maker!" said he.
"Not so long and wide the world is,
Not so rude and rough the way is,
That my wrath shall not attain him,
That my vengeance shall not reach him!"
   Then in swift pursuit departed,
Hiawatha and the hunters
On the trail of Pau-Puk-Keewis,
Through the forest, where he passed,
To the headlands where he rested;
But they found not Pau-Puk-Keewis,
Only in the trampled grasses,
In the whortleberry bushes,
Found the couch where he had rested,
Found the impress of his body.
From the lowlands far beneath them,
From the Muskoday, the meadow,
Pau-Puk-Keewis, turning backward,
Made a gesture of defiance,
Made a gesture of derision;
And aloud cried Hiawatha,
From the summit of the mountain:
"Not so long and wide the world is,
Not so rude and rough the way is,
But my wrath shall overtake you,
And my vengeance shall attain you!"
   Over rock and over river,
Through bush, and brake, and forest,
Ran the cunning Pau-Puk-Keewis;
Like an antelope he bounded,
Till he came unto a streamlet
In the middle of the forest,
To a streamlet still and tranquil,
That had overflowed its margin,

To a dam made by the beavers,
To a pond of quiet water,
Where knee-deep the trees were standing,
Where the water-lilies floated,
Where the rushes waved and whispered.

On the dam stood Pau-Puk-Keewis,
On the dam of trunks and branches,
Through whose chinks the water spouted,
O'er whose summit flowed the streamlet.
From the bottom rose the beaver,
Looked with two great eyes of wonder,
Eyes that seemed to ask a question,
At the stranger, Pau-Puk-Keewis.

On the dam stood Pau-Puk-Keewis,
O'er his ankles flowed the streamlet,
Flowed the bright and silvery water,
And he spake unto the beaver,
With a smile he spake in this wise:

"O my friend Ahmeek, the beaver,
Cool and pleasant is the water;
Let me dive into the water,
Let me rest there in your lodges;
Change me, too, into a beaver!"

Cautiously replied the beaver,
With reserve he thus made answer:
"Let me first consult the others,
Let me ask the other beavers."
Down he sank into the water,
Heavily sank he, as a stone sinks,
Down among the leaves and branches,
Brown and matted at the bottom.

On the dam stood Pau-Puk-Keewis,
O'er his ankles flowed the streamlet,
Spouted through the chinks below him
Dashed upon the stones beneath him,
Spread serene and calm before him,
And the sunshine and the shadows
Fell in flecks and gleams upon him,
Fell in little shining patches,
Through the waving, rustling branches.

From the bottom rose the beavers,
Silently above the surface
Rose one head and then another,
Till the pond seemed full of beavers,
Full of black and shining faces.

To the beavers Pau-Puk-Keewis
Spake entreating, said in this wise:
"Very pleasant is your dwelling,
O my friends! and safe from danger;
Can you not with all your cunning,
All your wisdom and contrivance,
Change me, too, into a beaver?"

"Yes!" replied Ahmeek, the beaver,
He the King of all the beavers,
"Let yourself slide down among us,
Down into the tranquil water."

Down into the pond among them
Silently sank Pau-Puk-Keewis;
Black became his shirt of deerskin,
Black his moccasins and leggings,
In a broad black tail behind him
Spread his foxtails and his fringes;
He was changed into a beaver.

"Make me large," said Pau-Puk-Keewis,
"Make me large and make me larger,
Larger than the other beavers."
"Yes," the beaver chief responded,
"When our lodge below you enter,
In our wigwam we will make you
Ten times larger than the others."

Thus into the clear, brown water
Silently sank Pau-Puk-Keewis;
Found the bottom covered over
With the trunks of trees and branches,
Hoards of food against the winter,
Piles and heaps against the famine;
Found the lodge with arching doorway,
Leading into spacious chambers.

Here they made him large and larger,
Made him largest of the beavers,

Ten times larger than the others.
"You shall be our ruler," said they;
"Chief and King of all the beavers."
        But not long had Pau-Puk-Keewis
Sat in state among the beavers,
When there came a voice of warning
From the watchman at his station,
In the water-flags and lilies,
Saying, "Here is Hiawatha!
Hiawatha with his hunters!"
        Then they heard a cry above them,
Heard a shouting and a tramping,
Heard a crashing and a rushing,
And the water round and o'er them
Sank and sucked away in eddies,
And they knew their dam was broken.
        On the lodge's roof the hunters
Leaped, and broke it all asunder;
Streamed the sunshine through the crevice,
Sprang the beavers through the doorway,
Hid themselves in deeper water,
In the channel of the streamlet;
But the mighty Pau-Puk-Keewis
Could not pass beneath the doorway;
He was puffed with pride and feeding,
He was swollen like a bladder.
        Through the roof looked Hiawatha,
Cried aloud, "O Pau-Puk-Keewis,
Vain are all your craft and cunning,
Vain your manifold disguises!
Well I know you, Pau-Puk-Keewis!"
        With their clubs they beat and bruised him,
Beat to death poor Pau-Puk-Keewis,
Pounded him as maize is pounded,
Till his skull was crushed to pieces.
        Six tall hunters, lithe and limber,
Bore him home on poles and branches,
Bore the body of the beaver;
But the ghost, the Jeebi in him,
Thought and felt as Pau-Puk-Keewis.

And it fluttered, strove, and struggled,
Waving hither, waving thither,
As the curtains of a wigwam
Struggle with their thongs of deep skin,
When the wintry wind is blowing;
Till it drew itself together,
Till it rose up from the body,
Till it took the form and features
Of the cunning Pau-Puk-Keewis
Vanishing into the forest.

But the wary Hiawatha
Saw the figure ere it vanished,
Saw the form of Pau-Puk-Keewis
Glide into the soft blue Shadow
Of the pine-trees of the forest;
Toward the squares of white beyond it,
Toward an opening in the forest,
Like a wind it rushed and panted,
Bending all the boughs before it,
And behind it, as the rain comes,
Came the steps of Hiawatha.

To a lake with many islands
Came the breathless Pau-Puk-Keewis,
Where among the water-lilies
Pishnekuh, the brant, was sailing;
Through the tufts of rushes floating,
Steering through the reedy islands.
Now their broad black beaks they lifted,
Now they plunged beneath the water,
Now they darkened in the shadow,
Now they brightened in the sunshine.

"Pishnekuh!" cried Pau-Puk-Keewis,
"Pishnekuh! my brothers!" said he,
"Change me to a brant with plumage,
With a shining neck and feathers,
Make me large, and make me larger,
Ten times larger than the others."

Straightway to a brant they changed him,
With two huge and dusky pinions,
With a bosom smooth and rounded,

With a bill like two great paddles,
Made him larger than the others,
Ten times larger than the largest,
Just as, shouting from the forest,
On the shore stood Hiawatha.

Up they rose with cry and clamor,
With a whir and beat of pinions,
Rose up from the reedy islands,
From the water-flags and lilies.
And they said to Pau-Puk-Keewis:
"In your flying, look not downward,
Take good heed and look not downward,
Lest some strange mischance should happen,
Lest some great mishap befall you!"

Fast and far they fled to northward,
Fast and far through mist and sunshine,
Fed among the moors and fenlands,
Slept among the reeds and rushes.

On the morrow as they journeyed,
Buoyed and lifted by the South-wind,
Wafted onward by the South-wind,
Blowing fresh and strong behind them,
Rose a sound of human voices,
Rose a clamor from beneath them,
From the lodges of a village,
From the people miles beneath them.

For the people of the village
Saw the flock of brant with wonder,
Saw the wings of Pau-Puk-Keewis
Flapping far up in the ether,
Broader than two doorway curtains.

Pau-Puk-Keewis heard the shouting,
Knew the voice of Hiawatha,
Knew the outcry of Iagoo.
And, forgetful of the warning,
Drew his neck in, and looked downward,
And the wind that blew behind him
Caught his mighty fan of feathers,
Sent him wheeling, whirling downward!

All in vain did Pau-Puk-Keewis
Struggle to regain his balance!
Whirling round and round and downward,
He beheld in turn the village
And in turn the flock above him,
Saw the village coming nearer,
And the flock receding farther,
Heard the voices growing louder,
Heard the shouting and the laughter;
Saw no more the flock above him,
Only saw the earth beneath him;
Dead out of the empty heaven,
Dead among the shouting people,
With a heavy sound and sullen,
Fell the brant with broken pinions.

But his soul, his ghost, his shadow,
Still survived as Pau-Puk-Keewis,
Took again the form and features
Of the handsome Yenadizze.
And again went rushing onward,
Followed fast by Hiawatha,
Crying: "Not so wide the world is,
Not so long and rough the way is,
But my wrath shall overtake you,
But my vengeance shall attain you!"

And so near he came, so near him,
That his hand was stretched to seize him,
His right hand to seize and hold him,
When the cunning Pau-Puk-Keewis
Whirled and spun about in circles,
Fanned the air into a whirlwind,
Danced the dust and leaves about him,
And amid the whirling eddies
Sprang into a hollow oak-tree,
Changed himself into a serpent,
Gliding out through root and rubbish.

With his right hand Hiawatha
Smote amain the hollow oak-tree,
Rent it into shreds and splinters,
Left it lying there in fragments.

But in vain; for Pau-Puk-Keewis,
Once again in human figure,
Full in sight ran on before him,
Sped away in gust and whirlwind,
On the shores of Gitche Gumee,
Westward by the Big-Sea-Water,
Came unto the rocky headlands,
To the Pictured Rocks of sandstone,[1]

[1] The reader will find a long description of the Pictured Rocks in Foster and Whitney's *Report on the Geology of Lake Superior Land District*, Part II, p. 124. From this I make the following extract:—

"The Pictured Rocks may be described in general terms as a series of sandstone bluffs extending along the shore of Lake Superior for about five miles, and rising, in most places vertically from the water, without any beach at the base, to a height varying from fifty to nearly two hundred feet. Were they simply a line of cliffs they might not, so far as relates to height or extent, be worthy of rank among great natural curiosities, although such an assemblage of rocky strata, washed by the waves of the great lake, would not, under any circumstances, be destitute of grandeur. To the voyager coasting along their base in his frail canoe they would at all times be an object of dread; the recoil of the surf, the rock-bound coast affording for miles no place of refuge, the lowering sky, the rising wind, all these would excite his apprehension, and induce him to ply a vigorous oar until the dreaded wall was passed. But in the Pictured Rocks there are two features which communicate to the scenery a wonderful and almost unique character. These are first, the curious manner in which the cliffs have been excavated and worn away by the action of the lake, which for centuries has dashed an ocean-like surf against their base; and second, the equally curious manner in which large portions of the surface have been colored by bands of brilliant hues.

"It is from the latter circumstances that the name by which these cliffs are known to the American traveller is derived; while that applied to them by the French voyagers ('Les Portals') is derived from the former, and by far the most striking peculiarity.

"The term *Pictured Rocks* has been in use for a great length of time; but when it was first applied we have been unable to discover. It would seem that the first travellers were more impressed with the novel and striking distribution of colors on the surface than with the astonishing variety of form into which the cliffs themselves have been worn. . . .

"Our voyagers had many legends to relate of the pranks of the *Menni-bojou* in these caverns, and in answer to our inquiries seemed disposed to fabricate stories without end of the achievements of this Indian deity."

Looking over lake and landscape.
And the Old Man of the Mountain,
He the Manito of Mountains,
Opened wide his rocky doorways,
Opened wide his deep abysses,
Giving Pau-Puk-Keewis shelter
In his caverns dark and dreary,
Bidding Pau-Puk-Keewis welcome
To his gloomy lodge of sandstone.

There without stood Hiawatha,
Found the doorways closed against him,
With his mittens, Minjekahwun,
Smote great caverns in the sandstone,
Cried aloud in tones of thunder,
"Open! I am Hiawatha!"
But the Old Man of the Mountain
Opened not, and made no answer
From the silent crags of sandstone,
From the gloomy rock abysses.

Then he raised his hands to heaven,
Called imploring on the tempest,
Called Waywassimo, the lightning,
And the thunder, Annemeekee;
And they came with night and darkness,
Sweeping down the Big-Sea-Water
From the distant Thunder Mountains;
And the trembling Pau-Puk-Keewis
Heard the footsteps of the thunder,
Saw the red eyes of the lightning,
Was afraid, and crouched and trembled.

Then Waywassimo, the lightning,
Smote the doorways of the caverns,
With his war club smote the doorways,
Smote the jutting crags of sandstone,
And the thunder, Annemeekee,
Shouted down into the caverns,
Saying, "Where is Pau-Puk-Keewis!"
And the crags fell, and beneath them
Dead among the rocky ruins
Lay the cunning Pau-Puk-Keewis,

Lay the handsome Yenadizze,
Slain in his own human figure.

Ended were his wild adventures,
Ended were his tricks and gambols,
Ended all his craft and cunning,
Ended all his mischief-making,
All his gambling and his dancing,
All his wooing of the maidens.

Then the noble Hiawatha
Took his soul, his ghost, his shadow,
Spake and said: "O Pau-Puk-Keewis,
Never more in human figure
Shall you search for new adventures;
Never more with jest and laughter
Dance the dust and leaves in whirlwinds;
But above there in the heavens
You shall soar and sail in circles;
I will change you to an eagle,
To Keneu, the great war-eagle,
Chief of all the fowls with feathers,
Chief of Hiawatha's chickens."

And the name of Pau-Puk-Keewis
Lingers still among the people,
Lingers still among the singers,
And among the story-tellers;
And in Winter, when the snowflakes
Whirl in eddies round the lodges,
When the wind in gusty tumult
O'er the smoke-flue pipes and whistles,
"There," they cry, "comes Pau-Puk-Keewis
He is dancing through the village,
He is gathering in his harvest!"

XVIII

THE DEATH OF KWASIND

Far and wide among the nations
Spread the name and fame of Kwasind;
No man dared to strive with Kwasind,

No man could compete with Kwasind.
But the mischievous Puk-Wudjies,
They the envious Little People,
They the fairies and the pygmies,
Plotted and conspired against him.
    "If this hateful Kwasind," said they,
"If this great, outrageous fellow
Goes on thus a little longer,
Tearing everything he touches,
Rending everything to pieces,
Filling all the world with wonder,
What becomes of the Puk-Wudjies?
Who will care for the Puk-Wudjies?
He will tread us down like mushrooms,
Drive us all into the water,
Give our bodies to be eaten
By the wicked Nee-ba-naw-baigs,
By the Spirits of the water!"
    So the angry Little People
All conspired against the Strong Man,
All conspired to murder Kwasind,
Yes, to rid the world of Kwasind,
The audacious, overbearing,
Heartless, haughty, dangerous Kwasind!
    Now this wondrous strength of Kwasind
In his crown alone was seated;
In his crown, too, was his weakness;
There alone could he be wounded,
Nowhere else could weapon pierce him,
Nowhere else could weapon harm him.
    Even there the only weapon
That could wound him, that could slay him,
Was the seed-cone of the pine-tree,
Was the blue cone of the fir-tree.
This was Kwasind's fatal secret,
Known to no man among mortals;
But the cunning Little People,
The Puk-Wudjies, knew the secret,
Knew the only way to kill him.
    So they gathered cones together,

Gathered seed-cones of the pine-tree,
Gathered blue cones of the fir-tree,
In the woods by Taquamenaw,
Brought them to the river's margin,
Heaped them in great piles together,
Where the red rocks from the margin
Jutting overhang the river.
There they lay in wait for Kwasind,
The malicious Little People.

'Twas an afternoon in Summer;
Very hot and still the air was,
Very smooth the gliding river,
Motionless the sleeping shadows;
Insects glistened in the sunshine,
Insects skated on the water,
Filled the drowsy air with buzzing,
With a far resounding war-cry.

Down the river came the Strong Man,
In his birch canoe came Kwasind,
Floating slowly down the current
Of the sluggish Taquamenaw,
Very languid with the weather,
Very sleepy with the silence.

From the overhanging branches,
From the tassels of the birch-trees,
Soft the Spirit of Sleep descended;
By his airy hosts surrounded,
His invisible attendants,
Came the Spirit of Sleep, Nepahwin;
Like the burnished Dush-kwo-neshe,
Like a dragon-fly he hovered
O'er the drowsy head of Kwasind.

To his ear there came a murmur
As of waves upon a seashore,
As of far-off tumbling waters,
As of wind among the pine-trees;
As he felt upon his forehead
Blows of little airy war-clubs,
Wielded by the slumbrous legions

Of the Spirit of Sleep, Nepahwin,
As of some one breathing on him.

At the first blow of their war-clubs
Fell a drowsiness on Kwasind;
At the second blow they smote him
Motionless his paddle rested;
At the third, before his vision
Reeled the landscape into darkness,
Very sound asleep was Kwasind.

So he floated down the river,
Like a blind man seated upright,
Floated down the Taquamenaw,
Underneath the trembling birch-trees,
Underneath the wooded headlands,
Underneath the war encampment
Of the pygmies, the Puk-Wudjies.

There they stood, all armed and waiting,
Hurled the pine-cones down upon him,
Struck him on his brawny shoulders,
On his crown defenceless struck him.
"Death to Kwasind!" was the sudden
War-cry of the Little People.

And he sideways swayed and tumbled,
Sideways fell into the river,
Plunged beneath the sluggish water
Headlong, as an otter plunges;
And the birch-canoe, abandoned,
Drifted empty down the river,
Bottom upwards swerved and drifted
Nothing more was seen of Kwasind.

But the memory of the Strong Man
Lingered long among the people,
And whenever through the forest
Raged and roared the wintry tempest,
And the branches tossed and troubled,
Creaked and groaned and split asunder,
"Kwasind!" cried they; "that is Kwasind!
He is gathering in his firewood!"

XIX

THE GHOSTS

Never stoops the soaring vulture
On his quarry in the desert,
On the sick or wounded bison,
But another vulture, watching
From his high aerial lookout,
Sees the downward plunge, and follows;
And a third pursues the second,
Coming from the invisible ether,
First a speck, and then a vulture,
Till the air is dark with pinions.

So disasters come not singly;
But as if they watched and waited,
Scanning one another's motions,
When the first descends, the others
Follow, follow, gathering flock-wise
Round their victim, sick and wounded,
First a shadow, then a sorrow,
Till the air is dark with anguish.

Now, o'er all the dreary Northland,
Mighty Peboan, the Winter,
Breathing on the lakes and rivers,
Into stone had changed their waters.
From his hair he shook the snowflakes,
Till the plains were strewn with whiteness,
One uninterrupted level,
As if, stooping, the Creator
With his hands had smoothed them over.

Through the forest, wide and wailing,
Roamed the hunter on his snowshoes;
In the village worked the women,
Pounded maize, or dressed the deer-skin;
And the young men played together
On the ice the noisy ball-play,
On the plain the dance of snowshoes.

One dark evening, after sundown,
In her wigwam Laughing Water

Sat with old Nokomis, waiting
For the steps of Hiawatha
Homeward from the hunt returning.

On their faces gleamed the firelight,
Painting them with streaks of crimson,
In the eyes of old Nokomis
Glimmered like the watery moonlight,
In the eyes of Laughing Water
Glistened like the sun in water;
And behind them crouched their shadows
In the corners of the wigwam,
And the smoke in wreaths above them,
Climbed and crowded through the smoke-flue.

Then the curtain of the doorway
From without was slowly lifted;
Brighter glowed the fire a moment,
And a moment swerved the smoke-wreath,
As two women entered softly,
Passed the doorway uninvited,
Without word of salutation,
Without sign of recognition,
Sat down in the farthest corner,
Crouching low among the shadows.

From their aspect and their garments,
Strangers seemed they in the village;
Very pale and haggard were they,
As they sat there sad and silent,
Trembling, cowering with the shadows.

Was it the wind above the smoke-flue,
Muttering down into the wigwam?
Was it the owl, the Koko-koho,
Hooting from the dismal forest?
Sure a voice said in the silence:
"These are corpses clad in garments,
These are ghosts that come to haunt you,
From the kingdom of Ponemah,
From the land of the Hereafter!"

Homeward now came Hiawatha
From his hunting in the forest,
With the snow upon his tresses,

And the red deer on his shoulders.
At the feet of Laughing Water
Down he threw his lifeless burden;
Nobler, handsomer she thought him,
Than when first he came to woo her,
First threw down the deer before her,
As a token of his wishes,
As a promise of the future.

Then he turned and saw the strangers,
Cowering, crouching with the shadows,
Said within himself, "Who are they?
What strange guests has Minnehaha?"
But he questioned not the strangers,
Only spake to bid them welcome
To his lodge, his food, his fireside.

When the evening meal was ready,
And the deer had been divided,
Both the pallid guests, the strangers,
Springing from among the shadows,
Seized upon the choicest portions,
Seized the white fat of the roebuck,
Set apart for Laughing Water,
For the wife of Hiawatha;
Without asking, without thanking,
Eagerly devoured the morsels,
Flitted back among the shadows
In the corner of the wigwam.

Not a word spake Hiawatha,
Not a motion made Nokomis,
Not a gesture Laughing Water;
Not a change came o'er their features,
Only Minnehaha softly
Whispered, saying, "They are famished;
Let them do what best delights them;
Let them eat, for they are famished."

Many a daylight dawned and darkened,
Many a night shook off the daylight
As the pine shakes off the snowflakes
From the midnight of its branches;
Day by day the guests unmoving

Sat there silent in the wigwam;
But by night, in the storm or starlight,
Forth they went into the forest,
Bringing firewood to the wigwam,
Bringing pine cones for the burning,
Always sad and always silent.

And whenever Hiawatha
Came from fishing or from hunting,
When the evening meal was ready,
And the food had been divided,
Gliding from their darksome corner
Came the pallid guests, the strangers,
Seized upon the choicest portions
Set aside for Laughing Water,
And without rebuke or question
Flitted back among the shadows.

Never once had Hiawatha
By a word or look reproved them;
Never once had old Nokomis
Made a gesture of impatience;
Never once had Laughing Water
Shown resentment at the outrage.
All had they endured in silence,
That the rights of guest and stranger,
That the virtue of free-giving,
By a look might not be lessened,
By a word might not be broken.

Once at midnight Hiawatha,
Ever wakeful, ever watchful,
In the wigwam, dimly lighted
By the brands that still were burning,
By the glimmering, flickering firelight,
Heard a sighing, oft repeated,
Heard a sobbing, as of sorrow.

From his couch rose Hiawatha,
From his shaggy hides of bison,
Pushed aside the deerskin curtain,
Saw the pallid guests, the shadows,
Sitting upright on their couches,
Weeping in the silent midnight.

And he said: "O guests! why is it
That your hearts are so afflicted,
That you sob so in the midnight?
Has perchance the old Nokomis,
Has my wife, my Minnehaha,
Wronged or grieved you by unkindness,
Failed in hospitable duties?"

Then the shadows ceased from weeping,
Ceased from sobbing and lamenting,
And they said, with gentle voices,
"We are ghosts of the departed,
Souls of those who once were with you.
From the realm of Chibiabos
Hither have we come to try you,
Hither have we come to warn you:

"Cries of grief and lamentation
Reach us in the Blessed Islands;
Cries of anguish from the living,
Calling back their friends departed,
Sadden us with useless sorrow.
Therefore have we come to try you:
No one knows us, no one heeds us.
We are but a burden to you,
And we see that the departed
Have no place among the living.

"Think of this, O Hiawatha!
Speak of it to all the people,
That henceforward and forever
They no more with lamentations
Sadden the souls of the departed
In the Islands of the Blessed.

"Do not lay such heavy burdens,
In the graves of those you bury,
Not such weight of furs and wampum,
Not such weight of pots and kettles,
For the spirits faint beneath them.
Only give them food to carry,
Only give them fire to light them.

"Four days is the spirit's journey
To the land of ghosts and shadows,

Four its lonely night encampments;
Four times must their fires be lighted.
Therefore, when the dead are buried,
Let a fire, as night approaches,
Four times on the grave be kindled,
That the soul upon its journey
May not lack the cheerful firelight,
May not grope about in darkness.
  "Farewell, noble Hiawatha!
We have put you to the trial,
To the proof have put your patience,
By the insult of our presence,
By the outrage of our actions.
We have found you great and noble.
Fail not in the greater trial,
Faint not in the harder struggle."
  When they ceased, a sudden darkness
Fell and filled the silent wigwam.
Hiawatha heard a rustle
As of garments trailing by him,
Heard the curtain of the doorway
Lifted by a hand he saw not,
Felt the cold breath of the night air,
For a moment saw the starlight;
But he saw the ghosts no longer,
Saw no more the wandering spirits
From the kingdom of Ponemah,
From the land of the Hereafter.

XX

THE FAMINE

O the long and dreary Winter!
O the cold and cruel Winter!
Ever thicker, thicker, thicker
Froze the ice on lake and river,
Ever deeper, deeper, deeper
Fell the snow o'er all the landscape,

Fell the covering snow, and drifted
Through the forest, round the village.
   Hardly from his buried wigwam
Could the hunter force a passage;
With his mittens and his snow-shoes
Vainly walked he through the forest,
Sought for bird or beast and found none,
Saw no track of deer or rabbit,
In the snow beheld no footprints,
In the ghastly, gleaming forest
Fell, and could not rise from weakness,
Perished there from cold and hunger.
   O the famine and the fever!
O the wasting of the famine!
O the blasting of the fever!
O the wailing of the children!
O the anguish of the women!
   All the earth was sick and famished;
Hungry was the air around them,
Hungry was the sky above them,
And the hungry stars in heaven
Like the eyes of wolves glared at them!
   Into Hiawatha's wigwam
Came two other guests, as silent
As the ghosts were, and as gloomy,
Waited not to be invited,
Did not parley at the doorway,
Sat there without word of welcome
In the seat of Laughing Water;
Looked with haggard eyes and hollow
At the face of Laughing Water.
   And the foremost said: "Behold me!
I am Famine, Bukadawin!"
And the other said: "Behold me!
I am Fever, Ahkosewin!"
   And the lovely Minnehaha
Shuddered as they looked upon her,
Shuddered at the words they uttered,
Lay down on her bed in silence,
Hid her face, but made no answer;

Lay there trembling, freezing, burning
At the looks they cast upon her,
At the fearful words they uttered.

Forth into the empty forest
Rushed the maddened Hiawatha;
In his heart was deadly sorrow,
In his face a stony firmness;
On his brow the sweat of anguish
Started, but it froze and fell not.

Wrapped in furs and armed for hunting,
With his mighty bow of ash-tree,
With his quiver full of arrows,
With his mittens, Minjekahwun,
Into the vast and vacant forest
On his snow-shoes strode he forward.

"Gitche Manito, the Mighty!"
Cried he with his face uplifted
In that bitter hour of anguish,
"Give your children food, O Father!
Give us food, or we must perish!
Give me food for Minnehaha,
For my dying Minnehaha!"

Through the far-resounding forest,
Through the forest vast and vacant
Rang that cry of desolation.
But there came no other answer
Than the echo of his crying,
Than the echo of the woodlands,
"Minnehaha! Minnehaha!"

All day long roved Hiawatha
In that melancholy forest,
Through the shadow of whose thickets,
In the pleasant days of Summer,
Of that ne'er forgotten Summer,
He had brought his young wife homeward
From the land of the Dacotahs;
When the birds sang in the thickets,
And the streamlets laughed and glistened,
And the air was full of fragrance,
And the lovely Laughing Water

Said with voice that did not tremble
"I will follow you, my husband!"
In the wigwam with Nokomis,
With those gloomy guests, that watched her,
With the Famine and the Fever,
She was lying, the Beloved,
She the dying Minnehaha.

"Hark!" she said; "I hear a rushing,
Hear a roaring and a rushing,
Hear the Falls of Minnehaha
Calling to me from a distance!"
"No, my child!" said old Nokomis,
" 'Tis the night-wind in the pine trees!"
"Look!" she said; "I see my father
Standing lonely at his doorway,
Beckoning to me from his wigwam
In the land of the Dacotahs!"
"No, my child!" said old Nokomis,
" 'Tis the smoke, that waves and beckons!"

"Ah!" said she, "the eyes of Pauguk
Glare upon me in the darkness,
I can feel his icy fingers
Clasping mine amid the darkness!
Hiawatha! Hiawatha!"

And the desolate Hiawatha,
Far away amid the forest,
Miles away among the mountains,
Heard that sudden cry of anguish,
Heard the voice of Minnehaha
Calling to him in the darkness,
"Hiawatha! Hiawatha!"

Over snowfields waste and pathless
Under snow-encumbered branches,
Homeward hurried Hiawatha,
Empty-handed, heavy-hearted,
Heard Nokomis moaning, wailing,
"Wahonowin! Wahonowin!
Would that I had perished for you,
Would that I were dead as you are!
Wahonowin! Wahonowin!"

And he rushed into the wigwam,
Saw the old Nokomis slowly
Rocking to and fro and moaning,
Saw his lovely Minnehaha
Lying dead and cold before him,
And his bursting heart within him
Uttered such a cry of anguish,
That the forest moaned and shuddered,
That the very stars in heaven
Shook and trembled with his anguish.

Then he sat down, still and speechless,
On the bed of Minnehaha,
At the feet of Laughing Water,
At those willing feet, that never
More would lightly run to meet him,
Never more would lightly follow.

With both hands his face he covered,
Seven long days and nights he sat there,
As if in a swoon he sat there,
Speechless, motionless, unconscious
Of the daylight or the darkness.

Then they buried Minnehaha;
In the snow a grave they made her,
In the forest deep and darksome,
Underneath the moaning hemlocks;
Clothed in her richest garments,
Wrapped in her robes of ermine;
Covered her with snow, like ermine,
Thus they buried Minnehaha.

And at night a fire was lighted,
On her grave four times was kindled,
For her soul upon its journey
To the Islands of the Blessed.
From his doorway Hiawatha
Saw it burning in the forest,
Lighting up the gloomy hemlocks;
From his sleepless bed uprising,
From the bed of Minnehaha,
Stood and watched it at the doorway,

That it might not be extinguished,
Might not leave her in the darkness.
  "Farewell!" said he, "Minnehaha!
Farewell, O my Laughing Water!
All my heart is buried with you,
All my thoughts go onward with you!
Come not back again to labor,
Come not back again to suffer,
Where the Famine and the Fever
Wear the heart and waste the body.
Soon my task will be completed,
Soon your footsteps I shall follow
To the Islands of the Blessed,
To the Kingdom of Ponemah,
To the Land of the Hereafter!"

XXI

THE WHITE MAN'S FOOT

In his lodge beside a river,
Close beside a frozen river,
Sat an old man, sad and lonely.
White his hair was as a snowdrift;
Dull and low his fire was burning,
And the old man shook and trembled,
Folded in his Waubewyon,
In his tattered whiteskin wrapper,
Hearing nothing but the tempest
As it roared along the forest,
Seeing nothing but the snowstorm,
As it whirled and hissed and drifted.
  All the coals were white with ashes,
And the fire was slowly dying,
As a young man, walking lightly,
At the open doorway entered.
Red with blood of youth his cheeks were,
Soft his eyes, as stars in Springtime,
Bound his forehead was with grasses,
Bound and plumed with scented grasses;

On his lips a smile of beauty,
Filling all the lodge with sunshine,
In his hand a bunch of blossoms
Filling all the lodge with sweetness.

"Ah, my son!" exclaimed the old man,
"Happy are my eyes to see you.
Sit here on the mat beside me,
Sit here by the dying embers,
Let us pass the night together.
Tell me of your strange adventures,
Of the lands where you have travelled;
I will tell you of my prowess,
Of my many deeds of wonder."

From his pouch he drew his peace-pipe,
Very old and strangely fashioned;
Made of red stone was the pipe-head,
And the stem a reed with feathers,
Filled the pipe with bark of willow,
Placed a burning coal upon it,
Gave it to his guest, the stranger,
And began to speak in this wise:
"When I blow my breath about me,
When I breathe upon the landscape,
Motionless are all the rivers,
Hard as stones becomes the water!"

And the young man answered, smiling:
"When I blow my breath about me,
When I breathe upon the landscape,
Flowers spring up o'er all the meadows,
Singing, onward rush the rivers!"

"When I shake my hoary tresses,"
Said the old man darkly frowning,
"All the land with snow is covered;
All the leaves from all the branches
Fall and fade and die and wither,
For I breathe, and lo! they are not.
From the waters and the marshes
Rise the wild goose and the heron,
Fly away to distant regions,
For I speak, and lo! they are not.

And where'er my footsteps wander,
All the wild beasts of the forest
Hide themselves in holes and caverns,
And the earth becomes as flintstone!"

"When I shake my flowing ringlets,"
Said the young man, softly laughing,
"Showers of rain fall warm and welcome,
Plants lift up their heads rejoicing,
Back unto their lakes and marshes
Come the wild goose and the heron,
Homeward shoots the arrowy swallow,
Sing the bluebird and the robin,
And where'er my footsteps wander,
All the meadows wave with blossoms,
All the woodlands ring with music,
All the trees are dark with foliage!"

While they spake, the night departed:
From the distant realms of Wabun,
From his shining lodge of silver,
Like a warrior robed and painted,
Came the sun, and said, "Behold me!
Gheezis, the great sun, behold me!"

Then the old man's tongue was speechless.
And the air grew warm and pleasant,
And upon the wigwam sweetly
Sang the bluebird and the robin,
And the stream began to murmur,
And a scent of growing grasses
Through the lodge was gently wafted.

And Segwun, the youthful stranger,
More distinctly in the daylight
Saw the icy face before him;
It was Peboan, the Winter!

From his eyes the tears were flowing,
As from melting lakes the streamlets,
And his body shrunk and dwindled
As the shouting sun ascended,
Till into the air it faded,
Till into the ground it vanished,
And the young man saw before him,

On the hearth-stone of the wigwam,
Where the fire had smoked and smouldered,
Saw the earliest flower of Springtime,
Saw the beauty of the Springtime,
Saw the Miskodeed in blossom.

Thus it was that in the North-land
After that unheard-of coldness,
That intolerable Winter,
Came the Spring with all its splendor,
All its birds and all its blossoms,
All its flowers and leaves and grasses.

Sailing on the wind to northward,
Flying in great flocks, like arrows,
Like huge arrows shot through heaven,
Passed the swan, the Mahnahbezee
Speaking almost as a man speaks;
And in long lines waving, bending
Like a bow-string snapped asunder,
Came the white goose, Waw-be-wawa:
And in pairs or singly flying,
Mahng the loon, with clangorous pinions,
The blue heron, the Shuh-shuh-gah,
And the grouse, the Mushkodasa.

In the thickets and the meadows
Piped the bluebird, the Owaissa,
On the summit of the lodges
Sang the Opechee, the robin,
In the covert of the pine-trees
Cooed the pigeon, the Omemee;
And the sorrowing Hiawatha,
Speechless in his infinite sorrow,
Heard their voices calling to him,
Went forth from his gloomy doorway,
Stood and gazed into the heavens,
Gazed upon the earth and waters.

From his wanderings far to eastward,
From the regions of the morning,
From the shining land of Wabun,
Homeward now returned Iagoo,
The great traveller, the great boaster,

Full of new and strange adventures,
Marvels many and many wonders.

And the people of the village
Listened to him as he told them
Of his marvellous adventures,
Laughing answered him in this wise:
"Ugh! it is indeed Iagoo!
No one else beholds such wonders!"

He had seen, he said, a water,
Bigger than the Big-Sea-Water,
Broader than the Gitche Gumee,
Bitter so that none could drink it!
At each other looked the warriors,
Looked the women at each other,
Smiled, and said, "It cannot be so!
Kaw!" they said, "It cannot be so!"

O'er it, said he, o'er this water
Came a great canoe with pinions,
A canoe with wings came flying,
Bigger than a grove of pine trees,
Taller than the tallest tree-tops!
And the old men and the women
Looked and tittered at each other;
"Kaw!" they said, "we don't believe it!"

From its mouth, he said, to greet him,
Came Waywassimo, the lightning,
Came the thunder, Annemeekee!
And the warriors and the women
Laughed aloud at poor Iagoo;
"Kaw!" they said, "what tales you tell us!"

In it, said he, came a people,
In the great canoe with pinions
Came, he said, a hundred warriors;
Painted white were all their faces
And with hair their chins were covered!
And the warriors and the women
Laughed and shouted in derision,
Like the ravens on the tree-tops,
Like the crows upon the hemlocks.

"Kaw!" they said, "what lies you tell us!
Do not think that we believe them!"
    Only Hiawatha laughed not,
But he gravely spake and answered
To their jeering and their jesting:
"True is all Iagoo tells us;
I have seen it in a vision,
Seen the great canoe with pinions,
Seen the people with white faces,
Seen the coming of this bearded
People of the wooden vessel
From the regions of the morning,
From the shining land of Wabun.
    "Gitche Manito, the Mighty,
The Great Spirit, the Creator,
Sends them hither on his errand,
Sends them to us with his message.
Wheresoe'er they move, before them
Swarms the stinging fly, the Ahmo.
Swarms the bee, the honey-maker;
Wheresoe'er they tread, beneath them
Springs a flower unknown among us,
Springs the White-man's Foot in blossom.
    "Let us welcome, then, the strangers,
Hail them as our friends and brothers,
And the heart's right hand of friendship
Give them when they come to see us.
Gitche Manito, the Mighty,
Said this to me in my vision.
    "I beheld, too, in that vision,
All the secrets of the future,
Of the distant days that shall be.
I beheld the westward marches
Of the unknown, crowded nations.
All the land was full of people,
Restless, struggling, toiling, striving,
Speaking many tongues, yet feeling
But one heart-beat in their bosoms.
In the woodlands rang their axes,
Smoked their towns in all the valleys,

Over all the lakes and rivers
Rushed their great canoes of thunder.
"Then a darker, drearier vision
Passed before me, vague and cloudlike
I beheld our nations scattered,
All forgetful of my counsels,
Weakened, warring with each other;
Saw the remnants of our people
Sweeping westward, wild and woful,
Like the cloud-rack of a tempest,
Like the withered leaves of Autumn!"

XXII

HIAWATHA'S DEPARTURE

By the shore of Gitche Gumee,
By the shining Big-Sea-Water,
At the doorway of his wigwam,
In the pleasant Summer morning,
Hiawatha stood and waited.
   All the air was full of freshness,
All the earth was bright and joyous,
And before him through the sunshine,
Westward toward the neighboring forest
Passed in golden swarms the Ahmo,
Passed the bees, the honey-makers,
Burning, singing in the sunshine.
   Bright above him shone the heavens,
Level spread the lake before him;
From its bosom leaped the sturgeon,
Sparkling, flashing in the sunshine;
On its margin the great forest
Stood reflected in the water,
Every treetop had its shadow,
Motionless beneath the water,
   From the brow of Hiawatha
Gone was every trace of sorrow,
As the fog from off the water,
As the mist from off the meadow.

With a smile of joy and triumph,
With a look of exultation,
As of one who in a vision
Sees what is to be, but is not,
Stood and waited Hiawatha.

Toward the sun his hands were lifted,[1]
Both the palms spread out against it,
And between the parted fingers
Fell the sunshine on his features,
Flecked with light his naked shoulders,
As it falls and flecks an oak tree
Through the rifted leaves and branches.

O'er the water floating, flying,
Something in the hazy distance,
Something in the mists of morning,
Loomed and lifted from the water,
Now seemed floating, now seemed flying,
Coming nearer, nearer, nearer.

Was it Shingebis, the diver?
Was it the pelican, the Shada?
Or the heron, the Shuh-shuh-gah?
Or the white goose, Waw-be-wawa,
With the water dripping, flashing,
From its glossy neck and feathers?

It was neither goose nor diver,
Neither pelican nor heron,
O'er the water floating, flying,
Through the shining mist of morning,
But a birch canoe with paddles,
Rising, sinking on the water,
Dripping, flashing in the sunshine;
And within it came a people
From the distant land of Wabun,
From the farthest realms of morning
Came the Black-Robe chief, the Prophet,
He the Priest of Prayer, the Paleface,
With his guides and his companions.

And the noble Hiawatha,

[1] In this manner, and with such salutations, was Father Marquette received by the Illinois. See his *Voyage et Découvertes,* Section V.

With his hands aloft extended,
Held aloft in sign of welcome,
Waited, full of exultation,
Till the birch canoe with paddles
Grated on the shining pebbles,
Stranded on the sandy margin,
Till the Black-Robe chief, the Paleface,
With the cross upon his bosom,
Landed on the sandy margin.

Then the joyous Hiawatha
Cried aloud and spake in this wise:
"Beautiful is the sun, O strangers,
When you come so far to see us!
All our town in peace awaits you,
All our doors stand open for you;
You shall enter all our wigwams,
For the heart's right hand we give you.

"Never bloomed the earth so gayly,
Never shone the sun so brightly,
As to-day they shine and blossom
When you come so far to see us!
Never was our lake so tranquil,
Nor so free from rocks and sandbars;
For our birch canoe in passing
Has removed both rock and sandbar.

"Never before had our tobacco
Such a sweet and pleasant flavor,
Never the broad leaves of our cornfields
Were so beautiful to look on,
As they seem to us this morning,
When you come so far to see us!"

And the Black-Robe chief made answer,
Stammered in his speech a little,
Speaking words yet unfamiliar:
"Peace be with you, Hiawatha,
Peace be with you and your people,
Peace of prayer, and peace of pardon,
Peace of Christ, and joy of Mary!"

Then the generous Hiawatha
Led the strangers to his wigwam,

Seated them on skins of bison,
Seated them on skins of ermine,
And the careful, old Nokomis
Brought them food in bowls of basswood,
Water brought in birchen dippers,
And the calumet, the peace-pipe,
Filled and lighted for their smoking.

All the old men of the village,
All the warriors of the nation,
All the Jossakeeds, the prophets,
The magicians, the Wabenos,
And the medicine-men, the Medas,
Came to bid the strangers welcome;
"It is well," they said, "O brothers,
That you come so far to see us!"

In a circle round the doorway,
With their pipes they sat in silence,
Waiting to behold the strangers,
Waiting to receive their message;
Till the Black-Robe chief, the Paleface,
From the wigwam came to greet them,
Stammering in his speech a little,
Speaking words yet unfamiliar;
"It is well," they said, "O brother,
That you come so far to see us!"

Then the Black-Robe chief, the prophet,
Told his message to the people,
Told the purport of his mission,
Told them of the Virgin Mary,
And her blessed Son, the Saviour,
How in distant lands and ages
He had lived on earth as we do;
How he fasted, prayed, and labored,
How the Jews, the tribe accursed,
Mocked him, scourged him, crucified him;
How he rose from where they laid him,
Walked again with his disciples,
And ascended into heaven.

And the chiefs made answer, saying:
"We have listened to your message,

We have heard your words of wisdom,
We will think on what you tell us.
It is well for us, O brothers,
That you come so far to see us!"
　　Then they rose up and departed
Each one homeward to his wigwam,
To the young men and the women
Told the story of the strangers
Whom the Master of Life had sent them
From the shining land of Wabun.

　　Heavy with the heat and silence
Grew the afternoon of Summer;
With a drowsy sound the forest
Whispered round the sultry wigwam.
With a sound of sleep the water
Rippled on the beach below it;
From the cornfields shrill and ceaseless
Sang the grasshopper, Pah-puk-keena;
And the guests of Hiawatha,
Weary with the heat of Summer,
Slumbered in the sultry wigwam.

　　Slowly o'er the simmering landscape
Fell the evening's dusk and coolness,
And the long and level sunbeams
Shot their spears into the forest,
Breaking through its shields of shadow,
Rushed into each secret ambush,
Searched each thicket, dingle, hollow;
Still the guests of Hiawatha
Slumbered in the silent wigwam.

　　From his place rose Hiawatha,
Bade farewell to old Nokomis,
Spake in whispers, spake in this wise,
Did not wake the guests, that slumbered:
　　"I am going, O Nokomis,
On a long and distant journey,
To the portals of the Sunset,
To the regions of the home-wind,
Of the Northwest wind, Keewaydin.
But these guests I leave behind me,

In your watch and ward I leave them;
See that never harm comes near them,
See that never fear molests them,
Never danger nor suspicion,
Never want of food or shelter,
In the lodge of Hiawatha!"
    Forth into the village went he,
Bade farewell to all the warriors,
Bade farewell to all the young men,
Spake persuading, spake in this wise:
    "I am going, O my people,
On a long and distant journey;
Many moons and many winters
Will have come, and will have vanished,
Ere I come again to see you.
But my guests I leave behind me;
Listen to their words of wisdom,
Listen to the truth they tell you,
For the Master of Life has sent them
From the land of light and morning!"
    On the shore stood Hiawatha,
Turned and waved his hand at parting;
On the clear and luminous water
Launched his birch canoe for sailing,
From the pebbles of the margin
Shoved it forth into the water;
Whispered to it, "Westward! westward!"
And with speed it darted forward.
    And the evening sun descending
Set the clouds on fire with redness,
Burned the broad sky, like a prairie,
Left upon the level water
One long track and trail of splendor,
Down whose stream, as down a river,
Westward, westward Hiawatha
Sailed into the fiery sunset,
Sailed into the purple vapors,
Sailed into the dusk of evening.
    And the people from the margin
Watched him floating, rising, sinking,

Till the birch canoe seemed lifted
High into that sea of splendor,
Till it sank into the vapors
Like the new moon slowly, slowly
Sinking in the purple distance.

And they said, "Farewell forever!"
Said, "Farewell, O Hiawatha!"
And the forests, dark and lonely,
Moved through all their depths of darkness,
Sighed, "Farewell, O Hiawatha!"
And the waves upon the margin
Rising, rippling on the pebbles,
Sobbed, "Farewell, O Hiawatha!"
And the heron, the Shuh-shuh-gah,
From her haunts among the fenlands,
Screamed, "Farewell, O Hiawatha!"

Thus departed Hiawatha!
Hiawatha the Beloved,
In the glory of the sunset,
In the purple mists of evening,
To the regions of the home-wind,
Of the Northwest wind, Keewaydin,
To the Islands of the Blessed,
To the Kingdom of Ponemah,
To the land of the Hereafter!

TALES OF A WAYSIDE INN

PRELUDE

THE WAYSIDE INN

ONE Autumn night, in Sudbury town,
Across the meadows bare and brown,
The windows of the wayside inn
Gleamed red with fire-light through the leaves
Of woodbine, hanging from the eaves
Their crimson curtains rent and thin.

As ancient is this hostelry
As any in the land may be,
Built in the old Colonial day,
When men lived in a grander way,
With ampler hospitality;
A kind of old Hobgoblin Hall,
Now somewhat fallen to decay,
With weather-stains upon the wall,
And stairways worn, and crazy doors,
And creaking and uneven floors,
And chimneys huge, and tiled and tall.

A region of repose it seems,
A place of slumber and of dreams,
Remote among the wooded hills!
For there no noisy railway speeds,
Its torch-race scattering smoke and gleeds;
But noon and night, the panting teams
Stop under the great oaks, that throw
Tangles of light and shade below,
On roofs and doors and window-sills.
Across the road the barns display
Their lines of stalls, their mows of hay,
Through the wide doors the breezes blow,
The wattled cocks strut to and fro,

And, half effaced by rain and shine,
The Red Horse prances on the sign.
Round this old-fashioned, quaint abode
Deep silence reigned, save when a gust
Went rushing down the county road,
And skeletons of leaves, and dust,
A moment quickened by its breath,
Shuddered and danced their dance of death,
And through the ancient oaks o'erhead
Mysterious voices moaned and fled.

But from the parlor of the inn
A pleasant murmur smote the ear,
Like water rushing through a weir;
Oft interrupted by the din
Of laughter and of loud applause,
And, in each intervening pause,
The music of a violin.
The fire-light, shedding over all
The splendor of its ruddy glow,
Filled the whole parlor large and low;
It gleamed on wainscot and on wall,
It touched with more than wonted grace
Fair Princess Mary's pictured face;
It bronzed the rafters overhead,
On the old spinet's ivory keys
It played inaudible melodies,
It crowned the sombre clock with flame,
The hands, the hours, the maker's name,
And painted with a livelier red
The Landlord's coat-of-arms again;
And, flashing on the window-pane,
Emblazoned with its light and shade
The jovial rhymes, that still remain,
Writ near a century ago,
By the great Major Molineaux,
Whom Hawthorne has immortal made.
Before the blazing fire of wood
Erect the rapt musician stood;
And ever and anon he bent

His head upon his instrument,
And seemed to listen, till he caught
Confessions of its secret thought,—
The joy, the triumph, the lament,
The exultation and the pain;
Then, by the magic of his art,
He soothed the throbbings of its heart,
And lulled it into peace again.

Around the fireside at their ease
There sat a group of friends, entranced
With the delicious melodies;
Who from the far-off noisy town
Had to the wayside inn come down,
To rest beneath its old oak-trees.
The fire-light on their faces glanced,
Their shadows on the wainscot danced,
And, though of different lands and speech,
Each had his tale to tell, and each
Was anxious to be pleased and please.
And while the sweet musician plays,
Let me in outline sketch them all,
Perchance uncouthly as the blaze
With its uncertain touch portrays
Their shadowy semblance on the wall.

But first the Landlord will I trace;
Grave in his aspect and attire;
A man of ancient pedigree,
A Justice of the Peace was he,
Known in all Sudbury as "The Squire."
Proud was he of his name and race,
Of old Sir William and Sir Hugh,
And in the parlor, full in view,
His coat-of-arms, well framed and glazed,
Upon the wall in colors blazed;
He beareth gules upon his shield,
A chevron argent in the field,
With three wolf's heads, and for the crest
A Wyvern part-per-pale addressed

Upon a helmet barred; below
The scroll reads, "By the name of Howe."
And over this, no longer bright,
Though glimmering with a latent light,
Was hung the sword his grandsire bore,
In the rebellious days of yore,
Down there at Concord in the fight.

A youth was there, of quiet ways,
A Student of old books and days,
To whom all tongues and lands were known,
And yet a lover of his own;
With many a social virtue graced,
And yet a friend of solitude;
A man of such a genial mood
The heart of all things he embraced,
And yet of such fastidious taste,
He never found the best too good.
Books were his passion and delight,
And in his upper room at home
Stood many a rare and sumptuous tome,
In vellum bound, with gold bedight,
Great volumes garmented in white,
Recalling Florence, Pisa, Rome.
He loved the twilight that surrounds
The border-land of old romance;
Where glitter hauberk, helm, and lance,
And banner waves, and trumpet sounds,
And ladies ride with hawk on wrist,
And mighty warriors sweep along,
Magnified by the purple mist,
The dusk of centuries and of song.
The chronicles of Charlemagne,
Of Merlin and the Mort d'Arthure,
Mingled together in his brain
With tales of Flores and Blanchefleur,
Sir Ferumbras, Sir Eglamour,
Sir Launcelot, Sir Morgadour,
Sir Guy, Sir Bevis, Sir Gawain.

A young Sicilian, too, was there:—
In sight of Etna born and bred,
Some breath of its volcanic air
Was glowing in his heart and brain,
And, being rebellious to his liege,
After Palermo's fatal siege,
Across the western seas he fled,
In good King Bomba's happy reign.
His face was like a summer night,
All flooded with a dusky light;
His hands were small; his teeth shone white
As sea-shells, when he smiled or spoke;
His sinews supple and strong as oak;
Clean shaven was he as a priest,
Who at the mass on Sunday sings,
Save that upon his upper lip
His beard, a good palm's length at least,
Level and pointed at the tip,
Shot sideways, like a swallow's wings.
The poets read he o'er and o'er,
And most of all the Immortal Four
Of Italy; and next to those,
The story-telling bard of prose,
Who wrote the joyous Tuscan tales
Of the Decameron, that make
Fiesole's green hills and vales
Remembered for Boccaccio's sake.
Much too of music was his thought;
The melodies and measures fraught
With sunshine and the open air,
Of vineyards and the singing sea
Of his beloved Sicily;
And much it pleased him to peruse
The songs of the Sicilian muse,—
Bucolic songs by Meli sung
In the familiar peasant tongue,
That made men say, "Behold! once more
The pitying gods to earth restore
Theocritus of Syracuse!"

A Spanish Jew from Alicant
With aspect grand and grave was there;
Vender of silks and fabrics rare,
And attar of rose from the Levant.
Like an old Patriarch he appeared,
Abraham or Isaac, or at least
Some later Prophet or High-Priest;
With lustrous eyes, and olive skin,
And, wildly tossed from cheeks and chin,
The tumbling cataract of his beard.
His garments breathed a spicy scent
Of cinnamon and sandal blent,
Like the soft aromatic gales
That meet the mariner, who sails
Through the Moluccas, and the seas
That wash the shores of Celebes.
All stories that recorded are
By Pierre Alphonse he knew by heart,
And it was rumored he could say
The Parables of Sandabar,
And all the Fables of Pilpay,
Or if not all, the greater part!
Well versed was he in Hebrew books,
Talmud and Targum, and the lore
Of Kabala; and evermore
There was a mystery in his looks;
His eyes seemed gazing far away,
As if in vision or in trance
He heard the solemn sackbut play,
And saw the Jewish maidens dance.

A Theologian, from the school
Of Cambridge on the Charles, was there;
Skilful alike with tongue and pen,
He preached to all men everywhere
The Gospel of the Golden Rule,
The New Commandment given to men,
Thinking the deed, and not the creed,
Would help us in our utmost need.
With reverent feet the earth he trod,

Nor banished nature from his plan,
But studied still with deep research
To build the Universal Church,
Lofty as is the love of God,
And ample as the wants of man.

A Poet, too, was there, whose verse
Was tender, musical, and terse;
The inspiration, the delight,
The gleam, the glory, the swift flight,
Of thoughts so sudden, that they seem
The revelations of a dream,
All these were his; but with them came
No envy of another's fame;
He did not find his sleep less sweet
For music in some neighboring street,
Nor rustling here in every breeze
The laurels of Miltiades.
Honor and blessings on his head
While living, good report when dead,
Who, not too eager for renown,
Accepts, but does not clutch, the crown!

Last the Musician, as he stood
Illumined by that fire of wood;
Fair-haired, blue-eyed, his aspect blithe,
His figure tall and straight and lithe,
And every feature of his face
Revealing his Norwegian race;
A radiance, streaming from within,
Around his eyes and forehead beamed,
The Angel with the violin,
Painted by Raphael, he seemed.
He lived in that ideal world
Whose language is not speech, but song;
Around him evermore the throng
Of elves and sprites their dances whirled;
The Strömkarl sang, the cataract hurled
Its headlong waters from the height;
And mingled in the wild delight
The scream of sea-birds in their flight,

The rumor of the forest trees,
The plunge of the implacable seas,
The tumult of the wind at night,
Voices of eld, like trumpets blowing,
Old ballads, and wild melodies
Through mist and darkness pouring forth,
Like Elivagar's river flowing
Out of the glaciers of the North.

The instrument on which he played
Was in Cremona's workshops made,
By a great master of the past,
Ere yet was lost the art divine:
Fashioned of maple and of pine,
That in Tyrolian forests vast
Had rocked and wrestled with the blast:
Exquisite was it in design,
Perfect in each minutest part,
A marvel of the lutist's art;
And in its hollow chamber, thus,
The maker from whose hands it came
Had written his unrivalled name,—
"Antonius Stradivarius."

And when he played, the atmosphere
Was filled with magic, and the ear
Caught echoes of that Harp of Gold,
Whose music had so weird a sound,
The hunted stag forgot to bound,
The leaping rivulet backward rolled,
The birds came down from bush and tree,
The dead came from beneath the sea,
The maiden to the harper's knee.

The music ceased; the applause was loud,
The pleased musician smiled and bowed;
The wood-fire clapped its hands of flame,
The shadows on the wainscot stirred,
And from the harpsichord there came
A ghostly murmur of acclaim,

A sound like that sent down at night
By birds of passage in their flight,
From the remotest distance heard.

Then silence followed; then began
A clamor for the Landlord's tale,—
The story promised them of old,
They said, but always left untold;
And he, although a bashful man,
And all his courage seemed to fail,
Finding excuse of no avail,
Yielded; and thus the story ran.

THE LANDLORD'S TALE

PAUL REVERE'S RIDE

Listen, my children, and you shall hear
Of the midnight ride of Paul Revere.
On the eighteenth of April, in Seventy-five;
Hardly a man is now alive
Who remembers that famous day and year.

He said to his friend, "If the British march
By land or sea from the town to-night,
Hang a lantern aloft in the belfry arch
Of the North Church tower as a signal light,—
One, if by land, and two, if by sea;
And I on the opposite shore will be,
Ready to ride and spread the alarm
Through every Middlesex village and farm,
For the country-folk to be up and to arm."

Then he said, "Good night!" and with muffled oar
Silently rowed to the Charlestown shore,
Just as the moon rose over the bay,
Where swinging wide at her moorings lay
The Somerset, British man-of-war;
A phantom ship, with each mast and spar
Across the moon like a prison bar,

And a huge black hulk, that was magnified
By its own reflection in the tide.

Meanwhile, his friend, through alley and street,
Wanders and watches with eager ears,
Till in silence around him he hears
The muster of men at the barrack door,
The sound of arms, and the tramp of feet,
And the measured tread of the grenadiers,
Marching down to their boats on the shore.

Then he climbed to the tower of the church,
Up the wooden stairs, with stealthy tread,
To the belfry-chamber overhead,
And startled the pigeons from their perch
On the sombre rafters, that round him made
Masses and moving shapes of shade—
Up the trembling ladder, steep and tall,
To the highest window in the wall,
Where he paused to listen and look down
A moment on the roofs of the town,
And the moonlight flowing over all.

Beneath, in the churchyard, lay the dead,
In their night-encampment on the hill,
Wrapped in silence so deep and still
That he could hear, like a sentinel's tread,
The watchful night-wind, as it went
Creeping along from tent to tent,
And seeming to whisper, "All is well!"
A moment only he feels the spell
Of the place and the hour, and the secret dread
Of the lonely belfry and the dead;
For suddenly all his thoughts are bent
On a shadowy something far away,
Where the river widens to meet the bay,—
A line of black that bends and floats
On the rising tide, like a bridge of boats.

Meanwhile, impatient to mount and ride,
Booted and spurred, with a heavy stride

On the opposite shore walked Paul Revere.
Now he patted his horse's side,
Now gazed at the landscape far and near,
Then, impetuous, stamped the earth,
And turned and tightened his saddle-girth;
But mostly he watched with eager search
The belfry-tower of the Old North Church,

As it rose above the graves on the hill,
Lonely and spectral and sombre and still,
And lo! as he looks, on the belfry's height
A glimmer, and then a gleam of light!
He springs to the saddle, the bridle he turns,
But lingers and gazes, till full on his sight
A second lamp in the belfry burns!

A hurry of hoofs in a village street,
A shape in the moonlight, a bulk in the dark,
And beneath, from the pebbles, in passing, a spark
Struck out by a steed flying fearless and fleet;
That was all! And yet, through the gloom and the light,
The fate of a nation was riding that night;
And the spark struck out by that steed, in his flight,
Kindled the land into flame with its heat.

He has left the village and mounted the steep,
And beneath him, tranquil and broad and deep,
Is the Mystic, meeting the ocean tides;
And under the alders, that skirt its edge,
Now soft on the sand, now loud on the ledge,
Is heard the tramp of his steed as he rides.

It was twelve by the village clock
When he crossed the bridge into Medford town.
He heard the crowing of the cock,
And the barking of the farmer's dog,
And felt the damp of the river fog,
That rises after the sun goes down.

It was one by the village clock,
When he galloped into Lexington
He saw the gilded weathercock
Swim in the moonlight as he passed,

And the meeting-house windows, blank and bare,
Gaze at him with a spectral glare,
As if they already stood aghast
At the bloody work they would look upon.

It was two by the village clock,
When he came to the bridge in Concord town.
He heard the bleating of the flock,
And the twitter of birds among the trees,
And felt the breath of the morning breeze
Blowing over the meadows brown.
And one was safe and asleep in his bed
Who at the bridge would be first to fall,
Who that day would be lying dead,
Pierced by a British musket-ball.

You know the rest. In the books you have read,
How the British Regulars fired and fled,—
How the farmers gave them ball for ball,
From behind each fence and farmyard wall,
Chasing the red-coats down the lane,
Then crossing the fields to emerge again
Under the trees at the turn of the road,
And only pausing to fire and load.

So through the night rode Paul Revere;
And so through the night went his cry of alarm
To every Middlesex village and farm,—
A cry of defiance and not of fear,
A voice in the darkness, a knock at the door,
And a word that shall echo forevermore!
For, borne on the night-wind of the Past,
Through all our history, to the last,
In the hour of darkness and peril and need,
The people will waken and listen to hear
The hurrying hoof-beats of that steed,
And the midnight message of Paul Revere.

INTERLUDE

The Landlord ended thus his tale,
Then rising took down from its nail

The sword that hung there, dim with dust,
And cleaving to its sheath with rust,
And said, "This sword was in the fight."
The Poet seized it, and exclaimed,
"It is the sword of a good knight,
Though homespun was his coat-of-mail;
What matter if it be not named
Joyeuse, Colada, Durindale,
Excalibar, or Aroundight,
Or other name the books record?
Your ancestor, who bore this sword
As Colonel of the Volunteers,
Mounted upon his old gray mare,
Seen here and there and everywhere,
To me a grander shape appears
Than old Sir William, or what not,
Clinking about in foreign lands
With iron gauntlets on his hands,
And on his head an iron pot!"

All laughed; the Landlord's face grew red
As his escutcheon on the wall;
He could not comprehend at all
The drift of what the Poet said;
For those who had been longest dead
Were always greatest in his eyes;
And he was speechless with surprise
To see Sir William's plumèd head
Brought to a level with the rest,
And made the subject of a jest.

And this perceiving, to appease
The Landlord's wrath, the others' fears,
The Student said, with careless ease,
"The ladies and the cavaliers,
The arms, the loves, the courtesies,
The deeds of high emprise, I sing!
Thus Ariosto says, in words
That have the stately stride and ring
Of armèd knights and clashing swords.
Now listen to the tale I bring;

Listen! though not to me belong
The flowing draperies of his song,
The words that rouse, the voice that charms.
The Landlord's tale was one of arms,
Only a tale of love is mine,
Blending the human and divine,
A tale of the Decameron, told
In Palmieri's garden old,
By Fiametta, laurel-crowned,
While her companions lay around,
And heard the intermingled sound
Of airs that on their errands sped,
And wild birds gossiping overhead,
And lisp of leaves, and fountain's fall,
And her own voice more sweet than all,
Telling the tale, which, wanting these,
Perchance may lose its power to please."

THE STUDENT'S TALE

THE FALCON OF SER FEDERIGO

One summer morning, when the sun was hot,
Weary with labor in his garden-plot,
On a rude bench beneath his cottage eaves,
Ser Federigo sat among the leaves
Of a huge vine, that, with its arms outspread,
Hung its delicious clusters overhead.
Below him, through the lovely valley, flowed
The river Arno, like a winding road,
And from its banks were lifted high in air
The spires and roofs of Florence called the Fair;
To him a marble tomb, that rose above
His wasted fortunes and his buried love.
For there, in banquet and in tournament,
His wealth had lavished been, his substance spent,
To woo and lose, since ill his wooing sped,
Donna Giovanna, who his rival wed,
Yet ever in his fancy reigned supreme,
The ideal woman of a young man's dream.

Then he withdrew, in poverty and pain,
To this small farm, the last of his domain,
His only comfort and his only care
To prune his vines, and plant the fig and pear;
His only forester and only guest
His falcon, faithful to him, when the rest,
Whose willing hands had found so light of yore
The brazen knocker of his palace door,
Had now no strength to lift the wooden latch,
That entrance gave beneath a roof of thatch.
Companion of his solitary ways,
Purveyor of his feasts on holidays,
On him this melancholy man bestowed
The love with which his nature overflowed.
And so the empty-handed years went round,
Vacant, though voiceful with prophetic sound,
And so, that summer morn, he sat and mused
With folded, patient hands, as he was used,
And dreamily before his half-closed sight
Floated the vision of his lost delight.
Beside him, motionless, the drowsy bird
Dreamed of the chase, and in his slumber heard
The sudden, scythe-like sweep of wings, that dare
The headlong plunge thro' eddying gulfs of air,
Then, starting broad awake upon his perch,
Tinkled his bells, like mass-bells in a church,
And, looking at his master, seemed to say,
"Ser Federigo, shall we hunt to-day?"
Ser Federigo thought not of the chase;
The tender vision of her lovely face,
I will not say he seems to see, he sees
In the leaf-shadows of the trellises
Herself, yet not herself; a lovely child
With flowing tresses, and eyes wide and wild,
Coming undaunted up the garden walk,
And looking not at him, but at the hawk.
"Beautiful falcon!" said he, "would that I
Might hold thee on my wrist, or see thee fly!"
The voice was hers, and made strange echoes start
Through all the haunted chambers of his heart,

As an æolian harp through gusty doors
Of some old ruin its wild music pours.

"Who is thy mother, my fair boy?" he said,
His hand laid softly on that shining head.
"Monna Giovanna.—Will you let me stay
A little while, and with your falcon play?
We live there, just beyond your garden wall,
In the great house behind the poplars tall."
So he spake on; and Federigo heard
As from afar each softly uttered word,
And drifted onward through the golden gleams
And shadows of the misty sea of dreams,
As mariners becalmed through vapors drift,
And feel the sea beneath them sink and lift,
And hear far off the mournful breakers roar,
And voices calling faintly from the shore!
Then, waking from his pleasant reveries,
He took the little boy upon his knees,
And told him stories of his gallant bird,
Till in their friendship he became a third.

Monna Giovanna, widowed in her prime,
Had come with friends to pass the summer time
In her grand villa, half-way up the hill,
O'erlooking Florence, but retired and still;
With iron gates, that opened through long lines
Of sacred ilex and centennial pines,
And terraced gardens, and broad steps of stone,
And sylvan deities, with moss o'ergrown,
And fountains palpitating in the heat,
And all Val d'Arno stretched beneath its feet.
Here in seclusion, as a widow may,
The lovely lady whiled the hours away,
Pacing in sable robes the statued hall,
Herself the stateliest statue among all,
And seeing more and more, with secret joy,
Her husband risen and living in her boy,
Till the lost sense of life returned again,
Not as delight, but as relief from pain.

Meanwhile the boy, rejoicing in his strength,
Stormed down the terraces from length to length;
The screaming peacock chased in hot pursuit,
And climbed the garden trellises for fruit.
But his chief pastime was to watch the flight
Of a gerfalcon, soaring into sight,
Beyond the trees that fringed the garden wall,
Then downward stooping at some distant call;
And as he gazed full often wondered he
Who might the master of the falcon be,
Until that happy morning, when he found
Master and falcon in the cottage ground.

And now a shadow and a terror fell
On the great house, as if a passing bell
Tolled from the tower, and filled each spacious room
With secret awe, and preternatural gloom;
The petted boy grew ill, and day by day
Pined with mysterious malady away.
The mother's heart would not be comforted;
Her darling seemed to her already dead,
And often, sitting by the sufferer's side,
"What can I do to comfort thee?" she cried.
At first the silent lips made no reply,
But, moved at length by her importunate cry,
"Give me," he answered with imploring tone,
"Ser Federigo's falcon for my own!"
No answer could the astonished mother make;
How could she ask, e'en for her darling's sake,
Such favor at a luckless lover's hand,
Well knowing that to ask was to command?
Well knowing, what all falconers confessed,
In all the land that falcon was the best,
The master's pride and passion and delight,
And the sole pursuivant of this poor knight.
But yet, for her child's sake, she could no less
Than give assent, to soothe his restlessness,
So promised, and then promising to keep
Her promise sacred, saw him fall asleep.

The morrow was a bright September morn;
The earth was beautiful as if newborn;
There was that nameless splendor everywhere,
That wild exhilaration in the air,
Which makes the passers in the city street
Congratulate each other as they meet.
Two lovely ladies, clothed in cloak and hood,
Passed through the garden gate into the wood,
Under the lustrous leaves, and through the sheen
Of dewy sunshine showering down between.
The one, close hooded, had the attractive grace
Which sorrow sometimes lends a woman's face;
Her dark eyes moistened with the mists that roll
From the gulf-stream of passion in the soul;
The other with her hood thrown back her hair
Making a golden glory in the air,
Her cheeks suffused with an auroral blush,
Her young heart singing louder than the thrush.
So walked, that morn, through mingled light and shade,
Each by the other's presence lovelier made,
Monna Giovanna and her bosom friend,
Intent upon their errand and its end.

They found Ser Federigo at his toil,
Like banished Adam, delving in the soil;
And when he looked and these fair women spied,
The garden suddenly was glorified;
His long-lost Eden was restored again,
And the strange river winding through the plain
No longer was the Arno to his eyes,
But the Euphrates watering Paradise!

Monna Giovanna raised her stately head,
And with fair words of salutation said:
"Ser Federigo, we come here as friends,
Hoping in this to make some poor amends
For past unkindness. I who ne'er before
Would even cross the threshold of your door,
I who in happier days such pride maintained,
Refused your banquets, and your gifts disdained,

This morning come, a self-invited guest,
To put your generous nature to the test,
And breakfast with you under your own vine."
To which he answered: "Poor desert of mine,
Not your unkindness call it, for if aught
Is good in me of feeling or of thought,
From you it comes, and this last grace outweighs
All sorrows, all regrets of other days."

And after further compliment and talk,
Among the dahlias in the garden walk
He left his guests; and to his cottage turned,
And as he entered for a moment yearned
For the lost splendors of the days of old,
The ruby glass, the silver and the gold,
And felt how piercing is the sting of pride,
By want embittered and intensified.
He looked about him for some means or way
To keep this unexpected holiday;
Searched every cupboard, and then searched again,
Summoned the maid, who came, but came in vain;
"The Signor did not hunt to-day," she said,
"There's nothing in the house but wine and bread."
Then suddenly the drowsy falcon shook
His little bells, with that sagacious look,
Which said, as plain as language to the ear,
"If anything is wanting, I am here!"
Yes, everything is wanting, gallant bird!
The master seized thee without further word,
Like thine own lure, he whirled thee round; ah me!
The pomp and flutter of brave falconry,
The bells, the jesses, the bright scarlet hood,
The flight and the pursuit o'er field and wood,
All these forevermore are ended now;
No longer victor, but the victim thou!

Then on the board a snow-white cloth he spread,
Laid on its wooden dish the loaf of bread,
Brought purple grapes with autumn sunshine hot,
The fragrant peach, the juicy bergamot;

Then in the midst a flask of wine he placed,
And with autumnal flowers the banquet graced.
Ser Federigo, would not these suffice
Without thy falcon stuffed with cloves and spice?

When all was ready, and the courtly dame
With her companion to the cottage came,
Upon Ser Federigo's brain there fell
The wild enchantment of a magic spell;
The room they entered, mean and low and small,
Was changed into a sumptuous banquet-hall,
With fanfares by aerial trumpets blown;
The rustic chair she sat on was a throne;
He ate celestial food, and a divine
Flavor was given to his country wine,
And the poor falcon, fragrant with his spice,
A peacock was, or bird of paradise.
When the repast was ended, they arose
And passed again into the garden-close.
Then said the lady, "Far too well I know,
Remembering still the days of long ago,
Though you betray it not, with what surprise
You see me here in this familiar wise.
You have no children, and you cannot guess
What anguish, what unspeakable distress
A mother feels, whose child is lying ill,
Nor how her heart anticipates his will.
And yet for this, you see me lay aside
All womanly reserve and check of pride,
And ask the thing most precious in your sight,
Your falcon, your sole comfort and delight,
Which if you find it in your heart to give,
My poor, unhappy boy perchance may live."

Ser Federigo listens, and replies,
With tears of love and pity in his eyes:
"Alas, dear lady! there can be no task
So sweet to me, as giving when you ask.
One little hour ago, if I had known
This wish of yours, it would have been my own.

But thinking in what manner I could best
Do honor to the presence of my guest,
I deemed that nothing worthier could be
Than what most dear and precious was to me,
And so my gallant falcon breathed his last
To furnish forth this morning our repast."

In mute contrition, mingled with dismay,
The gentle lady turned her eyes away,
Grieving that he such sacrifice should make,
And kill his falcon for a woman's sake,
Yet feeling in her heart a woman's pride,
That nothing she could ask for was denied;
Then took her leave, and passed out at the gate
With footsteps slow and soul disconsolate.

Three days went by, and lo! a passing-bell
Tolled from the little chapel in the dell;
Ten strokes Ser Federigo heard, and said,
Breathing a prayer, "Alas! her child is dead!"
Three months went by and lo! a merrier chime
Rang from the chapel bells at Christmas time;
The cottage was deserted, and no more
Ser Federigo sat beside its door,
But now, with servitors to do his will,
In the grand villa, half-way up the hill,
Sat at the Christmas feast, and at his side
Monna Giovanna, his belovèd bride,
Never so beautiful, so kind, so fair,
Enthroned once more in the old rustic chair,
High-perched upon the back of which there stood
The image of a falcon carved in wood,
And underneath the inscription, with a date,
"All things come round to him who will but wait."

INTERLUDE

Soon as the story reached its end,
One, over eager to commend,
Crowned it with injudicious praise;
And then the voice of blame found vent,

And fanned the embers of dissent
Into a somewhat lively blaze.

The Theologian shook his head;
"These old Italian tales," he said,
"From the much-praised Decameron down
Through all the rabble of the rest,
Are either trifling, dull, or lewd;
The gossip of a neighborhood
In some remote provincial town,
A scandalous chronicle at best!
They seem to me a stagnant fen,
Grown rank with rushes and with reeds.
Where a white lily, now and then,
Blooms in the midst of noxious weeds
And deadly nightshade on its banks."

To this the Student straight replied,
"For the white lily, many thanks!
One should not say, with too much pride,
Fountain, I will not drink of thee!
Nor were it grateful to forget,
That from these reservoirs and tanks
Even imperial Shakespeare drew
His Moor of Venice and the Jew
And Romeo and Juliet,
And many a famous comedy."

Then a long pause; till some one said,
"An Angel is flying overhead!"
At these words spake the Spanish Jew,
And murmured with an inward breath:
"God grant, if what you say is true
It may not be the Angel of Death!"

And then another pause; and then,
Stroking his beard, he said again:
"This brings back to my memory
A story in the Talmud told,
That book of gems, that book of gold,

Of wonders many and manifold,
A tale that often comes to me,
And fills my heart, and haunts my brain,
And never wearies nor grows old."

The Spanish Jew's Tale

THE LEGEND OF RABBI BEN LEVI

Rabbi Ben Levi, on the Sabbath, read
A volume of the Law, in which it said,
"No man shall look upon my face and live."
And as he read, he prayed that God would give
His faithful servant grace with mortal eye
To look upon His face and yet not die.

Then fell a sudden shadow on the page
And, lifting up his eyes, grown dim with age,
He saw the Angel of Death before him stand,
Holding a naked sword in his right hand.
Rabbi Ben Levi was a righteous man,
Yet through his veins a chill of terror ran.

With trembling voice he said, "What wilt thou here?"
The angel answered, "Lo! the time draws near
When thou must die; yet first, by God's decree,
Whate'er thou askest shall be granted thee."
Replied the Rabbi, "Let these living eyes
First look upon my place in Paradise."

Then said the Angel, "Come with me and look."
Rabbi Ben Levi closed the sacred book,
And rising, and uplifting his gray head,
"Give me thy sword," he to the Angel said,
"Lest thou shouldst fall upon me by the way."
The Angel smiled and hastened to obey,
Then led him forth to the Celestial Town,
And set him on the wall, whence, gazing down,
Rabbi Ben Levi, with his living eyes,
Might look upon his place in Paradise.

Then straight into the city of the Lord
The Rabbi leaped with the Death-Angel's sword,
And through the streets swept a sudden breath
Of something there unknown, which men call death.
Meanwhile the Angel stayed without, and cried,
"Come back!" To which the Rabbi's voice replied,
"No! in the name of God, whom I adore,
I swear that hence I will depart no more!"

Then all the Angels cried, "O Holy One,
See what the son of Levi here has done!
The kingdom of Heaven he takes by violence,
And in Thy name refuses to go hence!"
The Lord replied, "My Angels, be not wroth;
Did e'er the son of Levi break his oath?
Let him remain; for he with mortal eye
Shall look upon my face and yet not die."

Beyond the outer wall the Angel of Death
Heard the great voice, and said, with panting breath,
"Give back the sword, and let me go my way."
Whereat the Rabbi paused, and answered, "Nay!
Anguish enough already has it caused
Among the sons of men." And while he paused
He heard the awful mandate of the Lord
Resounding through the air, "Give back the sword!"

The Rabbi bowed his head in silent prayer;
Then said he to the dreadful Angel, "Swear,
No human eye shall look on it again;
But when thou takest away the souls of men,
Thyself unseen, and with an unseen sword,
Thou wilt perform the bidding of the Lord."

The Angel took the sword again, and swore,
And walks on earth unseen forevermore.

INTERLUDE

He ended: and a kind of spell
Upon the silent listeners fell.

His solemn manner and his words
Had touched the deep, mysterious chords,
That vibrate in each human breast
Alike, but not alike confessed.
The spiritual world seemed near;
And close above them, full of fear,
Its awful adumbration passed,
A luminous shadow, vague and vast,
They almost feared to look, lest there,
Embodied from the impalpable air
They might behold the Angel stand,
Holding the sword in his right hand.
At last, but in a voice subdued,
Not to disturb their dreamy mood,
Said the Sicilian: "While you spoke,
Telling your legend marvellous,
Suddenly in my memory woke
The thought of one, now gone from us,—
An old Abate, meek and mild,
My friend and teacher, when a child,
Who sometimes in those days of old
The legend of an Angel told,
Which ran, if I remember, thus."

THE SICILIAN'S TALE

KING ROBERT OF SICILY

Robert of Sicily, brother of Pope Urbane
And Valmond, Emperor of Allemaine,
Apparelled in magnificent attire,
With retinue of many a knight and squire,
On St. John's eve, at vespers, proudly sat
And heard the priests chant the Magnificat.
And as he listened, o'er and o'er again
Repeated, like a burden or refrain,
He caught the words, *"Deposuit potentes
De sede, et exaltavit humiles"*;
And slowly lifting up his kingly head
He to a learned clerk beside him said,

"What mean these words?" The clerk made answer
    meet,
"He has put down the mighty from their seat,
And has exalted them of low degree."
Thereat King Robert muttered scornfully,
" 'Tis well that such seditious words are sung
Only by priests and in the Latin tongue;
For unto priests and people be it known,
There is no power can push me from my throne!"
And leaning back, he yawned and fell asleep,
Lulled by the chant monotonous and deep.
When he awoke, it was already night;
The church was empty, and there was no light,
Save where the lamps, that glimmered few and faint,
Lighted a little space before some saint.
He started from his seat and gazed around,
But saw no living thing and heard no sound.
He groped towards the door, but it was locked;
He cried aloud, and listened, and then knocked.
And uttered awful threatenings and complaints,
And imprecations upon men and saints.
The sounds re-echoed from the roof and walls
As if dead priests were laughing in their stalls!

At length the sexton, hearing from without
The tumult of the knocking and the shout,
And thinking thieves were in the house of prayer,
Came with his lantern, asking, "Who is there?"
Half choked with rage, King Robert fiercely said,
"Open: 't is I, the King! Art thou afraid?"
The frightened sexton, muttering, with a curse,
"This is some drunken vagabond, or worse!"
Turned the great key and flung the portal wide;
A man rushed by him at a single stride,
Haggard, half naked, without hat or cloak,
Who neither turned, nor looked at him, nor spoke,
But leaped into the blackness of the night,
And vanished like a spectre from his sight.
Robert of Sicily, brother of Pope Urbane
And Valmond, Emperor of Allemaine,

Despoiled of his magnificent attire,
Bare-headed, breathless, and besprent with mire,
With sense of wrong and outrage desperate,
Strode on and thundered at the palace gate;
Rushed through the court-yard, thrusting in his rage
To right and left each seneschal and page,
And hurried up the broad and sounding stair,
His white face ghastly in the torches' glare.
From hall to hall he passed with breathless speed;
Voices and cries he heard, but did not heed,
Until at last he reached the banquet-room,
Blazing with light, and breathing with perfume.

There on the dais sat another king,
Wearing his robes, his crown, his signet-ring,
King Robert's self in features, form, and height,
But all transfigured with angelic light!
It was an Angel; and his presence there
With a divine effulgence filled the air,
An exultation, piercing the disguise,
Though none the hidden Angel recognize.

A moment speechless, motionless, amazed,
The throneless monarch on the Angel gazed,
Who met his looks of anger and surprise
With the divine compassion of his eyes;
Then said, "Who art thou? and why com'st thou here?"
To which King Robert answered, with a sneer,
"I am the King, and come to claim my own
From an impostor, who usurps my throne!"
And suddenly, at these audacious words,
Up sprang the angry guests, and drew their swords;
The Angel answered, with unruffled brow,
"Nay, not the King, but the King's Jester, thou
Henceforth shalt wear the bells and scalloped cape,
And for thy counsellor shalt lead an ape;
Thou shalt obey my servants when they call,
And wait upon my henchmen in the hall!"

Deaf to King Robert's threats and cries and prayers,
They thrust him from the hall and down the stairs;

A group of tittering pages ran before,
And as they opened wide the folding-door,
His heart failed, for he heard, with strange alarms,
The boisterous laughter of the men-at-arms,
And all the vaulted chamber roar and ring
With the mock plaudits of "Long live the King!"
Next morning, waking with the day's first beam,
He said within himself, "It was a dream!"
But the straw rustled as he turned his head,
There were the cap and bells beside his bed,
Around him rose the bare, discolored walls,
Close by, the steeds were champing in their stalls,
And in the corner, a revolting shape,
Shivering and chattering sat the wretched ape.
It was no dream; the world he loved so much
Had turned to dust and ashes at his touch!

Days came and went; and now returned again
To Sicily the old Saturnian reign;
Under the Angel's governance benign
The happy island danced with corn and wine,
And deep within the mountain's burning breast
Enceladus, the giant, was at rest.
Meanwhile King Robert yielded to his fate,
Sullen and silent and disconsolate.
Dressed in the motley garb that Jesters wear,
With looks bewildered and a vacant stare,
Close shaven above the ears, as monks are shorn,
By courtiers mocked, by pages laughed to scorn,
His only friend the ape, his only food
What others left,—he still was unsubdued.
And when the Angel met him on his way,
And half in earnest, half in jest, would say,
Sternly, though tenderly, that he might feel
The velvet scabbard held a sword of steel,
"Art thou the King?" the passion of his woe
Burst from him in resistless overflow,
And, lifting high his forehead, he would fling
The haughty answer back, "I am, I am the King!"

Almost three years were ended; when there came
Ambassadors of great repute and name
From Valmond, Emperor of Allemaine,
Unto King Robert, saying that Pope Urbane
By letter summoned them forthwith to come
On Holy Thursday to his city of Rome.
The Angel with great joy received his guests,
And gave them presents of embroidered vests,
And velvet mantles with rich ermine lined,
And rings and jewels of the rarest kind.
Then he departed with them o'er the sea
Into the lovely land of Italy,
Whose loveliness was more resplendent made
By the mere passing of that cavalcade,
With plumes, and cloaks, and housings, and the stir
Of jewelled bridle and of golden spur.

And lo! among the menials, in mock state,
Upon a piebald steed, with shambling gait,
His cloak of fox-tails flapping in the wind,
The solemn ape demurely perched behind,
King Robert rode, making huge merriment
In all the country towns through which they went.

The Pope received them with great pomp, and blare
Of bannered trumpets, on Saint Peter's square,
Giving his benediction and embrace,
Fervent, and full of apostolic grace.
While with congratulations and with prayers
He entertained the Angel unawares,
Robert, the Jester, bursting through the crowd,
Into their presence rushed, and cried aloud,
"I am the King! Look, and behold in me
Robert, your brother, King of Sicily!
This man, who wears my semblance to your eyes,
Is an impostor in a king's disguise.
Do you not know me? does no voice within
Answer my cry, and say we are akin?"
The Pope in silence, but with troubled mien,
Gazed at the Angel's countenance serene;

The Emperor, laughing, said, "It is strange sport
To keep a madman for thy Fool at court!"
And the poor, baffled Jester in disgrace
Was hustled back among the populace.

In solemn state the Holy Week went by,
And Easter Sunday gleamed upon the sky;
The presence of the Angel, with its light,
Before the sun rose, made the city bright,
And with new fervor filled the hearts of men,
Who felt that Christ indeed had risen again.
Even the Jester, on his bed of straw,
With haggard eyes the unwonted splendor saw,
He felt within a power unfelt before,
And, kneeling humbly on his chamber floor,
He heard the rushing garments of the Lord
Sweep through the silent air, ascending heavenward

And now the visit ending, and once more
Valmond returning to the Danube's shore,
Homeward the Angel journeyed, and again
The land was made resplendent with his train,
Flashing along the towns of Italy
Unto Salerno, and from there by sea.
And when once more within Palermo's wall,
And, seated on the throne in his great hall,
He heard the Angelus from convent towers,
As if the better world conversed with ours,
He beckoned to King Robert to draw nigher,
And with a gesture bade the rest retire;
And when they were alone, the Angel said,
"Art thou the King?" Then bowing down his head
King Robert crossed both hands upon his breast,
And meekly answered him: "Thou knowest best!
My sins as scarlet are; let me go hence,
And in some cloister's school of penitence,
Across those stones, that pave the way to heaven,
Walk barefoot, till my guilty soul is shriven!"
The Angel smiled, and from his radiant face
A holy light illumined all the place,

And through the open window, loud and clear,
They heard the monks chant in the chapel near,
Above the stir and tumult of the street:
"He has put down the mighty from their seat,
And has exalted them of low degree!"
And through the chant a second melody
Rose like the throbbing of a single string:
"I am an Angel, and thou art the King!"

King Robert, who was standing near the throne,
Lifted his eyes, and lo! he was alone!
But all apparelled as in days of old,
With ermined mantle and with cloth of gold;
And when his courtiers came, they found him there
Kneeling upon the floor, absorbed in silent prayer.

INTERLUDE

And then the blue-eyed Norseman told
A Saga of the days of old.
"There is," said he, "a wondrous book
Of Legends in the old Norse tongue,
Of the dead kings of Norroway,—
Legends that once were told or sung
In many a smoky fireside nook
Of Iceland, in the ancient day,
By wandering Saga-man or Scald;
Heimskringla is the volume called;
And he who looks may find therein
The story that I now begin."

And in each pause the story made
Upon his violin he played,
As an appropriate interlude,
Fragments of old Norwegian tunes
That bound in one the separate runes,
And held the mind in perfect mood,
Entwining and encircling all
The strange and antiquated rhymes
With melodies of olden times;

As over some half-ruined wall,
Disjointed and about to fall,
Fresh woodbines climb and interlace,
And keep the loosened stones in place.

THE MUSICIAN'S TALE

THE SAGA OF KING OLAF

I

The Challenge of Thor

I am the God Thor,
I am the War God,
I am the Thunderer!
Here in my Northland,
My fastness and fortress,
Reign I forever!

Here amid icebergs
Rule I the nations;
This is my hammer,
Miölner the mighty;
Giants and sorcerers
Cannot withstand it!

These are the gauntlets
Wherewith I wield it,
And hurl it afar off;
This is my girdle;
Whenever I brace it,
Strength is redoubled!

The light thou beholdest
Stream through the heavens,
In flashes of crimson,
Is but my red beard
Blown by the night-wind,
Affrighting the nations!

Jove is my brother;
Mine eyes are the lightning;
The wheels of my chariot
Roll in the thunder,
The blows of my hammer
Ring in the earthquake!

Force rules the world still,
Has ruled it, shall rule it;
Meekness is weakness,
Strength is triumphant,
Over the whole earth
Still is it Thor's-Day!

Thou art a God too,
O Galilean!
And thus singled-handed
Unto the combat,
Gauntlet or Gospel,
Here I defy thee!

II

King Olaf's Return

And King Olaf heard the cry,
Saw the red light in the sky,
    Laid his hand upon his sword,
As he leaned upon the railing,
And his ships went sailing, sailing
    Northward into Drontheim fiord.

There he stood as one who dreamed;
And the red light glanced and gleamed
    On the armor that he wore;
And he shouted, as the rifted
Streamers o'er him shook and shifted,
    "I accept thy challenge, Thor!"

To avenge his father slain,
And reconquer realm and reign,
    Came the youthful Olaf home,

Through the midnight sailing, sailing,
Listening to the wild wind's wailing,
   And the dashing of the foam.

To his thoughts the sacred name
Of his mother Astrid came,
   And the tale she oft had told
Of her flight by secret passes
Through the mountains and morasses,
   To the home of Hakon old.

Then strange memories crowded back
Of Queen Gunhild's wrath and wrack,
   And a hurried flight by sea;
Of grim Vikings, and their rapture
In the sea-fight, and the capture,
   And the life of slavery.

How a stranger watched his face
In the Esthonian market-place,
   Scanned his features one by one,
Saying, "We should know each other;
I am Sigurd, Astrid's brother,
   Thou art Olaf, Astrid's son!"

Then as Queen Allogia's page,
Old in honors, young in age,
   Chief of all her men-at-arms;
Till vague whispers, and mysterious,
Reached King Valdemar, the imperious,
   Filling him with strange alarms.

Then his cruisings o'er the seas,
Westward to the Hebrides,
   And to Scilly's rocky shore;
And the hermit's cavern dismal,
Christ's great name and rites baptismal,
   In the ocean's rush and roar.

All these thoughts of love and strife
Glimmered through his lurid life,
   As the star's intenser light.

Through the red flames o'er him trailing,
As his ships went sailing, sailing,
   Northward in the summer night.

Trained for either camp or court,
Skilful in each manly sport,
   Young and beautiful and tall;
Art of warfare, craft of chases,
Swimming, skating, snow-shoe races,
   Excellent alike in all.

When at sea, with all his rowers
He along the bending oars
   Outside of his ship could run.
He the Smalsor Horn ascended,
And the shining shield suspended
   On its summit, like a sun.

On the ship-rails he could stand,
Wield his sword with either hand,
   And at once two javelins throw;
At all feasts where ale was strongest,
Sat the merry monarch longest,
   First to come and last to go.

Norway never yet had seen
One so beautiful of mien,
   One so royal in attire,
When in arms completely furnished;
Harness gold-inlaid and burnished,
   Mantle like a flame of fire.

Thus came Olaf to his own,
When upon the night-wind blown
   Passed that cry along the shore;
And he answered, while the rifted
Streamers o'er him shook and shifted,
   "I accept thy challenge, Thor!"

III

Thora of Rimol

"Thora of Rimol! hide me! hide me!
Danger and shame and death betide me!
For Olaf the King is hunting me down
Through field and forest, through thorp and town!"
    Thus cried Jarl Hakon
    To Thora, the fairest of women.

"Hakon Jarl! for the love I bear thee
Neither shall shame nor death come near thee!
But the hiding-place wherein thou must lie
Is the cave underneath the swine in the sty."
    Thus to Jarl Hakon
    Said Thora, the fairest of women.

So Hakon Jarl and his base thrall Karker
Crouched in the cave, than a dungeon darker,
As Olaf came riding, with men in mail,
Through the forest roads into Orkadale,
    Demanding Jarl Hakon
    Of Thora, the fairest of women.

"Rich and honored shall be whoever
The head of Hakon Jarl shall dissever!"
Hakon heard him, and Karker the slave,
Through the breathing-holes of the darksome cave.
    Alone in her chamber
    Wept Thora, the fairest of women.

Said Karker, the crafty, "I will not slay thee!
For all the king's gold I will never betray thee!"
"Then why dost thou turn so pale, O churl,
And then again black as the earth?" said the Earl.
    More pale and more faithful
    Was Thora, the fairest of women.

From a dream in the night the thrall started, saying,
"Round my neck a gold ring King Olaf was laying!"

And Hakon answered, "Beware of the king!
He will lay round thy neck a blood-red ring."
    At the ring on her finger
    Gazed Thora, the fairest of women.

At daybreak slept Hakon with sorrows encumbered,
But screamed and drew up his feet as he slumbered;
The thrall in the darkness plunged with his knife,
And the Earl awakened no more in this life.
    But wakeful and weeping
    Sat Thora, the fairest of women.

At Nidarholm the priests are all singing,
Two ghastly heads on the gibbet are swinging;
One is Jarl Hakon's and one is his thrall's,
And the people are shouting from windows and walls;
    While alone in her chamber
    Swoons Thora, the fairest of women.

IV

Queen Sigrid the Haughty

Queen Sigrid the Haughty sat proud and aloft
In her chamber, that looked over meadow and croft.
    Heart's dearest,
    Why dost thou sorrow so?

The floor with tassels of fir was besprent,
Filling the room with their fragrant scent.

She heard the birds sing, she saw the sun shine,
The air of summer was sweeter than wine.

Like a sword without scabbard the bright river lay
Between her own kingdom and Norroway.

But Olaf the King had sued for her hand,
The sword would be sheathed, the river be spanned.

Her maidens were seated around her knee,
Working bright figures in tapestry.

And one was singing the ancient rune
Of Brynhilda's love and the wrath of Gudrun.

And through it, and round it, and over it all
Sounded incessant the waterfall.

The Queen in her hand held a ring of gold,
From the door of Ladé's Temple old.

King Olaf had sent her this wedding gift,
But her thoughts as arrows were keen and swift.

She had given the ring to her goldsmiths twain,
Who smiled, as they handed it back again.

And Sigrid the Queen, in her haughty way,
Said, "Why do you smile, my goldsmiths, say?"

And they answered: "O Queen! if the truth must be told,
The ring is of copper, and not of gold!"

The lightning flashed o'er her forehead and cheek,
She only murmured, she did not speak:

"If in his gifts he can faithless be,
There will be no gold in his love to me."

A footstep was heard on the outer stair,
And in strode King Olaf with royal air.

He kissed the Queen's hand, and he whispered of love,
And swore to be true as the stars are above.

But she smiled with contempt as she answered: "O King,
Will you swear it, as Odin once swore, on the ring?"

And the King: "O speak not of Odin to me,
The wife of King Olaf a Christian must be."

Looking straight at the King, with her level brows,
She said, "I keep true to my faith and my vows."

Then the face of King Olaf was darkened with gloom,
He rose in his anger and strode through the room.

"Why, then, should I care to have thee?" he said,—
"A faded old woman, a heathenish jade!"

His zeal was stronger than fear or love,
And he struck the Queen in the face with his glove.

Then forth from the chamber in anger he fled,
And the wooden stairway shook with his tread.

Queen Sigrid the Haughty said under her breath,
"This insult, King Olaf, shall be thy death!"
        Heart's dearest,
        Why dost thou sorrow so?

V

The Skerry of Shrieks

Now from all King Olaf's farms
            His men-at-arms
Gathered on the Eve of Easter;
To his house at Angvalds-ness
            Fast they press,
Drinking with the royal feaster.

Loudly through the wide-flung door
            Came the roar
Of the sea upon the Skerry;
And its thunder loud and near
            Reached the ear,
Mingling with their voices merry.

"Hark!" said Olaf to his Scald,
            Halfred the Bald,
"Listen to that song, and learn it!
Half my kingdom would I give,
            As I live,
If by such songs you would earn it!

"For of all the runes and rhymes
            Of all times,
Best I like the ocean's dirges,

When the old harper heaves and rocks,
       His hoary locks
Flowing and flashing in the surges!"

Halfred answered: "I am called
       The Unappalled!
Nothing hinders me or daunts me.
Hearken to me, then, O King,
       While I sing
The great Ocean Song that haunts me."

"I will hear your song sublime
       Some other time,"
Says the drowsy monarch, yawning,
And retires; each laughing guest
       Applauds the jest;
Then they sleep till day is dawning.

Pacing up and down the yard,
       King Olaf's guard
Saw the sea-mist slowly creeping
O'er the sands, and up the hill,
       Gathering still
Round the house where they were sleeping.

It was not the fog he saw
       Nor misty flaw,
That above the landscape brooded:
It was Eyvind Kallda's crew
       Of warlocks blue,
With their caps of darkness hooded!

Round and round the house they go,
       Weaving slow
Magic circles to encumber
And imprison in their ring
       Olaf the King,
As he helpless lies in slumber.

Then athwart the vapors dun
       The Easter sun
Streamed with one broad track of splendor!

In their real forms appeared
    The warlocks weird,
Awful as the witch of Endor.

Blinded by the light that glared,
    They groped and stared
Round about with steps unsteady;
From his window Olaf gazed,
    And, amazed,
"Who are these strange people?" said **he**.

"Eyvind Kallda and his men!"
    Answered then
From the yard a sturdy farmer;
While the men-at-arms apace
    Filled the place,
Busily buckling on their armor.

From the gates they sallied forth,
    South and north,
Scoured the island coast around them,
Seizing all the warlock band,
    Foot and hand
On the Skerry's rocks they bound them.

And at eve the king again
    Called his train,
And, with all the candles burning,
Silent sat and heard once more
    The sullen roar
Of the ocean tides returning.

Shrieks and cries of wild despair
    Filled the air,
Growing fainter as they listened.
Then the bursting surge alone
    Sounded on;—
Thus the sorcerers were christened!

"Sing, O Scald, your song sublime,
    Your ocean-rhyme,"
Cried King Olaf: "it will cheer me!"

Said the Scald, with pallid cheeks,
        "The Skerry of Shrieks
Sings too loud for you to hear me!"

VI

The Wraith of Odin

The guests were loud, the ale was strong,
King Olaf feasted late and long;
The hoary Scalds together sang;
O'erhead the smoky rafters rang.
        Dead rides Sir Morten of Fogelsang.

The door swung wide, with creak and din;
A blast of cold night-air came in,
And on the threshold shivering stood
A one-eyed guest, with cloak and hood.
        Dead rides Sir Morten of Fogelsang.

The King exclaimed, "O graybeard pale!
Come warm thee with this cup of ale."
The foaming draught the old man quaffed,
The noisy guests looked on and laughed.
        Dead rides Sir Morten of Fogelsang.

Then spake the King: "Be not afraid;
Sit here by me." The guest obeyed,
And, seated at the table, told
Tales of the sea, and Sagas old.
        Dead rides Sir Morten of Fogelsang.

And ever, when the tale was o'er,
The King demanded yet one more;
Till Sigurd the Bishop smiling said,
" 'Tis late, O King, and time for bed."
        Dead rides Sir Morten of Fogelsang.

The King retired; the stranger guest
Followed and entered with the rest.
The lights were out, the pages gone,
But still the garrulous guest spake on.
        Dead rides Sir Morten of Fogelsang.

As one who from a volume reads,
He spake of heroes and their deeds,
Of lands and cities he had seen,
And stormy gulfs that tossed between.
     Dead rides Sir Morten of Fogelsang.

Then from his lips in music rolled
The Havamal of Odin old,
With sounds mysterious as the roar
Of billows on a distant shore.
     Dead rides Sir Morten of Fogelsang.

"Do we not learn from runes and rhymes
Made by the gods in elder times,
And do not still the great Scalds teach
That silence better is than speech?"
     Dead rides Sir Morten of Fogelsang.

Smiling at this, the King replied,
"Thy lore is by thy tongue belied,
For never was I so enthralled
Either by Saga-man or Scald."
     Dead rides Sir Morten of Fogelsang.

The Bishop said, "Late hours we keep!
Night wanes, O King! 'tis time for sleep!"
Then slept the King, and when he woke
The guest was gone, the morning broke.
     Dead rides Sir Morten of Fogelsang.

They found the doors securely barred,
They found the watch-dog in the yard,
There was no footprint in the grass,
And none had seen the stranger pass.
     Dead rides Sir Morten of Fogelsang.

King Olaf crossed himself and said:
"I know that Odin the Great is dead;
Sure is the triumph of our Faith,
The one-eyed stranger was his wraith."
     Dead rides Sir Morten of Fogelsang.

VII

Iron-Beard

Olaf the King, one summer morn,
Blew a blast on his bugle-horn,
Sending his signal through the land of Drontheim.

And to the Hus-Ting held at Mere
Gathered the farmers far and near,
With their war weapons ready to confront him.

Ploughing under the morning star,
Old Iron-Beard in Yriar
Heard the summons, chuckling with a low laugh.

He wiped the sweat-drops from his brow,
Unharnessed his horses from the plough,
And clattering came on horseback to King Olaf.

He was the churliest of the churls;
Little he cared for king or earls;
Bitter as home-brewed ale were his foaming passions.

Hodden-gray was the garb he wore,
And by the Hammer of Thor he swore;
He hated the narrow town, and all its fashions.

But he loved the freedom of his farm,
His ale at night by the fireside warm,
Gudrun his daughter, with her flaxen tresses.

He loved his horses and his herds,
The smell of the earth, and the song of birds,
His well-filled barns, his brook with its water-cresses.

Huge and cumbersome was his frame;
His beard, from which he took his name,
Frosty and fierce, like that of Hymer the Giant.

So at the Hus-Ting he appeared,
The farmer of Yriar, Iron-Beard,
On horseback, with an attitude defiant.

And to King Olaf he cried aloud,
Out of the middle of the crowd,
That tossed about him like a stormy ocean:

"Such sacrifices shalt thou bring
To Odin and to Thor, O King,
As other kings have done in their devotion!"

King Olaf answered: "I command
This land to be a Christian land,
Here is my Bishop who the folk baptizes!

"But if you ask me to restore
Your sacrifices, stained with gore,
Then will I offer human sacrifices!

"Not slaves and peasants shall they be,
But men of note and high degree,
Such men as Orm of Lyra and Kar of Gryting!"

Then to their Temple strode he in,
And loud behind him heard the din
Of his men-at-arms and the peasants fiercely fighting.

There in the Temple, carved in wood,
The image of great Odin stood,
And other gods, with Thor supreme among them.

King Olaf smote them with the blade
Of his huge war-axe, gold inlaid,
And downward shattered to the pavement flung them.

At the same moment rose without,
From the contending crowd, a shout,
A mingled sound of triumph and of wailing.

And there upon the trampled plain
The farmer Iron-Beard lay slain,
Midway between the assailed and the assailing.

King Olaf from the doorway spoke:
"Choose ye between two things, my folk,
To be baptized or given up to slaughter!"

And seeing their leader stark and dead,
The people with a murmur said,
"O King, baptize us with thy holy water!"

So all the Drontheim land became
A Christian land in name and fame,
In the old gods no more believing and trusting.

And as a blood-atonement, soon
King Olaf wed the fair Gudrun;
And thus in peace ended the Drontheim Hus-Ting!

VIII

Gudrun

On King Olaf's bridal night
Shines the moon with tender light,
And across the chamber streams
    Its tide of dreams.

At the fatal midnight hour,
When all evil things have power,
In the glimmer of the moon
    Stands Gudrun.

Close against her heaving breast,
Something in her hand is pressed
Like an icicle, its sheen
    Is cold and keen.

On the cairn are fixed her eyes
Where her murdered father lies,
And a voice remote and drear
    She seems to hear.

What a bridal night is this!
Cold will be the dagger's kiss
Laden with the chill of death
    Is its breath.

Like the drifting snow she sweeps
To the couch where Olaf sleeps,
Suddenly he wakes and stirs,
  His eyes meet hers.

"What is that," King Olaf said,
"Gleams so bright above thy head?
Wherefore standest thou so white
  In pale moonlight?"

" 'Tis the bodkin that I wear
When at night I bind my hair;
It woke me falling on the floor;
  'Tis nothing more."

"Forests have ears, and fields have eyes;
Often treachery lurking lies
Underneath the fairest hair!
  Gudrun, beware!"

Ere the earliest peep of morn
Blew King Olaf's bugle-horn;
And forever sundered ride
  Bridegroom and bride!

IX

Thangbrand the Priest

Short of stature, large of limb,
 Burly face and russet beard,
All the women stared at him,
 When in Iceland he appeared.
  "Look!" they said,
  With nodding head,
"There goes Thangbrand, Olaf's Priest."

All the prayers he knew by rote,
 He could preach like Chrysostome,
From the Fathers he could quote,
 He had even been at Rome.
  A learned clerk,
  A man of mark,
Was this Thangbrand, Olaf's Priest.

He was quarrelsome and loud,
    And impatient of control,
Boisterous in the market crowd,
    Boisterous at the wassail-bowl,
        Everywhere
        Would drink and swear,
Swaggering Thangbrand, Olaf's Priest.

In his house this malcontent
    Could the King no longer bear,
So to Iceland he was sent
    To convert the heathen there,
        And away
        One summer day
Sailed this Thangbrand, Olaf's Priest.

There in Iceland, o'er their books
    Pored the people day and night,
But he did not like their looks,
    Nor the songs they used to write.
        "All this rhyme
        Is waste of time!"
Grumbled Thangbrand, Olaf's Priest.

To the alehouse, where he sat,
    Came the Scalds and Saga men;
Is it to be wondered at,
    That they quarrelled now and then,
        When o'er his beer
        Began to leer
Drunken Thangbrand, Olaf's Priest?

All the folk in Altafiord
    Boasted of their island grand;
Saying in a single word,
    "Iceland is the finest land
        That the sun
        Doth shine upon!"
Loud laughed Thangbrand, Olaf's Priest.

And he answered: "What's the use
  Of this bragging up and down,
When three women and one goose
  Make a market in your town!"
      Every Scald
      Satires scrawled
On poor Thangbrand, Olaf's Priest.

Something worse they did than that!
  And what vexed him most of all
Was a figure in shovel hat,
  Drawn in charcoal on the wall;
      With words that go
      Sprawling below,
"This is Thangbrand, Olaf's Priest."

Hardly knowing what he did,
  Then he smote them might and main,
Thorvald Veile and Veterlid
  Lay there in the alehouse slain.
      "To-day we are gold,
      To-morrow mould!"
Muttered Thangbrand, Olaf's Priest.

Much in fear of axe and rope,
  Back to Norway sailed he then.
"O, King Olaf! little hope
Is there of these Iceland men!"
      Meekly said,
      With bending head,
Pious Thangbrand, Olaf's Priest.

X

Raud the Strong

"All the old gods are dead,
All the wild warlocks fled;
But the White Christ lives and reigns,
And throughout my wide domains

His Gospel shall be spread!"
       On the Evangelists
       Thus swore King Olaf.

But still in dreams of the night
Beheld he the crimson light,
And heard the voice that defied
Him who was crucified,
And challenged him to the fight.
       To Sigurd the Bishop
       King Olaf confessed it.

And Sigurd the Bishop said,
"The old gods are not dead,
For the great Thor still reigns,
And among the Jarls and Thanes
The old witchcraft still is spread."
       Thus to King Olaf
       Said Sigurd the Bishop.

"Far north in the Salten Fiord,
By rapine, fire, and sword,
Lives the Viking, Raud the Strong;
All the Godoe Isles belong
To him and his heathen horde."
       Thus went on speaking
       Sigurd the Bishop.

"A warlock, a wizard is he,
And lord of the wind and the sea;
And whichever way he sails,
He has ever favoring gales,
By his craft in sorcery."
       Here the sign of the cross made
       Devoutly King Olaf.

"With rites that we both abhor,
He worships Odin and Thor;
So it cannot yet be said,
That all the old gods are dead,
And the warlocks are no more,"
       Flushing with anger
       Said Sigurd the Bishop.

Then King Olaf cried aloud:
"I will talk with this mighty Raud,
And along the Salten Fiord
Preach the Gospel with my sword,
Or be brought back in my shroud!"
　　So northward from Drontheim
　　Sailed King Olaf!

XI

Bishop Sigurd at Salten Fiord

Loud the angry wind was wailing
As King Olaf's ships came sailing
Northward out of Drontheim haven
　　To the mouth of Salten Fiord.

Though the flying sea-spray drenches
Fore and aft the rowers' benches,
Not a single heart is craven
　　Of the champions there on board.

All without the Fiord was quiet,
But within it storm and riot,
Such as on his Viking cruises
　　Raud the Strong was wont to ride.

And the sea through all its tide-ways
Swept the reeling vessels sideways,
As the leaves are swept through sluices,
　　When the flood-gates open wide.

" 'Tis the warlock! 'tis the demon
Raud!" cried Sigurd to the seamen;
"But the Lord is not affrighted
　　By the witchcraft of his foes."

To the ship's bow he ascended,
By his choristers attended,
Round him were the tapers lighted,
　　And the sacred incense rose.

On the bow stood Bishop Sigurd,
In his robes, as one transfigured,
And the Crucifix he planted
 High amid the rain and mist.

Then with holy water sprinkled
All the ship; the mass-bells tinkled;
Loud the monks around him chanted,
 Loud he read the Evangelist.

As into the Fiord they darted,
On each side the water parted;
Down a path like silver molten
 Steadily rowed King Olaf's ships;

Steadily burned all night the tapers,
And the White Christ through the vapors
Gleamed across the Fiord of Salten,
 As through John's Apocalypse,—

Till at last they reached Raud's dwelling
On the little isle of Gelling;
Not a guard was at the doorway,
 Not a glimmer of light was seen.

But at anchor, carved and gilded,
Lay the dragon-ship he builded;
'T was the grandest ship in Norway,
 With its crest and scales of green.

Up the stairway, softly creeping,
To the loft where Raud was sleeping,
With their fists they burst asunder
 Bolt and bar that held the door.

Drunken with sleep and ale they found him,
Dragged him from his bed and bound him,
While he stared with stupid wonder,
 At the look and garb they wore.

Then King Olaf said: "O Sea-King!
Little time have we for speaking,
Choose between the good and evil;
 Be baptized, or thou shalt die!"

But in scorn the heathen scoffer
Answered: "I disdain thine offer;
Neither fear I God nor Devil;
    Thee and thy Gospel I defy!"

Then between his jaws distended,
When his frantic struggles ended,
Through King Olaf's horn an adder
    Touched by fire, they forced to glide.

Sharp his tooth was as an arrow,
As he gnawed through bone and marrow;
But without a groan or shudder,
    Raud the Strong blaspheming died.

Then baptized they all that region
Swarthy Lap and fair Norwegian,
Far as swims the salmon, leaping,
    Up the streams of Salten Fiord.

In their temples Thor and Odin
Lay in dust and ashes trodden,
As King Olaf, onward sweeping,
    Preached the Gospel with his sword.

Then he took the carved and gilded
Dragon-ship that Raud had builded,
And the tiller single-handed,
    Grasping, steered into the main.

Southward sailed the sea-gulls o'er him,
Southward sailed the ship that bore him,
Till at Drontheim haven landed
    Olaf and his crew again.

XII

King Olaf's Christmas

At Drontheim, Olaf the King
Heard the bells of Yule-tide ring,
    As he sat in his banquet-hall,
Drinking the nut-brown ale.

With his bearded Berserks hale
    And tall.

Three days his Yule-tide feasts
He held with Bishops and Priests,
    And his horn filled up to the brim;
But the ale was never too strong,
Nor the Saga-man's tale too long,
    For him.

O'er his drinking-horn, the sign
He made of the cross divine,
    As he drank, and muttered his prayers;
But the Berserks evermore
Made the sign of the Hammer of Thor
    Over theirs.

The gleams of the fire-light dance
Upon helmet and hauberk and lance,
    And laugh in the eyes of the King;
And he cries to Halfred the Scald,
Gray-bearded, wrinkled, and bald,
    "Sing!"

"Sing me a song divine,
With a sword in every line,
    And this shall be thy reward."
And he loosened the belt at his waist,
And in front of the singer placed
    His sword.

"Quern-biter of Hakon the Good,
Wherewith at a stroke he hewed
    The millstone through and through,
And Foot-breadth of Thoralf the Strong,
Were neither so broad nor so long,
    Nor so true."

Then the Scald took his harp and sang,
And loud through the music rang
    The sound of that shining word;

And the harp-strings a clangor made,
As if they were struck with the blade
   Of a sword.

And the Berserks round about
Broke forth into a shout
   That made the rafters ring:
They smote with their fists on the board,
And shouted, "Long live the Sword,
   And the King!"

But the King said, "O my son,
I miss the bright word in one
   Of thy measures and thy rhymes."
And Halfred the Scald replied,
"In another 't was multiplied,
   Three times."

Then King Olaf raised the hilt
Of iron, cross-shaped and gilt,
   And said, "Do not refuse;
Count well the gain and the loss,
Thor's hammer or Christ's cross:
   Choose!"

And Halfred the Scald said, "This
In the name of the Lord I kiss,
   Who on it was crucified!"
And a shout went round the board,
"In the name of Christ the Lord,
   Who died!"

Then over the waste of snows
The noonday sun uprose,
   Through the driving mists revealed,
Like the lifting of the Host,
By incense-clouds almost
   Concealed.

On the shining wall a vast
And shadowy cross was cast
   From the hilt of the lifted sword,

And in foaming cups of ale
    The Berserks drank "Was-hael!
      To the Lord!"

XIII

The Building of the Long Serpent

Thorberg Skafting, master-builder,
    In his ship-yard by the sea,
Whistled, saying: " 'Twould bewilder
Any man but Thorberg Skafting,
    Any man but me!"

Near him lay the Dragon stranded,
    Built of old by Raud the Strong,
And King Olaf had commanded
He should build another Dragon,
    Twice as large and long.

Therefore whistled Thorberg Skafting,
    As he sat with half-closed eyes,
And his head turned sideways, drafting
That new vessel for King Olaf
    Twice the Dragon's size.

Round him busily hewed and hammered
    Mallet huge and heavy axe;
Workmen laughed and sang and clamored;
Whirred the wheels, that into rigging
    Spun the shining flax!

All this tumult heard the master,—
    It was music to his ear;
Fancy whispered all the faster,
"Men shall hear of Thorberg Skafting
    For a hundred year!"

Workmen sweating at the forges
    Fashioned iron bolt and bar,
Like a warlock's midnight orgies
Smoked and bubbled the black caldron
    With the boiling tar.

Did the warlocks mingle in it,
    Thorberg Skafting, any curse?
Could you not be gone a minute
But some mischief must be doing,
    Turning bad to worse?

'T was an ill wind that came wafting,
    From his homestead words of woe;
To his farm went Thorberg Skafting,
Oft repeating to his workmen,
    Build ye thus and so.

After long delays returning
    Came the master back by night
To his ship-yard longing, yearning,
Hurried he, and did not leave it
    Till the morning's light.

"Come and see my ship, my darling!"
    On the morrow said the King;
"Finished now from keel to carling
Never yet was seen in Norway
    Such a wondrous thing!"

In the ship-yard, idly talking,
    At the ship the workmen stared;
Some one, all their labor balking,
Down her sides had cut deep gashes,
    Not a plank was spared!

"Death be to the evil-doer!"
    With an oath King Olaf spoke;
"But rewards to his pursuer!"
And with wrath his face grew redder
    Than his scarlet cloak.

Straight the master-builder, smiling,
    Answered thus the angry King;
"Cease blaspheming and reviling,
Olaf, it was Thorberg Skafting
    Who has done this thing!"

Then he chipped and smoothed the planking,
    Till the King, delighted, swore,
With much lauding and much thanking,
"Handsomer is now my Dragon
    Than she was before!"

Seventy ells and four extended
    On the grass the vessel's keel;
High above it, gilt and splendid,
Rose the figure-head ferocious
    With its crest of steel.

Then they launched her from the tressels,
    In the ship-yard by the sea;
She was the grandest of all vessels,
Never ship was built in Norway
    Half so fine as she!

The Long Serpent was she christened,
    'Mid the roar of cheer on cheer!
They who to the Saga listened
Heard the name of Thorberg Skafting
    For a hundred year!

XIV

The Crew of the Long Serpent

Safe at anchor in Drontheim bay
King Olaf's fleet assembled lay,
    And, striped with white and blue,
Downward fluttered sail and banner,
As alights the screaming lanner;
Lustily cheered, in their wild manner,
    The Long Serpent's crew.

Her forecastle man was Ulf the Red;
Like a wolf's was his shaggy head,
    His teeth as large and white;
His beard, of gray and russet blended,
Round as a swallow's nest descended;
As standard-bearer he defended
    Olaf's flag in the fight.

Near him Kolbiorn had his place,
Like the King in garb and face,
   So gallant and so hale;
Every cabin-boy and varlet
Wondered at his cloak of scarlet;
Like a river, frozen and star-lit,
   Gleamed his coat of mail.

By the bulkhead, tall and dark,
Stood Thrand Rame of Thelemark,
   A figure gaunt and grand;
On his hairy arm imprinted
Was an anchor, azure-tinted;
Like Thor's hammer, huge and dinted
   Was his brawny hand.

Einar Tamberskelver, bare
To the winds his golden hair,
   By the mainmast stood;
Graceful was his form, and slender,
And his eyes were deep and tender
As a woman's, in the splendor
   Of her maidenhood.

In the fore hold Biorn and Bork
Watched the sailors at their work:
   Heavens! how they swore!
Thirty men they each commanded,
Iron-sinewed, horny-handed,
Shoulders broad, and chests expanded,
   Tugging at the oar.

These, and many more like these,
With King Olaf sailed the seas,
   Till the waters vast
Filled them with a vague devotion,
With the freedom and the motion,
With the roll and roar of ocean
   And the sounding blast.

When they landed from the fleet,
How they roared through Drontheim's street,
  Boisterous as the gale!
How they laughed and stamped and pounded,
Till the tavern roof resounded,
And the host looked on astounded
  As they drank the ale!

Never saw the wild North Sea
Such a gallant company
  Sail its billows blue!
Never, while they cruised and quarrelled,
Old King Gorm, or Blue-Tooth Harald,
Owned a ship so well apparelled,
  Boasted such a crew!

XV

A Little Bird in the Air

A little bird in the air
Is singing of Thyri the fair,
  The sister of Svend the Dane;
And the song of the garrulous bird
In the streets of the town is heard,
  And repeated again and again.
    Hoist up your sails of silk,
      And flee away from each other.

To King Burislaf, it is said,
Was the beautiful Thyri wed,
  And a sorrowful bride went she;
And after a week and a day,
She has fled away and away,
  From his town by the stormy sea.
    Hoist up your sails of silk,
      And flee away from each other.

They say, that through heat and through cold,
Through weald, they say, and through wold,
  By day and by night, they say,

She has fled; and the gossips report
She has come to King Olaf's court,
   And the town is all in dismay.
     Hoist up your sails of silk,
     And flee away from each other.

It is whispered King Olaf has seen,
Has talked with the beautiful Queen;
   And they wonder how it will end;
For surely, if here she remain,
It is war with King Svend the Dane,
   And King Burislaf the Vend!
     Hoist up your sails of silk,
     And flee away from each other.

O, greatest wonder of all!
It is published in hamlet and hall,
   It roars like a flame that is fanned!
The King—yes, Olaf the King—
Has wedded her with his ring,
   And Thyri is queen in the land!
     Hoist up your sails of silk,
     And flee away from each other.

XVI

Queen Thyri and the Angelica Stalks

Northward over Drontheim,
Flew the clamorous sea-gulls,
Sang the lark and linnet
   From the meadows green;

Weeping in her chamber,
Lonely and unhappy,
Sat the Drottning Thyri,
   Sat King Olaf's Queen.

In at all the windows
Streamed the pleasant sunshine,
On the roof above her
   Softly cooed the dove;

But the sound she heard not,
Nor the sunshine heeded,
For the thoughts of Thyri
   Were not thoughts of love.

Then King Olaf entered,
Beautiful as morning,
Like the sun at Easter
   Shone his happy face;

In his hand he carried
Angelicas uprooted,
With delicious fragrance
   Filling all the place.

Like a rainy midnight
Sat the Drottning Thyri,
Even the smile of Olaf
   Could not cheer her gloom;

Nor the stalks he gave her
With a gracious gesture,
And with words as pleasant
   As their own perfume.

In her hands he placed them,
And her jewelled fingers
Through the green leaves glistened
   Like the dews of morn;

But she cast them from her,
Haughty and indignant,
On the floor she threw them
   With a look of scorn.

"Richer presents," said she,
"Gave King Harald Gormson
To the Queen, my mother,
   Than such worthless weeds;

"When he ravaged Norway,
Laying waste the kingdom,
Seizing scatt and treasure
   For her royal needs.

"But thou darest not venture
Through the Sound to Vendland,
My domains to rescue
    From King Burislaf;

"Lest King Svend of Denmark,
Forked Beard, my brother,
Scatter all thy vessels
    As the wind the chaff."

Then up sprang King Olaf,
Like a reindeer bounding,
With an oath he answered
    Thus the luckless Queen:

"Never yet did Olaf
Fear King Svend of Denmark;
This right hand shall hale him
    By his forked chin!"

Then he left the chamber,
Thundering through the doorway,
Loud his steps resounded
    Down the outer stair.

Smarting with the insult,
Through the streets of Drontheim
Strode he red and wrathful,
    With his stately air.

All his ships he gathered,
Summoned all his forces,
Making his war levy
    In the region round;

Down the coast of Norway,
Like a flock of sea-gulls,
Sailed the fleet of Olaf
    Through the Danish Sound.

With his own hand fearless,
Steered he the Long Serpent,
Strained the creaking cordage,
    Bent each boom and gaff;

Till in Vendland landing,
The domains of Thyri
He redeemed and rescued
    From King Burislaf.

Then said Olaf, laughing,
"Not ten yoke of oxen
Have the power to draw us
    Like a woman's hair!

"Now will I confess it,
Better things are jewels
Than angelica stalks are
    For a Queen to wear."

XVII

King Svend of the Forked Beard

Loudly the sailors cheered
Svend of the Forked Beard,
As with his fleet he steered
    Southward to Vendland
Where with their courses hauled
All were together called,
Under the Isle of Svald
    Near to the mainland.

After Queen Gunhild's death,
So the old Saga saith,
Plighted King Svend his faith
    To Sigrid the Haughty;
And to avenge his bride,
Soothing her wounded pride,
Over the waters wide
    King Olaf sought he.

Still on her scornful face,
Blushing with deep disgrace,
Bore she the crimson trace
    Of Olaf's gauntlet;

Like a malignant star,
Blazing in heaven afar,
Red shone the angry scar
    Under her frontlet.

Oft to King Svend she spake,
"For thine own honor's sake
Shalt thou swift vengeance take
    On the vile coward!"
Until the King at last
Gusty and overcast,
Like a tempestuous blast
    Threatened and lowered.

Soon as the Spring appeared,
Svend of the Forked Beard
High his red standard reared,
    Eager for battle;
While every warlike Dane,
Seizing his arms again,
Left all unsown the grain,
    Unhoused the cattle.

Likewise the Swedish King
Summoned in hate a Thing,
Weapons and men to bring
    In aid of Denmark;
Eric, the Norseman, too,
As the war-tidings flew,
Sailed with a chosen crew
    From Lapland and Finmark.

So upon Easter day
Sailed the three kings away,
Out of the sheltered bay,
    In the bright season;
With them Earl Sigvald came,
Eager for spoil and fame;
Pity that such a name
    Stooped to such treason!

Safe under Svald at last,
Now were their anchors cast,
Safe from the sea and blast,
    Plotted the three kings;
While, with a base intent,
Southward Earl Sigvald went,
On a foul errand bent,
    Unto the Sea-kings.

Thence to hold on his course,
Unto King Olaf's force,
Lying within the hoarse
    Mouths of Stet-haven;
Him to ensnare and bring,
Unto the Danish king,
Who his dead corse would fling
    Forth to the raven!

XVIII

King Olaf and Earl Sigvald

On the gray sea-sands
King Olaf stands,
Northward and seaward
He points with his hands.

With eddy and whirl
The sea-tides curl,
Washing the sandals
Of Sigvald the Earl.

The mariners shout,
The ships swing about,
The yards are all hoisted,
The sails flutter out.

The war-horns are played,
The anchors are weighed,
Like moths in the distance
The sails flit and fade.

The sea is like lead,
The harbor lies dead,
As a corse on the sea-shore,
Whose spirit has fled!

On that fatal day,
The histories say,
Seventy vessels
Sailed out of the bay.

But soon scattered wide
O'er the billows they ride,
While Sigvald and Olaf
Sail side by side.

Cried the Earl: "Follow me,
I your pilot will be,
For I know all the channels
Where flows the deep sea!"

So into the strait
Where his foes lie in wait,
Gallant King Olaf
Sails to his fate!

Then the sea-fog veils
The ships and their sails;
Queen Sigrid the Haughty,
Thy vengeance prevails!

XIX

King Olaf's War-Horns

"Strike the sails!" King Olaf said;
"Never shall men of mine take flight
Never away from battle I fled,
Never away from my foes!
     Let God dispose
Of my life in the fight!"

"Sound the horns!" said Olaf the King;
And suddenly through the drifting brume
The blare of the horns began to ring
Like the terrible trumpet shock
 Of Regnarock,
On the Day of Doom!

Louder and louder the war-horns sang
Over the level floor of the flood;
All the sails came down with a clang,
And there in the mist overhead
 The sun hung red
As a drop of blood.

Drifting down on the Danish fleet
Three together the ships were lashed,
So that neither should turn and retreat:
In the midst, but in front of the rest
 The burnished crest
Of the Serpent flashed.

King Olaf stood on the quarter-deck,
With bow of ash and arrows of oak,
His gilded shield was without a fleck,
His helmet inlaid with gold,
 And in many a fold
Hung his crimson cloak.

On the forecastle Ulf the Red
Watched the lashing of the ships;
"If the Serpent lie so far ahead,
We shall have hard work of it here,"
 Said he with a sneer
On his bearded lips.

King Olaf laid an arrow on string,
"Have I a coward on board?" said he.
"Shoot it another way, O King!"
Sullenly answered Ulf,
 The old sea-wolf;
"You have need of me!"

In front came Svend, the King of the Danes,
Sweeping down with his fifty rowers;
To the right, the Swedish king with his thanes;
And on board of the Iron Beard
  Earl Eric steered
On the left with his oars.

"These soft Danes and Swedes," said the King,
"At home with their wives had better stay,
Than come within reach of my Serpent's sting;
But where Eric the Norsemen leads
  Heroic deeds
Will be done to-day!"

Then as together the vessels crashed,
Eric severed the cables of hide,
With which King Olaf's ships were lashed,
And left them to drive and drift
  With the currents swift
Of the outward tide.

Louder the war-horns growl and snarl,
Sharper the dragons bite and sting!
Eric the son of Hakon Jarl
A death-drink salt as the sea
  Pledges to thee,
Olaf the King!

XX

Einar Tamberskelver

It was Einar Tamberskelver
  Stood beside the mast;
From his yew-bow, tipped with silver,
  Flew the arrows fast;
Aimed at Eric unavailing,
  As he sat concealed,
Half behind the quarter-railing,
  Half behind his shield.

First an arrow struck the tiller,
   Just above his head;
"Sing, O Eyvind Skaldaspiller,"
   Then Earl Eric said,
"Sing the song of Hakon dying,
   Sing his funeral wail!"
And another arrow flying
   Grazed his coat of mail.

Turning to a Lapland yeoman,
   As the arrow passed,
Said Earl Eric, "Shoot that bowman
   Standing by the mast."
Sooner than the word was spoken
   Flew the yeoman's shaft;
Einar's bow in twain was broken,
   Einar only laughed.

"What was that?" said Olaf, standing
   On the quarter-deck.
"Something heard I like the stranding
   Of a shattered wreck."
Einar then, the arrow taking
   From the loosened string,
Answered, "That was Norway breaking
   From thy hand, O king!"

"Thou art but a poor diviner,"
   Straightway Olaf said;
"Take my bow, and swifter, Einar,
   Let thy shafts be sped."
Of his bows the fairest choosing,
   Reached he from above;
Einar saw the blood-drops oozing
   Through his iron glove.

But the bow was thin and narrow;
   At the first assay,
O'er his head he drew the arrow,
   Flung the bow away;

Said, with hot and angry temper
    Flushing in his cheek,
"Olaf! for so great a Kämper
    Are thy bows too weak!"

Then, with smile of joy defiant
    On his beardless lip,
Scaled he, light and self-reliant,
    Eric's dragon-ship.
Loose his golden locks were flowing,
    Bright his armor gleamed;
Like Saint Michael overthrowing
    Lucifer he seemed.

XXI

King Olaf's Death-Drink

All day has the battle raged,
All day have the ships engaged,
But not yet is assuaged
    The vengeance of Eric the Earl.

The decks with blood are red,
The arrows of death are sped,
The ships are filled with the dead,
    And the spears the champions hurl.

They drift as wrecks on the tide,
The grappling-irons are plied,
The boarders climb up the side,
    The shouts are feeble and few.

Ah! never shall Norway again
See her sailors come back o'er the main;
They all lie wounded or slain,
    Or asleep in the billows blue!

On the deck stands Olaf the King
Around him whistle and sing
The spears that the foemen fling,
    And the stones they hurl with their hands.

In the midst of the stones and the spears,
Kolbiorn, the marshal, appears,
His shield in the air he uprears,
    By the side of King Olaf he stands.

Over the slippery wreck
Of the Long Serpent's deck
Sweeps Eric with hardly a check,
    His lips with anger are pale;

He hews with his axe at the mast,
Till it falls, with the sails overcast,
Like a snow-covered pine in the vast
    Dim forests of Orkadale.

Seeking King Olaf then,
He rushes aft with his men,
As a hunter into the den,
    Of the bear, when he stands at bay.

"Remember Jarl Hakon!" he cries,
When lo! on his wondering eyes,
Two kingly figures arise,
    Two Olafs in warlike array!

Then Kolbiorn speaks in the ear
Of King Olaf a word of cheer,
In a whisper that none may hear,
    With a smile on his tremulous lip;

Two shields raised high in the air,
Two flashes of golden hair,
Two scarlet meteors' glare,
    And both have leaped from the ship.

Earl Eric's men in the boats
Seize Kolbiorn's shield as it floats,
And cry, from their hairy throats,
    "See! it is Olaf the King!"

While far on the opposite side
Floats another shield on the tide,
Like a jewel set in the wide
    Sea-current's eddying ring.

There is told a wonderful tale,
How the King stripped off his mail,
Like leaves of the brown sea-kale,
  As he swam beneath the main;

But the young grew old and gray,
And never, by night or by day,
In his kingdom of Norroway
  Was King Olaf seen again!

XXII

The Nun of Nidaros

In the convent of Drontheim,
Alone in her chamber
Knelt Astrid the Abbess,
At midnight, adoring,
Beseeching, entreating
The Virgin and Mother.

She heard in the silence
The voice of one speaking,
Without in the darkness.
In gusts of the night-wind
Now louder, now nearer,
Now lost in the distance.

The voice of a stranger
It seemed as she listened,
Of some one who answered,
Beseeching, imploring,
A cry from afar off
She could not distinguish.

The voice of Saint John,
The beloved disciple,
Who wandered and waited
The Master's appearance,
Alone in the darkness,
Unsheltered and friendless.

"It is accepted,
The angry defiance,
The challenge of battle!
It is accepted,
But not with the weapons
Of war that thou wieldest!

"Cross against corslet,
Love against hatred,
Peace-cry for war-cry!
Patience is powerful;
He that overcometh
Hath power o'er the nations.

"As torrents in summer,
Half dried in their channels,
Suddenly rise, though the
Sky is still cloudless,
For rain has been falling
Far off at their fountains;

"So hearts that are fainting
Grow full to o'erflowing,
And they that behold it
Marvel, and know not
That God at their fountains
Far off has been raining!

"Stronger than steel
Is the sword of the Spirit;
Swifter than arrows
The light of the truth is,
Greater than anger
Is love, and subdueth!

"Thou art a phantom,
A shape of the sea-mist,
A shape of the brumal
Rain, and the darkness
Fearful and formless;
Day dawns and thou art not!

"The dawn is not distant,
Nor is the night starless;
Love is eternal!
God is still God, and
His faith shall not fail us;
Christ is eternal!"

INTERLUDE

A strain of music closed the tale,
A low, monotonous, funeral wail,
That with its cadence, wild and sweet,
Made the long Saga more complete.

"Thank God," the Theologian said,
"The reign of violence is dead,
Or dying surely from the world;
While Love triumphant reigns instead,
And in a brighter sky o'erhead
His blessed banners are unfurled.
And most of all thank God for this:
The war and waste of clashing creeds
Now end in words, and not in deeds,
And no one suffers loss, or bleeds,
For thoughts that men call heresies.

"I stand without here in the porch,
I hear the bell's melodious din,
I hear the organ peal within,
I hear the prayer, with words that scorch
Like sparks from an inverted torch,
I hear the sermon upon sin,
With threatenings of the last account.
And all, translated in the air,
Reach me but as our dear Lord's Prayer,
And as the Sermon on the Mount.

"Must it be Calvin, and not Christ?
Must it be Athanasian creeds,
Or holy water, books and beads?
Must struggling souls remain content
With councils and decrees of Trent?

And can it be enough for these
The Christian Church the year embalms
With evergreens and boughs of palms,
And fills the air with litanies?

"I know that yonder Pharisee
Thanks God that he is not like me;
In my humiliation dressed,
I only stand and beat my breast,
And pray for human charity.

"Not to one church alone, but seven,
The voice prophetic spake from heaven;
And unto each the promise came,
Diversified, but still the same;
For him that overcometh are
The new name written on the stone,
The raiment white, the crown, the throne,
And I will give him the Morning Star!

"Ah! to how many Faith has been
No evidence of things unseen,
But a dim shadow, that recasts
The creed of the Phantasiasts,
For whom no Man of Sorrows died,
For whom the Tragedy Divine
Was but a symbol and a sign,
And Christ a phantom crucified!

"For others a diviner creed
Is living in the life they lead.
The passing of their beautiful feet
Blesses the pavement of the street,
And all their looks and words repeat
Old Fuller's saying, wise and sweet,
Not as a vulture, but a dove,
The Holy Ghost came from above.

"And this brings back to me a tale
So sad the hearer well may quail,
And question if such things can be;

Yet in the chronicles of Spain
Down the dark pages runs this stain,
And naught can wash them white again,
So fearful is the tragedy."

THE THEOLOGIAN'S TALE

TORQUEMADA

In the heroic days when Ferdinand
And Isabella ruled the Spanish land,
And Torquemada, with his subtle brain,
Ruled them, as Grand Inquisitor of Spain,
In a great castle near Valladolid,
Moated and high and by fair woodlands hid,
There dwelt, as from the chronicles we learn,
An old Hidalgo proud and taciturn,
Whose name has perished with his towers of stone,
And all his actions save this one alone;
This one, so terrible, perhaps 'twere best
If it, too, were forgotten with the rest;
Unless, perchance, our eyes can see therein
The martyrdom triumphant o'er the sin;
A double picture, with its gloom and glow,
The splendor overhead, the death below.

This sombre man counted each day as lost
On which his feet no sacred threshold crossed;
And when he chanced the passing Host to meet,
He knelt and prayed devoutly in the street;
Oft he confessed; and with each mutinous thought,
As with wild beasts at Ephesus, he fought.
In deep contrition scourged himself in Lent,
Walked in processions, with his head down bent,
At plays of Corpus Christi oft was seen,
And on Palm Sunday bore his bough of green.
His only pastime was to hunt the boar
Through tangled thickets of the forest hoar,
Or with his jingling mules to hurry down
To some grand bull-fight in the neighboring town,

Or in the crowd with lighted taper stand,
When Jews were burned, or banished from the land.
Then stirred within him a tumultuous joy;
The demon whose delight is to destroy
Shook him, and shouted with a trumpet tone,
"Kill! kill! and let the Lord find out his own!"

And now, in that old castle in the wood,
His daughters, in the dawn of womanhood,
Returning from their convent school, had made
Resplendent with their bloom the forest shade,
Reminding him of their dead mother's face,
When first she came into that gloomy place,—
A memory in his heart as dim and sweet
As moonlight in a solitary street,
Where the same rays, that lift the sea, are thrown
Lovely but powerless upon walls of stone.

These two fair daughters of a mother dead
Were all the dream had left him as it fled.
A joy at first, and then a growing care,
As if a voice within him cried, "Beware!"
A vague presentiment of impending doom,
Like ghostly footsteps in a vacant room,
Haunted him day and night; a formless fear
That death to some one of his house was near,
With dark surmises of a hidden crime,
Made life itself a death before its time.
Jealous, suspicious, with no sense of shame,
A spy upon his daughters he became;
With velvet slippers, noiseless on the floors,
He glided softly through half-open doors;

Now in the room, and now upon the stair,
He stood beside them ere they were aware;
He listened in the passage when they talked,
He watched them from the casement when they walked,
He saw the gypsy haunt the river's side,
He saw the monk among the corktrees glide;
And, tortured by the mystery and the doubt
Of some dark secret, past his finding out,

Baffled he paused; then reassured again
Pursued the flying phantom of his brain.
He watched them even when they knelt in church;
And then, descending lower in his search,
Questioned the servants, and with eager eyes
Listened incredulous to their replies;
The gypsy? none had seen her in the wood!
The monk? a mendicant in search of food!

At length the awful revelation came,
Crushing at once his pride of birth and name,
The hopes his yearning bosom forward cast,
And the ancestral glories of the past;
All fell together, crumbling in disgrace,
A turret rent from battlement to base.
His daughters talking in the dead of night
In their own chamber, and without a light,
Listening, as he was wont, he overheard,
And learned the dreadful secret, word by word;
And hurrying from his castle, with a cry
He raised his hands to the unpitying sky,
Repeating one dread word, till bush and tree
Caught it, and shuddering answered, "Heresy!"

Wrapped in his cloak, his hat drawn o'er his face,
Now hurrying forward, now with lingering pace,
He walked all night the alleys of his park,
With one unseen companion in the dark,
The Demon who within him lay in wait,
And by his presence turned his love to hate,
Forever muttering in an undertone,
"Kill! kill! and let the Lord find out his own!"
Upon the morrow, after early Mass,
While yet the dew was glistening on the grass,
And all the woods were musical with birds,
The old Hidalgo, uttering tearful words,
Walked homeward with the Priest, and in his room
Summoned his trembling daughters to their doom.
When questioned, with brief answers they replied,
Nor when accused evaded or denied;

Expostulations, passionate appeals,
All that the human heart most fears or feels,
In vain the Priest with earnest voice essayed,
In vain the father threatened, wept, and prayed;
Until at last he said, with haughty mien,
"The Holy Office, then, must intervene!"

And now the Grand Inquisitor of Spain,
With all the fifty horsemen of his train,
His awful name resounding like the blast
Of funeral trumpets, as he onward passed,
Came to Valladolid, and there began
To harry the rich Jews with fire and ban.
To him the Hidalgo went, and at the gate
Demanded audience on affairs of state,
And in a secret chamber stood before
A venerable graybeard of fourscore,
Dressed in the hood and habit of a friar;
Out of his eyes flashed a consuming fire,
And in his hand the mystic horn he held,
Which poison and all noxious charms dispelled.
He heard in silence the Hidalgo's tale,
Then answered in a voice that made him quail:
"Son of the Church! when Abraham of old
To sacrifice his only son was told,
He did not pause to parley nor protest,
But hastened to obey the Lord's behest.
In him it was accounted righteousness;
The Holy Church expects of thee no less!"

A sacred frenzy seized the father's brain,
And Mercy from that hour implored in vain.
Ah! who will e'er believe the words I say?
His daughters he accused, and the same day
They both were cast into the dungeon's gloom,
That dismal antechamber of the tomb,
Arraigned, condemned, and sentenced to the flame,
The secret torture and the public shame.
Then to the Grand Inquisitor once more
The Hidalgo went, more eager than before,

And said: "When Abraham offered up his son,
He clave the wood wherewith it might be done.
By his example taught, let me too bring
Wood from the forest for my offering!"
And the deep voice, without a pause replied:
"Son of the Church! by faith now justified,
Complete thy sacrifice, even as thou wilt;
The Church absolves thy conscience from all guilt!"

Then this most wretched father went his way
Into the woods, that round his castle lay,
Where once his daughters in their childhood played
With their young mother in the sun and shade.
Now all the leaves had fallen; the branches bare
Made a perpetual moaning in the air,
And screaming from their eyries overhead
The ravens sailed athwart the sky of lead.
With his own hands he lopped the boughs and bound
Fagots, that crackled with foreboding sound,
And on his mules, caparisoned and gay
With bells and tassels, sent them on their way.

Then with his mind on one dark purpose bent,
Again to the Inquisitor he went,
And said: "Behold, the fagots I have brought,
And now, lest my atonement be as naught,
Grant me one more request, one last desire,—
With my own hand to light the funeral fire!"
And Torquemada answered from his seat,
"Son of the Church! Thine offering is complete;
Her servants through all ages shall not cease
To magnify thy deed. Depart in peace!"

Upon the market-place, builded of stone
The scaffold rose, whereon Death claimed his own.
At the four corners, in stern attitude,
Four statues of the Hebrew Prophets stood,
Gazing with calm indifference in their eyes
Upon this place of human sacrifice,
Round which was gathering fast the eager crowd,
With clamor of voices dissonant and loud,

And every roof and window was alive
With restless gazers, swarming like a hive.
The church-bells tolled, the chant of monks drew near,
Loud trumpets stammered forth their notes of fear,
A line of torches smoked along the street,
There was a stir, a rush, a tramp of feet,
And, with its banners floating in the air,
Slowly the long procession crossed the square,
And, to the statues of the Prophets bound,
The victims stood, with fagots piled around.
Then all the air a blast of trumpets shook,
And louder sang the monks with bell and book,
And the Hidalgo, lofty, stern, and proud,
Lifted his torch, and, bursting through the crowd,
Lighted in haste the fagots, and then fled,
Lest those imploring eyes should strike him dead!

O pitiless skies! why did your clouds retain
For peasants' fields their floods of hoarded rain?
O pitiless earth! why opened no abyss
To bury in its chasm a crime like this?

That night, a mingled column of fire and smoke
Fron the dark thickets of the forest broke,
And, glaring o'er the landscape leagues away,
Made all the fields and hamlets bright as day.
Wrapped in a sheet of flame the castle blazed,
And as the villagers in terror gazed,
They saw the figure of that cruel knight
Lean from a window in the turret's height,
His ghastly face illumined with the glare,
His hands upraised above his head in prayer,
Till the floor sank beneath him, and he fell
Down the black hollow of that burning well.

Three centuries and more above his bones
Have piled the oblivious years like funeral stones;
His name has perished with him, and no trace
Remains on earth of his afflicted race;
But Torquemada's name, with clouds o'ercast,
Looms in the distant landscape of the Past,

Like a burnt tower upon a blackened heath,
Lit by the fires of burning woods beneath!

INTERLUDE

Thus closed the tale of guilt and gloom,
That cast upon each listener's face
Its shadow, and for some brief space
Unbroken silence filled the room.
The Jew was thoughtful and distressed;
Upon his memory thronged and pressed
The persecution of his race,
Their wrongs and sufferings and disgrace;
His head was sunk upon his breast,
And from his eyes alternate came
Flashes of wrath and tears of shame.

The student first the silence broke,
As one who long has lain in wait,
With purpose to retaliate,
And thus he dealt the avenging stroke.
"In such a company as this,
A tale so tragic seems amiss,
That by its terrible control
O'ermasters and drags down the soul
Into a fathomless abyss.
The Italian Tales that you disdain,
Some merry Night of Straparole,
Or Machiavelli's Belphagor,
Would cheer us and delight us more,
Give greater pleasure and less pain
Than your grim tragedies of Spain!"

And here the poet raised his hand,
With such entreaty and command,
It stopped discussion at its birth,
And said: "The story I shall tell
Has meaning in it, if not mirth;
Listen, and hear what once befell
The merry birds of Killingworth!"

The Poet's Tale

THE BIRDS OF KILLINGWORTH

It was the season, when through all the land
  The merle and mavis build, and building sing
Those lovely lyrics, written by His hand,
  Whom Saxon Cædmon calls the Blithe-heart King;
When on the boughs the purple buds expand,
  The banners of the vanguard of the Spring,
And rivulets, rejoicing, rush and leap,
And wave their fluttering signals from the steep.

The robin and the blue-bird, piping loud,
  Filled all the blossoming orchards with their glee;
The sparrows chirped as if they still were proud
  Their race in Holy Writ should mentioned be;
And hungry crows assembled in a crowd,
  Clamored their piteous prayer incessantly,
Knowing who hears the ravens cry, and said:
"Give us, O Lord, this day our daily bread!"

Across the Sound the birds of passage sailed,
  Speaking some unknown language strange and sweet
Of tropic isle remote, and passing hailed
  The village with the cheers of all their fleet;
Or quarrelling together, laughed and railed
  Like foreign sailors, landed in the street
Of seaport town, and with outlandish noise
Of oaths and gibberish frightening girls and boys.

Thus came the jocund Spring in Killingworth,
  In fabulous days, some hundred years ago;
And thrifty farmers, as they tilled the earth,
  Heard with alarm the cawing of the crow,
That mingled with the universal mirth,
  Cassandra-like, prognosticating woe;
They shook their heads, and doomed with dreadful words
To swift destruction the whole race of birds.

And a town-meeting was convened straightway
    To set a price upon the guilty heads
Of these marauders, who in lieu of pay,
    Levied black-mail upon the garden beds
And corn-fields, and beheld without dismay
    The awful scarecrow, with his fluttering shreds;
The skeleton that waited at their feast,
Whereby their sinful pleasure was increased.

Then from his house, a temple painted white,
    With fluted columns, and a roof of red,
The Squire came forth, august and splendid sight!
    Slowly descending, with majestic tread,
Three flights of steps, nor looking left nor right,
    Down the long street he walked, as one who said,
"A town that boasts inhabitants like me
Can have no lack of good society!"

The Parson, too, appeared, a man austere,
    The instinct of whose nature was to kill;
The wrath of God he preached from year to year,
    And read, with fervor, Edwards on the Will;
His favorite pastime was to slay the deer
    In summer on some Adirondack hill;
E'en now, while walking down the rural lane,
He lopped the wayside lilies with his cane.

From the Academy, whose belfry crowned
    The hill of Science with its vane of brass,
Came the Preceptor, gazing idly round,
    Now at the clouds, and now at the green grass,
And all absorbed in reveries profound
    Of fair Almira in the upper class
Who was, as in a sonnet he had said,
As pure as water, and as good as bread.

And next the Deacon issued from his door,
    In his voluminous neck-cloth, white as snow;
A suit of sable bombazine he wore;
    His form was ponderous, and his step was slow;

There never was so wise a man before;
    He seemed the incarnate "Well, I told you so!"
And to perpetuate his great renown
There was a street named after him in town.

These came together in the new town-hall,
    With sundry farmers from the region round.
The Squire presided, dignified and tall,
    His air impressive and his reasoning sound;
Ill fared it with the birds, both great and small;
    Hardly a friend in all that crowd they found,
But enemies enough, who every one
Charged them with all the crimes beneath the sun.

When they had ended, from his place apart,
    Rose the Preceptor, to redress the wrong,
And, trembling like a steed before the start,
    Looked round bewildered on the expectant throng;
Then thought of fair Almira, and took heart
    To speak out what was in him, clear and strong,
Alike regardless of their smile or frown,
And quite determined not to be laughed down.

"Plato, anticipating the Reviewers,
    From his republic banished without pity
The Poets; in this little town of yours,
    You put to death, by means of a Committee,
The ballad-singers and the Troubadours,
    The street-musicians of the heavenly city,
The birds, who make sweet music for us all
In our dark hours, as David did for Saul.

"The thrush that carols at the dawn of day
    From the green steeples of the piny wood;
The oriole in the elm; the noisy jay,
    Jargoning like a foreigner at his food;
The blue-bird balanced on some topmost spray,
    Flooding with melody the neighborhood;
Linnet and meadow-lark, and all the throng
That dwell in nests, and have the gift of song.

"You slay them all! and wherefore? for the gain
    Of a scant handful more or less of wheat,
Or rye, or barley, or some other grain,
    Scratched up at random by industrious feet,
Searching for worm or weevil after rain!
    Or a few cherries, that are not so sweet
As are the songs these univited guests
Sing at their feast with comfortable breasts.

"Do you ne'er think what wondrous beings these?
    Do you ne'er think who made them, and who taught
The dialect they speak, where melodies
    Alone are the interpreters of thought?
Whose household words are songs in many keys,
    Sweeter than instrument of man e'er caught!
Whose habitations in the tree-tops even
Are half-way houses on the road to heaven!

"Think, every morning when the sun peeps through
    The dim, leaf-latticed windows of the grove,
How jubilant the happy birds renew
    Their old, melodious madrigals of love!
And when you think of this, remember too
    'T is always morning somewhere, and above
The awakening continents, from shore to shore,
Somewhere the birds are singing evermore.

"Think of your woods and orchards without birds!
    Of empty nests that cling to boughs and beams
As in an idiot's brain remembered words
    Hang empty 'mid the cobwebs of his dreams!
Will bleat of flocks or bellowing of herds
    Make up for the lost music, when your teams
Drag home the stingy harvest, and no more
The feathered gleaners follow to your door?

"What! would you rather see the incessant stir
    Of insects in the windrows of the hay,
And hear the locust and the grasshopper
    Their melancholy hurdy-gurdies play?

Is this more pleasant to you than the whir
  Of meadow-lark, and its sweet roundelay,
Or twitter of little field-fares, as you take
Your nooning in the shade of bush and brake?

"You call them thieves and pillagers; but know
  They are the wingèd wardens of your farms,
Who from the cornfields drive the insidious foe,
  And from your harvests keep a hundred harms;
Even the blackest of them all, the crow,
  Renders good service as your man-at-arms,
Crushing the beetle in his coat of mail,
And crying havoc on the slug and snail.

"How can I teach your children gentleness,
  And mercy to the weak, and reverence
For Life, which, in its weakness or excess,
  Is still a gleam of God's omnipotence,
Or Death, which, seeming darkness, is no less
  The selfsame light, although averted hence,
When by your laws, your actions, and your speech,
You contradict the very things I teach?"

With this he closed; and through the audience went
  A murmur, like the rustle of dead leaves;
The farmers laughed and nodded and some bent
  Their yellow heads together like their sheaves;
Men have no faith in fine-spun sentiment
  Who put their trust in bullocks and in beeves.
The birds were doomed; and, as the record shows,
A bounty offered for the heads of crows.

There was another audience out of reach,
  Who had no voice nor vote in making laws,
But in the papers read his little speech,
  And crowned his modest temples with applause;
They made him conscious, each one more than each,
  He still was victor, vanquished in their cause.
Sweetest of all the applause he won from thee,
O fair Almira at the Academy!

And so the dreadful massacre began
  O'er fields and orchards, and o'er woodland crests,
The ceaseless fusillade of terror ran,
  Dead fell the birds, with blood-stains on their breasts,
Or wounded crept away from sight of man,
  While the young died of famine in their nests;
A slaughter to be told in groans, not words,
The very St. Bartholomew of Birds!

The summer came, and all the birds were dead;
  The days were like hot coals; the very ground
Was burned to ashes; in the orchards fed
  Myriads of caterpillars, and around
The cultivated fields and garden beds
  Hosts of devouring insects crawled, and found
No foe to check their march, till they had made
The land a desert without leaf or shade.

Devoured by worms, like Herod, was the town,
  Because, like Herod, it had ruthlessly
Slaughtered the Innocents. From the trees spun down
  The canker-worms upon the passers-by,
Upon each woman's bonnet, shawl, and gown,
  Who shook them off with just a little cry;
They were the terror of each favorite walk,
The endless theme of all the village talk.

The farmers grew impatient, but a few
  Confessed their error, and would not complain,
For after all, the best thing one can do
  When it is raining, is to let it rain.
Then they repealed the law, although they knew
  It would not call the dead to life again;
As school-boys, finding their mistake too late,
Draw a wet sponge across the accusing slate.

That year in Killingworth the Autumn came
  Without the light of his majestic look,
The wonder of the falling tongues of flame,
  The illumined pages of his Dooms-Day book.

A few lost leaves blushed crimson with their shame,
  And drowned themselves despairing in the brook,
While the wild wind went moaning everywhere,
Lamenting the dead children of the air!

But the next Spring a stranger sight was seen,
  A sight that never yet by bard was sung,
As great a wonder as it would have been
  If some dumb animal had found a tongue!
A wagon, overarched with evergreen,
  Upon whose boughs were wicker cages hung,
All full of singing birds, came down the street,
Filling the air with music wild and sweet.

From all the country round these birds were brought,
  By order of the town, with anxious quest,
And, loosened from their wicker prisons, sought
  In woods and fields the places they loved best,
Singing loud canticles, which many thought
  Were satires to the authorities addressed,
While others, listening in green lanes, averred
Such lovely music never had been heard!

But blither still and louder carolled they
  Upon the morrow, for they seemed to know
It was the fair Almira's wedding day,
  And everywhere, around, above, below,
When the Preceptor bore his bride away,
  Their songs burst forth in joyous overflow,
And a new heaven bent over a new earth
Amid the sunny farms of Killingworth.

FINALE

The hour was late; the fire burned low,
The landlord's eyes were closed in sleep,
And near the story's end a deep
Sonorous sound at times was heard,
As when the distant bagpipes blow.
At this all laughed; the landlord stirred,

As one awaking from a swound,
And, gazing anxiously around,
Protested that he had not slept,
But only shut his eyes, and kept
His ears attentive to each word.

Then all arose, and said "Good Night."
Alone remained the drowsy Squire
To rake the embers of the fire,
And quench the waning parlor light;
While from the windows, here and there,
The scattered lamps a moment gleamed,
And the illumined hostel seemed
The constellation of the Bear,
Downward, athwart the misty air,
Sinking and setting toward the sun.
Far off the village clock struck one.

VOICES OF THE NIGHT

Prelude

Pleasant it was, when woods were green,
　　And winds were soft and low,
To lie amid some sylvan scene,
Where, the long drooping boughs between,
Shadows dark and sunlight sheen
　　Alternate come and go;

Or where the denser grove receives
　　No sunlight from above,
But the dark foliage interweaves
In one unbroken roof of leaves,
Underneath whose sloping eaves
　　The shadows hardly move.

Beneath some patriarchal tree
　　I lay upon the ground;
His hoary arms uplifted he,
And all the broad leaves over me
Clapped their little hands in glee,
　　With one continuous sound;—

A slumberous sound,—a sound that brings
　　The feelings of a dream,—
As of innumerable wings,
As, when a bell no longer swings,
Faint the hollow murmur rings
　　O'er meadow, lake, and stream.

And dreams of that which cannot die,
　　Bright visions, came to me,
As lapped in thought I used to lie,
And gaze into the summer sky,
Where the sailing clouds went by,
　　Like ships upon the sea;

Dreams that the soul of youth engage
   Ere Fancy has been quelled;
Old legends of the monkish page,
Traditions of the saint and sage,
Tales that have the rime of age,
   And chronicles of Eld.

And, loving still these quaint old themes,
   Even in the city's throng
I feel the freshness of the streams,
That, crossed by shades and sunny gleams,
Water the green land of dreams,
   The holy land of song.

Therefore at Pentecost, which brings
   The Spring, clothed like a bride,
When nestling buds unfold their wings,
And bishop's-caps have golden rings,
Musing upon many things,
   I sought the woodlands wide.

The green trees whispered low and mild;
   It was a sound of joy!
They were my playmates when a child,
And rocked me in their arms so wild!
Still they looked at me and smiled,
   As if I were a boy;

And ever whispered, mild and low,
   "Come, be a child once more!"
And waved their long arms to and fro,
And beckoned solemnly and slow;
O, I could not choose but go
   Into the woodlands hoar;

Into the blithe and breathing air,
   Into the solemn wood.
Solemn and silent everywhere!
Nature with folded hands seemed there,
Kneeling at her evening prayer!
   Like one in prayer I stood.

Before me rose an avenue
  Of tall and sombrous pines;
Abroad their fan-like branches grew,
And, where the sunshine darted through,
Spread a vapor soft and blue,
  In long and sloping lines.

And, falling on my weary brain,
  Like a fast-falling shower,
The dreams of youth came back again;
Low lispings of the summer rain,
Dropping on the ripened grain,
  As once upon the flower.

Visions of childhood! Stay, O stay!
  Ye were so sweet and wild!
And distant voices seemed to say:—
"It cannot be! They pass away!
Other themes demand thy lay;
  Thou art no more a child!

"The land of Song within thee lies,
  Watered by living springs;
The lids of Fancy's sleepless eyes
Are gates unto that Paradise,
Holy thoughts, like stars, arise,
  Its clouds are angels' wings.

"Learn, that henceforth thy song shall be,
  Not mountains capped with snow,
Nor forests sounding like the sea,
Nor rivers flowing ceaselessly,
Where the woodlands bend to see
  The bending heavens below.

"There is a forest where the din
  Of iron branches sounds!
A mighty river roars between,
And whosoever looks therein,
Sees the heavens all black with sin,—
  Sees not its depths, nor bounds.

"Athwart the swinging branches cast,
  Soft rays of sunshine pour;
Then comes the fearful wintry blast;
Our hopes, like withered leaves, fall fast;
Pallid lips say, 'It is past!
  We can return no more!'

"Look, then, into thine heart, and write!
  Yes, into Life's deep stream!
All forms of sorrow and delight,
All solemn Voices of the Night,
That can soothe thee, or affright,—
  Be these henceforth thy theme."

HYMN TO THE NIGHT

Ἀσπασίη, τϱιλλιστος

I heard the trailing garments of the Night
  Sweep through her marble halls!
I saw her sable skirts all fringed with light
  From the celestial walls!

I felt her presence, by its spell of might,
  Stoop o'er me from above;
The calm, majestic presence of the Night,
  As of the one I love.

I heard the sounds of sorrow and delight,
  The manifold, soft chimes,
That fill the haunted chambers of the Night,
  Like some old poet's rhymes.

From the cool cisterns of the midnight air
  My spirit drank repose;
The fountain of perpetual peace flows there,—
  From those deep cisterns flows.

O holy Night! from thee I learn to bear
  What man has borne before!
Thou layest thy finger on the lips of Care
  And they complain no more.

Peace! Peace! Orestes-like I breathe this prayer!
　Descend with broad-winged flight,
The welcome, the thrice-prayed for, the most fair,
　The best-beloved Night!

A Psalm of Life

WHAT THE HEART OF THE YOUNG MAN SAID TO THE PSALMIST

Tell me not, in mournful numbers,
　"Life is but an empty dream!"
For the soul is dead that slumbers,
　And things are not what they seem.

Life is real! Life is earnest!
　And the grave is not its goal;
"Dust thou art, to dust returnest,"
　Was not spoken of the soul.

Not enjoyment, and not sorrow,
　Is our destined end or way;
But to act, that each to-morrow
　Finds us farther than to-day.

Art is long, and Time is fleeting,
　And our hearts, though stout and brave,
Still, like muffled drums, are beating
　Funeral marches to the grave.

In the world's broad field of battle,
　In the bivouac of Life,
Be not like dumb, driven cattle!
　Be a hero in the strife!

Trust no Future, howe'er pleasant!
　Let the dead Past bury its dead!
Act,—act in the living Present!
　Heart within, and God o'erhead!

Lives of great men all remind us
　We can make our lives sublime,
And, departing, leave behind us
　Footprints on the sands of time;

Footprints, that perhaps another,
   Sailing o'er life's solemn main,
A forlorn and shipwrecked brother,
   Seeing, shall take heart again.

Let us, then, be up and doing,
   With a heart for any fate;
Still achieving, still pursuing
   Learn to labor and to wait.

THE REAPER AND THE FLOWERS

There is a Reaper, whose name is Death,
   And, with his sickle keen,
He reaps the bearded grain at a breath,
   And the flowers that grow between.

"Shall I have nought that is fair?" saith he,.
   "Have nought but the bearded grain?
Though the breath of these flowers is sweet to me,
   I will give them all back again."

He gazed at the flowers with tearful eyes,
   He kissed their drooping leaves;
It was for the Lord of Paradise
   He bound them in his sheaves.

"My Lord has need of these flowerets gay,"
   The Reaper said, and smiled;
"Dear tokens of the earth are they,
   Where he was once a child.

"They shall all bloom in fields of light,
   Transplanted by my care,
And saints, upon their garments white,
   These sacred blossoms wear."

And the mother gave, in tears and pain,
   The flowers she most did love;
She knew she should find them all again
   In the fields of light above.

O, not in cruelty, not in wrath,
  The Reaper came that day;
'T was an angel visited the green earth,
  And took the flowers away.

THE LIGHT OF STARS

The night is come, but not too soon;
  And sinking silently,
All silently, the little moon
  Drops down behind the sky.

There is no light in earth or heaven,
  But the cold light of stars;
And the first watch of night is given
  To the red planet Mars.

Is it the tender star of love?
  The star of love and dreams?
O no! from that blue tent above,
  A hero's armor gleams.

And earnest thoughts within me rise,
  When I behold afar,
Suspended in the evening skies,
  The shield of that red star.

O star of strength! I see thee stand
  And smile upon my pain;
Thou beckonest with thy mailèd hand,
  And I am strong again.

Within my breast there is no light,
  But the cold light of stars;
I give the first watch of the night
  To the red planet Mars.

The star of the unconquered will,
  He rises in my breast,
Serene, and resolute, and still,
  And calm, and self-possessed.

And thou, too, whosoe'er thou art,
    That readest this brief psalm,
As one by one thy hopes depart,
    Be resolute and calm.

O fear not in a world like this,
    And thou shalt know ere long,
Know how sublime a thing it is
    To suffer and be strong.

FOOTSTEPS OF ANGELS

When the hours of Day are numbered,
    And the voices of the Night
Wake the better soul, that slumbered,
    To a holy, calm delight;

Ere the evening lamps are lighted,
    And, like phantoms grim and tall,
Shadows from the fitful fire-light
    Dance upon the parlor wall;

Then the forms of the departed
    Enter at the open door;
The beloved, the true-hearted,
    Come to visit me once more;

He, the young and strong, who cherished
    Noble longings for the strife,
By the roadside fell and perished,
    Weary with the march of life!

They, the holy ones and weakly,
    Who the cross of suffering bore,
Folded their pale hands so meekly,
    Spake with us on earth no more!

And with them the Being Beauteous
    Who unto my youth was given,
More than all things else to love me,
    And is now a saint in heaven.

With a slow and noiseless footstep
   Comes that messenger divine,
Takes the vacant chair beside me,
   Lays her gentle hand in mine.

And she sits and gazes at me
   With those deep and tender eyes,
Like the stars, so still and saint-like,
   Looking downward from the skies.

Uttered not, yet comprehended,
   Is the spirit's voiceless prayer,
Soft rebukes, in blessings ended,
   Breathing from her lips of air.

O, though oft depressed and lonely,
   All my fears are laid aside,
If I but remember only
   Such as these have lived and died!

FLOWERS

Spake full well, in language quaint and olden,
   One who dwelleth by the castled Rhine,
When he called the flowers, so blue and golden,
   Stars, that in earth's firmament do shine.

Stars they are, wherein we read our history,
   As astrologers and seers of eld;
Yet not wrapped about with awful mystery,
   Like the burning stars, which they beheld.

Wondrous truths, and manifold as wondrous,
   God hath written in those stars above;
But not less in the bright flowerets under us
   Stands the revelation of his love.

Bright and glorious is that revelation,
   Written all over this great world of ours;
Making evident our own creation,
   In these stars of earth,—these golden flowers.

And the Poet, faithful and far-seeing,
    Sees, alike in stars and flowers, a part
Of the selfsame, universal being,
    Which is throbbing in his brain and heart.

Gorgeous flowerets in the sunlight shining,
    Blossoms flaunting in the eye of day,
Tremulous leaves, with soft and silver lining,
    Buds that open only to decay;

Brilliant hopes, all woven in gorgeous tissues,
    Flaunting gayly in the golden light;
Large desires, with most uncertain issues,
    Tender wishes, blossoming at night!

These in flowers and men are more than seeming;
    Workings are they of the selfsame powers,
Which the Poet, in no idle dreaming,
    Seeth in himself and in the flowers.

Everywhere about us are they glowing,
    Some like stars, to tell us Spring is born;
Others, their blue eyes with tears o'erflowing,
    Stand like Ruth amid the golden corn;

Not alone in Spring's armorial bearing,
    And in Summer's green-emblazoned field,
But in arms of brave old Autumn's wearing,
    In the center of his brazen shield;

Not alone in meadows and green alleys,
    On the mountain-top, and by the brink
Of sequestered pools in woodland valleys,
    Where the slaves of Nature stoop to drink;

Not alone in her vast dome of glory,
    Not on graves of bird and beast alone,
But in old cathedrals, high and hoary,
    On the tombs of heroes, carved in stone;

In the cottage of the rudest peasant,
    In ancestral homes, whose crumbling towers,
Speaking of the Past unto the Present,
    Tell us of the ancient Games of Flowers;

In all places, then, and in all seasons,
    Flowers expand their light and soul-like wings,
Teaching us, by most persuasive reasons,
    How akin they are to human things.

And with childlike, credulous affection
    We behold their tender buds expand;
Emblems of our own great resurrection,
    Emblems of the bright and better land.

THE BELEAGUERED CITY

I have read, in some old marvellous tale,
    Some legend strange and vague,
That a midnight host of spectres pale
    Beleaguered the walls of Prague.

Beside the Moldau's rushing stream,
    With the wan moon overhead,
There stood, as in an awful dream,
    The army of the dead.

White as a sea-fog, landward bound,
    The spectral camp was seen,
And, with a sorrowful, deep sound,
    The river flowed between.

No other voice nor sound was there,
    No drum, nor sentry's pace;
The mist-like banners clasped the air,
    As clouds with clouds embrace.

But, when the old cathedral bell
    Proclaimed the morning prayer,
The white pavilions rose and fell
    On the alarmèd air.

Down the broad valley fast and far
    The troubled army fled;
Up rose the glorious morning star,
    The ghastly host was dead.

I have read, in the marvellous heart of man,
    That strange and mystic scroll,
That an army of phantoms vast and wan
    Beleaguer the human soul.

Encamped beside Life's rushing stream,
    In Fancy's misty light,
Gigantic shapes and shadows gleam
    Portentous through the night.

Upon its midnight battle-ground
    The spectral camp is seen,
And, with a sorrowful, deep sound,
    Flows the River of Life between.

No other voice, nor sound is there,
    In the army of the grave;
No other challenge breaks the air,
    But the rushing of Life's wave.

And, when the solemn and deep church-bell
    Entreats the soul to pray,
The midnight phantoms feel the spell,
    The shadows sweep away.

Down the broad Vale of Tears afar
    The spectral camp is fled;
Faith shineth as a morning star,
    Our ghastly fears are dead.

MIDNIGHT MASS FOR THE DYING YEAR

    Yes, the Year is growing old,
        And his eye is pale and bleared!
    Death, with frosty hand and cold,
        Plucks the old man by the beard,
            Sorely,—sorely!

    The leaves are falling, falling,
        Solemnly and slow;
    Caw! caw! the rooks are calling,
        It is a sound of woe,
            A sound of woe!

Through woods and mountain passes
  The winds, like anthems, roll;
They are chanting solemn masses,
  Singing, "Pray for this poor soul,
      Pray,—pray!"

And the hooded clouds, like friars,
  Tell their beads in drops of rain,
And patter their doleful prayers;—
  But their prayers are all in vain,
      All in vain!

There he stands in the foul weather,
  The foolish, fond Old Year,
Crowned with wild flowers and with heather,
  Like weak, despisèd Lear,
      A king,—a king!

Then comes the summer-like day,
  Bids the old man rejoice!
His joy! his last! O, the old man gray,
  Loveth that ever-soft voice,
      Gentle and low.

To the crimson woods he saith,—
  To the voice gentle and low
Of the soft air, like a daughter's breath,—
  "Pray do not mock me so!
      Do not laugh at me!"

And now the sweet day is dead;
  Cold in his arms it lies;
No stain from its breath is spread
  Over the glassy skies,
      No mist or stain!

Then, too, the Old Year dieth,
  And the forests utter a moan,
Like the voice of one who crieth
  In the wilderness alone,
      "Vex not his ghost!"

Then comes, with an awful roar
    Gathering and sounding on,
The storm-wind from Labrador,
    The wind Euroclydon,
        The storm-wind!

Howl! howl! and from the forest
    Sweep the red leaves away!
Would the sins that thou thus abhorrest,
    O Soul! could thus decay
        And be swept away!

For there shall come a mightier blast,
    There shall be a darker day;
And the stars from heaven down cast,
    Like red leaves be swept away!
        Kyrie, eleyson!
        Christe, eleyson!

EARLIER POEMS

[These poems were written for the most part during my college
life, and all of them before the age of nineteen. Some have found
their way into schools, and seem to be successful. Others lead a
vagabond and precarious existence in the corners of newspapers; or
have changed their names and run away to seek their fortunes
beyond the sea. I say, with the Bishop of Avranches, on a similar
occasion: "I cannot be displeased to see these children of mine,
which I have neglected, and almost exposed, brought from their
wanderings in lanes and alleys, and safely lodged, in order to go
forth into the world together in a more decorous garb."]

An April Day

When the warm sun, that brings
Seed-time and harvest, has returned again,
'T is sweet to visit the still wood, where springs
    The first flower of the plain.

I love the season well,
When forest glades are teeming with bright forms,
Nor dark and many-folded clouds foretell
    The coming-on of storms.

From the earth's loosened mould
The sapling draws its sustenance, and thrives;
Though stricken to the heart with winter's cold,
    The drooping tree revives.

The softly-warbled song
Comes from the pleasant woods, and colored wings
Glance quick in the bright sun, that moves along
    The forest openings.

When the bright sunset fills
The silver woods with light, the green slope throws
Its shadows in the hollows of the hills,
    And wide the upland glows.

And, when the eve is born,
In the blue lake the sky, o'er-reaching far,
Is hollowed out, and the moon dips her horn,
    And twinkles many a star.

Inverted in the tide,
Stand the gray rocks, and trembling shadows throw,
And the fair trees look over, side by side,
    And see themselves below.

Sweet April!—many a thought
Is wedded unto thee, as hearts are wed;
Nor shall they fail, till, to its autumn brought,
    Life's golden fruit is shed.

AUTUMN

With what glory comes and goes the year!
The buds of spring, those beautiful harbingers
Of sunny skies and cloudless times, enjoy
Life's newness, and earth's garniture spread out;
And when the silver habit of the clouds
Comes down upon the autumn sun and with
A sober gladness the old year takes up
His bright inheritance of golden fruits,
A pomp and pageant fill the splendid scene.

There is a beautiful spirit breathing now
Its mellow richness on the clustered trees,
And, from a beaker full of richest dyes,
Pouring new glory on the autumn woods,
And dipping in warm light the pillared clouds.
Morn on the mountain, like a summer bird,
Lifts up her purple wing, and in the vales
The gentle wind, a sweet and passionate wooer,
Kisses the blushing leaf, and stirs up life
Within the solemn woods of ash deep-crimsoned,
And silver beech, and maple yellow-leaved,
Where autumn, like a faint old man, sits down
By the wayside a-weary. Through the trees
The golden robin moves. The purple finch,
That on wild cherry and red cedar feeds,
A winter bird, comes with its plaintive whistle,
And pecks by the witch-hazel, whilst aloud,
From cottage roofs the warbling bluebird sings,
And merrily, with oft-repeated stroke,
Sounds from the threshing-floor the busy flail.

O what a glory doth this world put on
For him who, with a fervent heart, goes forth
Under the bright and glorious sky, and looks
On duties well performed, and days well spent!
For him the wind, ay, and the yellow leaves,
Shall have a voice, and give him eloquent teachings;
He shall so hear the solemn hymn, that Death
Has lifted up for all, that he shall go
To his long resting-place without a tear.

WOODS IN WINTER

When winter winds are piercing chill,
    And through the hawthorn blows the gale,
With solemn feet I tread the hill,
    That overbrows the lonely vale.

O'er the bare upland, and away
    Through the long reach of desert woods,

The embracing sunbeams chastely play,
  And gladden these deep solitudes.

Where, twisted round the barren oak,
  The summer vine in beauty clung,
And summer winds the stillness broke,
  The crystal icicle is hung.

Where, from their frozen urns, mute springs
  Pour out the river's gradual tide,
Shrilly the skater's iron rings,
  And voices fill the woodland side.

Alas! how changed from the fair scene,
  When birds sang out their mellow lay,
And winds were soft, and woods were green,
  And the song ceased not with the day.

But still wild music is abroad,
  Pale, desert woods! within your crowd,
And gathering winds, in hoarse accord,
  Amid the vocal reeds pipe loud.

Chill airs and wintry winds! my ear
  Has grown familiar with your song;
I hear it in the opening year,—
  I listen and it cheers me long.

HYMN OF THE MORAVIAN NUNS OF BETHLEHEM

AT THE CONSECRATION OF PULASKI'S BANNER

When the dying flame of day
Through the chancel shot its ray,
Far the glimmering tapers shed
Faint light on the cowlèd head;
And the censer burning swung,
Where, before the altar, hung
The blood-red banner, that with prayer
Had been consecrated there.
And the nuns' sweet hymn was heard the while,
Sung low in the dim, mysterious aisle.

"Take thy banner! May it wave
Proudly o'er the good and brave;
When the battle's distant wail
Breaks the sabbath of our vale,
When the clarion's music thrills
To the hearts of these lone hills,
When the spear in conflict shakes,
And the strong lance shivering breaks.

"Take thy banner! and, beneath
The battle-cloud's encircling wreath,
Guard it!—till our homes are free!
Guard it!—God will prosper thee!
In the dark and trying hour,
In the breaking forth of power,
In the rush of steeds and men,
His right hand will shield thee then.

"Take thy banner! But, when night
Closes round the ghastly fight,
If the vanquished warrior bow,
Spare him!—By our holy vow,
By our prayers and many tears,
By the mercy that endears.
Spare him!—he our love hath shared!
Spare him!—as thou wouldst be spared!

"Take thy banner!—and if e'er
Thou shouldst press the soldier's bier,
And the muffled drum should beat
To the tread of mournful feet,
Then this crimson flag shall be
Martial cloak and shroud for thee."

The warrior took that banner proud
And it was his martial cloak and shroud!

SUNRISE ON THE HILLS

I stood upon the hills, when heaven's wide arch
Was glorious with the sun's returning march,

And woods were brightened, and soft gales
Went forth to kiss the sun-clad vales.
The clouds were far beneath me;—bathed in light,
They gathered mid-way round the wooded height,
And, in their fading glory shone
Like hosts in battle overthrown,
As many a pinnacle, with shifting glance,
Through the gray mist thrust up its shattered lance,
And rocking on the cliff was left
The dark pine blasted, bare, and cleft.
The veil of cloud was lifted, and below
Glowed the rich valley, and the river's flow
Was darkened by the forest's shade,
Or glistened in the white cascade;
Where upward, in the mellow blush of day,
The noisy bittern wheeled his spiral way.

I heard the distant waters dash,
I saw the current whirl and flash
And richly, by the blue lake's silver beach,
The woods were bending with a silent reach.
Then o'er the vale, with gentle swell,
The music of the village bell
Came sweetly to the echo-giving hills,
And the wild horn, whose voice the woodland fills,
Was ringing to the merry shout,
That faint and far the glen sent out,
Where, answering to the sudden shot, thin smoke,
Through thick-leaved branches, from the dingle broke.

If thou art worn and hard beset
With sorrows, that thou wouldst forget,
If thou wouldst read a lesson, that will keep
Thy heart from fainting and thy soul from sleep,
Go to the woods and hills!—no tears
Dim the sweet look that Nature wears.

THE SPIRIT OF POETRY

There is a quiet spirit in these woods,
That dwells where'er the gentle south wind blows;
Where, underneath the white-thorn, in the glade,

The wild flowers bloom, or, kissing the soft air,
The leaves above their sunny palms outspread.
With what a tender and impassioned voice
It fills the nice and delicate ear of thought,
When the fast-ushering star of morning comes
O'er-riding the gray hills with golden scarf;
Or when the cowled and dusky-sandalled Eve,
In mourning weeds, from out the western gate,
Departs with silent pace! That spirit moves
In the green valley, where the silver brook,
From its full laver, pours the white cascade;
And, babbling low amid the tangled woods,
Slips down through moss-grown stones with endless laughter.
And frequent, on the everlasting hills,
Its feet go forth, when it doth wrap itself
In all the dark embroidery of the storm,
And shouts the stern, strong wind. And here, amid
The silent majesty of these deep woods,
Its presence shall uplift thy thoughts from earth,
As to the sunshine and the pure, bright air
Their tops the green trees lift. Hence gifted bards
Have ever loved the calm and quiet shades.
For them there was an eloquent voice in all
The sylvan pomp of woods, the golden sun,
The flowers, the leaves, the river on its way,
Blue skies, and silver clouds, and gentle winds,—
The swelling upland, where the sidelong sun
Aslant the wooded slope, at evening goes,—
Groves, through whose broken roof the sky looks in,
Mountain, and shattered cliff, and sunny vale,
The distant lake, fountains,—and mighty trees,
In many a lazy syllable, repeating
Their old poetic legends to the wind.

And this is the sweet spirit that doth fill
The world; and, in these wayward days of youth,
My busy fancy oft embodies it,
As a bright image of the light and beauty
That dwell in nature,—of the heavenly forms
We worship in our dreams, and the soft hues

That stain the wild bird's wing, and flush the clouds
When the sun sets. Within her eye
The heaven of April, with its changing light,
And when it wears the blue of May, is hung,
And on her lip the rich, red rose. Her hair
Is like the summer tresses of the trees,
When twilight makes them brown, and on her cheek
Blushes the richness of an autumn sky,
With ever-shifting beauty. Then her breath,
It is so like the gentle air of Spring,
As, from the morning's dewy flowers, it comes
Full of their fragrance, that it is a joy
To have it round us,—and her silver voice
Is the rich music of a summer bird,
Heard in the still night, with its passionate cadence.

BURIAL OF THE MINNISINK

On sunny slope and beechen swell,
The shadowed light of evening fell;
And, where the maple's leaf was brown,
With soft and silent lapse came down
The glory, that the wood receives,
At sunset, in its brazen leaves.

Far upward in the mellow light
Rose the blue hills. One cloud of white,
Around a far uplifted cone,
In the warm blush of evening shone;
An image of the silver lakes,
By which the Indian's soul awakes.

But soon a funeral hymn was heard
Where the soft breath of evening stirred
The tall, gray forest; and a band
Of stern in heart, and strong in hand,
Came winding down beside the wave,
To lay the red chief in his grave.

They sang, that by his native bowers
He stood, in the last moon of flowers
And thirty snows had not yet shed
Their glory on the warrior's head;
But, as the summer fruit decays,
So died he in those naked days.

A dark cloak of the roebuck's skin
Covered the warrior, and within
Its heavy folds the weapons, made
For the hard toils of war, were laid;
The cuirass, woven of plaited reeds,
And the broad belt of shells and beads.

Before, a dark-haired virgin train
Chanted the death dirge of the slain;
Behind, the long procession came
Of hoary men and chiefs of fame,
With heavy hearts, and eyes of grief,
Leading the war-horse of their chief.

Stripped of his proud and martial dress,
Uncurbed, unreined, and riderless,
With darting eye, and nostril spread,
And heavy and impatient tread,
He came; and oft that eye so proud
Asked for his rider in the crowd.

They buried the dark chief, they freed
Beside the grave his battle steed;
And swift an arrow cleaved its way
To his stern heart! One piercing neigh
Arose,—and, on the dead man's plain,
The rider grasps his steed again.

TRANSLATIONS

[Don Jorge Manrique, the author of the following poem, flourished in the last half of the fifteenth century. He followed the profession of arms, and died on the field of battle. Mariana, in his History of Spain, makes honorable mention of him, as being present at the siege of Uclés; and speaks of him as "a youth of estimable qualities, who in this war gave brilliant proofs of his valor. He died young; and was thus cut off from long exercising his great virtues, and exhibiting to the world the light of his genius, which was already known to fame." He was mortally wounded in a skirmish near Cañavete, in the year 1479.

The name of Rodrigo Manrique, the father of the poet, Conde de Paredes and Maestre de Santiago, is well known in Spanish history and song. He died in 1476; according to Mariana, in the town of Uclés; but, according to the poem of his son, in Ocaña. It was his death that called forth the poem upon which rests the literary reputation of the younger Manrique. In the language of his historian, "Don Jorge Manrique, in an elegant Ode, full of poetic beauties, rich embellishments of genius, and high moral reflections, mourned the death of his father as with a funeral hymn." This praise is not exaggerated. The poem is a model in its kind. Its conception is solemn and beautiful; and, in accordance with it, the style moves on—calm, dignified, and majestic.]

COPLAS DE MANRIQUE

FROM THE SPANISH

O let the soul her slumbers break
Let thought be quickened, and awake;
Awake to see
How soon this life is past and gone,
And death comes softly stealing on,
How silently!

Swiftly our pleasures glide away,
Our hearts recall the distant day
With many sighs;
The moments that are speeding fast
We heed not, but the past,—the past,—
More highly prize.

Onward its course the present keeps
Onward the constant current sweeps,
Till life is done;

And, did we judge of time aright,
The past and future in their flight
Would be as one.

Let no one fondly dream again,
That Hope and all her shadowy train
Will not decay;
Fleeting as were the dreams of old,
Remembered like a tale that's told,
They pass away.

Our lives are rivers, gliding free
To that unfathomed, boundless sea,
The silent grave!
Thither all earthly pomp and boast
Roll, to be swallowed up and lost
In one dark wave.

Thither the mighty torrents stray,
Thither the brook pursues its way,
And tinkling rill.
There all are equal. Side by side
The poor man and the son of pride
Lie calm and still.

I will not here invoke the throng
Of orators and sons of song,
The deathless few;
Fiction entices and deceives,
And, sprinkled o'er her fragrant leaves,
Lies poisonous dew.

To One alone my thoughts arise,
The Eternal Truth,—the Good and Wise,—
To Him I cry,
Who shared on earth our common lot,
But the world comprehended not
His deity.

This world is but the rugged road
Which leads us to the bright abode
Of peace above;

So let us choose that narrow way,
Which leads no traveller's foot astray
From realms of love.

Our cradle is the starting-place,
In life we run the onward race,
And reach the goal;
When, in the mansions of the blest,
Death leaves to its eternal rest
The weary soul.

Did we but use it as we ought,
This world would school each wandering thought
To its high state.
Faith wings the soul beyond the sky,
Up to that better world on high,
For which we wait.

Yes,—the glad messenger of love,
To guide us to our home above,
The Saviour came;
Born amid mortal cares and fears,
He suffered in this vale of tears
A death of shame.

Behold of what delusive worth
The bubbles we pursue on earth,
The shapes we chase,
Amid a world of treachery!
They vanish ere death shuts the eye,
And leave no trace.

Time steals them from us,—chances strange,
Disastrous accidents, and change,
That come to all;
Even in the most exalted state,
Relentless sweeps the stroke of fate;
The strongest fall.

Tell me,—the charms that lovers seek
In the clear eye and blushing cheek,
The hues that play

O'er rosy lip and brow of snow,
When hoary age approaches slow,
Ah, where are they?

The cunning skill, the curious arts,
The glorious strength that youth imparts
In life's first stage;
These shall become a heavy weight
When Time swings wide his outward gate
To weary age.

The noble blood of Gothic name,
Heroes emblazoned high to fame,
In long array;
How, in the onward course of time,
The landmarks of that race sublime
Were swept away!

Some, the degraded slaves of lust,
Prostrate and trampled in the dust
Shall rise no more;
Others, by guilt and crime, maintain
The scutcheon, that, without a stain,
Their fathers bore.

Wealth and the high estate of pride,
With what untimely speed they glide,
How soon depart!
Bid not the shadowy phantoms stay,
The vassals of a mistress they,
Of fickle heart.

These gifts in Fortune's hands are found;
Her swift revolving wheel turns round,
And they are gone!
No rest the inconstant goddess knows,
But changing, and without repose,
Still hurries on.

Even could the hand of avarice save
Its gilded baubles, till the grave
Reclaimed its prey,

Let none on such poor hopes rely,
Life, like an empty dream, flits by
And where are they?

Earthly desires and sensual lust
Are passions springing from the dust,—
They fade and die;
But, in the life beyond the tomb,
They seal the immortal spirit's doom
Eternally!

The pleasures and delights, which mask
In treacherous smiles life's serious task,
What are they, all,
But the fleet coursers of the chase,
And death an ambush in the race,
Wherein we fall?

No foe, no dangerous pass, we heed,
Brook no delay,—but onward speed
With loosened rein;
And, when the fatal snare is near,
We strive to check our mad career,
But strive in vain.

Could we new charms to age impart
And fashion with a cunning art
The human face,
As we can clothe the soul with light,
And make the glorious spirit bright
With heavenly grace,—

How busily each passing hour
Should we exert that magic power!
What ardor show,
To deck the sensual slave of sin,
Yet leave the freeborn soul within,
In weeds of woe!

Monarchs, the powerful and the strong,
Famous in history and in song
Of olden time,

Saw, by the stern decrees of fate,
Their kingdoms lost, and desolate
Their race sublime.

Who is the champion? who the strong?
Pontiff and priest, and sceptred throng?
On these shall fall
As heavily the hand of Death,
As when it stays the shepherd's breath
Beside his stall.

I speak not of the Trojan name,
Neither its glory nor its shame
Has met our eyes;
Nor of Rome's great and glorious dead
Though we have heard so oft, and read
Their histories.

Little avails it now to know
Of ages passed so long ago,
Nor how they rolled;
Our theme shall be of yesterday,
Which to oblivion sweeps away,
Like days of old.

Where is the King, Don Juan? Where
Each royal prince and noble heir
Of Aragon?
Where are the courtly gallantries?
The deeds of love and high emprise
In battle done?

Tourney and joust, that charmed the eye,
And scarf, and gorgeous panoply,
And nodding plume,—
What were they but a pageant scene?
What but the garlands, gay and green,
That deck the tomb?

Where are the high-born dames, and where
Their gay attire and jewelled hair,
And odors sweet?

Where are the gentle knights, that came
To kneel, and breathe love's ardent flame,
Low at their feet?

Where is the song of Troubadour?
Where are the lute and gay tambour
They loved of yore?
Where is the mazy dance of old,
The flowing robes, inwrought with gold,
The dancers wore?

And he who next the sceptre swayed,
Henry, whose royal court displayed,
Such power and pride;
O, in what winning smiles arrayed,
The world its various pleasures laid
His throne beside!

But O! how false and full of guile
That world, which wore so soft a smile
But to betray!
She, that had been his friend before,
Now from the fated monarch tore
Her charms away.

The countless gifts,—the stately walls,
The royal palaces, and halls
All filled with gold;
Plate with armorial bearings wrought,
Chambers with ample treasures fraught
Of wealth untold;

The noble steeds, and harness bright,
And gallant lord, and stalwart knight,
In rich array,—
Where shall we seek them now? Alas!
Like the bright dewdrops on the grass,
They passed away.

His brother, too, whose factious zeal
Usurped the sceptre of Castile,
Unskilled to reign;

What a gay, brilliant court had he,
When all the flower of chivalry
Was in his train!

But he was mortal; and the breath
That flamed from the hot forge of Death
Blasted his years;
Judgment of God! that flame by thee,
When raging fierce and fearfully,
Was quenched in tears!

Spain's haughty Constable,—the true
And gallant Master, whom we knew
Most loved of all.
Breathe not a whisper of his pride,—
He on the gloomy scaffold died,
Ignoble fall!

The countless treasures of his care,
His hamlets green, and cities fair,
His mighty power,—
What were they all but grief and shame,
Tears and a broken heart, when came
The parting hour?

His other brothers, proud and high,
Masters, who, in prosperity,
Might rival kings;
Who made the bravest and the best
The bondsmen of their high behest,
Their underlings;

What was their prosperous estate,
When high exalted and elate
With power and pride?
What, but a transient gleam of light,
A flame, which, glaring at its height,
Grew dim and died?

So many a duke of royal name,
Marquis and count of spotless fame,
And baron brave,

That might the sword of empire wield,
All these, O Death, hast thou concealed
In the dark grave!

Their deeds of mercy and of arms,
In peaceful days, or war's alarms,
When thou dost show,
O Death, thy stern and angry face,
One stroke of thy all-powerful mace
Can overthrow.

Unnumbered hosts, that threaten nigh,
Pennon and standard flaunting high,
And flag displayed;
High battlements intrenched around,
Bastion, and moated wall, and mound,
And palisade,

And covered trench, secure and deep,—
All these cannot one victim keep,
O Death, from thee,
When thou dost battle in thy wrath,
And the strong shafts pursue their path
Unerringly.

O World! so few the years we live,
Would that the life which thou dost give
Were life indeed!
Alas! thy sorrows fall so fast,
Our happiest hour is when at last
The soul is freed.

Our days are covered o'er with grief,
And sorrows neither few nor brief
Veil all in gloom;
Left desolate of real good,
Within this cheerless solitude
No pleasures bloom.

Thy pilgrimage begins in tears,
And ends in bitter doubts and fears,
Or dark despair;

Midway so many toils appear,
That he who lingers longest here
Knows most of care.

Thy goods are bought with many a groan,
By the hot sweat of toil alone,
And weary hearts;
Fleet-footed is the approach of woe,
But with a lingering step and slow
Its form departs.

And he, the good man's shield and shade,
To whom all hearts their homage paid,
As Virtue's son,—
Roderic Manrique,—he whose name
Is written on the scroll of Fame,
Spain's champion;

His signal deeds and prowess high
Demand no pompous eulogy,—
Ye saw his deeds!
Why should their praise in verse be sung?
The name, that dwells on every tongue,
No minstrel needs.

To friends a friend;—how kind to all
The vassals of this ancient hall
And feudal fief!
To foes how stern a foe was he!
And to the valiant and the free
How brave a chief!

What prudence with the old and wise:
What grace in youthful gayeties;
In all how sage!
Benignant to the serf and slave,
He showed the base and falsely brave
A lion's rage.

His was Octavian's prosperous star,
The rush of Cæsar's conquering car
At battle's call;

His, Scipio's virtue; his, the skill
And the indomitable will
Of Hannibal.

His was a Trajan's goodness,—his
A Titus' noble charities
And righteous laws;
The arm of Hector, and the might
Of Tully, to maintain the right
In truth's just cause;

The clemency of Antonine,
Aurelius' countenance divine.
Firm, gentle, still;
The eloquence of Adrian,
And Theodosius' love to man,
And generous will;

In tented field and bloody fray,
An Alexander's vigorous sway
And stern command;
The faith of Constantine; ay, more,
The fervent love Camillus bore
His native land.

He left no well-filled treasury,
He heaped no pile of riches high,
Nor massive plate;
He fought the Moors, and, in their fall,
City and tower and castled wall
Were his estate.

Upon the hard-fought battle-ground,
Brave steeds and gallant riders found
A common grave;
And there the warrior's hand did gain
The rents, and the long vassal train,
That conquest gave.

And if, of old, his halls displayed
The honored and exalted grade
His worth had gained,

So, in the dark, disastrous hour,
Brothers and bondsmen of his power
His hand sustained.

After high deeds, not left untold,
In the stern warfare, which of old
'T was his to share,
Such noble leagues he made, that more
And fairer regions, than before,
His guerdon were.

These are the records, half effaced,
Which, with the hand of youth, he traced
On history's page;
But with fresh victories he drew
Each fading character anew
In his old age.

By his unrivalled skill, by great
And veteran service to the state,
By worth adored,
He stood, in his high dignity,
The proudest knight of chivalry,
Knight of the Sword.

He found his cities and domains
Beneath a tyrant's galling chains
And cruel power;
But, by fierce battle and blockade,
Soon his own banner was displayed
From every tower.

By the tried valor of his hand,
His monarch and his native land
Were nobly served;
Let Portugal repeat the story,
And proud Castile, who shared the glory
His arms deserved.

And when so oft, for weal or woe,
His life upon the fatal throw
Had been cast down;

When he had served, with patriot zeal,
Beneath the banner of Castile,
His sovereign's crown;

And done such deeds of valor strong,
That neither history nor song
Can count them all;
Then, on Ocaña's castled rock,
Death at his portal came to knock,
With sudden call,—

Saying, "Good Cavalier, prepare
To leave this world of toil and care
With joyful mien;
Let thy strong heart of steel this day
Put on its armor for the fray,—
The closing scene.

"Since thou hast been, in battle strife,
So prodigal of health and life,
For earthly fame,
Let virtue nerve thy heart again;
Loud on the last stern battle-plain
They call thy name.

"Think not the struggle that draws near
Too terrible for man,—nor fear
To meet the foe;
Nor let thy noble spirit grieve,
Its life of glorious fame to leave
On earth below.

"A life of honor and of worth
Has no eternity on earth,—
'T is but a name;
And yet its glory far exceeds
That base and sensual life, which leads
To want and shame.

"The eternal life, beyond the sky,
Wealth cannot purchase, nor the high
And proud estate;

The soul in dalliance laid,—the spirit
Corrupt with sin,—shall not inherit
A joy so great.

"But the good monk, in cloistered cell,
Shall gain it by his book and bell,
His prayers and tears;
And the brave knight, whose arm endures
Fierce battle, and against the Moors
His standard rears.

"And thou, brave knight, whose hand has poured
The life-blood of the Pagan horde
O'er all the land,
In heaven shalt thou receive, at length,
The guerdon of thine earthly strength
And dauntless hand.

"Cheered onward by this promise sure,
Strong in the faith entire and pure
Thou dost profess,
Depart,—thy hope is certainty,—
The third—the better life on high
Shalt thou possess."

"O Death, no more, no more delay:
My spirit longs to flee away,
And be at rest;
The will of Heaven my will shall be,—
I bow to the divine decree,
To God's behest.

"My soul is ready to depart,
No thought rebels, the obedient heart
Breathes forth no sigh;
The wish on earth to linger still
Were vain, when 't is God's sovereign will
That we shall die.

"O thou, that for our sins didst take
A human form, and humbly make
Thy home on earth;

Thou, that to thy divinity
A human nature didst ally
By mortal birth,

"And in that form didst suffer here
Torment, and agony, and fear,
So patiently;
By thy redeeming grace alone,
And not for merits of my own,
O, pardon me!"

As thus the dying warrior prayed,
Without one gathering mist or shade
Upon his mind;
Encircled by his family,
Watched by affection's gentle eye,
So soft and kind;

His soul to Him, who gave it, rose;
God lead it to its long repose,
Its glorious rest!
And, though the warrior's sun has set,
Its light shall linger round us yet,
Bright, radiant, blest.[1]

[1] This poem of Manrique is a great favorite in Spain. No less than four poetic Glosses, or running commentaries, upon it have been published, no one of which, however, possesses great poetic merit. That of the Carthusian monk, Rodrigo de Valddepeñas, is the best. It is known as the *Glosa del Cartujo*. There is also a prose Commentary by Luis de Aranda.

The following stanzas of the poem were found in the author's pocket, after his death on the field of battle:—

"O World! so few the years we live,
    Would that the life which thou dost give
    Were life indeed!
Alas! thy sorrows fall so fast,
Our happiest hour is when at last
    The soul is freed.

"Our days are covered o'er with grief,
    And sorrows neither few nor brief
    Veil all in gloom;

The Good Shepherd

FROM THE SPANISH OF LOPE DE VEGA

Shepherd! that with thine amorous, sylvan song
Hast broken the slumber which encompassed me,—
That mad'st thy crook from the accursed tree,
On which thy powerful arms were stretched so long!
Lead me to mercy's ever flowing fountains;
For thou my shepherd, guard, and guide shalt be;
I will obey thy voice, and wait to see
Thy feet all beautiful upon the mountains.
Here, Shepherd!—thou who for thy flock art dying,
O, wash away these scarlet sins, for thou
Rejoicest at the contrite sinner's vow.
O, wait!—to thee my weary soul is crying,—
Wait for me!—Yet why ask it, when I see,
With feet nailed to the cross, thou'rt waiting still for me!

To-morrow

FROM THE SPANISH OF LOPE DE VEGA

Lord, what am I, that, with unceasing care,
Thou didst seek after me,—that thou didst wait,
Wet with unhealthy dews, before my gate,
And pass the gloomy nights of winter there?

Left desolate of real good,
Within this cheerless solitude
No pleasures bloom.
"Thy pilgrimage begins in tears,
And ends in bitter doubts and fears,
Or dark despair;
Midway so many toils appear,
That he who lingers longest here
Knows most of care.
"Thy goods are bought with many a groan,
By the hot sweat of toil alone,
And weary hearts;
Fleet-footed is the approach of woe,
But with a lingering step and slow
Its form departs."

O strange delusion!—that I did not greet
Thy blest approach, and O, to Heaven how lost,
If my ingratitude's unkindly frost
Has chilled the bleeding wounds upon thy feet.
How oft my guardian angel gently cried,
"Soul, from thy casement look, and thou shalt see
How he persists to knock and wait for thee!"
And, O! how often to that voice of sorrow,
"To-morrow we will open," I replied,
And when the morrow came I answered still, "To-morrow."

THE NATIVE LAND

FROM THE SPANISH OF FRANCISCO DE ALDANA

Clear fount of light! my native land on high,
Bright with a glory that shall never fade!
Mansion of truth! without a veil or shade,
Thy holy quiet meets the spirit's eye.
There dwells the soul in its ethereal essence,
Gasping no longer for life's feeble breath;
But, sentinelled in heaven, its glorious presence
With pitying eye beholds, yet fears not, death.
Beloved country! banished from thy shore,
A stranger in this prison-house of clay,
The exiled spirit weeps and sighs for thee!
Heavenward the bright perfections I adore
Direct, and the sure promise cheers the way,
That, whither love aspires, there shall my dwelling be.

THE IMAGE OF GOD

FROM THE SPANISH OF FRANCISCO DE ALDANA

O Lord! that seest, from yon starry height,
Centred in one the future and the past,
Fashioned in thine own image, see how fast
The world obscures in me what once was bright!
Eternal Sun! the warmth which thou hast given,

To cheer life's flowery April, fast decays;
Yet, in the hoary winter of my days,
Forever green shall be my trust in Heaven.
Celestial King! O let thy presence pass
Before my spirit, and an image fair
Shall meet that look of mercy from on high,
As the reflected image in a glass
Doth meet the look of him who seeks it there,
And owes its being to the gazer's eye.

THE BROOK

FROM THE SPANISH

Laugh of the mountain!—lyre of bird and tree!
Pomp of the meadow! mirror of the morn!
The soul of April, unto whom are born
The rose and jessamine, leaps wild in thee!
Although, where'er thy devious current strays,
The lap of earth with gold and silver teems
To me thy clear proceeding brighter seems
Than golden sands, that charm each shepherd's gaze.
How without guile thy bosom, all transparent
As the pure crystal, lets the curious eye
Thy secrets scan, thy smooth, round pebbles count!
How, without malice murmuring, glides thy current!
O sweet simplicity of days gone by!
Thou shun'st the haunts of man, to dwell in limpid fount!

THE CELESTIAL PILOT

FROM DANTE. PURGATORIO, II

And now, behold! as at the approach of morning,
Through the gross vapors, Mars grows fiery red
Down in the west upon the ocean floor,

Appeared to me,—may I again behold it!—
A light along the sea, so swiftly coming,
Its motion by no flight of wing is equalled.

And when therefrom I had withdrawn a little
Mine eyes, that I might question my conductor,
Again I saw it brighter grown and larger.

Thereafter, on all sides of it, appeared
I knew not what of white, and underneath,
Little by little, there came forth another.

My master yet had uttered not a word,
While the first brightness into wings unfolded;
But, when he clearly recognized the pilot,

He cried aloud: "Quick, quick, and bow the knee!
Behold the Angel of God! fold up thy hands!
Henceforward shalt thou see such officers!

"See, how he scorns all human arguments,
So that no oar he wants nor other sail
Than his own wings, between so distant shores!

"See, how he holds them, pointed straight to heaven,
Fanning the air with the eternal pinions,
That do not moult themselves like mortal hair!"

And then, as nearer and more near us came
The Bird of Heaven, more glorious he appeared,
So that the eye could not sustain his presence,

But down I cast it; and he came to shore
With a small vessel, gliding swift and light,
So that the water swallowed naught thereof.

Upon the stern stood the Celestial Pilot!
Beatitude seemed written in his face!
And more than a hundred spirits sat within.

"In exitu Israel out of Egypt!"
Thus sang they all together in one voice,
With whatso in that Psalm is after written.

Then made he sign of holy rood upon them,
Whereat all cast themselves upon the shore,
And he departed swiftly as he came.

THE TERRESTRIAL PARADISE

FROM DANTE. PURGATORIO, XXVIII

Longing already to search in and round
The heavenly forest, dense and living-green,
Which to the eyes tempered the new-born day,

Withouten more delay I left the bank,
Crossing the level country slowly, slowly,
Over the soil, that everywhere breathed fragrance,

A gently-breathing air, that no mutation
Had in itself, smote me upon the forehead,
No heavier blow, than of a pleasant breeze.

Whereat the tremulous branches readily
Did all of them bow downward towards that side
Where its first shadow casts the Holy Mountain;

Yet not from their upright direction bent
So that the little birds upon their tops
Should cease the practice of their tuneful art;

But, with full-throated joy, the hours of prime
Singing received they in the midst of foliage
That made monotonous burden to their rhymes,

Even as from branch to branch it gathering swells,
Through the pine forests on the shore of Chiassi,
When Æolus unlooses the Sirocco.

Already my slow steps had led me on
Into the ancient wood so far, that I
Could see no more the place where I had entered.

And lo! my farther course cut off a river,
Which, towards the left hand, with its little waves,
Bent down the grass, that on its margin sprang.

All waters that on earth most limpid are,
Would seem to have within themselves some mixture,
Compared with that, which nothing doth conceal,

Although it moves on with a brown, brown current,
Under the shade perpetual, that never
Ray of the sun lets in, nor of the moon.

BEATRICE

FROM DANTE. PURGATORIO, XXX, XXXI

Even as the Blessed, in the new covenant,
Shall rise up quickened, each one from his grave,
Wearing again the garments of the flesh,

So, upon that celestial chariot,
A hundred rose *ad vocem tanti senis,*
Ministers and messengers of life eternal.

They all were saying: "*Benedictus qui venis,*"
And scattering flowers above and round about,
"*Manibus o date lilia plenis.*"

I once beheld, at the approach of day,
The orient sky all stained with roseate hues,
And the other heaven with light serene adorned,

And the sun's face uprising, overshadowed,
So that, by temperate influence of vapors,
The eye sustained his aspect for long while;

Thus in the bosom of a cloud of flowers,
Which from those hands angelic were thrown up
And down descended inside and without,

With crown of olive o'er a snow-white veil,
Appeared a lady, under a green mantle,
Vested in colors of the living flame.

.   .   .   .

Even as the snow, among the living rafters
Upon the back of Italy, congeals,
Blown on and beaten by Sclavonian winds,

And then, dissolving, filters through itself,
Whene'er the land, that loses shadow, breathes,
Like as a taper melts before a fire,

Even such I was, without a sigh or tear,
Before the song of those who chime forever
After the chiming of the eternal spheres;

But, when I heard in those sweet melodies
Compassion for me, more than had they said,
"O wherefore, lady, dost thou thus consume him?"

The ice, that was about my heart congealed,
To air and water changed, and, in my anguish,
Through lips and eyes came gushing from my breast.

    .   .   .   .

Confusion and dismay, together mingled,
Forced such a feeble "Yes!" out of my mouth,
To understand it one had need of sight.

Even as a cross-bow breaks, when 't is discharged,
Too tensely drawn the bow-string and the bow,
And with less force the arrow hits the mark;

So I gave way under this heavy burden,
Gushing forth into bitter tears and sighs,
And the voice, fainting, flagged upon its passage.

Spring

FROM THE FRENCH OF CHARLES D'ORLÉANS

XV. Century

Gentle Spring!—in sunshine clad,
  Well dost thou thy power display!
For Winter maketh the light heart sad,
  And thou,—thou makest the sad heart gay.
He sees thee, and calls to his gloomy train,
The sleet, and the snow, and the wind, and the rain;
And they shrink away, and they flee in fear,
  When thy merry step draws near.

Winter giveth the fields and the trees, so old,
  Their beards of icicles and snow;
And the rain, it raineth so fast and cold,
  We must cower over the embers low;
And, snugly housed from the wind and weather,
Mope like birds that are changing feather.
But the storm retires, and the sky grows clear,
  When thy merry step draws near.

Winter maketh the sun in the gloomy sky
  Wrap him round with a mantle of cloud;
But, Heaven be praised, thy step is nigh;
  Thou tearest away the mournful shroud,
And the earth looks bright, and Winter surly,
Who has toiled for naught both late and early,
Is banished afar by the new-born year,
  When thy merry step draws near.

THE CHILD ASLEEP

FROM THE FRENCH

Sweet babe! true portrait of thy father's face,
  Sleep on the bosom that thy lips have pressed!
Sleep, little one; and closely, gently place
  Thy drowsy eyelid on thy mother's breast.

Upon that tender eye, my little friend,
  Soft sleep shall come, that cometh not to me!
I watch to see thee, nourish thee, defend;—
  'T is sweet to watch for thee,—alone for thee!

His arms fall down; sleep sits upon his brow;
  His eye is closed; he sleeps, nor dreams of harm.
Wore not his cheek the apple's ruddy glow,
  Would you not say he slept on Death's cold arm?

Awake, my boy!—I tremble with affright!
  Awake, and chase this fatal thought!—Unclose
Thine eye but for one moment on the light!
  Even at the price of thine, give me repose!

Sweet error!—he but slept,—I breathe again;—
   Come, gentle dreams, the hour of sleep beguile!
O! when shall he, for whom I sigh in vain,
   Beside me watch to see thy waking smile?

THE GRAVE

FROM THE ANGLO-SAXON

For thee was a house built
Ere thou wast born,
For thee was a mould meant
Ere thou of mother camest.
But it is not made ready,
Nor its depth measured,
Nor is it seen
How long it shall be.
Now I bring thee
Where thou shalt be;
Now I shall measure thee,
And the mould afterwards.

Thy house is not
Highly timbered,
It is unhigh and low;
When thou art therein
The heel-ways are low,
The side-ways unhigh.
The roof is built
Thy breast full nigh,
So thou shalt in mould
Dwell full cold,
Dimly and dark.

Doorless is that house,
And dark it is within;
There thou art fast detained
And Death hath the key.
Loathsome is that earth-house,

And grim within to dwell.
There thou shalt dwell,
And worms shall divide thee.

Thus thou art laid,
And leavest thy friends;
Thou hast no friend,
Who will come to thee,
Who will ever see
How that house pleaseth thee;
Who will ever open
The door for thee,
And descend after thee,
For soon thou art loathsome
And hateful to see.

KING CHRISTIAN

A NATIONAL SONG OF DENMARK

FROM THE DANISH OF JOHANNES EVALD

KING CHRISTIAN stood by the lofty mast
    In mist and smoke;
His sword was hammering so fast,
Through Gothic helm and brain it passed;
Then sank each hostile hulk and mast,
    In mist and smoke.
"Fly!" shouted they, "fly, he who can!
Who braves of Denmark's Christian
    The stroke?"

Nils Juel gave heed to the tempest's roar,
    Now is the hour!
He hoisted his blood-red flag once more,
And smote upon the foe full sore
And shouted loud, through the tempest's roar,
    "Now is the hour!"
"Fly!" shouted they, "for shelter fly!
Of Denmark's Juel who can defy
    The power?"

North Sea! a glimpse of Wessel rent
    Thy murky sky!
Then champions to thine arms were sent;
Terror and Death glared where he went;
From the waves was heard a wail, that rent
    Thy murky sky!
From Denmark, thunders Tordenskiol',
Let each to Heaven commend his soul,
    And fly!

Path of the Dane to fame and might!
    Dark-rolling wave!
Receive thy friend, who, scorning flight,
Goes to meet danger with despite,
Proudly as thou the tempest's might
    Dark-rolling wave!
And amid pleasures and alarms,
And war and victory, be thine arms
    My grave! [1]

THE HAPPIEST LAND

FRAGMENT OF A MODERN BALLAD

FROM THE GERMAN

There sat one day in quiet,
    By an alehouse on the Rhine,
Four hale and hearty fellows,
    And drank the precious wine.

The landlord's daughter filled their cups,
    Around the rustic board;
Then sat they all so calm and still,
    And spake not one rude word.

[1] Nils Juel was a celebrated Danish Admiral, and Peder Wessel a Vice-Admiral, who for his great prowess received the popular title of Tordenskiold, or *Thunder shield*. In childhood he was a tailor's apprentice, and rose to his high rank before the age of twenty-eight, when he was killed in a duel.

But, when the maid departed,
  A Swabian raised his hand,
And cried, all hot and flushed with wine,
  "Long live the Swabian land!

"The greatest kingdom upon earth
  Cannot with that compare;
With all the stout and hardy men
  And the nut-brown maidens there."

"Ha!" cried a Saxon, laughing,—
  And dashed his beard with wine;
"I had rather live in Lapland,
  Than that Swabian land of thine!

"The goodliest land on all this earth,
  It is the Saxon land!
There have I as many maidens
  As fingers on this hand!"

"Hold your tongues! both Swabian and Saxon!"
  A bold Bohemian cries;
"If there's a heaven upon this earth,
  In Bohemia it lies.

"There the tailor blows the lute,
  And the cobbler blows the horn,
And the miner blows the bugle,
  Over mountain gorge and bourn."

.   .

And then the landlord's daughter
  Up to heaven raised her hand
And said, "Ye may no more contend,—
  There lies the happiest land!"

THE WAVE

FROM THE GERMAN OF TIEDGE

"Whither, thou turbid wave?
Whither, with so much haste,
As if a thief wert thou!"

"I am the Wave of Life,
Stained with my margin's dust;
From the struggle and the strife
Of the narrow stream I fly
To the Sea's immensity,
To wash from me the slime
Of the muddy banks of Time."

THE DEAD

FROM THE GERMAN OF KLOPSTOCK

How they so softly rest,
All, all the holy dead,
Unto whose dwelling-place
Now doth my soul draw near!
How they so softly rest,
All in their silent graves,
Deep to corruption
Slowly down-sinking!

And they no longer weep,
Here, where complaint is still!
And they no longer feel,
Here, where all gladness flies!
And, by the cypresses
Softly o'ershadowed,
Until the Angel
Calls them, they slumber!

THE BIRD AND THE SHIP

FROM THE GERMAN OF MÜLLER

"The rivers rush into the sea,
By castle and town they go;
The winds behind them merrily
Their noisy trumpets blow.

"The clouds are passing far and high,
We little birds in them play;
And everything, that can sing and fly,
Goes with us, and far away.

"I greet thee, bonny boat! Whither, or whence,
  With thy fluttering golden band?"—
"I greet thee, little bird! To the wide sea
  I haste from the narrow land.

"Full and swollen is every sail;
  I see no longer a hill,
I have trusted all to the sounding gale,
  And it will not let me stand still.

"And wilt thou, little bird, go with us?
  Thou mayest stand on the mainmast tall,
For full to sinking is my house
  With merry companions all."—

"I need not and seek not company,
  Bonny boat, I can sing all alone;
For the mainmast tall too heavy am I,
  Bonny boat, I have wings of my own.

"High over the sails, high over the mast,
  Who shall gainsay these joys?
When thy merry companions are still, at last,
  Thou shalt hear the sound of my voice.

"Who neither may rest, nor listen may,
  God bless them every one!
I dart away, in the bright blue day,
  And the golden fields of the sun.

"Thus do I sing my weary song,
  Wherever the four winds blow;
And this same song, my whole life long,
  Neither Poet nor Printer may know."

WHITHER?

FROM THE GERMAN OF MÜLLER

I heard a brooklet gushing
  From its rocky fountain near,
Down into the valley rushing,
  So fresh and wondrous clear.

I know not what came o'er me
   Nor who the counsel gave;
But I must hasten downward,
   All with my prilgrim-stave;

Downward, and ever farther,
   And ever the brook beside;
And ever fresher murmured,
   And ever clearer, the tide.

Is this the way I was going?
   Whither, O brooklet, say!
Thou hast, with thy soft murmur,
   Murmured my senses away.

What do I say of a murmur?
   That can no murmur be;
'T is the water-nymphs, that are singing
   Their roundelays under me.

Let them sing, my friend, let them murmur,
   And wander merrily near;
The wheels of a mill are going
   In every brooklet clear.

BEWARE!

FROM THE GERMAN

I know a maiden fair to see,
   Take care!
She can both false and friendly be,
   Beware! Beware!
   Trust her not,
She is fooling thee!

She has two eyes, so soft and brown,
   Take care!
She gives a side-glance and looks down,
   Beware! Beware!
   Trust her not,
She is fooling thee!

And she has hair of a golden hue,
  Take care!
And what she says, it is not true,
  Beware! Beware!
   Trust her not,
She is fooling thee!

She has a bosom as white as snow,
  Take care!
She knows how much it is best to show,
  Beware! Beware!
   Trust her not,
She is fooling thee!

She gives thee a garland woven fair,
  Take care!
It is a fool's-cap for thee to wear,
  Beware! Beware!
   Trust her not,
She is fooling thee!

SONG OF THE BELL

FROM THE GERMAN

Bell! thou soundest merrily,
When the bridal party
 To the church doth hie!
Bell! thou soundest solemnly,
When, on Sabbath morning,
 Fields deserted lie!

Bell! thou soundest merrily;
Tellest thou at evening,
 Bed-time draweth nigh!
Bell! thou soundest mournfully
Tellest thou the bitter
 Parting hath gone by!

Say! how canst thou mourn?
How canst thou rejoice?
 Thou art but metal dull!

And yet all our sorrowings,
And all our rejoicings,
　Thou dost feel them all!

God hath wonders many,
Which we cannot fathom,
　Placed within thy form!
When the heart is sinking,
Thou alone canst raise it,
　Trembling in the storm!

THE CASTLE BY THE SEA

FROM THE GERMAN OF UHLAND

"Hast thou seen that lordly castle,
　That Castle by the Sea?
Golden and red above it
　The clouds float gorgeously.

"And fain it would stoop downward
　To the mirrored wave below;
And fain it would soar upward
　In the evening's crimson glow."

"Well have I seen that castle,
　That Castle by the Sea,
And the moon above it standing,
　And the mist rise solemnly."

"The winds and the waves of ocean,
　Had they a merry chime?
Didst thou hear, from those lofty chambers,
　The harp and the minstrel's rhyme?"

"The winds and the waves of ocean,
　They rested quietly,
But I heard on the gale a sound of wail,
　And tears came to mine eye."

"And sawest thou on the turrets
　The King and his royal bride?
And the wave of their crimson mantles?
　And the golden crown of pride?

"Led they not forth, in rapture,
　　A beauteous maiden there?
Resplendent as the morning sun,
　　Beaming with golden hair?"

"Well saw I the ancient parents,
　　Without the crown of pride;
They were moving slow, in weeds of woe,
　　No maiden was by their side!"

THE BLACK KNIGHT

FROM THE GERMAN OF UHLAND

'T was Pentecost, the Feast of Gladness,
When woods and fields put off all sadness.
　　Thus began the King and spake:
"So from the halls
Of ancient Hofburg's walls,
　　A luxuriant Spring shall break."

Drums and trumpets echo loudly,
Wave the crimson banners proudly.
　　From balcony the King looked on;
In the play of spears,
Fell all the cavaliers,
　　Before the monarch's stalwart son.

To the barrier of the fight
Rode at last a sable Knight.
　　"Sir Knight! your name and scutcheon, say!"
"Should I speak it here,
Ye would stand aghast with fear;
　　I am a Prince of mighty sway!"

When he rode into the lists,
The arch of heaven grew black with mists,
　　And the castle 'gan to rock.
At the first blow,
Fell the youth from saddle-bow,
　　Hardly rises from the shock.

Pipe and viol call the dances,
Torch-light through the high halls glances;
  Waves a mighty shadow in;
With manner bland
Doth ask the maiden's hand,
  Doth with her the dance begin;

Danced in sable iron sark,
Danced a measure weird and dark,
  Coldly clasped her limbs around.
From breast and hair
Down fall from her the fair
  Flowerets, faded, to the ground.

To the sumptuous banquet came
Every Knight and every Dame.
  'Twixt son and daughter all distraught,
With mournful mind
The ancient King reclined,
  Gazed at them in silent thought.

Pale the children both did look,
But the guest a beaker took;
  "Golden wine will make you whole!"
The children drank,
Gave many a courteous thank;
  "O that draught was very cool!"

Each the father's breast embraces,
Son and daughter; and their faces
  Colorless grow utterly.
Whichever way
Looks the fear-struck father gray,
  He beholds his children die.

"Woe! the blessed children both
Takest thou in the joy of youth;
  Take me, too, the joyless father!"
Spake the grim Guest,
From his hollow, cavernous breast,
  "Roses in the spring I gather!"

SONG OF THE SILENT LAND

FROM THE GERMAN OF SALIS

Into the Silent Land!
Ah! who shall lead us thither?
Clouds in the evening sky more darkly gather,
And shattered wrecks lie thicker on the strand.
Who leads us with a gentle hand
Thither, O thither,
Into the Silent Land?

Into the Silent Land!
To you, ye boundless regions
Of all perfection! Tender morning visions
Of beauteous souls! The Future's pledge
          and band!
Who in Life's battle firm doth stand,
Shall bear Hope's tender blossoms
Into the Silent Land!

O Land! O Land!
For all the broken-hearted
The mildest herald by our fate allotted,
Beckons, and with inverted torch doth stand
To lead us with a gentle hand
Into the land of the great Departed,
Into the Silent Land!

L'ENVOI

Ye voices, that arose,
After the Evening's close,
And whispered to my restless heart repose!

Go, breathe it in the ear
Of all who doubt and fear,
And say to them, "Be of good cheer!"

Ye sounds, so low and calm,
That in the groves of balm
Seemed to me like an angel's psalm!

Go, mingle yet once more
With the perpetual roar
Of the pine forest dark and **hoar!**

Tongues of the dead, not lost,
But speaking from death's frost,
Like fiery tongues at Pentecost!

Glimmer, as funeral lamps,
Amid the chills and damps
Of the vast plain where Death encamps!

BALLADS AND OTHER POEMS

The Skeleton in Armor

[The following Ballad was suggested to me while riding on the seashore at Newport. A year or two previous a skeleton had been dug up at Fall River, clad in broken and corroded armor; and the idea occurred to me of connecting it with the Round Tower at Newport, generally known hitherto as the Old Wind-Mill, though now claimed by the Danes as a work of their early ancestors. Professor Rafn, in the *Mémoires de la Société Royale des Antiquaires du Nord* for 1838-1839, says:—

"There is no mistaking in this instance the style in which the more ancient stone edifices of the North were constructed, the style which belongs to the Roman or ante-Gothic architecture, and which, especially after the time of Charlemagne, diffused itself from Italy over the whole of the West and North of Europe, where it continued to predominate until the close of the 12th century; that style, which some authors have, from one of its most striking characteristics, called the round-arch style, the same which in England is denominated Saxon and sometimes Norman architecture.

"On the ancient structure in Newport there are no ornaments remaining, which might possibly have served to guide us in assigning the probable date of its erection. That no vestige whatever is found of the pointed arch, nor any approximation to it, is indicative of an earlier rather than of a later period. From such characteristics as remain, however, we can scarcely form any other inference than one, in which I am persuaded that all, who are familiar with Old-Northern architecture, will concur, THAT THIS BUILDING WAS ERECTED AT A PERIOD DECIDEDLY NOT LATER THAN THE 12TH CENTURY. This remark applies, of course, to the original building only, and not to the alterations that it subsequently received; for there are several such alterations in the upper part of the building which cannot be mistaken, and which were most likely occasioned by its being adapted in modern times to various uses, for example as the substructure of a wind-mill, and latterly as a hay magazine. To the same times may be referred the windows, the fireplace, and the apertures made above the columns. That this building could not have been erected for a wind-mill is what an architect will easily discern."

I will not enter into a discussion of the point. It is sufficiently well established for the purposes of a ballad; though doubtless many an honest citizen of Newport, who has passed his days within sight of the Round Tower, will be ready to exclaim with Sancho, "God bless me! did I not warn you to have a care of what you were doing,

for that it was nothing but a wind-mill; and nobody could mistake
it, but one who had the like in his head."]

"SPEAK! speak! thou fearful guest,
Who, with thy hollow breast
Still in rude armor drest,
          Comest to daunt me!
Wrapt not in Eastern balms,
But with thy fleshless palms
Stretched, as if asking alms,
          Why dost thou haunt me?"

Then, from those cavernous eyes
Pale flashes seemed to rise,
As when the Northern skies
          Gleam in December;
And, like the water's flow
Under December's snow,
Came a dull voice of woe
          From the heart's chamber.

"I was a Viking old!
My deeds, though manifold,
No Skald in song has told,
          No Saga taught thee!
Take heed, that in thy verse
Thou dost the tale rehearse,
Else dread a dead man's curse
          For this I sought thee.

"Far in the Northern Land,
By the wild Baltic's strand,
I, with my childish hand,
          Tamed the gerfalcon;
And, with my skates fast-bound,
Skimmed the half-frozen Sound,
That the poor whimpering hound
          Trembled to walk on.

"Oft to his frozen lair
Tracked I the grisly bear,
While from my path the hare
          Fled like a shadow;

Oft through the forest dark
Followed the were-wolf's bark,
Until the soaring lark
    Sang from the meadow.

"But when I older grew,
Joining a corsair's crew,
O'er the dark sea I flew
    With the marauders.
Wild was the life we led;
Many the souls that sped,
Many the hearts that bled
    By our stern orders.

"Many a wassail-bout
Wore the long Winter out;
Often our midnight shout
    Set the cocks crowing,
As we the Berserk's tale
Measured in cups of ale,
Draining the oaken pail,
    Filled to o'erflowing.

"Once as I told in glee
Tales of the stormy sea,
Soft eyes did gaze on me,
    Burning yet tender;
And as the white stars shine
On the dark Norway pine,
On that dark heart of mine
    Fell their soft splendor.

"I wooed the blue-eyed maid,
Yielding, yet half afraid,
And in the forest's shade
    Our vows were plighted.
Under its loosened vest
Fluttered her little breast,
Like birds within their nest
    By the hawk frighted.

"Bright in her father's hall
Shields gleamed upon the wall,
Loud sang the minstrels all,
    Chaunting his glory;
When of old Hildebrand
I asked his daughter's hand,
Mute did the minstrels stand
    To hear my story.

"While the brown ale he quaffed,
Loud then the champion laughed.
And as the wind gusts waft
    The sea-foam brightly,
So the loud laugh of scorn,
Out of those lips unshorn,
From the deep drinking-horn
    Blew the foam lightly.

"She was a Prince's child,
I but a Viking wild,
And though she blushed and smiled
    I was discarded!
Should not the dove so white
Follow the sea-mew's flight,
Why did they leave that night
    Her nest unguarded?

"Scarce had I put to sea,
Bearing the maid with me,—
Fairest of all was she
    Among the Norsemen!—
When on the white sea-strand,
Waving his armèd hand,
Saw we old Hildebrand,
    With twenty horsemen.

"Then launched they to the blast,
Bent like a reed each mast,
Yet we were gaining fast,
    When the wind failed us,

And with a sudden flaw
Came round the gusty Skaw,
So that our foe we saw
    Laugh as he hailed us.

"And as to catch the gale
Round veered the flapping sail,
Death! was the helmsman's hail
    Death without quarter!
Mid-ships with iron keel
Struck we her ribs of steel;
Down her black hulk did reel
    Through the black water!

"As with his wings aslant,
Sails the fierce cormorant,
Seeking some rocky haunt,
    With his prey laden,
So toward the open main,
Beating to sea again,
Through the wild hurricane
    Bore I the maiden.

"Three weeks we westward bore,
And when the storm was o'er,
Cloud-like we saw the shore
    Stretching to lee-ward;
There for my lady's bower
Built I the lofty tower,
Which, to this very hour,
    Stands looking seaward.

"There lived we many years;
Time dried the maiden's tears;
She had forgot her fears,
    She was a mother;
Death closed her mild blue eyes,
Under that tower she lies;
Ne'er shall the sun arise
    On such another!

"Still grew my bosom then,
Still as a stagnant fen!
Hateful to me were men,
    The sunlight hateful!
In the vast forest here,
Clad in my warlike gear,
Fell I upon my spear,
    O, death was grateful!

"Thus, seamed with many scars
Bursting these prison bars,
Up to its native stars
    My soul ascended!
There from the flowing bowl
Deep drinks the warrior's soul,
Skoal! [1] to the Northland! *Skoal!"*
    —Thus the tale ended.

THE WRECK OF THE HESPERUS

'Twas the schooner Hesperus,
    That sailed the wintry sea;
And the skipper had taken his little daughter,
    To bear him company.

Blue were her eyes as the fairy-flax,
    Her cheeks like the dawn of day,
And her bosom white as the hawthorn buds
    That ope in the month of May.

The skipper he stood beside the helm,
    His pipe was in his mouth,
And he watched how the veering flaw did blow
    The smoke now West, now South.

Then up and spake an old Sailòr,
    Had sailed the Spanish Main,
"I pray thee, put into yonder port,
    For I fear a hurricane.

[1] In Scandinavia this is the customary salutation when drinking a health. I have slightly changed the orthography of the word, in order to preserve the correct pronunciation.

"Last night the moon had a golden ring,
    And to-night no moon we see!"
The skipper he blew a whiff from his pipe,
    And a scornful laugh laughed he.

Colder and colder blew the wind,
    A gale from the North-east;
The snow fell hissing in the brine,
    And the billows frothed like yeast.

Down came the storm, and smote amain,
    The vessel in its strength;
She shuddered and paused, like a frightened steed,
    Then leaped her cable's length.

"Come hither! come hither! my little daughtèr,
    And do not tremble so;
For I can weather the roughest gale
    That ever wind did blow."

He wrapped her warm in his seaman's coat
    Against the stinging blast;
He cut a rope from a broken spar,
    And bound her to the mast.

"O father! I hear the church-bells ring,
    O say, what may it be?"
" 'T is a fog-bell on a rock-bound coast!"
    And he steered for the open sea.

"O father! I hear the sound of guns,
    O say, what may it be?"
"Some ship in distress, that cannot live
    In such an angry sea!"

"O father! I see a gleaming light,
    O say, what may it be?"
But the father answered never a word,
    A frozen corpse was he.

Lashed to the helm, all stiff and stark,
    With his face turned to the skies,
The lantern gleamed through the gleaming snow
    On his fixed and glassy eyes.

Then the maiden clasped her hands and prayed
    That savèd she might be;
And she thought of Christ, who stilled the wave,
    On the Lake of Galilee.

And fast through the midnight dark and drear,
    Through the whistling sleet and snow,
Like a sheeted ghost, the vessel swept
    Towards the reef of Norman's Woe.

And ever the fitful gusts between
    A sound came from the land;
It was the sound of the trampling surf,
    On the rocks and the hard sea-sand.

The breakers were right beneath her bows,
    She drifted a dreary wreck,
And a whooping billow swept the crew
    Like icicles from her deck.

She struck where the white and fleecy waves
    Looked soft as carded wool,
But the cruel rocks, they gored her side
    Like the horns of an angry bull.

Her rattling shrouds, all sheathed in ice,
    With the masts went by the board;
Like a vessel of glass, she stove and sank,
    Ho! ho! the breakers roared!

At daybreak, on the bleak sea-beach,
    A fisherman stood aghast,
To see the form of a maiden fair,
    Lashed close to a drifting mast.

The salt sea was frozen on her breast,
    The salt tears in her eyes;
And he saw her hair, like the brown sea-weed,
    On the billows fall and rise.

Such was the wreck of the Hesperus,
    In the midnight and the snow!
Christ save us all from a death like this
    On the reef of Norman's Woe!

The Luck of Edenhall

FROM THE GERMAN OF UHLAND

[The tradition upon which this ballad is founded, and the "shards of the Luck of Edenhall," still exists in England. The goblet is in the possession of Sir Christopher Musgrave, Bart., of Eden Hall, Cumberland; and is not so entirely shattered as the ballad leaves it.]

Of Edenhall, the youthful Lord
Bids sound the festal trumpet's call.
He rises at the banquet board,
And cries, 'mid the drunken revellers all,
"Now bring me the Luck of Edenhall!"

The butler hears the words with pain,
The house's oldest seneschal,
Takes slow from its silken cloth again
The drinking glass of crystal tall;
They call it the Luck of Edenhall.

Then said the Lord, "This glass to praise,
Fill with red wine from Portugal!"
The gray-beard with trembling hand obeys;
A purple light shines over all,
It beams from the Luck of Edenhall.

Then speaks the Lord, and waves it light,
"This glass of flashing crystal tall
Gave to my sires the Fountain-Sprite;
She wrote in it, *If this glass doth fall,
Farewell then, O Luck of Edenhall!*

" 'T was right a goblet the Fate should be
Of the joyous race of Edenhall!
Deep draughts drink we right willingly;
And willingly ring, with merry call,
Kling! klang! to the Luck of Edenhall!"

First rings it deep, and full, and mild,
Like to the song of a nightingale;
Then like the roar of a torrent wild;
Then mutters at last like the thunder's fall,
The glorious Luck of Edenhall.

"For its keeper takes a race of might,
The fragile goblet of crystal tall;
It has lasted longer than is right;
Kling! klang!—with a harder blow than all
Will I try the Luck of Edenhall!"

As the goblet ringing flies apart,
Suddenly cracks the vaulted hall;
And through the rift, the wild flames start;
The guests in dust are scattered all,
With the breaking Luck of Edenhall!

In storms the foe, with fire and sword;
He in the night had scaled the wall,
Slain by the sword lies the youthful Lord,
But holds in his hand the crystal tall,
The shattered Luck of Edenhall.

On the morrow the butler gropes alone,
The gray-beard in the desert hall,
He seeks his Lord's burnt skeleton,
He seeks in the dismal ruin's fall
The shards of the Luck of Edenhall.

"The stone wall," saith he, "doth fall aside,
Down must the stately columns fall;
Glass is this earth's Luck and Pride;
In atoms shall fall this earthy ball
One day like the Luck of Edenhall!"

THE ELECTED KNIGHT

FROM THE DANISH

[The following strange and somewhat mystical ballad is from
Nyerup and Rahbek's *Danske Viser* of the Middle Ages. It seems to
refer to the first preaching of Christianity in the North, and to the
institution of Knight-Errantry. The three maidens I suppose to be
Faith, Hope, and Charity. The irregularities of the original have
been carefully preserved in the translation.]

Sir Oluf he rideth over the plain,
    Full seven miles broad and seven miles wide,
But never, ah never can meet with the man
    A tilt with him dare ride.

He saw under the hillside
    A Knight full well equipped;
His steed was black, his helm was barred;
    He was riding at full speed.

He wore upon his spurs
    Twelve little golden birds;
Anon he spurred his steed with a clang,
    And there sat all the birds and sang.

He wore upon his spurs
    Twelve little golden wheels;
Anon in eddies the wild wind blew,
    And round and round the wheels they flew.

He wore before his breast
    A lance that was poised in rest;
And it was sharper than diamond-stone,
    It made Sir Oluf's heart to groan.

He wore upon his helm,
    A wreath of ruddy gold;
And that gave him the Maidens three.
    The youngest was fair to behold.

Sir Oluf questioned the Knight eftsoon
    If he were come from heaven down;
"Art thou Christ of Heaven," quoth he,
    "So will I yield me unto thee."

'I am not Christ the Great,
    Thou shalt not yield thee yet;
I am an Unknown Knight,
    Three modest Maidens have me bedight."

"Art thou a Knight elected,
    And have three Maidens thee bedight;
So shalt thou ride a tilt this day,
    For all the Maidens' honor!"

The first tilt they together rode
    They put their steeds to the test;
The second tilt they together rode,
    They proved their manhood best.

The third tilt they together rode,
   Neither of them would yield;
The fourth tilt they together rode,
   They both fell on the field.

Now lie the lords upon the plain,
   And their blood runs unto death;
Now sit the Maidens in the high tower,
   The youngest sorrows till death.

THE CHILDREN OF THE LORD'S SUPPER

FROM THE SWEDISH OF BISHOP TEGNÉR

Pentecost, day of rejoicing, had come. The church of the
   village
Gleaming stood in the morning's sheen. On the spire of the
   belfry,
Tipped with a vane of metal, the friendly flames of the
   Spring sun
Glanced like the tongues of fire, beheld by Apostles afore-
   time.
Clear was the heaven and blue, and May, with her cap
   crowned with roses,
Stood in her holiday dress in the fields, and the wind and
   the brooklet
Murmured gladness and peace, God's-peace! With lips rosy-
   tinted
Whispered the race of the flowers, and merry on balancing
   branches
Birds were singing their carol, a jubilant hymn to the Highest.
Swept and clean was the churchyard. Adorned like a leaf-
   woven arbor
Stood its old-fashioned gate; and within upon each cross of
   iron
Hung was a fragrant garland, new twined by the hands of
   affection.
Even the dial, that stood on a hillock among the departed,
(There full a hundred years had it stood), was embellished
   with blossoms.

Like to the patriarch hoary, the sage of his kith and the
    hamlet,
Who on his birthday is crowned by children and children's
    children,
So stood the ancient prophet, and mute with his pencil of
    iron,
Marked on the tablet of stone, and measured the time and
    its changes,
While all around at his feet, an eternity slumbered in quiet.
Also the church within was adorned, for this was the season
When the young, their parents' hope, and the loved-ones of
    heaven,
Should at the foot of the altar renew the vows of their
    baptism.
Therefore each nook and corner was swept and cleaned, and
    the dust was
Blown from the walls and ceilings, and from the oil-painted
    benches.
There stood the church like a garden; the Feast of the Leafy
    Pavilions [1]
Saw we in living presentment. From noble arms on the church
    wall
Grew forth a cluster of leaves, and the preacher's pulpit of
    oakwood
Budded once more anew, as aforetime the rod before Aaron.
Wreathed thereon was the Bible with leaves, and the dove,
    washed with silver,
Under its canopy fastened, had on it a necklace of wind-
    flowers.
But in front of the choir, round the altar-piece painted by
    Hörberg,[2]
Crept a garland gigantic; and bright-curling tresses of angels
Peeped, like the sun from a cloud, from out of the shadowy
    leaf-work.
Likewise the lustre of brass, new-polished, blinked from the
    ceiling,

[1] The Feast of the Tabernacles; in Swedish, *Löfhydaohögtiden*, the
Leaf-huts'-high-tide.
[2] The peasant-painter of Sweden. He is known chiefly by his altar-
pieces in the village churches.

And for lights there were lilies of Pentecost set in the sockets.

> Loud rang the bells already; the thronging crowd was assembled
Far from valleys and hills, to list to the holy preaching.
Hark! then roll forth at once the mighty tones from the organ,
Hover like voices from God, aloft like invisible spirits.
Like as Elias in heaven, when he cast off from him his mantle,
Even so cast off the soul its garments of earth; and with one voice
Chimed in the congregation, and sang an anthem immortal
Of the sublime Wallin,[1] of David's harp in the North-land
Tuned to the choral of Luther; the song on its powerful pinions
Took every living soul, and lifted it gently to heaven,
And every face did shine like the Holy One's face upon Tabor.
Lo! there entered then into the church the Reverend Teacher.
Father he hight and he was in the parish; a christianly plainness
Clothed from his head to his feet the old man of seventy winters.
Friendly was he to behold, and glad as the heralding angel
Walked he among the crowds, but still a contemplative grandeur
Lay on his forehead as clear, as on moss-covered gravestone a sunbeam.
As in his inspiration (an evening twilight that faintly
Gleams in the human soul, even now, from the day of creation)
Th' Artist, the friend of heaven, imagines Saint John when in Patmos,
Gray, with his eyes uplifted to heaven, so seemed then the old man;
Such was the glance of his eye, and such were his tresses of silver.
All the congregation arose in the pews that were numbered.

---

[1] A distinguished pulpit-orator and poet. He is particularly remarkable for the beauty and sublimity of his psalms.

But with a cordial look, to the right and the left hand, the
old man,
Nodding all hail and peace, disappeared in the innermost
chancel.

Simply and solemnly now proceeded the Christian service,
Singing and prayer, and at last an ardent discourse from the
old man.
Many a moving word and warning, that out of the heart
came,
Fell like the dew of the morning, like manna on those in the
desert.
Afterwards, when all was finished, the Teacher re-entered
the chancel,
Followed therein by the young. On the right hand the boys
had their places,
Delicate figures, with close-curling hair and cheeks rosy-
blooming.
But on the left hand of these, there stood the tremulous
lilies,
Tinged with the blushing light of the morning, the diffident
maidens,—
Folding their hands in prayer, and their eyes cast down on
the pavement.
Now came, with question and answer, the catechism. In the
beginning
Answered the children with troubled and faltering voice, but
. the old man's
Glances of kindness encouraged them soon, and the doctrines
eternal
Flowed, like the waters of fountains, so clear from lips unpolluted.
Whene'er the answer was closed, and as oft as they named
the Redeemer,
Lowly louted the boys, and lowly the maidens all courtesied.
Friendly the Teacher stood, like an angel of light there
among them,
And to the children explained he the holy, the highest, in
few words,

Thorough, yet simple and clear, for sublimity always is
    simple,
Both in sermon and song, a child can seize on its meaning.
Even as the green-growing bud is unfolded when Springtide
    approaches,
Leaf by leaf is developed, and warmed by the radiant sun-
    shine,
Blushes with purple and gold, till at last the perfected blos-
    som
Opens its odorous chalice, and rocks with its crown in the
    breezes,
So was unfolded here the Christian lore of salvation,
Line by line from the soul of childhood. The fathers and
    mothers
Stood behind them in tears, and were glad at each well-
    worded answer.

  Now went the old man up to the altar;—and straightway
    transfigured
(So did it seem unto me) was then the affectionate Teacher.
Like the Lord's Prophet sublime, and awful as Death and
    as Judgment
Stood he, the God-commissioned, the soul-searcher, earth-
    ward descending.
Glances, sharp as a sword, into hearts that to him were
    transparent
Shot he; his voice was deep, was low like the thunder afar
    off.
So on a sudden transfigured he stood there, he spake and he
    questioned.

  "This is the faith of the Fathers, the faith the Apostles de-
    livered,
This is moreover the faith whereunto I baptized you, while
    still ye
Lay on your mothers' breasts, and nearer the portals of
    heaven.
Slumbering received you then the Holy Church in its bosom;
Wakened from sleep are ye now, and the light in its radiant
    splendor

Rains from the heaven downward;—to-day on the threshold
    of childhood
Kindly she frees you again, to examine and make your elec-
    tion,
For she knows nought of compulsion, and only conviction
    desireth.
This is the hour of your trial, the turning-point of existence,
Seed for the coming days; without revocation departeth
Now from your lips the confession; Bethink ye, before ye
    make answer!
Think not, O think not with guile to deceive the questioning
    Teacher.
Sharp is his eye to-day, and a curse ever rests upon falsehood.
Enter not with a lie on Life's journey; the multitude hears
    you,
Brothers and sisters and parents, what dear upon earth is
    and holy
Standeth before your sight as a witness; the Judge everlast-
    ing
Looks from the sun down upon you, and angels in waiting
    beside him
Grave your confession in letters of fire, upon tablets eternal.
Thus then,—believe ye in God, in the Father who this world
    created?
Him who redeemed it, the Son, and the Spirit where both
    are united?
Will ye promise me here, (a holy promise!) to cherish
God more than all things earthly, and every man as a
    brother?
Will ye promise me here, to confirm your faith by your
    living,
Th' heavenly faith of affection! to hope, to forgive, and to
    suffer,
Be what it may your condition, and walk before God in up-
    rightness?
Will ye promise me this before God and man?"—With a
    clear voice
Answered the young men Yes! and Yes! with lips softly-
    breathing

Answered the maidens eke. Then dissolved from the brow
    of the Teacher
Clouds with the thunders therein, and he spake in accents
    more gentle,
Soft as the evening's breath, as harps by Babylon's rivers.

"Hail, then, hail to you all! To the heirdom of heaven
    be ye welcome!
Children no more from this day, but by covenant brothers
    and sisters!
Yet,—for what reason not children? Of such is the kingdom
    of heaven.
Here upon earth an assemblage of children, in heaven one
    Father,
Ruling them all as his household,—forgiving in turn and
    chastising,
That is of human life a picture, as Scripture has taught us.
Blessed are the pure before God! Upon purity and upon
    virtue
Resteth the Christian Faith; she herself from on high is de-
    scended.
Strong as a man and pure as a child, is the sum of the doc-
    trine
Which the Divine One taught, and suffered and died on the
    cross for.
O! as ye wander this day from childhood's sacred asylum
Downward and ever downward, and deeper in Age's chill
    valley,
O! how soon will ye come,—too soon!—and long to turn
    backward
Up to its hill-tops again, to the sun-illumined, where Judg-
    ment
Stood like a father before you, and Pardon, clad like a
    mother,
Gave you her hand to kiss, and the loving heart was for-
    given,
Life was a play and your hands grasped after the roses of
    heaven!
Seventy years have I lived already; the Father eternal

Gave me gladness and care; but the loveliest hours of ex
 istence,
When I have steadfastly gazed in their eyes, I have in
 stantly known them,
Known them all again;—they were my childhood's acquaint
 ance.
Therefore take from henceforth, as guides in the paths of
 existence,
Prayer, with her eyes raised to heaven, and Innocence, bride
 of a man's childhood.
Innocence, child beloved, is a guest from the world of the
 blessed,
Beautiful, and in her hand a lily; on life's roaring billows
Swings she in safety, she heedeth them not, in the ship she
 is sleeping.
Calmly she gazes around in the turmoil of men; in the
 desert
Angels descend and minister unto her; she herself knoweth
Naught of her glorious attendance; but follows faithful and
 humble,
Follows so long as she may her friend; O do not reject her,
For she cometh from God and she holdeth the keys of the
 heavens.—
Prayer is Innocence' friend; and willingly flyeth incessant
'Twixt the earth and the sky, the carrier-pigeon of heaven.
Son of Eternity, fettered in Time, and an exile, the Spirit
Tugs at his chains evermore, and struggles like flames ever
 upward.
Still he recalls with emotion his Father's manifold mansions,
Thinks of the land of his fathers, where blossomed more
 freshly the flowers,
Shone a more beautiful sun, and he played with the wingèd
 angels.
Then grows the earth too narrow, too close; and homesick
 for heaven
Longs the wanderer again; and the Spirit's longings are wor-
 ship;
Worship is called his most beautiful hour, and its tongue is
 entreaty.
Ah! when the infinite burden of life descendeth upon us,

Crushes to earth our hope, and, under the earth, in the
     graveyard,—

Then it is good to pray unto God; for his sorrowing children
Turns he ne'er from his door, but he heals and helps and
     consoles them.

Yet is it better to pray when all things are prosperous with
     us,

Pray in fortunate days, for life's most beautiful Fortune
Kneels down before the Eternal's throne; and, with hands
     interfolded,

Praises, thankful and moved, the only giver of blessings.

Or do ye know, ye children, one blessing that comes not
     from Heaven?

What has mankind forsooth, the poor! that it has not re-
     ceived?

Therefore, fall in the dust and pray! The seraphs adoring
Cover with pinions six their face in the glory of him who
Hung his masonry pendant on naught, when the world he
     created.

Earth declareth his might, and the firmament uttereth his
     glory.

Races blossom and die, and stars fall downward from
     heaven,

Downward like withered leaves; at the last stroke of mid-
     night, millenniums

Lay themselves down at his feet, and he sees them, but
     counts them as nothing.

Who shall stand in his presence? The wrath of the judge is
     terrific,

Casting the insolent down at a glance. When he speaks in
     his anger

Hillocks skip like the kid, and mountains leap like the roe-
     buck.

Yet,—why are ye afraid, ye children? This awful avenger,
Ah! is a merciful God! God's voice was not in the earth-
     quake,

Not in the fire, nor the storm, but it was in the whispering
     breezes.

Love is the root of creation; God's essence; worlds without
     number

Lie in his bosom like children; he made them for this pur-
pose only.
Only to love and to be loved again, he breathed forth his
spirit
Into the slumbering dust, and upright standing, it laid its
Hand on its heart, and felt it was warm with a flame out of
heaven.
Quench, O quench not that flame! It is the breath of your
being.
Love is life, but hatred is death. Not father, nor mother
Loved you, as God has loved you; for 't was that you may be
happy
Gave he his only Son. When he bowed down his head in the
death-hour
Solemnized Love its triumph; the sacrifice then was com-
pleted.
Lo! then was rent on a sudden the vail of the temple, di-
viding
Earth and heaven apart, and the dead from their sepulchres
rising
Whispered with pallid lips and low in the ears of each other
Th' answer, but dreamed of before, to creation's enigma,—
Atonement!
Depths of Love are Atonement's depths, for Love is Atone-
ment.
Therefore, child of mortality, love thou the merciful Father;
Wish what the Holy One wishes, and not from fear, but
affection;
Fear is the virtue of slaves; but the heart that loveth is
willing;
Perfect was before God, and perfect is Love, and Love only.
Lovest thou God as thou oughtest, then lovest thou likewise
thy brethren;
One is the sun in heaven, and one, only one, is Love also.
Bears not each human figure the godlike stamp on his fore-
head?
Readest thou not in his face thine origin? Is he not sailing
Lost like thyself on an ocean unknown, and is he not guided
By the same stars that guide thee? Why shouldst thou hate
then thy brother?

Hateth he thee, forgive! For 't is sweet to stammer one letter
Of the Eternal's language;—on earth it is called Forgiveness!
Knowest thou Him, who forgave, with the crown of thorns
    round his temples?
Earnestly prayed for his foes, for his murderers? Say, dost
    thou know him?
Ah! thou confessest his name, so follow likewise his example,
Think of thy brother no ill, but throw a veil over his failings,
Guide the erring aright; for the good, the heavenly shepherd
Took the lost lamb in his arms, and bore it back to its
    mother.
This is the fruit of Love, and it is by its fruits that we
    know it.
Love is the creature's welfare, with God; but Love among
    mortals
Is but an endless sigh! He longs, and endures, and stands
    waiting,
Suffers and yet rejoices, and smiles with tears on his eyelids.
Hope,—so is called upon earth, his recompense,—Hope, the
    befriending,
Does what she can, for she points evermore up to heaven,
    and faithful
Plunges her anchor's peak in the depths of the grave, and be-
    neath it
Paints a more beautiful world, a dim, but a sweet play of
    shadows!
Races, better than we, have leaned on her wavering promise,
Having naught else but Hope. Then praise we our Father in
    heaven,
Him, who has given us more; for to us has Hope been trans-
    figured,
Groping no longer in night; she is Faith, she is living as-
    surance.
Faith is enlightened Hope; she is light, is the eye of affection,
Dreams of the longing interprets, and carves their visions
    in marble.
Faith is the sun of life; and her countenance shines like the
    Hebrew's,
For she has looked upon God; the heaven on its stable
    foundation

Draws she with chains down to earth, and the New Jeru-
    salem sinketh
Splendid with portals twelve in golden vapors descending.
There enraptured she wanders, and looks at the figure ma-
    jestic,
Fears not the wingèd crowd, in the midst of them all is her
    homestead.
Therefore love and believe; for works will follow spon-
    taneous
Even as day does the sun; the Right from the Good is an
    offspring,
Love in a bodily shape; and Christian works are no more
    than
Animate Love and faith, as flowers are the animate spring-
    tide.
Works do follow us all unto God; there stand and bear wit-
    ness
Not what they seemed,—but what they were only. Blessed
    is he who
Hears their confession secure; they are mute upon earth
    until death's hand
Opens the mouth of the silent. Ye children, does Death e'er
    alarm you?
Death is the brother of Love, twin-brother is he, and is only
More austere to behold. With a kiss upon lips that are
    fading
Takes he the soul and departs, and rocked in the arms of
    affection,
Places the ransomed child, new born, 'fore the face of its
    father.
Sounds of his coming already I hear,—see dimly his pinions,
Swart as the night, but with stars strewn upon them! I fear
    not before him.
Death is only release, and in mercy is mute. On his bosom,
Freer breathes, in its coolness, my breast; and face to face
    standing
Look I on God as he is, a sun unpolluted by vapors;
Look on the light of the ages I loved, the spirits majestic,
Nobler, better than I; they stand by the throne all trans-
    figured,

Vested in white, and with harps of gold, and are singing an
 anthem,
Writ in the climate of heaven, in the language spoken by
 angels.
You, in like manner, ye children beloved, he one day shall
 gather,
Never forgets he the weary;—then welcome, ye loved ones,
 hereafter!
Meanwhile forget not the keeping of vows, forget not the
 promise,
Wander from holiness onward to holiness; earth shall ye
 heed not;
Earth is but dust and heaven is light; I have pledged you to
 heaven.
God of the Universe, hear me! thou fountain of Love everlasting,
Hark to the voice of thy servant! I send up my prayer to
 thy heaven!
Let me hereafter not miss at thy throne one spirit of all
 these,
Whom thou hast given me here! I have loved them all like
 a father.
May they bear witness for me, that I taught them the way
 of salvation,
Faithful, so far as I knew of thy word; again may they
 know me,
Fall on their Teacher's breast, and before thy face may I
 place them,
Pure as they now are, but only more tried, and exclaiming
 with gladness,
Father, lo! I am here, and the children, whom thou hast
 given me!"

 Weeping he spake in these words; and now at the beck of
 the old man
Knee against knee they knitted a wreath round the altar's
 enclosure.
Kneeling he read them the prayers of the consecration, and
 softly

With him the children read; at the close, with tremulous
accents,
Asked he the peace of heaven, a benediction upon them.
Now should have ended his task for the day; the following
Sunday
Was for the young appointed to eat of the Lord's holy
Supper.
Sudden, as struck from the clouds, stood the Teacher silent
and laid his
Hand on his forehead, and cast his looks upward; while
thoughts high and holy
Flew through the midst of his soul, and his eyes glanced
with wonderful brightness.
"On the next Sunday, who knows! perhaps I shall rest in
the grave-yard!
Some one perhaps of yourselves, a lily broken untimely,
Bow down his head to the earth; why delay I? the hour is
accomplished.
Warm is the heart;—I will so! for to-day grows the harvest
of heaven.
What I began accomplish I now; for what failing therein is
I, the old man, will answer to God and the reverend father.
Say to me only, ye children, ye denizens new-come in heaven,
Are ye ready this day to eat of the bread of Atonement?
What it denoteth, that know ye full well, I have told it you
often.
Of the new covenant a symbol it is, of Atonement a token,
'Stablished between earth and heaven. Man by his sins and
transgressions
Far hath wandered from God, from his essence. 'T was in
the beginning
Fast by the Tree of Knowledge he fell, and it hangs its
crown o'er the
Fall to this day; in the Thought is the Fall; in the Heart
the Atonement.
Infinite is the Fall, the Atonement infinite likewise.
See! behind me, as far as the old man remembers, and for-
ward,
Far as Hope in her flight can reach with her wearied pin-
ions,

Sin and Atonement incessant go through the lifetime of
mortals.

Brought forth is sin full-grown; but Atonement sleeps in our
bosoms

Still as the cradled babe; and dreams of heaven and of
angels,

Cannot awake to sensation; is like the tones in the harp's
strings,

Spirits imprisoned, that wait evermore the deliverer's finger.

Therefore, ye children beloved, descended the Prince of
Atonement,

Woke the slumberer from sleep, and she stands now with
eyes all resplendent,

Bright as the vault of the sky, and battles with Sin and
o'ercomes her,

Downward to earth he came and transfigured, thence re-
ascended,

Not from the heart in like wise, for there he still lives in the
Spirit,

Loves and atones evermore. So long as Time is, is Atonement.

Therefore with reverence receive this day her visible token.

Tokens are dead if the things do not live. The light everlasting

Unto the blind man is not, but is born of the eye that has
vision.

Neither in bread nor in wine, but in the heart that is hallowed

Lieth forgiveness enshrined; the intention alone of amend-
ment,

Fruits of the earth ennobles to heavenly things, and re-
moves all

Sin and the guerdon of sin. Only Love with his arms wide
extended,

Penitence weeping and praying: the Will that is tried, and
whose gold flows

Purified forth from the flame; in a word, mankind by Atonement

Breaketh Atonement's bread, and drinketh Atonement's
wine-cup.

But he who cometh up hither, unworthy, with hate in his
bosom,

Scoffing at men and at God, is guilty of Christ's blessed
body,

And the Redeemer's blood! To himself he eateth and drinketh

Death and doom! And from this, preserve us, thou Heavenly
Father!

Are ye ready, ye children, to eat of the bread of Atonement?"

Thus with emotion he asked, and together answered the
children

Yes! with deep sobs interrupted. Then read he the due sup-
plications,

Read the Form of Communion, and in chimed the organ
and anthem;

O! Holy Lamb of God, who takest away our transgressions,

Hear us! give us thy peace! have mercy, have mercy upon
us!

Th' old man, with trembling hand, and heavenly pearls on
his eyelids,

Filled now the chalice and paten, and dealt round the mystical symbols.

O! then seemed it to me as if God, with the broad eye of
midday,

Clearer looked in at the windows, and all the trees in the
churchyard

Bowed down their summits of green, and the grass on the
graves 'gan to shiver.

But in the children (I noted it well; I knew it) there ran a

Tremor of holy rapture along through their icy cold mem-
bers.

Decked like an altar before them, there stood the green
earth, and above it

Heaven opened itself, as of old, before Stephen; they saw
there

Radiant in glory the Father, and on his right hand the Redeemer.

Under them hear they the clang of harpstrings, and angels
from gold clouds

Beckon to them like brothers, and fan with their pinions of
    purple.

Closed was the Teacher's task, and with heaven in their
    hearts and their faces,
Up rose the children all, and each bowed him, weeping full
    sorely,
Downward to kiss that reverend hand, but all of them
    pressed he
Moved to his bosom, and laid, with a prayer, his hands full
    of blessings,
Now on the holy breast, and now on the innocent tresses.

POEMS ON SLAVERY

[The following poems, with one exception, were written at sea, in
the latter part of October. I had not then heard of Dr. Channing's
death. Since that event the poem addressed to him is no longer
appropriate. I have decided, however, to let it remain as it was written,
a feeble testimony of my admiration for a great and good man.]

TO WILLIAM E. CHANNING

The pages of thy book I read,
    And as I closed each one,
My heart, responding, ever said,
    "Servant of God! well done!"

Well done! Thy words are great and bold;
    At times they seem to me,
Like Luther's, in the days of old,
    Half-battles for the free.

Go on, until this land revokes
    The old and chartered Lie,
The feudal curse, whose whips and yokes
    Insult humanity.

A voice is ever at thy side
    Speaking in tones of might,
Like the prophetic voice, that cried
    To John in Patmos, "Write!"

Write! and tell out this bloody tale;
  Record this dire eclipse,
This Day of Wrath, this Endless Wail,
  This dread Apocalypse!

THE SLAVE'S DREAM

Beside the ungathered rice he lay,
  His sickle in his hand;
His breast was bare, his matted hair
  Was buried in the sand.
Again, in the mist and shadow of sleep,
  He saw his Native Land.

Wide through the landscape of his dreams
  The lordly Niger flowed;
Beneath the palm-trees on the plain
  Once more a king he strode,
And heard the tinkling caravans
  Descend the mountain-road.

He saw once more his dark-eyed queen
  Among her children stand;
They clasped his neck, they kissed his cheeks,
  They held him by the hand!—
A tear burst from the sleeper's lids
  And fell into the sand.

And then at furious speed he rode
  Along the Niger's bank;
His bridle-reins were golden chains,
  And, with a martial clank,
At each leap he could feel his scabbard of steel
  Smiting his stallion's flank.

Before him, like a blood-red flag,
  The bright flamingoes flew;
From morn till night he followed their flight,
  O'er plains where the tamarind grew,
Till he saw the roofs of Caffre huts,
  And the ocean rose to view.

At night he heard the lion roar,
  And the hyena scream,
And the river-horse, as he crushed the reeds
  Beside some hidden stream;
And it passed, like a glorious roll of drums,
  Through the triumph of his dream.

The forests, with their myriad tongues,
  Shouted of liberty;
And the Blast of the Desert cried aloud,
  With a voice so wild and free,
That he started in his sleep and smiled
  At their tempestuous glee.

He did not feel the driver's whip,
  Nor the burning heat of day;
For Death had illumined the Land of Sleep,
  And his lifeless body lay
A worn-out fetter, that the soul
  Had broken and thrown away!

THE GOOD PART

That Shall Not Be Taken Away

She dwells by Great Kenhawa's side,
  In valleys green and cool;
And all her hope and all her pride
  Are in the village school.

Her soul, like the transparent air
  That robes the hills above,
Though not of earth, encircles there
  All things with arms of love.

And thus she walks among her girls
  With praise and mild rebukes;
Subduing e'en rude village churls
  By her angelic looks.

She reads to them at eventide
    Of One who came to save;
To cast the captive's chains aside
    And liberate the slave.

And oft the blessed time foretells
    When all men shall be free;
And musical, as silver bells,
    Their falling chains shall be.

And following her belovèd Lord,
    In decent poverty,
She makes her life one sweet record
    And deed of charity.

For she was rich, and gave up all
    To break the iron bands
Of those who waited in her hall,
    And labored in her lands.

Long since beyond the Southern Sea
    Their outbound sails have sped,
While she, in meek humility,
    Now earns her daily bread.

It is their prayers, which never cease,
    That clothe her with such grace;
Their blessing is the light of peace
    That shines upon her face.

THE SLAVE IN THE DISMAL SWAMP

In dark fens of the Dismal Swamp
    The hunted Negro lay;
He saw the fire of the midnight camp,
And heard at times a horse's tramp
    And a bloodhound's distant bay.

Where will-o'-the-wisps and glow-worms shine,
    In bulrush and in brake;
Where waving mosses shroud the pine,
And the cedar grows, and the poisonous vine
    Is spotted like the snake;

Where hardly a human foot could pass,
  Or a human heart would dare,
On the quaking turf of the green morass
He crouched in the rank and tangled grass,
  Like a wild beast in his lair.

A poor old slave, infirm and lame;
  Great scars deformed his face;
On his forehead he bore the brand of shame,
And the rags, that hid his mangled frame,
  Were the livery of disgrace.

All things above were bright and fair,
  All things were glad and free;
Lithe squirrels darted here and there,
And wild birds filled the echoing air
  With songs of Liberty.

On him alone was the doom of pain,
  From the morning of his birth;
On him alone the Curse of Cain
Fell, like a flail on the garnered grain,
  And struck him to the earth.

THE SLAVE SINGING AT MIDNIGHT

Loud he sang the psalm of David!
He, a Negro and enslavèd,
Sang of Israel's victory,
Sang of Zion, bright and free.

In that hour, when night is calmest,
Sang he from the Hebrew Psalmist,
In a voice so sweet and clear
That I could not choose but hear,

Songs of triumph, and ascriptions,
Such as reached the swart Egyptians,
When upon the Red Sea coast
Perished Pharaoh and his host.

And the voice of his devotion
Filled my soul with strange emotion;
For its tones by turns were glad,
Sweetly solemn, wildly sad.

Paul and Silas, in their prison,
Sang of Christ, the Lord arisen,
And an earthquake's arm of might.
Broke their dungeon-gates at night.

But, alas! what holy angel
Brings the Slave this glad evangel?
And what earthquake's arm of might
Breaks his dungeon-gates at night?

THE WITNESSES

In Ocean's wide domains,
　　Half buried in the sands,
Like skeletons in chains,
　　With shackled feet and hands.

Beyond the fall of dews,
　　Deeper than plummet lies,
Float ships, with all their crews,
　　No more to sink nor rise.

There the black Slave-ship swims,
　　Freighted with human forms,
Whose fettered, fleshless limbs
　　Are not the sport of storms.

These are the bones of Slaves;
　　They gleam from the abyss;
They cry, from yawning waves,
　　"We are the Witnesses!"

Within Earth's wide domains
　　Are markets for men's lives;
Their necks are galled with chains.
　　Their wrists are cramped with gyves.

Dead bodies, that the kite
  In deserts makes its prey;
Murders, that with affright
  Scare schoolboys from their play!

All evil thoughts and deeds;
  Anger, and lust, and pride;
The foulest, rankest weeds,
  That choke Life's groaning tide!

These are the woes of Slaves;
  They glare from the abyss;
They cry, from unknown graves,
  "We are the Witnesses!"

THE QUADROON GIRL

The Slaver in the broad lagoon
  Lay moored with idle sail;
He waited for the rising moon,
  And for the evening gale.

Under the shore his boat was tied
  And all her listless crew
Watched the gray alligator slide
  Into the still bayou.

Odors of orange flowers, and spice,
  Reached them from time to time,
Like airs that breathe from Paradise
  Upon a world of crime.

The Planter, under his roof of thatch,
  Smoked thoughtfully and slow;
The Slaver's thumb was on the latch,
  He seemed in haste to go.

He said, "My ship at anchor rides
  In yonder broad lagoon;
I only wait the evening tides,
  And the rising of the moon."

Before them, with her face upraised,
  In timid attitude,
Like one half curious, half amazed,
  A Quadroon maiden stood.

Her eyes were large, and full of light,
  Her arms and neck were bare;
No garment she wore save a kirtle bright,
  And her own long, raven hair.

And on her lips there played a smile
  As holy, meek, and faint,
As lights in some cathedral aisle
  The features of a saint.

"The soil is barren,—the farm is old;"
  The thoughtful Planter said;
Then looked upon the Slaver's gold,
  And then upon the maid.

His heart within him was at strife
  With such accursèd gains;
For he knew whose passions gave her life,
  Whose blood ran in her veins.

But the voice of nature was too weak;
  He took the glittering gold!
Then pale as death grew the maiden's cheek,
  Her hands as icy cold.

The Slaver led her from the door,
  He led her by the hand,
To be his slave and paramour
  In a strange and distant land!

THE WARNING

Beware! The Israelite of old, who tore
  The lion in his path,—when, poor and blind,
He saw the blessed light of heaven no more,
  Shorn of his noble strength and forced to grind
In prison, and at last led forth to be
A pander to Philistine revelry,—

Upon the pillars of the temple laid
  His desperate hands, and in its overthrow
Destroyed himself, and with him those who made
  A cruel mockery of his sightless woe;
The poor, blind Slave, the scoff and jest of all,
Expired, and thousands perished in the fall!

There is a poor, blind Samson in this land,
  Shorn of his strength, and bound in bonds of steel,
Who may, in some grim revel, raise his hand,
  And shake the pillars of this Commonweal,
Till the vast Temple of our liberties
A shapeless mass of wreck and rubbish lies.

THE SPANISH STUDENT

DRAMATIS PERSONÆ

VICTORIAN⎱ . . . . *Students of Alcalá.*
HYPOLITO ⎰

THE COUNT OF LARA⎱ . . . *Gentlemen of Madrid.*
DON CARLOS ⎰

THE ARCHBISHOP OF TOLEDO.

A CARDINAL.

BELTRAN CRUZADO . . . . . *Count of the Gypsies.*

BARTOLOMÉ ROMAN . . . . . *A young Gypsy.*

THE PADRE CURA OF GUADARRAMA

PEDRO CRESPO . . . . *Alcalde.*

PANCHO . . . . *Alguacil.*

FRANCISCO . . . . *Lara's servant.*

CHISPA . . . . *Victorian's servant.*

BALTASAR . . . . *Innkeeper.*

PRECIOSA . . . . *A Gypsy girl.*

ANGELICA . . . . *A poor girl.*

MARTINA . . . . *The Padre Cura's niece.*

DOLORES . . . . *Preciosa's maid.*

Gypsies, Musicians, etc.

ACT I

SCENE I. *The* COUNT OF LARA'S *chambers. Night. The* COUNT *in his dressing-gown, smoking and conversing with* DON CARLOS.

LARA

You were not at the play to-night, Don Carlos;
How happened it?

DON CARLOS
I had engagements elsewhere.
Pray who was there?

LARA

Why, all the town and court.
The house was crowded; and the busy fans
Among the gayly dressed and perfumed ladies
Fluttered like butterflies among the flowers.
There was the Countess of Medina Celi;
The Goblin Lady with her Phantom Lover,
Her Lindo Don Diego; Doña Sol,
And Doña Serafina, and her cousins.

DON CARLOS

What was the play?

LARA

It was a dull affair;
One of those comedies in which you see,
As Lope says,[1] the history of the world
Brought down from Genesis to the Day of Judgment.
There were three duels fought in the first act,
Three gentlemen receiving deadly wounds,
Laying their hands upon their hearts, and saying,
"O, I am dead!" a lover in a closet,
An old hidalgo, and a gay Don Juan,
A Doña Inez with a black mantilla
Followed at twilight by an unknown lover,
Who looks intently where he knows she is not!

DON CARLOS

Of course, the Preciosa danced to-night?

LARA

And never better. Every footstep fell
As lightly as a sunbeam on the water.
I think the girl extremely beautiful.

[1] *As Lope says.*

"La cólera
de un Español sentado no se templa,
sino le representan en dos horas
hasta el final juicio desde el Génesis."
Lope de Vega.

DON CARLOS

Almost beyond the privilege of woman!
I saw her in the Prado yesterday.
Her step was royal,—queen-like,—and her face
As beautiful as a saint's in Paradise.

LARA

May not a saint fall from her Paradise,
And be no more a saint?

DON CARLOS
Why do you ask?

LARA

Because I have heard it said this angel fell,
And, though she is a virgin outwardly,
Within she is a sinner; like those panels
Of doors and altar-pieces the old monks
Painted in convents, with the Virgin Mary
On the outside, and on the inside Venus!

DON CARLOS

You do her wrong; indeed, you do her wrong!
She is as virtuous as she is fair.

LARA

How credulous you are! Why, look you, friend,
There's not a virtuous woman in Madrid,
In this city whole! And would you persuade me
That a mere dancing-girl, who shows herself,
Nightly, half-naked, on the stage, for money,
And with voluptuous motions fires the blood
Of inconsiderate youth, is to be held
A model for her virtue?

DON CARLOS
You forget

She is a Gypsy girl.

LARA
And therefore won

The easier.

DON CARLOS

Nay, not to be won at all!
The only virtue that a Gypsy prizes
Is chastity. That is her only virtue.
Dearer than life she holds it. I remember
A Gypsy woman, a vile, shameless bawd,
Whose craft was to betray the young and fair;
And yet this woman was above all bribes.
And when a noble lord, touched by her beauty,
The wild and wizard beauty of her race,
Offered her gold to be what she made others,
She turned upon him, with a look of scorn,
And smote him in the face!

LARA

And does that prove
That Preciosa is above suspicion?

DON CARLOS

It proves a nobleman may be repulsed
When he thinks conquest easy. I believe
That woman, in her deepest degradation,
Holds something sacred, something undefiled,
Some pledge and keepsake of her higher nature,
And, like the diamond in the dark, retains
Some quenchless gleam of the celestial light!

LARA

Yet Preciosa would have taken the gold.

DON CARLOS (*rising*)

I do not think so.

LARA

I am sure of it.
But why this haste? Stay yet a little longer,
And fight the battles of your Dulcinea.

DON CARLOS

'Tis late. I must begone, for if I stay
You will not be persuaded.

LARA

Yes; persuade me.

DON CARLOS

No one so deaf as he who will not hear!

LARA

No one so blind as he who will not see!

DON CARLOS

And so good-night. I wish you pleasant dreams,
And greater faith in woman. [*Exit.*

LARA

Greater faith!
I have the greatest faith; for I believe
Victorian is her lover. I believe
That I shall be to-morrow; and thereafter
Another, and another, and another,
Chasing each other through her zodiac,
As Taurus chases Aries.
(*Enter* FRANCISCO *with a casket*)
Well, Francisco,
What speed with Preciosa?

FRANCISCO

None, my lord.
She sends your jewels back, and bids me tell you
She is not to be purchased by your gold.

LARA

Then I will try some other way to win her.
Pray, dost thou know Victorian?

FRANCISCO

Yes, my lord,
I saw him at the jeweller's to-day.

LARA

What was he doing there?

FRANCISCO

I saw him buy
A golden ring, that had a ruby in it.

LARA

Was there another like it?

FRANCISCO

One so like it
I could not choose between them.

LARA

It is well.
To-morrow morning bring that ring to me.
Do not forget. Now light me to my bed. [*Exeunt.*

SCENE II. *A street in Madrid. Enter* CHISPA, *followed by musicians, with a bagpipe, guitars, and other instruments.*

CHISPA

Abernuncio Satanas! [1] and a plague on all lovers who ramble about at night, drinking the elements, instead of sleeping quietly in their beds. Every dead man to his cemetery, say I; and every friar to his monastery. Now, here's my master, Victorian, yesterday a cow-keeper, and to-day a gentleman; yesterday a student, and to-day a lover; and I must be up later than the nightingale, for as the abbot sings so must the sacristan respond. God grant he may soon be married, for then shall all this serenading cease. Ay, marry! marry! marry! Mother, what does marry mean? It means to spin, to bear children, and to weep, my daughter! And of a truth, there is something more in matrimony than the wedding-ring. (*To the musicians.*) And now, gentlemen, Pax vobiscum! as the ass said to the cabbages. Pray, walk this way; and don't hang down your heads. It is no disgrace to have an old father and a ragged shirt. Now, look you, you are gentlemen who lead the life of crickets; you enjoy hunger by day and noise by night. Yet, I beseech you, for this once be not loud, but pathetic; for it is a serenade to a damsel in bed, and not to the Man in the Moon. Your object is not to arouse and terrify, but to soothe and bring lulling dreams. Therefore, each shall not play upon his instrument as if it were the only one in the universe, but gently, and

[1] *Abernuncio Satanas.*
"Digo, Señora, respondeió Sancho, lo que tengo dicho, que de los azotes abernuncio. Abernuncio, habeis del decir, Sancho, y no como decis, dijo el Duque."—*Don Quixote,* Part II, ch. 35.

with a certain modesty according with the others. Pray, how may I call thy name, friend?

FIRST MUSICIAN

Gerónimo Gil, at your service.

CHISPA

Every tub smells of the wine that is in it. Pray, Gerónimo, is not Saturday an unpleasant day with thee?

FIRST MUSICIAN

Why so?

CHISPA

Because I have heard it said that Saturday is an unpleasant day with those who have but one shirt. Moreover, I have seen thee at the tavern, and if thou canst run as fast as thou canst drink, I should like to hunt hares with thee. What instrument is that?

FIRST MUSICIAN

An Aragonese bagpipe.

CHISPA

Pray, art thou related to the bagpiper of Bujalance, who asked a maravedí for playing, and ten for leaving off?

FIRST MUSICIAN

No, your honor.

CHISPA

I am glad of it. What other instruments have we?

SECOND AND THIRD MUSICIANS

We play the bandurria.

CHISPA

A pleasing instrument. And thou?

FOURTH MUSICIAN

The fife.

CHISPA

I like it; it has a cheerful, soul-stirring sound, that soars up to my lady's window like the song of a swallow. And you others?

OTHER MUSICIANS

We are the singers, please your honor.

CHISPA

You are too many. Do you think we are going to sing mass in the cathedral of Córdova? Four men can make but little use of one shoe, and I see not how you can all sing in one song. But follow me along the garden wall. That is the way my master climbs to the lady's window. It is by the Vicar's skirts that the devil climbs into the belfry. Come, follow me, and make no noise. [*Exeunt.*

SCENE III. PRECIOSA'S *chamber. She stands at the open window.*

PRECIOSA

How slowly through the lilac-scented air
Descends the tranquil moon! Like thistle-down
The vapory clouds float in the peaceful sky;
And sweetly from yon hollow vaults of shade
The nightingales breathe out their souls in song.
And hark! what songs of love, what soul-like sounds,
Answer them from below!

SERENADE

Stars of the summer night!
    Far in yon azure deeps,
Hide, hide your golden light!
    She sleeps!
My lady sleeps!
    Sleeps!

Moon of the summer night!
    Far down yon western steeps,
Sink, sink in silver light!
    She sleeps!
My lady sleeps!
    Sleeps!

Wind of the summer night!
　　Where yonder woodbine creeps,
　Fold, fold thy pinions light!
　　　She sleeps!
　My lady sleeps!
　　　Sleeps!

Dreams of the summer night!
　　Tell her, her lover keeps
Watch! while in slumbers light
　　　She sleeps!
　My lady sleeps!
　　　Sleeps!

(*Enter* VICTORIAN *by the balcony*)

VICTORIAN

Poor, little dove! Thou tremblest like a leaf!

PRECIOSA

I am so frightened! 'T is for thee I tremble!
I hate to have thee climb that wall by night!
Did no one see thee?

VICTORIAN

　　　　　None, my love, but thou.

PRECIOSA

'T is very dangerous; and when thou art gone
I chide myself for letting thee come here
Thus stealthily by night. Where hast thou been?
Since yesterday I have no news from thee.

VICTORIAN

Since yesterday I've been in Alcalá.
Ere long the time will come, sweet Preciosa,
When that dull distance shall no more divide us;
And I no more shall scale thy wall by night
To steal a kiss from thee, as I do now.

PRECIOSA

An honest thief, to steal but what thou givest.

VICTORIAN

And we shall sit together unmolested,
And words of true love pass from tongue to tongue,
As singing birds from one bough to another.

PRECIOSA

That were a life indeed to make time envious!
I knew that thou wouldst visit me to-night.
I saw thee at the play.

VICTORIAN

Sweet child of air!
Never did I behold thee so attired
And garmented in beauty as to-night!
What hast thou done to make thee look so fair?

PRECIOSA

Am I not always fair?

VICTORIAN

Ay, and so fair
That I am jealous of all eyes that see thee,
And wish that they were blind.

PRECIOSA

I heed them not;
When thou art present, I see none but thee!

VICTORIAN

There's nothing fair nor beautiful, but takes
Something from thee, that makes it beautiful.

PRECIOSA

And yet thou leavest me for those dusty books.

VICTORIAN

Thou comest between me and those books too often!
I see thy face in everything I see!
The paintings in the chapel wear thy looks,
The canticles are changed to sarabands,
And with the learnèd doctors of the schools
I saw thee dance cachuchas.

PRECIOSA

In good sooth,
I dance with learnèd doctors of the schools
To-morrow morning.

VICTORIAN

And with whom, I pray?

PRECIOSA

A grave and reverend Cardinal, and his Grace
The Archbishop of Toledo.

VICTORIAN

What mad jest
Is this?

PRECIOSA

It is no jest; indeed it is not.

VICTORIAN

Prithee, explain thyself.

PRECIOSA

Why, simply thus.
Thou knowest the Pope has sent here into Spain
To put a stop to dances on the stage.

VICTORIAN

I have heard it whispered.

PRECIOSA

Now the Cardinal,
Who for this purpose comes, would fain behold
With his own eyes these dances; and the Archbishop
Has sent for me—

VICTORIAN

That thou may'st dance before them.
Now viva la cachucha! It will breathe
The fire of youth into these gray old men!
'Twill be thy proudest conquest!

PRECIOSA

Saving one;
And yet I fear these dances will be stopped,
And Preciosa be once more a beggar.

VICTORIAN

The sweetest beggar that e'er asked for alms;
With such beseeching eyes, that when I saw thee
I gave my heart away!

PRECIOSA

Dost thou remember
When first we met?

VICTORIAN

It was at Córdova,
In the cathedral garden. Thou wast sitting
Under the orange trees, beside a fountain.

PRECIOSA

'T was Easter-Sunday. The full-blossomed trees
Filled all the air with fragrance and with joy.
The priests were singing, and the organ sounded,
And then anon the great cathedral bell.
It was the elevation of the Host.
We both of us fell down upon our knees,
Under the orange boughs, and prayed together.
I never had been happy till that moment.

VICTORIAN

Thou blessed angel!

PRECIOSA

And when thou wast gone
I felt an aching here. I did not speak
To any one that day. But from that day
Bartolomé grew hateful unto me.

VICTORIAN

Remember him no more. Let not his shadow
Come between thee and me. Sweet Preciosa!
I loved thee even then, though I was silent!

PRECIOSA

I thought I ne'er should see thy face again.
Thy farewell had a sound of sorrow in it.

VICTORIAN

That was the first sound in the song of love!
Scarce more than silence is, and yet a sound.
Hands of invisible spirits touch the strings
Of that mysterious instrument, the soul,
And play the prelude of our fate. We hear
The voice prophetic, and are not alone.

PRECIOSA

That is my faith. Dost thou believe these warnings?

VICTORIAN

So far as this. Our feelings and our thoughts
Tend ever on, and rest not in the Present.
As drops of rain fall into some dark well,
And from below comes a scarce audible sound,
So fall our thoughts into the dark Hereafter,
And their mysterious echo reaches us.

PRECIOSA

I have felt it so, but found no words to say it!
I cannot reason; I can only feel!
But thou hast language for all thoughts and feelings.
Thou art a scholar; and sometimes I think
We cannot walk together in this world!
The distance that divides us is too great!
Henceforth thy pathway lies among the stars;
I must not hold thee back.

VICTORIAN

Thou little sceptic!
Dost thou still doubt? What I most prize in woman
Is her affections, not her intellect!
The intellect is finite; but the affections
Are infinite, and cannot be exhausted.
Compare me with the great men of the earth;

Why, a pygmy among giants!
lovest,—mark me! I say lovest,
of thy sex excels thee not!
f the affections is thy world,
man's ambition. In that stillness
wnich most becomes a woman, calm and holy,
Thou sittest by the fireside of the heart,
Feeding its flame. The element of fire
Is pure. It cannot change nor hide its nature,
But burns as brightly in a Gypsy camp
As in a palace hall. Art thou convinced?

PRECIOSA

Yes, that I love thee, as the good love heaven;
But not that I am worthy of that heaven.
How shall I more deserve it?

VICTORIAN

Loving more.

PRECIOSA

I cannot love thee more; my heart is full.

VICTORIAN

Then let it overflow, and I will drink it,
As in the summer-time the thirsty sands
Drink the swift waters of the Manzanares,
And still do thirst for more.

A WATCHMAN (*in the street*)

Ave Maria

Purissima! 'Tis midnight and serene!

VICTORIAN

Hear'st thou that cry?

PRECIOSA

It is a hateful sound,
To scare thee from me!

VICTORIAN

As the hunter's horn
Doth scare the timid stag, or bark of hounds
The moor-fowl from his mate.

PRECIOSA

Pray, do not go!

VICTORIAN

I must away to Alcalá to-night.
Think of me when I am away.

PRECIOSA

Fear not!
I have no thoughts that do not think of thee.

VICTORIAN (*giving her a ring*)

And to remind thee of my love, take this;
A serpent, emblem of Eternity;
A ruby,—say, a drop of my heart's blood.

PRECIOSA

It is an ancient saying, that the ruby
Brings gladness to the wearer, and preserves
The heart pure, and if laid beneath the pillow,
Drives away evil dreams. But then, alas!
It was a serpent tempted Eve to sin.

VICTORIAN

What convent of barefooted Carmelites
Taught thee so much theology?

PRECIOSA (*laying her hand upon his mouth*)

Hush! Hush!
Good-night! and may all holy angels guard thee!

VICTORIAN

Good-night! good-night! Thou art my guardian angel!
I have no other saint than thou to pray to!
(*He descends by the balcony*)

PRECIOSA

Take care, and do not hurt thee. Art thou safe?

VICTORIAN (*from the garden*)

Safe as my love for thee! But art thou safe?
Others can climb a balcony by moonlight
As well as I. Pray, shut thy window close;
I am jealous of the perfumed air of night
That from this garden climbs to kiss thy lips.

PRECIOSA (*throwing down her handkerchief*)
Thou silly child! Take this to blind thine eyes.
It is my benison!

VICTORIAN
And brings to me
Sweet fragrance from thy lips, as the soft wind
Wafts to the out-bound mariner the breath
Of the belovèd land he leaves behind.

PRECIOSA
Make not thy voyage long.

VICTORIAN
To-morrow night
Shall see me safe returned. Thou art the star
To guide me to an anchorage. Good-night!
My beauteous star! My star of love, good-night!

PRECIOSA
Good-night!

WATCHMAN (*at a distance*) ·
Ave Maria Purissima!

SCENE IV. *An inn on the road to Alcalá.* BALTASAR *asleep on a bench. Enter* CHISPA.

CHISPA
And here we are, half-way to Alcalá, between cocks and midnight. Body o' me! what an inn this is! The lights out, and the landlord asleep. Holá! ancient Baltasar!

BALTASAR (*waking*)
Here I am.

CHISPA
Yes, there you are, like a one-eyed Alcalde in a town without inhabitants. Bring a light, and let me have supper.

BALTASAR
Where is your master?

CHISPA

Do not trouble yourself about him. We have stopped a moment to breathe our horses; and, if he chooses to walk up and down in the open air, looking into the sky as one who hears it rain, that does not satisfy my hunger, you know. But be quick, for I am in a hurry, and every man stretches his legs according to the length of his coverlet. What have we here?

BALTASAR (*setting a light on the table*)

Stewed rabbit.

CHISPA (*eating*)

Conscience of Portalegre! Stewed kitten, you mean!

BALTASAR

And a pitcher of Pedro Ximenes, with a roasted pear in it.

CHISPA (*drinking*)

Ancient Baltasar, amigo! You know how to cry wine and sell vinegar. I tell you this is nothing but Vino Tinto of La Mancha, with a tang of the swine-skin.

BALTASAR

I swear to you by Saint Simon and Judas, it is all as I say.

CHISPA

And I swear to you, by Saint Peter and Saint Paul, that it is no such thing. Moreover, your supper is like the hidalgo's dinner, very little meat, and a great deal of tablecloth.

BALTASAR

Ha! ha! ha!

CHISPA

And more noise than nuts.

BALTASAR

Ha! ha! ha! You must have your joke, Master Chispa. But shall I not ask Don Victorian in, to take a draught of the Pedro Ximenes?

CHISPA

No; you might as well say, "Don't-you-want-some?" to a dead man.

BALTASAR

Why does he go so often to Madrid?

CHISPA

For the same reason that he eats no supper. He is in love. Were you ever in love, Baltasar?

BALTASAR

I was never out of it, good Chispa. It has been the torment of my life.

CHISPA

What! are you on fire, too, old hay-stack? Why, we shall never be able to put you out.

VICTORIAN (*without*)

Chispa!

CHISPA

Go to bed, Pero Grullo, for the cocks are crowing.

VICTORIAN

Ea! Chispa! Chispa!

CHISPA

Ea! Señor. Come with me, ancient Baltasar, and bring water for the horses. I will pay for the supper to-morrow.

[*Exeunt.*

SCENE V. VICTORIAN'S *chambers at Alcalá.* HYPOLITO *asleep in an arm-chair. He awakes slowly.*

HYPOLITO

I must have been asleep! ay, sound asleep!
And it was all a dream. O sleep, sweet!
Whatever form thou takest, thou art fair,
Holding unto our lips thy goblet filled

Out of Oblivion's well, a healing draught!
The candles have burned low; it must be late.
Where can Victorian be? Like Fray Carrillo,[1]
The only place in which one cannot find him
Is his own cell. Here's his guitar, that seldom
Feels the caresses of its master's hand.
Open thy silent lips, sweet instrument!
And make a dull midnight merry with a song.

(*He plays and sings*)
Padre Francisco![2]
Padre Francisco!
What do you want of Padre Francisco?
Here is a pretty young maiden
Who wants to confess her sins!
Open the door and let her come in,
I will shrive her from every sin.
(*Enter* VICTORIAN)

VICTORIAN

Padre Hypolito! Padre Hypolito!

HYPOLITO

What do you want of Padre Hypolito?

VICTORIAN

Come, shrive me straight; for, if love be a sin,
I am the greatest sinner that doth live.

[1] *Fray Carrillo*. The allusion here is to a Spanish Epigram.
"Siempre Fray Carrillo estás
cansándonos acá fuera:
quien en tu celda estuviera
para no verte jamas!"
Böhl de Faber. Floresta, No. 611

[2] *Padre Francisco*. This is from an Italian popular song.
" 'Padre Francesco,
Padre Francesco!'
—Cosa volete del Padre Francesco—
'V' è una bella ragazzina
Che si vuole confessar!'
Fatte l'entrare, fatte l'entrare!
Che la voglio confessare."
*Kopisch. Volksthmümliche. Poesien aus allen
Mun darten Italiens und seiner Inseln*,
p. 194.

I will confess the sweetest of all crimes,
A maiden wooed and won.

HYPOLITO

The same old tale
Of the old woman in the chimney corner
Who, while the pot boils, says, "Come here, my child;
I'll tell thee a story of my wedding-day."

VICTORIAN

Nay, listen, for my heart is full; so full
That I must speak.

HYPOLITO

Alas! that heart of thine
Is like a scene in the old play; the curtain
Rises to solemn music, and lo! enter
The eleven thousand virgins of Cologne!

VICTORIAN

Nay, like the Sibyl's volumes, thou shouldst say;
Those that remained, after the six were burned,
Being held more precious than the nine together.
But listen to my tale. Dost thou remember
The Gypsy girl we saw at Córdova
Dance the Romalis in the market-place?

HYPOLITO

Thou meanest Preciosa.

VICTORIAN

Ay, the same.
Thou knowest how her image haunted me
Long after we returned to Alcalá.
She's in Madrid.

HYPOLITO

I know it.

VICTORIAN

And I'm in love.

HYPOLITO

And therefore in Madrid when thou shouldst be
In Alcalá.

VICTORIAN

O pardon me, my friend,
If I so long have kept this secret from thee;
But silence is the charm that guards such treasures,
And, if a word be spoken ere the time,
They sink again, they were not meant for us.

HYPOLITO

Alas! alas! I see thou art in love.
Love keeps the cold out better than a cloak.
It serves for food and raiment. Give a Spaniard
His mass, his olla, and his Doña Luisa,—
Thou knowest the proverb. But pray tell me, lover,
How speeds thy wooing? Is the maiden coy?
Write her a song, beginning with an *Ave;*
Sing as the monk sang to the Virgin Mary,

> *Ave! cujus calcem clare* [1]
> *Nec centenni commendare*
> *Sciret Seraph studio!*

VICTORIAN

Pray, do not jest! This is no time for it!
I am in earnest!

HYPOLITO

Seriously enamored?
What, ho! The Primus of great Alcalá
Enamored of a Gypsy? Tell me frankly,
How meanest thou?

VICTORIAN

I mean it honestly.

---

[1] *Ave! cujus calcem clare.*
From a monkish hymn of the twelfth century, in Sir Alexander
Croke's *Essay on the Origin, Progress and Decline of Rhyming Latin
Verse*, p. 109.

HYPOLITO

Surely thou wilt not marry her!

VICTORIAN

Why not?

HYPOLITO

She was betrothed to one Bartolomé
If I remember rightly, a young Gypsy
Who danced with her at Córdova.

VICTORIAN

They quarrelled,
And so the matter ended.

HYPOLITO

But in truth
Thou wilt not marry her.

VICTORIAN

In truth I will.
The angels sang in heaven when she was born!
She is a precious jewel I have found
Among the filth and rubbish of the world.
I'll stoop for it; but when I wear it here,
Set on my forehead like the morning star,
The world may wonder, but it will not laugh.

HYPOLITO

If thou wear'st nothing else upon thy forehead,
'T will be indeed a wonder.

VICTORIAN

Out upon thee,
With thy unseasonable jests! Pray, tell me,
Is there no virtue in the world?

HYPOLITO

Not much.
What, think'st thou, is she doing at this moment;
Now, while we speak of her?

VICTORIAN

She lies asleep,
And, from her parted lips, her gentle breath
Comes like the fragrance from the lips of flowers.
Her tender limbs are still, and, on her breast,
The cross she prayed to, ere she fell asleep,
Rises and falls with the soft tide of dreams,
Like a light barge safe moored.

HYPOLITO

Which means, in prose,
She's sleeping with her mouth a little open!

VICTORIAN

O, would I had the old magician's glass
To see her as she lies in child-like sleep!

HYPOLITO

And wouldst thou venture?

VICTORIAN

Ay, indeed I would!

HYPOLITO

Thou art courageous. Hast thou e'er reflected
How much lies hidden in that one word, *now?*

VICTORIAN

Yes; all the awful mystery of Life!
I oft have thought, my dear Hypolito,
That could we, by some spell of magic, change
The world and its inhabitants to stone,
In the same attitudes they are now in,
What fearful glances downward might we cast
Into the hollow chasms of human life!
What groups should we behold about the deathbed,
Putting to shame the group of Niobe!
What joyful welcomes, and what sad farewells!
What stony tears in those congealèd eyes!
What visible joy or anguish in those cheeks!
What bridal pomps, and what funereal shows!
What foes, like gladiators, fierce and struggling!
What lovers with their marble lips together!

HYPOLITO

Ay, there it is! and, if I were in love,
That is the very point I most should dread.
This magic glass, these magic spells of thine,
Might tell a tale were better left untold.
For instance, they might show us thy fair cousin,
The lady Violante, bathed in tears
Of love and anger, like the maid of Colchis,
Whom thou, another faithless Argonaut,
Having won that golden fleece, a woman's love,
Desertest for this Glaucè.

VICTORIAN

        Hold thy peace:
She cares not for me. She may wed another,
Or go into a convent, and, thus dying,
Marry Achilles in the Elysian Fields.

HYPOLITO (*rising*)

And so, good-night! Good-morning, I should say.

(*Clock strikes three*)

Hark! how the loud and ponderous mace of Time
Knocks at the golden portals of the day!
And so, once more, good-night!
We'll speak more largely
Of Preciosa when we meet again.
Get thee to bed, and the magician, Sleep,
Shall show her to thee, in his magic glass,
In all her loveliness. Good-night!   [*Exit.*

VICTORIAN

        Good-night!
But not to bed; for I must read awhile.

(*Throws himself into the arm-chair which* HYPOLITO *has left,
and lays a large book open upon his knees.*)

Must read, or sit in reverie and watch
The changing color of the waves that break
Upon the idle seashore of the mind!
Visions of Fame! that once did visit me,

Making night glorious with your smile, where are ye?
O, who shall give me, now that ye are gone,
Juices of those immortal plants that bloom
Upon Olympus, making us immortal?
Or teach me where that wondrous mandrake grows
Whose magic root, torn from the earth with groans,
At midnight hour, can scare the fiends away,
And make the mind prolific in its fancies?
I have the wish, but want the will to act!
Souls of great men departed! Ye whose words
Have come to light from the swift river of Time,
Like Roman swords found in the Tagus' bed,
Where is the strength to wield the arms ye bore?
From the barred visor of Antiquity
Reflected shines the eternal light of Truth,
As from a mirror! All the means of action—
The shapeless masses—the materials—
Lie everywhere about us. What we need
Is the celestial fire to change the flint
Into transparent crystal, bright and clear.
That fire is genius! The rude peasant sits
At evening in his smoky cot, and draws
With charcoal uncouth figures on the wall.
The son of genius comes, foot-sore with travel,
And begs a shelter from the inclement night.
He takes the charcoal from the peasant's hand,
And, by the magic of his touch at once
Transfigured, all its hidden virtues shine,
And, in the eyes of the astonished clown,
It gleams a diamond! Even thus transformed,
Rude popular traditions and old tales
Shine as immortal poems, at the touch
Of some poor, houseless, homeless, wandering bard,
Who had but a night's lodging for his pains.
But there are brighter dreams than those of Fame,
Which are the dreams of Love! Out of the heart
Rises the bright ideal of these dreams,
As from some woodland fount a spirit rises
And sinks again into its silent deeps,
Ere the enamored knight can touch her robe!

'T is this ideal that the soul of man,
Like the enamored knight beside the fountain,
Waits for upon the margin of Life's stream;
Waits to behold her rise from the dark waters,
Clad in mortal shape! Alas! how many
Must wait in vain! The stream flows evermore,
But from its silent deeps no spirit rises!
Yet I, born under a propitious star,
Have found the bright ideal of my dreams.
Yes! she is ever with me. I can feel,
Here, as I sit at midnight and alone,
Her gentle breathing! on my breast can feel
The pressure of her head! God's benison
Rest ever on it! Close those beauteous eyes,
Sweet Sleep! and all the flowers that bloom at night
With balmy lips breathe in her ears my name!

(*Gradually sinks asleep*)

ACT II

SCENE I. PRECIOSA'S *chamber. Morning.* PRECIOSA *and* AN-
GELICA.

PRECIOSA

Why will you go so soon? Stay yet awhile.
The poor too often turn away unheard
From hearts that shut against them with a sound
That will be heard in heaven. Pray, tell me more
Of your adversities. Keep nothing from me.
What is your landlord's name?

ANGELICA

The Count of Lara.

PRECIOSA

The Count of Lara? O, beware that man!
Mistrust his pity,—hold no parley with him!
And rather die an outcast in the streets
Than touch his gold.

ANGELICA

You know him, then!

PRECIOSA

As much
As any woman may, and yet be pure.
As you would keep your name without a blemish,
Beware of him!

ANGELICA

Alas! what can I do?
I cannot choose my friends. Each word of kindness,
Come whence it may, is welcome to the poor.

PRECIOSA

Make me your friend. A girl so young and fair
Should have no friends but those of her own sex.
What is your name?

ANGELICA
Angelica.

PRECIOSA

That name
Was given you, that you might be an angel
To her who bore you! When your infant smile
Made her home Paradise, you were her angel.
O, be an angel still! She needs that smile.
So long as you are innocent, fear nothing.
No one can harm you! I am a poor girl,
Whom chance has taken from the public streets
I have no other shield than mine own virtue:
That is the charm which has protected me!
Amid a thousand perils, I have worn it
Here on my heart! It is my guardian angel.

(ANGELICA *rising*)

I thank you for this counsel, dearest lady.

PRECIOSA

Thank me by following it.

ANGELICA
Indeed I will.

PRECIOSA

Pray, do not go. I have much more to say.

ANGELICA

My mother is alone. I dare not leave her.

PRECIOSA

Some other time, then, when we meet again.
You must not go away with words alone.

(*Gives her a purse*)

Take this. Would it were more.

ANGELICA

　　　　　　　　I thank you, lady.

PRECIOSA

No thanks. To-morrow come to me again.
I dance to-night,—perhaps for the last time.
But what I gain, I promise shall be yours,
If that can save you from the Count of Lara.

ANGELICA

O, my dear lady! how shall I be grateful
For so much kindness?

PRECIOSA

　　　　　　　I deserve no thanks.
Thank Heaven, not me.

ANGELICA

　　　　　　Both Heaven and you.

PRECIOSA

　　　　　　　　　　　Farewell!

Remember that you come again to-morrow.

ANGELICA

I will. And may the blessed Virgin guard you,
And all good angels. 　　　　　　　　　[*Exit.*

PRECIOSA

May they guard thee too,
And all the poor; for they have need of angels.
Now bring me, dear Dolores, my basquiña,
My richest maja dress,—my dancing dress,
And my most precious jewels! Make me look
Fairer than night e'er saw me! I've a prize
To win this day, worthy of Preciosa!

(*Enter* BELTRAN CRUZADO)

CRUZADO

Ave Maria!

PRECIOSA

O God! my evil genius!
What seekest thou here to-day?

CRUZADO

Thyself,—my child.

PRECIOSA

What is thy will with me?

CRUZADO

Gold! gold!

PRECIOSA

I gave thee yesterday; I have no more.

CRUZADO

The gold of the Busné,—give me his gold!

PRECIOSA

I gave the last in charity to-day.

CRUZADO

That is a foolish lie.

PRECIOSA

It is the truth.

CRUZADO

Curses upon thee! Thou art not my child!
Hast thou given gold away, and not to me?
Not to thy father? To whom, then?

PRECIOSA

To one
Who needs it more.

CRUZADO

No one can need it more.

PRECIOSA

Thou art not poor.

CRUZADO

What, I, who lurk about
In dismal suburbs and unwholesome lanes;
I, who am housed worse than the galley slave;
I, who am fed worse than the kennelled hound;
I, who am clothed in rags,—Beltran Cruzado,—
Not poor!

PRECIOSA

Thou hast a stout heart and strong hands.
Thou canst supply thy wants; what wouldst thou more?

CRUZADO

The gold of the Busné! [1] give me his gold!

PRECIOSA

Beltran Cruzado! hear me once for all,
I speak the truth. So long as I had gold,
I gave it to thee freely, at all times,
Never denied thee; never had a wish
But to fulfil thine own. Now go in peace!
Be merciful, be patient, and, ere long,
Thou shalt have more.

CRUZADO

And if I have it not,
Thou shalt no longer dwell here in rich chambers,
Wear silken dresses, feed on dainty food,
And live in idleness; but go with me,
Dance the Romalis in the public streets,
And wander wild again o'er field and fell;
For here we stay not long.

[1] *The gold of Busné.*
Busné is the name given by the Gypsies to all who are not of their race.

PRECIOSA
What! march again?

CRUZADO

Ay, with all speed. I hate the crowded town!
I cannot breathe shut up within its gates!
Air,—I want air, and sunshine, and blue sky,
The feeling of the breeze upon my face,
The feeling of the turf beneath my feet,
And no walls but the far-off mountain tops.
Then I am free and strong,—once more myself,
Beltran Cruzado, Count of the Calés! [1]

PRECIOSA

God speed thee on thy march!—I cannot go.

CRUZADO

Remember who I am, and who thou art!
Be silent and obey! Yet one thing more.
Bartolomé Román—

PRECIOSA (*with emotion*)
O I beseech thee!

If my obedience and blameless life,
If my humility and meek submission
In all things hitherto, can move in thee
One feeling of compassion, if thou art
Indeed my father, and canst trace in me
One look of her who bore me, or one tone
That doth remind thee of her, let it plead
In my behalf, who am a feeble girl,
Too feeble to resist, and do not force me
To wed that man! I am afraid of him!
I do not love him! On my knees I beg thee
To use no violence, nor do in haste
What cannot be undone!

CRUZADO
O child, child, child!

Thou hast betrayed thy secret, as a bird

[1] *Count of the Calés.*
The Gypsies call themselves Calés. See Borrow's valuable and extremely interesting work, *The Zincali; or an Account of the Gypsies in Spain.* London, 1841.

Betrays her nest, by striving to conceal it.
I will not leave thee here in the great city
To be a grandee's mistress. Make thee ready
To go with us; and until then remember
A watchful eye is on thee.   [*Exit*.

PRECIOSA
Woe is me!

I have a strange misgiving in my heart!
But that one deed of charity I'll do,
Befall what may; they cannot take that from me.   [*Exit*.

SCENE II. *A room in the* ARCHBISHOP'S *Palace, The* ARCH-
    BISHOP *and a* CARDINAL *seated*.

ARCHBISHOP

Knowing how near it touched the public morals,
And that our age is grown corrupt and rotten
By such excesses, we have sent to Rome,
Beseeching that his Holiness would aid
In curing the gross surfeit of the time,
By seasonable stop put here in Spain
To bull-fights and lewd dances on the stage.
All this you know.

CARDINAL
Know and approve.

ARCHBISHOP
And farther,

That, by a mandate from his Holiness,
The first have been suppressed.

CARDINAL
I trust forever.

It was a cruel sport.

ARCHBISHOP
A barbarous pastime,

Disgraceful to the land that calls itself
Most Catholic and Christian.

CARDINAL
Yet the people

Murmur at this; and, if the public dances

Should be condemned upon too slight occasion,
Worse ills might follow than the ills we cure.
As *Panem et Circenses* was the cry,
Among the Roman populace of old,
So *Pan y Toros* is the cry in Spain.
Hence I would act advisedly herein,
And therefore have induced your grace to see
These national dances, ere we interdict them.

(*Enter a Servant*)

SERVANT

The dancing-girl, and with her the musicians
Your grace was pleased to order, wait without.

ARCHBISHOP

Bid them come in. Now shall your eyes behold
In what angelic yet voluptuous shape
The Devil came to tempt Saint Anthony.

(*Enter* PRECIOSA, *with a mantle thrown over her head. She
advances slowly, in a modest, half-timid attitude.*)

CARDINAL (*aside*)

O, what a fair and ministering angel
Was lost to heaven when this sweet woman fell!

PRECIOSA (*kneeling before the* ARCHBISHOP)

I have obeyed the order of your grace.
If I intrude upon your better hours,
I proffer this excuse, and here beseech
Your holy benediction.

ARCHBISHOP

May God bless thee,
And lead thee to a better life. Arise.

CARDINAL (*aside*)

Her acts are modest, and her words discreet!
I did not look for this. Come hither, child.
Is thy name Preciosa?

PRECIOSA

Thus I am called.

CARDINAL

That is a Gypsy name. Who is thy father?

PRECIOSA

Beltran Cruzado, Count of the Calés.

ARCHBISHOP

I have a dim remembrance of that man;
He was a bold and reckless character
A sun-burnt Ishmael!

CARDINAL
Dost thou remember
Thy earlier days?

PRECIOSA
Yes; by the Darro's side
My childhood passed. I can remember still
The river, and the mountains capped with snow;
The villages, where, yet a little child,
I told the traveller's fortune in the street;
The smuggler's horse, the brigand and the shepherd;
The march across the moor; the halt at noon;
The red fire of the evening camp, that lighted
The forest where we slept; and, farther back,
As in a dream or in some former life,
Gardens and palace walls.

ARCHBISHOP
'T is the Alhambra,
Under whose towers the Gypsy camp was pitched.
But the time wears; and we would see thee dance.

PRECIOSA

Your grace shall be obeyed.
(*She lays aside her mantilla. The music of the cachucha
is played, and the dance begins. The* ARCHBISHOP *and the*
CARDINAL *look on with gravity and an occasional frown;
then make signs to each other; and, as the dance continues,
become more and more pleased and excited; and at length
rise from their seats, throw their caps in the air, and
applaud vehemently as the scene closes.*)

SCENE III. *The Prado. A long avenue of trees leading to the gate of Atocha. On the right the dome and spires of a convent. A fountain. Evening.* DON CARLOS *and* HYPOLITO *meeting.*

DON CARLOS

Holá! good-evening, Don Hypolito.

HYPOLITO

And a good-evening to my friend, Don Carlos,
Some lucky star has led my steps this way.
I was in search of you.

DON CARLOS

Command me always.

HYPOLITO

Do you remember, in Quevedo's Dreams,
The miser, who, upon the Day of Judgment,
Asks if his money-bags would rise? [1]

DON CARLOS

I do;

But what of that?

HYPOLITO

I am that wretched man.

DON CARLOS

You mean to tell me yours have risen empty?

HYPOLITO

And amen! said my Cid Campeador. [2]

DON CARLOS

Pray, how much need you?

[1] *Asks if his money-bags would rise.*
"¿Y volviéndome á un lado, vi á un Avariento, que estaba pregun-tando á otro, (que porhaber sido emblasamado, y estar léxos sus tripas no hablaba, porque no habian llegado si habian de resucitar aquel dia todos los enterrados) si resucitarian unos bolsones suyos?"— *El Sueño de las Calaveras.*

[2] *And amen! said my Cid Campeador.*
A line from the ancient *Poema del Cid.*
"Amen, dixo Mio Cid el Campeador.''
Line 3044.

HYPOLITO

Some half dozen ounces

Which, with due interest—

DON CARLOS (*giving his purse*)

What, am I a Jew

To put my moneys out at usury?
Here is my purse.

HYPOLITO

Thank you. A pretty purse,

Made by the hand of some fair Madrileña;
Perhaps a keepsake.

DON CARLOS

No, 't is at your service.

HYPOLITO

Thank you again. Lie there, good Chrysostom,
And with thy golden mouth remind me often,
I am the debtor of my friend.

DON CARLOS

But tell me,

Come you to-day from Alcalá?

HYPOLITO

This moment.

DON CARLOS

And pray, how fares the brave Victorian?

HYPOLITO

Indifferent well; that is to say, not well.
A damsel has ensnared him with the glances
Of her dark, roving eyes, as herdsmen catch
A steer of Andalusia with a lazo.
He is in love.

DON CARLOS

And is it faring ill

To be in love?

HYPOLITO
In his case very ill.

DON CARLOS
Why so?

HYPOLITO
For many reasons. First and foremost,
Because he is in love with an ideal,
A creature of his own imagination;
A child of air; an echo of his heart;
And like a lily on a river floating,
She floats upon the river of his thoughts! [1]

DON CARLOS
A common thing with poets. But who is
This floating lily? For, in fine, some woman,
Some living woman,—not a mere ideal,—
Must wear the outward semblance of his thought.
Who is it? Tell me.

HYPOLITO
Well, it is a woman!
But, look you, from the coffer of his heart
He brings forth precious jewels to adorn her,
As pious priests adorn some favorite saint
With gems and gold, until at length she gleams
One blaze of glory. Without these, you know,
And the priest's benediction, 't is a doll.

DON CARLOS
Well, well! who is this doll?

HYPOLITO
Why, who do you think?

DON CARLOS
His cousin Violante.

[1] *The river of his thoughts.* This expression is from Dante;
"Si she chiaro
Per essa scenda della mente il fiume."
Byron had likewise used the expression; though I do not recollect
in which of his poems.

HYPOLITO
Guess again.
To ease his laboring heart, in the last storm
He threw her overboard, with all her ingots.

DON CARLOS
I cannot guess; so tell me who it is.

HYPOLITO
Not I.

DON CARLOS
Why not?

HYPOLITO (*mysteriously*)
Why? Because Mari Franca [1]
Was married four leagues out of Salamanca!

DON CARLOS
Jesting aside, who is it?

HYPOLITO
Preciosa.

DON CARLOS
Impossible! The Count of Lara tells me
She is not virtuous.

HYPOLITO
Did I say she was?
The Roman Emperor Claudius had a wife
Whose name was Messalina, as I think;
Valeria Messalina was her name.
But hist! I see him yonder through the trees,
Walking as in a dream.

DON CARLOS
He comes this way.

---

[1] *Mari Franca.* A common Spanish proverb, used to turn aside a
question one does not wish to answer:
"Porque casó Mari Franca
quatro leguas de Salamanca."

HYPOLITO

It has been truly said by some wise man,
That money, grief, and love cannot be hidden.

(*Enter* VICTORIAN *in front*)

VICTORIAN

Where'er thy step has passed is holy ground;
These groves are sacred! I behold thee walking
Under these shadowy trees, where we have walked
At evening, and I feel thy presence now;
Feel that the place has taken a charm from thee,
And is forever hallowed.

HYPOLITO

Mark him well!
See how he strides away with lordly air,
Like that odd guest of stone, that grim Commander
Who comes to sup with Juan in the play.

DON CARLOS

What ho! Victorian!

HYPOLITO

Wilt thou sup with us?

VICTORIAN

Holá! amigos! Faith, I did not see you.
How fares Don Carlos?

DON CARLOS

At your service ever.

VICTORIAN

How is that young and green-eyed Gaditana
That you both wot of?

DON CARLOS

Ay, soft, emerald eyes! [1]
She has gone back to Cadiz.

---

[1] *Ay, soft, emerald eyes*. The Spaniards, with good reason, consider this color of the eye as beautiful, and celebrate it in song; as, for example in the well known *Vallanccio;*

> "Ay ojuelos verdes,
> ay los mis ojuelos,
> ay hagan los cielos

HYPOLITO

Ay de mi!

VICTORIAN

You are much to blame for letting her go back.
A pretty girl; and in her tender eyes
Just that soft shade of green we sometimes see
In evening skies.

HYPOLITO

But, speaking of green eyes,

Are thine green?

VICTORIAN

Not a whit. Why so?

HYPOLITO

I think

The slightest shade of green would be becoming,
For thou art jealous.

VICTORIAN

No, I am not jealous.

HYPOLITO

Thou shouldst be.

VICTORIAN

Why?

HYPOLITO

Because thou art in love.

And they who are in love are always jealous.
Therefore thou shouldst be.

VICTORIAN

Marry, is that all?

Farewell; I am in haste. Farewell, Don Carlos.
Thou sayst I should be jealous?

----

que de mi te acuerdes!

.   .   .

Tengo confianza
de mis verdes ojos."
        Böhl de Faber. Floresta, No. 255.

Dante speaks of Beatrice's eyes as emeralds. *Purgatorie,* xxxi. 116.
Lami says, in his *Annotazioni,* "Erano i suoi occhi d' un turchino
verdiccio, simile a quel del mare."

HYPOLITO

Ay, in truth
I fear there is reason. Be upon thy guard,
I hear it whispered that the Count of Lara
Lays siege to the same citadel.

VICTORIAN

Indeed!
Then he will have his labor for his pains.

HYPOLITO

He does not think so, and Don Carlos tells me
He boasts of his success.

VICTORIAN

How's this, Don Carlos?

DON CARLOS

Some hints of it I heard from his own lips.
He spoke but lightly of the lady's virtue,
As a gay man might speak.

VICTORIAN

Death and damnation!
I'll cut his lying tongue out of his mouth,
And throw it to my dog! But no, no, no!
This cannot be. You jest, indeed you jest.
Trifle with me no more. For otherwise
We are no longer friends. And so, farewell!   [*Exit*

HYPOLITO

Now what a coil is here! The Avenging Child [1]
Hunting the traitor Quadros to his death,
And the great Moor Calaynos, when he rode
To Paris for the ears of Oliver,
Were nothing to him! O hot-headed youth!
But come; we will not follow. Let us join
The crowd that pours into the Prado. There
We shall find merrier company; I see
The Marialonzos and the Almavivas,
And fifty fans, that beckon me already.   [*Exeunt.*

---

[1] *The Avenging Child.* See the ancient Ballads of *El Infante Vengador* and *Calaynos.*

SCENE IV. PRECIOSA'S *chamber. She is sitting, with a book in her hand, near a table on which are flowers. A bird singing in its cage. The* COUNT OF LARA *enters behind unperceived.*

PRECIOSA (*reads*)

All are sleeping, weary heart! [1]
Thou, thou only sleepless art!

Heigho! I wish Victorian were here.
I know not what makes me so restless!

(*The bird sings*)

Thou little prisoner with thy motley coat,
That from thy vaulted, wiry dungeon singest,
Like thee I am a captive, and, like thee,
I have a gentle gaoler. Lack-a-day!

All are sleeping, weary heart!
Thou, thou only sleepless art!
All this throbbing, all this aching,
Evermore shall keep thee waking,
For a heart in sorrow breaking
Thinketh ever of its smart!

Thou speakest truly, poet! and methinks
More hearts are breaking in this world of ours
Than one would say. In distant villages
And solitudes remote, where winds have wafted
The barbèd seeds of love, or birds of passage
Scattered them in their flight, do they take root,
And grow in silence, and in silence perish.
Who hears the falling of the forest leaf?
Or who takes note of every flower that dies?
Heigho! I wish Victorian would come.
Dolores!

(*Turns to lay down her book and perceives the* COUNT)

Ha!

LARA
Señora, pardon me!

[1] *All are sleeping.* From the Spanish. *Böhl's Floresta*, No. 282.

PRECIOSA

How's this? Dolores!

LARA

Pardon me—

PRECIOSA

Dolores!

LARA

Be not alarmed; I found no one in waiting.
If I have been too bold—

PRECIOSA (*turning her back upon him*)
You are too bold!
Retire! retire, and leave me!

LARA
My dear lady,
First hear me! I beseech you, let me speak!
'T is for your good I come.

PRECIOSA (*turning toward him with indignation*)
Begone! Begone!
You are the Count of Lara, but your deeds
Would make the statues of your ancestors
Blush on their tombs! Is it Castilian honor,
Is it Castilian pride, to steal in here
Upon a friendless girl, to do her wrong?
O shame! shame! shame that you, a nobleman,
Should be so little noble in your thoughts
As to send jewels here to win my love,
And think to buy my honor with your gold!
I have no words to tell you how I scorn you!
Begone! The sight of you is hateful to me!
Begone, I say!

LARA
Be calm; I will not harm you.

PRECIOSA

Because you dare not.

LARA

I dare anything!
Therefore beware! You are deceived in me.
In this false world, we do not always know
Who are our friends and who our enemies,
We all have enemies, and all need friends.
Even you, fair Preciosa, here at court
Have foes, who seek to wrong you.

PRECIOSA

If to this
I owe the honor of the present visit,
You might have spared the coming. Having spoken,
Once more I beg you, leave me to myself.

LARA

I thought it but a friendly part to tell you
What strange reports are current here in town.
For my own self, I do not credit them;
But there are many who, not knowing you,
Will lend a readier ear.

PRECIOSA

There was no need
That you should take upon yourself the duty
Of telling me these tales.

LARA

Malicious tongues
Are ever busy with your name.

PRECIOSA

Alas!
I have no protectors. I am a poor girl,
Exposed to insults and unfeeling jests.
They wound me, yet I cannot shield myself.
I give no cause for these reports, I live
Retired; am visited by none.

LARA

By none?
O, then, indeed, you are much wronged!

PRECIOSA

How mean you?

LARA

Nay, nay; I will not wound your gentle soul
By the report of idle tales.

PRECIOSA

Speak out!
What are these idle tales? You need not spare me.

LARA

I will deal frankly with you. Pardon me;
This window, as I think, looks toward the street,
And this into the Prado, does it not?
In yon high house, beyond the garden wall,—
You see the roof there just above the trees,—
There lives a friend, who told me yesterday,
That on a certain night,—be not offended
If I too plainly speak,—he saw a man
Climb to your chamber window. You are silent!
I would not blame you, being young and fair—
(*He tries to embrace her. She starts back and draws a
    dagger from her bosom*)

PRECIOSA

Beware! beware! I am a Gypsy girl!
Lay not your hand upon me. One step nearer
And I will strike!

LARA

Pray you, put up that dagger.
Fear not.

PRECIOSA

I do not fear. I have a heart
In whose strength I can trust.

LARA

Listen to me.
I come here as your friend,—I am your friend,—
And by a single word can put a stop
To all those idle tales, and make your name

Spotless as lilies are. Here on my knees,
Fair Preciosa! on my knees I swear
I love you even to madness, and that love
Has driven me to break the rules of custom,
And force myself unasked into your presence.

(VICTORIAN *enters behind*)

PRECIOSA

Rise, Count of Lara! That is not the place
For such as you are. It becomes you not
To kneel before me. I am strangely moved
To see one of your rank thus low and humbled;
For your sake I will put aside all anger,
All unkind feeling, all dislike, and speak
In gentleness, as most becomes a woman,
And as my heart now prompts me. I no more
Will hate you, for all hate is painful to me.
But if, without offending modesty
And that reserve which is a woman's glory,
I may speak freely, I will teach my heart
To love you.

LARA

O sweet angel!

PRECIOSA

Ay, in truth
Far better than you love yourself or me.

LARA

Give me some sign of this,—the slightest token.
Let me but kiss your hand.

PRECIOSA

Nay, come no nearer.
The words I utter are its sign and token.
Misunderstand me not! Be not deceived!
The love wherewith I love you is not such
As you would offer me. For you come here
To take from me the only thing I have,
My honor. You are wealthy, you have friends
And kindred, and a thousand pleasant hopes
That fill your heart with happiness; but I

Am poor, and friendless, having but one treasure,
And you would take that from me, and for what?
To flatter your own vanity, and make me
What you would most despise. O Sir, such love,
That seeks to harm me, cannot be true love.
Indeed it cannot. But my love for you
Is of a different kind. It seeks your good.
It is a holier feeling. It rebukes
Your earthly passion, your unchaste desires,
And bids you look into your heart, and see
How you do wrong that better nature in you,
And grieve your soul with sin.

LARA
                    I swear to you,
I would not harm you; I would only love you.
I would not take your honor, but restore it,
And in return I ask but some slight mark
Of your affection. If indeed you love me,
As you confess you do, O let me thus
With this embrace—

VICTORIAN (*rushing forward*)
                    Hold! hold! This is too much.
What means this outrage?

LARA
                    First, what right have you
To question thus a nobleman of Spain?

VICTORIAN
I too am noble, and you are no more!
Out of my sight!

LARA
            Are you the master here?

VICTORIAN
Ay, here and elsewhere, when the wrong of others
Gives me the right!

PRECIOSA (*to* LARA)
            Go! I beseech you, go!

VICTORIAN

I shall have business with you, Count, anon!

LARA

You cannot come too soon! [*Exit.*

PRECIOSA

Victorian!
O we have been betrayed!

VICTORIAN

Ha! ha! betrayed!
'T is I have been betrayed, not we!—not we!

PRECIOSA

Dost thou imagine—

VICTORIAN

I imagine nothing;
I see how 't is thou whilest the time away
When I am gone!

PRECIOSA

O speak not in that tone!
It wounds me deeply.

VICTORIAN

'T was not meant to flatter.

PRECIOSA

Too well thou knowest the presence of that man
Is hateful to me!

VICTORIAN

Yet I saw thee stand
And listen to him, when he told his love.

PRECIOSA

I did not heed his words.

VICTORIAN

Indeed thou didst,
And answeredst them with love.

PRECIOSA

Hadst thou heard all—

VICTORIAN

I heard enough.

PRECIOSA

Be not so angry with me.

VICTORIAN

I am not angry; I am very calm.

PRECIOSA

If thou wilt let me speak—

VICTORIAN

Nay, say no more.
I know too much already. Thou art false!
I do not like these Gypsy marriages!
Where is the ring I gave thee?

PRECIOSA

In my casket.

VICTORIAN

There let it rest! I would not have thee wear it;
I thought thee spotless, and thou art polluted!

PRECIOSA

I call the Heavens to witness—

VICTORIAN

Nay, nay, nay!
Take not the name of Heaven upon thy lips!
They are forsworn!

PRECIOSA

Victorian! dear Victorian!

VICTORIAN

I gave up all for thee; myself, my fame,
My hopes of fortune, ay, my very soul!
And thou hast been my ruin! Now go on!
Laugh at my folly with thy paramour,
And, sitting on the Count of Lara's knee,
Say what a poor, fond fool Victorian was!

(*He casts her from him and rushes out*)

PRECIOSA

And this from thee!

(*Scene closes*)

SCENE V. *The* COUNT OF LARA'S *rooms. Enter the* COUNT.

LARA

There 's nothing in this world so sweet as love,
And next to love the sweetest thing is hate!
I've learned to hate, and therefore am revenged.
A silly girl to play the prude with me!
The fire that I have kindled—

(*Enter* FRANCISCO)
Well, Francisco.

What tidings from Don Juan?

FRANCISCO
Good, my lord;

He will be present.

LARA

And the Duke of Lermos?

FRANCISCO

Was not at home.

LARA

How with the rest?

FRANCISCO

I've found

The men you wanted. They will all be there,
And at the given signal raise a whirlwind
Of such discordant noises, that the dance
Must cease for lack of music.

LARA

Bravely done.

Ah! little dost thou dream, sweet Preciosa,
What lies in wait for thee. Sleep shall not close
Thine eyes this night! Give me my cloak and sword.

[*Exeunt.*

SCENE VI. *A retired spot beyond the city gates. Enter*
VICTORIAN *and* HYPOLITO.

VICTORIAN

O shame! O shame! Why do I walk abroad
By daylight, when the very sunshine mocks me,
And voices, and familiar sights and sounds
Cry, "Hide thyself"! O what a thin partition
Doth shut out from the curious world the knowledge
Of evil deeds that have been done in darkness!
Disgrace has many tongues. My fears are windows,
Through which all eyes seem gazing. Every face
Expresses some suspicion of my shame,
And in derision seems to smile at me!

HYPOLITO

Did I not caution thee? Did I not tell thee
I was but half persuaded of her virtue?

VICTORIAN

And yet, Hypolito, we may be wrong,
We may be over-hasty in condemning!
The Count of Lara is a cursèd villain.

HYPOLITO

And therefore is she cursed, loving him.

VICTORIAN

She does not love him. 'T is for gold! for gold!

HYPOLITO

Ay, but remember, in the public streets
He shows a golden ring the Gypsy gave him,
A serpent with a ruby in its mouth.

VICTORIAN

She had that ring from me! God! she is false!
But I will be revenged! The hour is passed.
Where stays the coward?

HYPOLITO

            Nay, he is no coward;
A villain, if thou wilt, but not a coward.
I've seen him play with swords; it is his pastime,

And therefore be not over-confident,
He'll task thy skill anon. Look, here he comes.

(*Enter* LARA *followed by* FRANCISCO)

LARA

Good-evening, gentlemen.

HYPOLITO
Good-evening, Count.

LARA

I trust I have not kept you long in waiting.

VICTORIAN

Not long and yet too long. Are you prepared?

LARA

I am.

HYPOLITO

It grieves me much to see this quarrel
Between you, gentlemen. Is there no way
Left open to accord this difference,
But you must make one with your swords?

VICTORIAN
No! none!

I do entreat thee, dear Hypolito,
Stand not between me and my foe. Too long
Our tongues have spoken. Let these tongues of steel
End our debate. Upon your guard, Sir Count!

(*They fight.* VICTORIAN *disarms the* COUNT)

Your life is mine; and what shall now withhold me
From sending your vile soul to its account?

LARA

Strike! strike!

VICTORIAN

You are disarmed. I will not kill you.
I will not murder you. Take up your sword.

(FRANCISCO *hands the* COUNT *his sword, and* HYPOLITO
interposes)

HYPOLITO

Enough! Let it end here! The Count of Lara
Has shown himself a brave man, and Victorian
A generous one, as ever. Now be friends.
Put up your swords; for, to speak frankly to you,
Your cause of quarrel is too slight a thing
To move you to extremes.

LARA

I am content.
I sought no quarrel. A few hasty words,
Spoken in the heat of blood, have led to this.

VICTORIAN

Nay, something more than that.

LARA

I understand you.
Therein I did not mean to cross your path.
To me the door stood open, as to others.
But, had I known the girl belonged to you,
Never would I have sought to win her from you.
The truth stands now revealed; she has been false
To both of us.

VICTORIAN

Ay, false as hell itself.

LARA

In truth I did not seek her; she sought me;
And told me how to win her, telling me
The hours when she was oftenest left alone.

VICTORIAN

Say, can you prove this to me? O pluck out
These awful doubts, that goad me into madness!
Let me know all! all! all!

LARA

You shall know all.
Here is my page, who was the messenger
Between us. Question him. Was it not so,
Francisco?

FRANCISCO

Ay, my lord.

LARA

If farther proof
Is needful, I have here a ring she gave me.

VICTORIAN

Pray let me see that ring! It is the same!

(*Throws it upon the ground, and tramples upon it*)

Thus may she perish who once wore that ring!
Thus do I spurn her from me; do thus trample
Her memory in the dust! O Count of Lara,
We both have been abused, been much abused!
I thank you for your courtesy and frankness.
Though, like the surgeon's hand, yours gave me pain,
Yet it has cured my blindness, and I thank you.
I now can see the folly I have done,
Though 't is, alas! too late. So fare you well!
To-night I leave this hateful town for ever.
Regard me as your friend. Once more, farewell!

HYPOLITO

Farewell, Sir Count.

[*Exeunt* VICTORIAN *and* HYPOLITO.

LARA

Farewell! farewell!
Thus have I cleared the field of my worst foe!
I have none else to fear; the fight is done,
The citadel is stormed, the victory won!

[*Exit with* FRANCISCO.

SCENE VII. *A lane in the suburbs. Night. Enter* CRUZADO
and BARTOLOMÉ.

CRUZADO

And so, Bartolomé, the expedition failed. But where wast
thou for the most part?

BARTOLOMÉ

In the Guadarrama mountains, near San Ildefonso.

CRUZADO

And thou bringest nothing back with thee? Didst thou rob no one?

BARTOLOMÉ

There was no one to rob, save a party of students from Segovia, who looked as if they would rob us, and a jolly little friar, who had nothing in his pockets but a missal and a loaf of bread.

CRUZADO

Pray, then, what brings thee back to Madrid?

BARTOLOMÉ

First tell me what keeps thee here?

CRUZADO

Preciosa.

BARTOLOMÉ

And she brings me back. Hast thou forgotten thy promise?

CRUZADO

The two years are not passed yet. Wait patiently. The girl shall be thine.

BARTOLOMÉ

I hear she has a Busné lover.

CRUZADO

That is nothing.

BARTOLOMÉ

I do not like it. I hate him,—the son of a Busné harlot. He goes in and out, and speaks with her alone, and I must stand aside, and wait his pleasure.

CRUZADO

Be patient, I say. Thou shalt have thy revenge. When the time comes, thou shalt waylay him.

BARTOLOMÉ

Meanwhile, show me her house.

CRUZADO

Come this way. But thou wilt not find her. She dances at the play to-night.

BARTOLOMÉ

No matter. Show me the house.

[*Exeunt.*

SCENE VIII. *The theatre. The orchestra plays the cachucha.
Sound of castanets behind the scenes. The curtain rises
and discovers* PRECIOSA *in the attitude of commencing the
dance. The cachucha. Tumult; hisses; cries of "Brava!"
and "Afuera!" She falters and pauses. The music stops.
General confusion.* PRECIOSA *faints.*

SCENE IX. *The* COUNT OF LARA'S *chambers.* LARA *and his
friends at supper.*

LARA

So, Caballeros, once more many thanks!
You have stood by me bravely in this matter.
Pray fill your glasses.

DON JUAN

Did you mark, Don Luis,
How pale she looked, when first the noise began,
And then stood still, with her large eyes dilated!
Her nostrils spread! her lips apart! her bosom
Tumultuous as the sea!

DON LUIS

I pitied her.

LARA

Her pride is humbled; and this very night
I mean to visit her.

DON JUAN

Will you serenade her?

LARA

No music! no more music!

DON LUIS

Why not music?
It softens many hearts.

LARA

Not in the humor
She now is in. Music would madden her.

DON JUAN

Try golden cymbals.

DON LUIS

Yes, try Don Dinero!
A mighty wooer is your Don Dinero.

LARA

To tell the truth, then, I have bribed her maid.
But, Caballeros, you dislike this wine.
A bumper and away; for the night wears.
A health to Preciosa!

(*They rise and drink*)

ALL

Preciosa.

LARA (*holding up his glass*)

Thou bright and flaming minister of Love!
Thou wonderful magician! who hast stolen
My secret from me, and 'mid sighs of passion
Caught from my lips, with red and fiery tongue,
Her precious name! O never more henceforth
Shall mortal lips press thine; and never more
A mortal name be whispered in thine ear.
Go! keep my secret!

(*Drinks and dashes the goblet down*)

DON JUAN

Ite! missa est!

(*Scene Closes*)

SCENE X. *Street and garden wall. Night. Enter* CRUZADO *and* BARTOLOMÉ.

CRUZADO

This is the garden wall, and above it yonder, is her house.
The window in which thou seest the light is her window.
But we will not go in now.

BARTOLOMÉ

Why not?

CRUZADO

Because she is not at home.

BARTOLOMÉ

No matter; we can wait. But how is this? The gate is bolted. (*Sound of guitars and voices in a neighboring street.*) Hark! There comes her lover with his infernal serenade! Hark!

SONG

Good-night! [1] Good-night, beloved!
  I come to watch o'er thee!
To be near thee,—to be near thee,
  Alone is peace for me.

Thine eyes are stars of morning,
  Thy lips are crimson flowers!
Good-night! Good-night, beloved,
  While I count the weary hours.

CRUZADO

They are not coming this way.

BARTOLOMÉ

Wait, they begin again.

SONG (*coming nearer*)

Ah! thou moon that shinest
  Argent-clear above!
All night long enlighten
  My sweet lady-love!
Moon that shinest,
All night long enlighten us!

BARTOLOMÉ

Woe be to him, if he comes this way!

CRUZADO

Be quiet, they are passing down the street.

SONG (*dying away*)

The nuns in the cloister
  Sang to each other;

[1] *Good-night.* From the Spanish; as are likewise the songs immediately following, and that which commences the first scene of Act III.

For so many sisters
  Is there not one brother?
Ay, for the partridge, mother;
  The cat has run away with the partridge!
Puss! puss! puss!

BARTOLOMÉ

Follow that! follow that! Come with me. Puss! puss!

(*Exeunt. On the opposite side enter the* COUNT OF LARA *and gentlemen with* FRANCISCO)

LARA

The gate is fast. Over the wall, Francisco,
And draw the bolt. There, so, and so, and over.
Now, gentlemen, come in, and help me scale
Yon balcony. How now? Her light still burns.
Move warily. Make fast the gate, Francisco.

(*Exeunt. Re-enter* CRUZADO *and* BARTOLOMÉ)

BARTOLOMÉ

They went in at the gate. Hark! I hear them in the garden. (*Tries the gate.*) Bolted again! Vive Cristo! Follow me over the wall.

(*They climb the wall*)

SCENE XI. PRECIOSA'S *bed-chamber. Midnight. She is sleeping in an arm-chair, in an undress,* DOLORES *watching her.*

DOLORES

She sleeps at last!

(*Opens the window and listens*)

           All silent in the street
And in the garden. Hark!

PRECIOSA (*in her sleep*)
           I must go hence.
Give me my cloak!

DOLORES
He comes! I hear his footsteps!

PRECIOSA

Go tell them that I cannot dance to-night;
I am too ill! Look at me! See the fever
That burns upon my cheek! I must go hence.
I am too weak to dance.

(*Signal from the garden*)

DOLORES (*from the window*)
Who's there?

VOICE (*from below*)

A friend.

DOLORES

ʳ will undo the door. Wait till I come.

PRECIOSA

I must go hence. I pray you do not harm me!
Shame! shame! to treat a feeble woman thus!
Be you but kind, I will do all things for you.
I'm ready now,—give me my castanets.
Where is Victorian? Oh, those hateful lamps!
They glare upon me like an evil eye.
I cannot stay. Hark! how they mock at me!
They hiss at me like serpents! Save me! save me!

(*She wakes*)

How late is it, Dolores?

DOLORES

It is midnight.

PRECIOSA

We must be patient. Smooth this pillow for me.
(*She sleeps again. Noise from the garden, and voices*)

VOICE

Muera!

ANOTHER VOICE
O villains! villains!

LARA
So! have at you!

VOICE

Take that!

LARA

O, I am wounded!

DOLORES (*shutting the window*)
Jesu Maria!

ACT III

SCENE I. *A cross-road through a wood. In the background a distant village spire.* VICTORIAN *and* HYPOLITO, *as travelling students, with guitars, sitting under the trees.* HYPOLITO *plays and sings.*

SONG
Ah, Love!
Perjured, false, treacherous Love!
Enemy
Of all that mankind may not rue!
Most untrue
To him who keeps most faith with thee.
Woe is me!
The falcon has the eyes of the dove,
Ah, Love!
Perjured, false, treacherous Love!

VICTORIAN
Yes, love is ever busy with his shuttle,
Is ever weaving into life's dull warp
Bright, gorgeous flowers and scenes Arcadian;
Hanging our gloomy prison-house about
With tapestries, that make its walls dilate
In never-ending vistas of delight.

HYPOLITO
Thinking to walk in those Arcadian pastures,
Thou hast run thy noble head against the wall.

SONG (*continued*)
Thy deceits
Give us clearly to comprehend,
Whither tend
All thy pleasures, all the sweets!
They are cheats,

Thorns below and flowers above,
  Ah, Love!
Perjured, false, treacherous Love!

VICTORIAN

A very pretty song. I thank thee for it.

HYPOLITO

It suits thy case.

VICTORIAN

            Indeed, I think it does.
What wise man wrote it?

HYPOLITO

            Lopez Maldonado.

VICTORIAN

In truth, a pretty song.

HYPOLITO

            With much truth in it.
I hope thou wilt profit by it; and in earnest
Try to forget this lady of thy love.

VICTORIAN

I will forget her! All dear recollections
Pressed in my heart, like flowers within a book,
Shall be torn out, and scattered to the winds!
I will forget her! But perhaps hereafter,
When she shall learn how heartless is the world,
A voice within her will repeat my name,
And she will say, "He was indeed my friend!"
O, would I were a soldier, not a scholar,
That the loud march, the deafening beat of drums,
The shattering blast of the brass-throated trumpet,
The din of arms, the onslaught and the storm,
And a swift death, might make me deaf forever
To the upbraidings of this foolish heart!

HYPOLITO

Then let that foolish heart upbraid no more!
To conquer love, one need but will to conquer.

VICTORIAN

Yet, good Hypolito, it is in vain
I throw into Oblivion's sea the sword
That pierces me; for, like Excalibar,
With gemmed and flashing hilt, it will not sink.
There rises from below a hand that grasps it,
And waves it in the air; and wailing voices
Are heard along the shore.

HYPOLITO

And yet at last
Down sank Excalibar to rise no more.
This is not well. In truth, it vexes me.
Instead of whistling to the steeds of Time,
To make them jog on merrily with life's burden,
Like a dead weight thou hangest on the wheels.
Thou art too young, too full of lusty health
To talk of dying.

VICTORIAN

Yet I fain would die!
To go through life, unloving and unloved;
To feel that thirst and hunger of the soul
We cannot still; that longing, that wild impulse,
And struggle after something we have not
And cannot have; the effort to be strong;
And, like the Spartan boy, to smile, and smile,
While secret wounds do bleed beneath our cloaks;
All this the dead feel not,—the dead alone!
Would I were with them!

HYPOLITO

We shall all be soon.

VICTORIAN

It cannot be too soon; for I am weary
Of the bewildering masquerade of Life,
Where strangers walk as friends, and friends as strangers;
Where whispers overheard betray false hearts;
And through the mazes of the crowd we chase
Some form of loveliness, that smiles, and beckons,
And cheats us with fair words, only to leave us

A mockery and a jest; maddened,—confused,—
Not knowing friend from foe.

HYPOLITO
Why seek to know?
Enjoy the merry shrove-tide of thy youth!
Take each fair mask for what it gives itself,
Nor strive to look beneath it.

VICTORIAN
I confess,
That were the wiser part. But Hope no longer
Comforts my soul. I am a wretched man,
Much like a poor and shipwrecked mariner,
Who, struggling to climb up into the boat,
Has both his bruised and bleeding hands cut off,
And sinks again into the weltering sea,
Helpless and hopeless!

HYPOLITO
Yet thou shalt not perish.
The strength of thine own arm is thy salvation.
Above thy head, through rifted clouds, there shines
A glorious star. Be patient. Trust thy star!

(Sound of a village bell in the distance)

VICTORIAN
Ave Maria! I hear the sacristan
Ringing the chimes from yonder village belfry!
A solemn sound, that echoes far and wide
Over the red roofs of the cottages,
And bids the laboring hind a-field, the shepherd,
Guarding his flock, the lonely muleteer,
And all the crowd in village streets, stand still,
And breathe a prayer unto the blessed Virgin!

HYPOLITO
Amen! amen! Not half a league from hence
The village lies.

VICTORIAN
This path will lead us to it,
Over the wheat fields, where the shadows sail

Across the running sea, now green, now blue,
And, like an idle mariner on the main,
Whistles the quail. Come, let us hasten on.

[*Exeunt.*

SCENE II. *Public square in the village of Guadarrama. The
Ave Maria still tolling. A crowd of villagers, with their
hats in their hands, as if in prayer. In front, a group of
Gypsies. The bell rings a merrier peal. A Gypsy dance.
Enter* PANCHO, *followed by* PEDRO CRESPO.

PANCHO

Make room, ye vagabonds and Gypsy thieves!
Make room for the Alcalde and for me!

PEDRO CRESPO

Keep silence all! I have an edict here
From our most gracious lord, the King of Spain,
Jerusalem, and the Canary Islands,
Which I shall publish in the marketplace.
Open your ears and listen!

(*Enter the* PADRE CURA *at the door of his cottage*)

Padre Cura,
Good-day! and, pray you, hear this edict read.

PADRE CURA

Good-day, and God be with you! Pray, what is it?

PEDRO CRESPO

An act of banishment against the Gypsies!

(*Agitation and murmurs in the crowd*)

PANCHO

Silence!

PEDRO CRESPO (*reads*)
"I hereby order and command,
That the Egyptian and Chaldean strangers,
Known by the name of Gypsies, shall henceforth
Be banished from the realm, as vagabonds
And beggars; and if, after seventy days,
Any be found within our kingdom's bounds,

They shall receive a hundred lashes each;
The second time, shall have their ears cut off;
The third, be slaves for life to him who takes them,
Or burnt as heretics. Signed, I, the King."
Vile miscreants and creatures unbaptized!
You hear the law! Obey and disappear!

PANCHO

And if in seventy days you are not gone,
Dead or alive I make you all my slaves.

(*The Gypsies go out in confusion, showing signs of fear and discontent.* PANCHO *follows*)

PADRE CURA

A righteous law! A very righteous law!
Pray you, sit down.

PEDRO CRESPO
                I thank you heartily.

(*They seat themselves on a bench at the* PADRE CURA'S *door. Sound of guitars heard at a distance, approaching during the dialogue which follows*)

A very righteous judgment, as you say.
Now tell me, Padre Cura,—you know all things,—
How came these Gypsies into Spain?

PADRE CURA
                                Why, look you;
They came with Hercules from Palestine,
And hence are thieves and vagrants, Sir Alcalde,
As the Simoniacs from Simon Magus.
And, look you, as Fray Jayme Bleda says,
There are a hundred marks to prove a Moor
Is not a Christian, so 't is with the Gypsies.
They never marry, never go to mass,
Never baptize their children, nor keep Lent,
Nor see the inside of a church,—nor—nor—

PEDRO CRESPO
Good reasons, good, substantial reasons all!
No matter for the other ninety-five.

They should be burnt, I see it plain enough,
They should be burnt.

(*Enter* VICTORIAN *and* HYPOLITO *playing*)

PADRE CURA
               And pray, whom have we here?

PEDRO CRESPO
More vagrants! By Saint Lazarus, more vagrants!

HYPOLITO
Good-evening, gentlemen! Is this Guadarrama?

PADRE CURA
Yes, Guadarrama, and good-evening to you.

HYPOLITO
We seek the Padre Cura of the village;
And, judging from your dress and reverend mien,
You must be he.

PADRE CURA
               I am. Pray, what's your pleasure?

HYPOLITO
We are poor students, travelling in vacation.
You know this mark?

(*Touching the wooden spoon in his hatband*)

PADRE CURA (*joyfully*)
               Ay, know it, and have worn it.

PEDRO CRESPO (*aside*)
Soup-eaters! by the mass! The worst of vagrants!
And there is no law against them. Sir, your servant.
                                        [*Exit.*

PADRE CURA
Your servant, Pedro Crespo.

HYPOLITO
                    Padre Cura,
From the first moment I beheld your face,
I said within myself, "This is the man!"
There is a certain something in your looks,
A certain scholar-like and studious something,—

You understand,—which cannot be mistaken;
Which marks you as a very learned man,
In fine, as one of us.

VICTORIAN (*aside*)
              What impudence!

HYPOLITO
As we approached, I said to my companion,
"That is the Padre Cura; mark my words!"
Meaning your Grace. "The other man," said I,
"Who sits so awkwardly upon the bench,
Must be the sacristan."

PADRE CURA
              Ah! said you so?
Why, that was Pedro Crespo, the alcalde!

HYPOLITO
Indeed! you much astonish me. His air
Was not so full of dignity and grace
As an alcalde's should be.

PADRE CURA
              That is true.
He is out of humor with some vagrant Gypsies,
Who have their camp here in the neighborhood.
There is nothing so undignified as anger.

HYPOLITO
The Padre Cura will excuse our boldness,
If, from his well-known hospitality,
We crave a lodging for the night.

PADRE CURA
                        I pray you!
You do me honor! I am but too happy
To have such guests beneath my humble roof.
It is not often that I have occasion
To speak with scholars; and *Emollit mores,*
Nec sinit esse feros, Cicero says.

HYPOLITO
'T is Ovid, is it not?

PADRE CURA
No, Cicero.

HYPOLITO
Your Grace is right. You are the better scholar.
Now what a dunce was I to think it Ovid!
But hang me if it is not!   (*Aside.*)

PADRE CURA
Pass this way.
He was a very great man, was Cicero!
Pray you, go in, go in! no ceremony.

[*Exeunt.*

SCENE III. *A room in the* PADRE CURA's *house. Enter the*
PADRE *and* HYPOLITO.

PADRE CURA
So then, Señor, you come from Alcalá.
I am glad to hear it. It was there I studied.

HYPOLITO
And left behind an honored name, no doubt.
How may I call your Grace?

PADRE CURA
Gerónimo
De Santillana, at your Honor's service.

HYPOLITO
Descended from the Marquis Santillana?
From the distinguished poet?

PADRE CURA
From the Marquis,
Not from the poet.

HYPOLITO
Why, they were the same.
Let me embrace you! O some lucky star
Has brought me hither! Yet once more!—once more!
Your name is ever green in Alcalá,
And our professor, when we are unruly,
Will shake his hoary head, and say, "Alas!
It was not so in Santillana's time!"

PADRE CURA

I did not think my name remembered there.

HYPOLITO

More than remembered; it is idolized.

PADRE CURA

Of what professor speak you?

HYPOLITO
                    Timoneda.

PADRE CURA

I don't remember any Timoneda.

HYPOLITO

A grave and sombre man, whose beetling brow
O'erhangs the rushing current of his speech
As rocks o'er rivers hang. Have you forgotten?

PADRE CURA

Indeed, I have. O, those were pleasant days,
Those college days! I ne'er shall see the like!
I had not buried then so many hopes!
I had not buried then so many friends!
I've turned my back on what was then before me;
And the bright faces of my young companions
Are wrinkled like my own, or are no more.
Do you remember Cueva?

HYPOLITO
                    Cueva? Cueva?

PADRE CURA

Fool that I am! He was before your time.
You're a mere boy, and I am an old man.

HYPOLITO

I should not like to try my strength with you.

PADRE CURA

Well, well. But I forget; you must be hungry.
Martina! ho! Martina! 'T is my niece.

(*Enter* MARTINA)

HYPOLITO

You may be proud of such a niece as that.
I wish I had a niece. *Emollit mores.* (*Aside*)
He was a very great man, was Cicero!
Your servant, fair Martina.

MARTINA
Servant, sir.

PADRE CURA

This gentleman is hungry. See thou to it.
Let us have supper.

MARTINA
'Twill be ready soon.

PADRE CURA

And bring a bottle of my Val-de-Peñas
Out of the cellar. Stay; I'll go myself,
Pray you, Señor, excuse me. [*Exit.*

HYPOLITO
Hist! Martina!
One word with you. Bless me! what handsome **eyes**!
To-day there have been Gypsies in the village,
Is it not so?

MARTINA
There have been Gypsies here.

HYPOLITO

Yes, and they told your fortune.

MARTINA (*embarrassed*)
Told my fortune?

HYPOLITO

Yes, yes; I know they did. Give me your hand.
I'll tell you what they said. They said,—they said,
The shepherd boy that loved you was a clown,
And him you should not marry. Was it not?

MARTINA (*surprised*)
How know you that?

HYPOLITO
O, I know more than that.
What a soft, little hand! And then they said,
A cavalier from court, handsome, and tall
And rich, should come one day to marry you,
And you should be a lady. Was it not?
He has arrived, the handsome cavalier.
(*Tries to kiss her. She runs off. Enter* VICTORIAN, *with a letter.*)

VICTORIAN
The muleteer has come.

HYPOLITO
So soon?

VICTORIAN
I found him
Sitting at supper by the tavern door,
And, from a pitcher that he held aloft
His whole arm's length, drinking the blood-red wine.

HYPOLITO
What news from Court?

VICTORIAN
He brought this letter only. (*Reads*)
O cursed perfidy! Why did I let
That lying tongue deceive me? Preciosa,
Sweet Preciosa! how art thou avenged!

HYPOLITO
What news is this, that makes thy cheek turn pale,
And thy hand tremble?

VICTORIAN
O, most infamous!
The Count of Lara is a damnèd villain!

HYPOLITO
That is no news, forsooth.

VICTORIAN
He strove in vain
To steal from me the jewel of my soul,
The love of Preciosa. Not succeeding,

He swore to be revenged; and set on foot
A plot to ruin her, which has succeeded,
She has been hissed and hooted from the stage,
Her reputation stained by slanderous lies
Too foul to speak of; and, once more a beggar,
She roams a wanderer over God's green earth,
Housing with Gypsies!

HYPOLITO
To renew again
The Age of Gold, and make the shepherd swains
Desperate with love, like Gasper Gil's Diana.
Redit et Virgo!

VICTORIAN
Dear Hypolito,
How have I wronged that meek, confiding heart!
I will go seek for her; and with my tears
Wash out the wrong I've done her!

HYPOLITO
O beware!
Act not that folly o'er again.

VICTORIAN
Ay, folly,
Delusion, madness, call it what thou wilt,
I will confess my weakness,—I still love her!
Still fondly love her!

(*Enter the* PADRE CURA)

HYPOLITO
Tell us, Padre Cura,
Who are these Gypsies in the neighborhood?

PADRE CURA
Beltran Cruzado and his crew.

VICTORIAN
Kind Heaven,
I thank thee! She is found! is found again!

HYPOLITO
And have they with them a pale, beautiful girl,
Called Preciosa?

PADRE CURA

Ay, a pretty girl.
The gentleman seems moved.

HYPOLITO

Yes, moved with hunger,
He is half famished with this long day's journey.

PADRE CURA

Then, pray you, come this way.
The supper waits.

[*Exeunt.*

SCENE IV. *A post-house on the road to Segovia, not far from
the village of Guadarrama. Enter* CHISPA, *cracking a whip,
and singing the cachucha.*

CHISPA

Halloo! Don Fulano! Let us have horses, and quickly.
Alas, poor Chispa! what a dog's life dost thou lead! I thought,
when I left my old master Victorian, the student, to serve
my new master Don Carlos, the gentleman, that I, too, should
lead the life of a gentleman; should go to bed early, and get
up late. For when the abbot plays cards, what can you expect
of the friars? But, in running away from the thunder, I have
run into the lightning. Here I am in hot chase after my master
and his Gypsy girl. And a good beginning of the week it is,
as he said who was hanged on Monday morning.

(*Enter* DON CARLOS)

DON CARLOS

Are not the horses ready yet?

CHISPA

I should think not, for the hostler seems to be asleep. Ho!
within there! Horses! horses! horses! (*He knocks at the
gate with his whip, and enter* MOSQUITO, *putting on his
jacket.*)

MOSQUITO

Pray, have a little patience. I'm not a musket.

CHISPA

Health and pistareens! I'm glad to see you come on dancing, padre! Pray, what's the news?

MOSQUITO

You cannot have fresh horses, because there are none.

CHISPA

Cachiporra! Throw that bone to another dog. Do I look like your aunt?

MOSQUITO

No; she has a beard.

CHISPA

Go to! go to!

MOSQUITO

Are you from Madrid?

CHISPA

Yes; and going to Estramadura. Get us horses.

MOSQUITO

What's the news at Court?

CHISPA

Why, the latest news is, that I am going to set up a coach, and I have already bought the whip.

(*Strikes him round the legs*)

MOSQUITO

Oh! oh! you hurt me!

DON CARLOS

Enough of this folly. Let us have horses. (*Gives money to* MOSQUITO.) It is almost dark; and we are in haste. But tell me, has a band of Gypsies passed this way of late?

MOSQUITO

Yes; and they are still in the neighborhood.

DON CARLOS

And where?

MOSQUITO

Across the fields yonder, in the woods near Guadarrama.

[*Exit.*

DON CARLOS

Now this is lucky. We will visit the Gypsy camp.

CHISPA

Are you not afraid of the evil eye? [1] Have you a stag's horn with you?

DON CARLOS

Fear not. We will pass the night at the village.

CHISPA

And sleep like the Squires of Hernan Daza, nine under one blanket.

DON CARLOS

I hope we may find the Preciosa among them.

CHISPA

Among the Squires?

DON CARLOS

No; among the Gypsies, blockhead!

CHISPA

I hope we may; for we are giving ourselves trouble enough on her account. Don't you think so? However, there is no catching trout without wetting one's trousers. Yonder come the horses.   [*Exeunt.*

[1] *The evil eye.* "In the Gitano language, casting the evil eye is called *Querelar nasula,* which simply means making sick, and which, according to the common superstition, is accomplished by casting an evil look at people, especially children, who from the tenderness of their constitution, are supposed to be more easily blighted than those of a mature age. After receiving the evil glance, they fall sick, and die in a few hours.

"The Spaniards have very little to say respecting the evil eye, though the belief in it is very prevalent, especially in Andalusia, amongst the lower orders. A stag's horn is considered a good safeguard, and on that account a small horn, tipped with silver, is frequently attached to the children's necks by means of a cord braided from the hair of a black mare's tail. Should the evil glance be cast, it is imagined that the horn receives it, and instantly snaps asunder. Such horns may be purchased in some of the silversmiths' shops at Seville."

BORROW'S *Zincali.* Vol. I. ch. ix.

SCENE V. *The Gypsy camp in the forest. Night. Gypsies working at a forge. Others playing cards by the firelight.*

GYPSIES (*at the forge sing*)
On the top of the mountain I stand,[1]
With a crown of red gold in my hand,
Wild Moors come trooping over the lea,
O how from their fury shall I flee, flee, flee?
O how from their fury shall I flee?

FIRST GYPSY (*playing*)
Down with your John-Dorados, my pigeon. Down with your John-Dorados, and let us make an end.

GYPSIES (*at the forge sing*)
Loud sang the Spanish cavalier,
And thus the ditty ran;
God send the Gypsy lassie here,
And not the Gypsy man.

FIRST GYPSY (*playing*)
There you are in your morocco!

SECOND GYPSY
One more game. The Alcalde's doves against the Padre Cura's new moon.

---

[1] *On the top of a mountain I stand.*
This and the following scraps of song are from Borrow's *Zincali; or, an Account of the Gypsies in Spain.*
The Gypsy words in the same scene may be thus interpreted:
John-Dorados, pieces of gold.
Pigeon, a simpleton.
In your morocco, stripped.
Doves, sheets.
Moon, a shirt.
Chirelin, a thief.
Murcigalleros, those who steal at nightfall.
Rastilleros, foot-pads.
Hermit, highway-robber.
Planets, candles.
Commandments, the fingers.
Saint Martin asleep, to rob a person asleep.
Lanterns, eyes.
Goblin, police officer.
Papagayo, a spy.
Vineyards and Dancing John, to take flight.

FIRST GYPSY

Have at you, Chirelin.

GYPSIES (*at the forge sing*)
At midnight, when the moon began
To show her silver flame,
There came to him no Gypsy man,
The Gypsy lassie came.

(*Enter* BELTRAN CRUZADO)

CRUZADO

Come hither, Murcigalleros and Rastilleros; leave work, leave play; listen to your orders for the night. (*Speaking to the right.*) You will get you to the village, mark you, by the stone cross.

GYPSIES

Ay!

CRUZADO (*to the left*)

And you, by the pole with the hermit's head upon it.

GYPSIES

Ay!

CRUZADO

As soon as you see the planets are out, in with you, and be busy with the ten commandments, under the sly, and Saint Martin asleep. D' ye hear?

GYPSIES

Ay!

CRUZADO

Keep your lanterns open, and, if you see a goblin or a papagayo, take to your trampers. "Vineyards and Dancing John" is the word. Am I comprehended?

GYPSIES

Ay! ay!

CRUZADO

Away, then!

(*Exeunt severally.* CRUZADO *walks up the stage, and disappears among the trees. Enter* PRECIOSA.)

PRECIOSA

How strangely gleams through the gigantic trees
The red light of the forge! Wild, beckoning shadows
Stalk through the forest ever and anon
Rising and bending with the flickering flame,
Then flitting into darkness! So within me
Strange hopes and fears do beckon to each other,
My brightest hopes giving dark fears a being,
As the light does the shadow. Woe is me!
How still it is about me, and how lonely!

(BARTOLOMÉ *rushes in*)

BARTOLOMÉ

Ho! Preciosa!

PRECIOSA

O, Bartolomé!
Thou here?

BARTOLOMÉ

Lo! I am here.

PRECIOSA

Whence comest thou?

BARTOLOMÉ

From the rough ridges of the wild Sierra,
From caverns in the rocks, from hunger, thirst,
And fever! Like a wild wolf to the sheepfold
Come I for thee, my lamb.

PRECIOSA

O touch me not!
The Count of Lara's blood is on thy hands!
The Count of Lara's curse is on thy soul!
Do not come near me! Pray, begone from here!
Thou art in danger! They have set a price
Upon thy head!

BARTOLOMÉ

Ay, and I've wandered long
Among the mountains; and for many days
Have seen no human face, save the rough swineherd's.
The wind and rain have been my sole companions.

I shouted to them from the rocks thy name,
And the loud echo sent it back to me,
Till I grew mad. I could not stay from thee,
And I am here! Betray me, if thou wilt.

PRECIOSA

Betray thee? I betray thee?

BARTOLOMÉ

Preciosa!
I come for thee! for thee I thus brave death!
Fly with me o'er the borders of this realm!
Fly with me!

PRECIOSA

Speak of that no more. I cannot.
I am thine no longer.

BARTOLOMÉ

O, recall the time
When we were children! how we played together,
How we grew up together; how we plighted
Our hearts unto each other, even in childhood!
Fulfil thy promise, for the hour has come.
I am hunted from the kingdom, like a wolf!
Fulfil thy promise.

PRECIOSA

'T was my father's promise,
Not mine. I never gave my heart to thee,
Nor promised thee my hand!

BARTOLOMÉ

False tongue of woman!
And heart more false!

PRECIOSA

Nay, listen unto me.
I will speak frankly. I have never loved thee;
I cannot love thee. This is not my fault,
It is my destiny. Thou art a man
Restless and violent. What wouldst thou with me,
A feeble girl, who have not long to live,
Whose heart is broken? Seek another wife,

Better than I, and fairer; and let not
Thy rash and headlong moods estrange her from thee.
Thou art unhappy in this hopeless passion.
I never sought thy love; never did aught
To make thee love me. Yet I pity thee,
And most of all I pity thy wild heart,
That hurries thee to crimes and deeds of blood.
Beware, beware of that.

BARTOLOMÉ
For thy dear sake,
I will be gentle. Thou shalt teach me patience.

PRECIOSA
Then take this farewell, and depart in peace;
Thou must not linger here.

BARTOLOMÉ
Come, come with me!

PRECIOSA
Hark! I hear footsteps.

BARTOLOMÉ
I entreat thee, come.

PRECIOSA
Away! It is in vain.

BARTOLOMÉ
Wilt thou not come?

PRECIOSA
Never!

BARTOLOMÉ
Then woe, eternal woe, upon thee,
Thou shalt not be another's. Thou shalt die.   [*Exit*.

PRECIOSA
All holy angels keep me in this hour!
Spirit of her who bore me, look upon me!
Mother of God, the glorified, protect me!
Christ and the saints, be merciful unto me!
Yet why should I fear death? What is it to die?
To leave all disappointment, care, and sorrow,

To leave all falsehood, treachery, and unkindness,
All ignominy, suffering, and despair,
And be at rest for ever! O, dull heart,
Be of good cheer! When thou shalt cease to beat,
Then shalt thou cease to suffer and complain!

(*Enter* VICTORIAN *and* HYPOLITO *behind*)

VICTORIAN

'T is she! Behold, how beautiful she stands
Under the tent-like trees!

HYPOLITO
         A woodland nymph!

VICTORIAN

I pray thee, stand aside. Leave me.

HYPOLITO
                Be wary,
Do not betray thyself too soon.

VICTORIAN (*disguising his voice*)
              Hist! Gypsy!

PRECOSIA (*aside, with emotion*)

That voice! that voice from heaven! O speak again!
Who is it calls?

VICTORIAN

A friend.

PRECOSIA (*aside*)
            'T is he! 'T is he!
I thank thee, Heaven, that thou hast heard my prayer
And sent me this protector! Now be strong,
Be strong, my heart! I must dissemble here.
False friend or true?

VICTORIAN
            A true friend to the true.
Fear not; come hither. So; can you tell fortunes?

PRECIOSA

Not in the dark. Come nearer to the fire.
Give me your hand. It is not crossed, I see.

VICTORIAN (*putting a piece of gold into her hand*)
There is the cross.

PRECIOSA
Is 't silver?

VICTORIAN
No, 't is gold.

PRECIOSA
There's a fair lady at the Court, who loves you,
And for yourself alone.

VICTORIAN
Fie! the old story!
Tell me a better fortune for my money;
Not this old woman's tale!

PRECIOSA
You are passionate
And this same passionate humor in your blood
Has marred your fortune. Yes; I see it now;
The line of life is crossed by many marks.
Shame! shame! O you have wronged the maid who loved you!
How could you do it?

VICTORIAN
I never loved a maid;
For she I loved was then a maid no more.

PRECIOSA
How know you that?

VICTORIAN
A little bird in the air
Whispered the secret.

PRECIOSA
There, take back your gold!
Your hand is cold, like a deceiver's hand!
There is no blessing in its charity!
Make her your wife, for you have been abused;
And you shall mend your fortunes, mending hers.

VICTORIAN (*aside*)
How like an angel's speaks the tongue of woman,
When pleading in another's cause her own!—

That is a pretty ring upon your finger.
Pray give it me. (*Tries to take the ring.*)

PRECIOSA

No; never from my hand
Shall that be taken!

VICTORIAN

Why, 't is but a ring.
I'll give it back to you; or, if I keep it,
Will give you gold to buy you twenty such.

PRECIOSA

Why would you have this ring?

VICTORIAN

A traveller's fancy,
A whim, and nothing more. I would fain keep it
As a memento of the Gypsy camp
In Guadarrama, and the fortune-teller
Who sent me back to wed a widowed maid.
Pray, let me have the ring.

PRECIOSA

No, never! never!
I will not part with it, even when I die;
But bid my nurse fold my pale fingers thus,
That it may not fall from them. 'T is a token
Of a beloved friend, who is no more.

VICTORIAN

How? dead?

PRECIOSA

Yes; dead to me; and worse than dead.
He is estranged! And yet I keep this ring.
I will rise with it from my grave hereafter,
To prove to him that I was never false.

VICTORIAN (*aside*)

Be still, my swelling heart! one moment, still!
Why, 't is the folly of a love-sick girl.
Come, give it me, or I will say 't is mine,
And that you stole it.

PRECIOSA

O, you will not dare
To utter such a fiendish lie!

VICTORIAN

Not dare?
Look in my face, and say if there is aught
I have not dared, I would not dare for thee!
(She rushes into his arms)

PRECIOSA

'T is thou! 't is thou! Yes; yes; my heart's elected!
My dearest-dear Victorian! my soul's heaven!
Where hast thou been so long? Why didst thou leave me?

VICTORIAN

Ask me not now, my dearest Preciosa.
Let me forget we ever have been parted!

PRECIOSA

Hadst thou not come—

VICTORIAN

I pray thee, do not chide me!

PRECIOSA

I should have perished here among these Gypsies.

VICTORIAN

Forgive me, sweet! for what I made thee suffer.
Think'st thou this heart could feel a moment's joy,
Thou being absent? O, believe it not!
Indeed, since that sad hour I have not slept,
For thinking of the wrong I did to thee!
Dost thou forgive me? Say, wilt thou forgive me?

PRECIOSA

I have forgiven thee. Ere those words of anger
Were in the book of Heaven writ down against thee,
I had forgiven thee.

VICTORIAN

I'm the veriest fool
That walks the earth, to have believed thee false.
It was the Count of Lara—

PRECIOSA

That bad man
Has worked me harm enough. Hast thou not heard—

VICTORIAN

I have heard all. And yet speak on, speak on!
Let me but hear thy voice, and I am happy;
For every tone, like some sweet incantation,
Calls up the buried past to plead for me.
Speak, my beloved, speak into my heart,
Whatever fills and agitates thine own.

(*They walk aside*)

HYPOLITO

All gentle quarrels in the pastoral poets,
All passionate love scenes in the best romances,
All chaste embraces on the public stage,
All soft adventures, which the liberal stars
Have winked at, as the natural course of things,
Have been surpassed here by my friend, the student,
And this sweet Gypsy lass, fair Preciosa!

PRECIOSA

Señor Hypolito! I kiss your hand.
Pray, shall I tell your fortune?

HYPOLITO

Not to-night;
For, should you treat me as you did Victorian,
And send me back to marry maids forlorn,
My wedding day would last from now till Christmas.

CHISPA (*within*)

What ho! the Gypsies, ho! Beltran Cruzado!
Halloo! halloo! halloo! halloo!

(*Enters booted, with a whip and lantern*)

VICTORIAN

What now?

Why such a fearful din? Hast thou been robbed?

CHISPA

Ay, robbed and murdered; and good-evening to you,
My worthy masters.

VICTORIAN
Speak; what brings thee here?

CHISPA (*to* PRECIOSA)
Good news from Court; good news! Beltran Cruzado,
The Count of the Calés, is not your father,
But your true father has returned to Spain
Laden with wealth. You are no more a Gypsy.

VICTORIAN
Strange as a Moorish tale!

CHISPA
And we have all
Been drinking at the tavern to your health,
As wells drink in November, when it rains.

VICTORIAN
Where is the gentleman?

CHISPA
As the old song says,
His body is in Segovia,
His soul is in Madrid.

PRECIOSA
Is this a dream? O, if it be a dream,
Let me sleep on, and do not wake me yet!
Repeat thy story! Say I'm not deceived!
Say that I do not dream! I am awake;
This is the Gypsy camp; this is Victorian,
And this his friend, Hypolito! Speak! speak!
Let me not wake and find it all a dream!

VICTORIAN
It is a dream, sweet child! a waking dream,
A blissful certainty, a vision bright
Of that rare happiness, which even on earth
Heaven gives to those it loves. Now art thou rich,
As thou wast ever beautiful and good;
And I am now the beggar.

PRECIOSA (*giving him her hand*)
I have still
a hand to give.

CHISPA (*aside*)

               And I have two to take.
I've heard my grandmother say, that Heaven gives almonds
To those who have no teeth. That's nuts to crack.
I've teeth to spare, but where shall I find almonds?

VICTORIAN

What more of this strange story?

CHISPA

                     Nothing more.
Your friend, Don Carlos, is now at the village,
Showing to Pedro Crespo, the Alcalde,
The proofs of what I tell you. The old hag,
Who stole you in your childhood, has confessed;
And probably they'll hang her for the crime,
To make the celebration more complete.

VICTORIAN

No; let it be a day of general joy;
Fortune comes well to all, that comes not late.
Now let us join Don Carlos.

HYPOLITO

                 So farewell,
The student's wandering life! Sweet serenades,
Sung under ladies' windows in the night,
And all that makes vacation beautiful!
To you, ye cloistered shades of Alcalá,
To you, ye radiant visions of romance,
Written in books, but here surpassed by truth,
The Bachelor Hypolito returns,
And leaves the Gypsy with the Spanish Student.

SCENE VI. *A pass in the Guadarrama mountains. Early morn-
    ing. A muleteer crosses the stage, sitting sideways on his
    mule, and lighting a paper cigar with flint and steel.*

SONG

    If thou art sleeping, maiden,[1]
      Awake and open thy door,
    'T is the break of day, and we must away
      O'er meadow, and mount, and moor.

[1] *If thou art sleeping, maiden.* From the Spanish, as it is likewise
the song of the Contrabandista on page 528.

Wait not to find thy slippers,
But come with thy naked feet;
We shall have to pass through the dewy
grass,
And waters wide and fleet.

(*Disappears down the pass. Enter a Monk. A Shepherd appears on the rocks above.*)

MONK

Ave Maria, gratia plena. Olá! good man!

SHEPHERD

Olá!

MONK

Is this the road to Segovia?

SHEPHERD

It is, your reverence.

MONK

How far is it?

SHEPHERD

I do not know.

MONK

What is that yonder in the valley?

SHEPHERD

San Ildefonso.

MONK

A long way to breakfast.

SHEPHERD

Ay, marry.

MONK

Are there robbers in these mountains?

SHEPHERD

Yes, and worse than that.

MONK

What?

SHEPHERD

Wolves.

MONK

Santa Maria! Come with me to San Ildefonso, and thou shalt be well rewarded.

SHEPHERD

What wilt thou give me?

MONK

An Agnus Dei and my benediction.

(*They disappear. A mounted Contrabandista passes, wrapped in his cloak, and a gun at his saddle-bow. He goes down the pass singing.*)

SONG

Worn with speed is my good steed,
And I march me hurried, worried;
Onward, caballito mio,
With the white star in thy forehead!
Onward, for here comes the Ronda,
And I hear their rifles crack!
Ay, jaléo! Ay, ay, jaléo!
Ay, jaléo! They cross our track.

(*Song dies away. Enter* PRECIOSA, *on horseback, attended by* VICTORIAN, HYPOLITO, DON CARLOS, *and* CHISPA, *on foot, and armed.*)

VICTORIAN

This is the highest point. Here let us rest.
See, Preciosa, see how all about us
Kneeling, like hooded friars, the misty mountains
Receive the benediction of the sun!
O glorious sight!

PRECIOSA

Most beautiful indeed!

HYPOLITO

Most wonderful!

VICTORIAN

And in the vale below,
Where yonder steeples flash like lifted halberds,
San Ildefonso, from its noisy belfries,

Sends up a salutation to the morn,
As if an army smote their brazen shields,
And shouted victory!

PRECIOSA
And which way lies
Segovia?

VICTORIAN
At a great distance yonder.
Dost thou not see it?

PRECIOSA
No. I do not see it.

VICTORIAN
The merest flaw that dents the horizon's edge.
There, yonder!

HYPOLITO
'T is a notable old town,
Boasting an ancient Roman aqueduct,
And an Alcázar, builded by the Moors,
Wherein, you may remember, poor Gil Blas
Was fed on *Pan del Rey*. O, many a time
Out of its grated windows have I looked
Hundreds of feet plumb down to the Eresma,
That, like a serpent through the valley creeping,
Glides at its foot.

PRECIOSA
O, yes! I see it now,
Yet rather with my heart than with mine eyes,
So faint it is. And all my thoughts sail thither,
Freighted with prayers and hopes, and forward urged
Against all stress of accident, as, in
The Eastern Tale, against the wind and tide,
Great ships were drawn to the Magnetic Mountains,
And there were wrecked, and perished in the sea! (*She weeps.*)

VICTORIAN
O gentle spirit! Thou didst bear unmoved
Blasts of adversity and frosts of fate!
But the first ray of sunshine that falls on thee
Melts thee to tears! O, let thy weary heart

Lean upon mine! and it shall faint no more,
Nor thirst, nor hunger; but be comforted
And filled with my affection.

PRECIOSA
Stay no longer!
My father waits. Methinks I see him there,
Now looking from the window, and now watching
Each sound of wheels or foot-fall in the street,
And saying, "Hark! She comes!" O father! father!

(*They descend the pass.* CHISPA *remains behind*)

CHISPA

I have a father, too, but he is a dead one. Alas and alack-a-day! Poor was I born, and poor do I remain. I neither win nor lose. Thus I wag through the world, half the time on foot, and the other half walking; and always as merry as a thunderstorm in the night. And so we plough along, as the fly said to the ox. Who knows what may happen? Patience, and shuffle the cards! I am not yet so bald, that you can see my brains; and perhaps, after all, I shall some day go to Rome, and come back Saint Peter. Benedicite!   [*Exit.*

(*A pause. Then enter* BARTOLOMÉ *wildly, as if in pursuit, with a carbine in his hand.*)

BARTOLOMÉ
They passed this way! I hear their horses' hoofs!
Yonder I see them! Come, sweet caramillo,
This serenade shall be the Gypsy's last!
(*Fires down the pass*)
Ha! ha! Well whistled, my sweet caramillo!
Well whistled!—I have missed her!—O, my God!
(*The shot is returned.* BARTOLOMÉ *falls.*)

THE BELFRY OF BRUGES, AND OTHER POEMS

CARILLON

In the ancient town of Bruges,
In the quaint old Flemish city,
As the evening shades descended,
Low and loud and sweetly blended,
Low at times and loud at times,
And changing like a poet's rhymes,
Rang the beautiful wild chimes
From the Belfry in the market
Of the ancient town of Bruges.

Then, with deep sonorous clangor
Calmly answering their sweet anger,
When the wrangling bells had ended,
Slowly struck the clock eleven,
And, out of the silent heaven,
Silence on the town descended.
Silence, silence everywhere,
On the earth and in the air,
Save that footsteps here and there
Of some burgher home returning,
By the street lamps faintly burning,
For a moment woke the echoes
Of the ancient town of Bruges.

But amid my broken slumbers
Still I heard those magic numbers,
As they loud proclaimed the flight
And stolen marches of the night;
Till their chimes in sweet collision
Mingled with each wandering vision,
Mingled with the fortune-telling
Gypsy-bands of dreams and fancies,
Which amid the waste expanses

Of the silent land of trances
Have their solitary dwelling.
All else seemed asleep in Bruges,
In the quaint old Flemish city.

And I thought how like these chimes
Are the poet's airy rhymes,
All his rhymes and roundelays,
His conceits, and songs, and ditties,
From the belfry of his brain,
Scattered downward, though in vain,
On the roofs and stones of cities!
For by night the drowsy ear
Under its curtains cannot hear,
And by day men go their ways,
Hearing the music as they pass,
But deeming it no more, alas!
Than the hollow sound of brass.

Yet, perchance a sleepless wight,
Lodging at some humble inn
In the narrow lanes of life,
When the dusk and hush of night
Shut out the incessant din
Of daylight and its toil and strife,
May listen with a calm delight
To the poet's melodies,
Till he hears, or dreams he hears,
Intermingled with the song,
Thoughts that he has cherished long;
Hears amid the chime and singing
The bells of his own village ringing,
And wakes, and finds his slumberous eyes
Wet with most delicious tears.

Thus dreamed I, as by night I lay
In Bruges, at the Fleur-de-blé,
Listening with a wild delight
To the chimes that, through the night,
Rang their changes from the Belfry
Of that quaint old Flemish city.

The Belfry of Bruges

In the market-place of Bruges stands the belfry old and
brown;
Thrice consumed and thrice rebuilded, still it watches o'er
the town.

As the summer morn was breaking, on that lofty tower I
stood,
And the world threw off the darkness, like the weeds of widow-
hood.

Thick with towns and hamlets studded, and with streams and
vapors gray,
Like a shield embossed with silver, round and vast the landscape lay.

At my feet the city slumbered. From its chimneys, here and
there,
Wreaths of snow-white smoke, ascending, vanished, ghost-
like, into air.

Not a sound rose from the city at that early morning hour,
But I heard a heart of iron beating in the ancient tower.

From their nests beneath the rafters sang the swallows wild
and high;
And the world, beneath me sleeping, seemed more distant
than the sky.

Then most musical and solemn, bringing back the olden times,
With their strange, unearthly changes rang the melancholy
chimes,

Like the psalms from some old cloister, when the nuns sing
in the choir;
And the great bell tolled among them, like the chanting of a
friar.

Visions of the days departed, shadowy phantoms filled my
brain;
They who live in history only seemed to walk the earth again;

All the Foresters of Flanders,[1]—mighty Baldwin Bras de Fer,
Lyderick du Bucq and Cressy, Philip, Guy de Dampierre.

I beheld the pageants splendid that adorned those days of
old;
Stately dames, like queens attended,[2] knights who bore the
Fleece of Gold; [3]

Lombard and Venetian merchants with deep-laden argosies;
Ministers from twenty nations; more than royal pomp and
ease.

[1] *All the Foresters of Flanders*. The title of Foresters was given to
the early governors of Flanders, appointed by the kings of France.
Lyderick du Bucq, in the days of Clotaire the Second, was the first of
them; and Beaudoin Bras-de-Fer, who stole away the fair Judith,
daughter of Charles the Bald, from the French court, and married
her in Bruges, was the last. After him, the title of Forester was
changed to that of Count. Philippe d'Alsace, Guy de Dampierre, and
Louis de Crécy, coming later in the order of time, were therefore
rather Counts than Foresters. Philippe went twice to the Holy Land
as a Crusader, and died of the plague at St. Jean-d'Acre shortly after
the capture of the city by the Christians. Guy de Dampierre died in
the prison of Compiègne. Louis de Crécy was son and successor of
Robert de Béthune, who strangled his wife, Yolande de Bourgogne,
with the bridle of his horse, for having poisoned, at the age of eleven
years, Charles, his son by his first wife, Blanche d'Anjou.

[2] *Stately dames like queens attended*. When Philippe-le-Bel, King
of France, visited Flanders with his queen, she was so astonished at
the magnificence of the dames of Bruges, that she exclaimed, "Je
croyais être seule reine ici, mais il paraît que ceux de Flandre qui se
trouvent dans nos prisons sont tous des princes, car leurs femmes
sont habillées comme des princesses et des reines."

When the burgomasters of Ghent, Bruges, and Ypres went to Paris
to pay homage to King John, in 1351, they were received with great
pomp and distinction; but, being invited to a festival, they observed
that their seats at table were not furnished with cushions; whereupon,
to make known their displeasure at this want of regard to their
dignity, they folded their richly embroidered cloaks and seated themselves upon them. On rising from table, they left their cloaks behind
them, and, being informed of their apparent forgetfulness, Simon
van Eertrycke, burgomaster of Bruges, replied, "We Flemings are not
in the habit of carrying away our cushions after dinner."

[3] *Knights who bore the Fleece of Gold*, Philippe de Bourgogne,
surnamed Le Bon, espoused Isabella of Portugal on the 10th of
January, 1430, and on the same day instituted the famous order of
the Fleece of Gold.

I beheld proud Maximilian, kneeling humbly on the
    ground;
I beheld the gentle Mary,[1] hunting with her hawk and
    hound;

And her lighted bridal-chamber, where a duke slept with the
    queen,
And the armèd guard around them, and the sword unsheathed
    between.

I beheld the Flemish weavers, with Namur and Juliers bold,
Marching homeward from the bloody battle of the Spurs of
    Gold;[2]

[1] *I beheld the gentle Mary.* Marie de Valois, Duchess of Burgundy,
was left by the death of her father, Charles-le-Téméraire, at the age
of twenty, the richest heiress of Europe. She came to Bruges, as
Countess of Flanders, in 1477, and in the same year was married by
proxy to the Archduke Maximilian. According to the custom of the
time, the Duke of Bavaria, Maximilian's substitute, slept with the
princess. They were both in complete dress, separated by a naked
sword, and attended by four armed guards. Marie was adored by
her subjects for her gentleness and her many other virtues.

Maximilian was son of the Emperor Frederick the Third, and is
the same person mentioned afterwards in the poem of *Nuremberg*
as the Kaiser Maximilian, and the hero of Pfinzing's poem of *Teuerdank.* Having been imprisoned by the revolted burghers of Bruges,
they refused to release him till he consented to kneel in the public
square, and to swear on the Holy Evangelists and the body of Saint
Donatus that he would not take vengeance upon them for their
rebellion.

[2] *The bloody battle of the Spurs of Gold.* This battle, the most
memorable in Flemish history, was fought under the walls of Courtray,
on the 11th of July, 1302, between the French and the Flemings, the
former commanded by Robert, Comte d'Artois, and the latter by
Guillaume de Juliers, and Jean, Comte de Namur. The French army
was completely routed, with a loss of twenty thousand infantry and
seven thousand cavalry; among whom were sixty-three princes, dukes,
and counts, seven hundred lords-banneret, and eleven hundred noble-
men. The flower of the French nobility perished on that day, to which
history has given the name of the *Journée des Eperons d'Or,* from the
great number of golden spurs found on the field of battle. Seven
hundred of them were hung up as a trophy in the church of Notre
Dame de Courtray; and, as the cavaliers of that day wore but a
single spur each, these vouched to God for the violent and bloody
death of seven hundred of his creatures.

Saw the fight at Minnewater,[1] saw the White Hoods moving
    west,
Saw great Artevelde victorious scale the Golden Dragon's
    nest.[2]

And again the whiskered Spaniard all the land with terror
    smote;
And again the wild alarum sounded from the tocsin's throat;

Till the bell of Ghent responded o'er lagoon and dike of sand,
"I am Roland! I am Roland! there is victory in the land!"

Then the sound of drums aroused me. The awakened city's
    roar
Chased the phantoms I had summoned back into their graves
    once more.

[1] *Saw the fight at Minnewater.* When the inhabitants of Bruges
were digging a canal at Minnewater, to bring the waters of the Lys
from Deynze to their city, they were attacked and routed by the
citizens of Ghent, whose commerce would have been much injured
by the canal. They were led by Jean Lyons, captain of a military
company at Ghent, called the *Chapperons Blancs.* He had great
sway over the turbulent populace, who, in those prosperous times
of the city, gained an easy livelihood by laboring two or three days
in the week, and had the remaining four or five to devote to public
affairs. The fight at Minnewater was followed by open rebellion
against Louis de Maele, the Count of Flanders and Protector of
Bruges. His superb château of Wondelghem was pillaged and burnt;
and the insurgents forced the gates of Bruges, and entered in triumph,
with Lyons mounted at their head. A few days afterwards he died
suddenly, perhaps by poison.

Meanwhile the insurgents received a check at the village of Nevèle;
and two hundred of them perished in the church, which was burned
by the Count's orders. One of the chiefs, Jean de Lannoy, took
refuge in the belfry. From the summit of the tower he held forth
his purse filled with gold, and begged for deliverance. It was in
vain. His enemies cried to him from below to save himself as best
he might; and, half suffocated with smoke and flame, he threw
himself from the tower and perished at their feet. Peace was soon
afterwards established, and the Count retired to faithful Bruges.

[2] *The Golden Dragon's nest.* The Golden Dragon, taken from the
church of St. Sophia, at Constantinople, in one of the Crusades, and
placed on the belfry of Bruges, was afterwards transported to Ghent
by Philip van Artevelde, and still adorns the belfry of that city.

The inscription on the alarm-bell at Ghent is, *"Mynen naem is
Roland: als ik klep is er brand, and als ik luy is er victorie in het
land."* My name is Roland; when I toll there is fire, and when I ring
there is victory in the land.

Hours had passed away like minutes; and, before I was aware,
Lo! the shadow of the belfry crossed the sun illumined
   square.

MISCELLANEOUS

A Gleam of Sunshine

This is the place. Stand still, my steed,
   Let me review the scene,
And summon from the shadowy Past
   The forms that once have been.

The Past and Present here unite
   Beneath Time's flowing tide
Like footprints hidden by a brook,
   But seen on either side.

Here runs the highway to the town;
   There the green lane descends,
Through which I walked to church with thee,
   O gentlest of my friends!

The shadow of the linden-trees
   Lay moving on the grass;
Between them and the moving boughs,
   A shadow, thou didst pass.

Thy dress was like the lilies,
   And thy heart as pure as they:
One of God's holy messengers
   Did walk with me that day.

I saw the branches of the trees
   Bend down thy touch to meet,
The clover-blossoms in the grass
   Rise up to kiss thy feet.

"Sleep, sleep to-day, tormenting cares,
   Of earth and folly born!"
Solemnly sang the village choir
   On that sweet Sabbath morn.

Through the closed blinds the golden sun
    Poured in a dusty beam,
Like the celestial ladder seen,
    By Jacob in his dream.

And ever and anon, the wind,
    Sweet-scented with the hay,
Turned o'er the hymn-book's fluttering leaves
    That on the window lay.

Long was the good man's sermon,
    Yet it seemed not so to me;
For he spake of Ruth the beautiful,
    And still I thought of thee.

Long was the prayer he uttered,
    Yet it seemed not so to me;
For in my heart I prayed with him,
    And still I thought of thee.

But now, alas! the place seems changed;
    Thou art no longer here;
Part of the sunshine of the scene
    With thee did disappear.

Though thoughts, deep-rooted in my heart,
    Like pine-trees dark and high,
Subdue the light of noon, and breathe
    A low and ceaseless sigh;

This memory brightens o'er the past,
    As when the sun, concealed
Behind some cloud that near us hangs,
    Shines on a distant field.

THE ARSENAL AT SPRINGFIELD

This is the Arsenal. From floor to ceiling,
    Like a huge organ, rise the burnished arms;
But from their silent pipes no anthem pealing
    Startles the villages with strange alarms.

Ah! what a sound will rise, how wild and dreary,
　　When the death-angel touches those swift keys!
What loud lament and dismal Miserere
　　Will mingle with their awful symphonies!

I hear even now the infinite fierce chorus,
　　The cries of agony, the endless groan,
Which, through the ages that have gone before us,
　　In long reverberations reach our own.

On helm and harness rings the Saxon hammer,
　　Through Cimbric forest roars the Norseman's song,
And loud, amid the universal clamor,
　　O'er distant deserts sounds the Tartar gong.

I hear the Florentine, who from his palace
　　Wheels out his battle-bell with dreadful din,
And Aztec priests upon their teocallis
　　Beat the wild war-drums made of serpent's skin;

The tumult of each sacked and burning village;
　　The shout that every prayer for mercy drowns;
The soldiers' revels in the midst of pillage;
　　The wail of famine in beleaguered towns;

The bursting shell, the gateway wrenched asunder,
　　The rattling musketry, the clashing blade;
And ever and anon, in tones of thunder,
　　The diapason of the cannonade.

Is it, O man, with such discordant noises,
　　With such accursed instruments as these,
Thou drownest Nature's sweet and kindly voices,
　　And jarrest the celestial harmonies?

Were half the power, that fills the world with terror,
　　Were half the wealth, bestowed on camps and courts,
Given to redeem the human mind from error,
　　There were no need of arsenals nor forts:

The warrior's name would be a name abhorrèd!
　　And every nation, that should lift again
Its hand against a brother, on its forehead
　　Would wear for evermore the curse of Cain!

Down the dark future, through long generations,
    The echoing sounds grow fainter and then cease;
And like a bell, with solemn, sweet vibrations,
    I hear once more the voice of Christ say, "Peace!"

Peace! and no longer from its brazen portals
    The blast of War's great organ shakes the skies!
But beautiful as songs of the immortals,
    The holy melodies of love arise.

THE NORMAN BARON

Dans les moments de la vie où la réflexion devient plus calme et plus profonde, où l'intérêt et l'avarice parlent moins haut que la raison, dans les instants de chagrin domestique, de maladie, et de péril de mort, les nobles se repentirent de posséder des serfs, comme d'une chose peu agréable à Dieu, qui avait créé tous les hommes à son image.

THIERRY: CONQUETE DE L'ANGLETERRE.

In his chamber, weak and dying,
Was the Norman baron lying;
Loud, without, the tempest thundered,
    And the castle turret shook.

In this fight was Death the gainer,
Spite of vassal and retainer,
And the lands his sires had plundered,
    Written in the Doomsday Book.

By his bed a monk was seated,
Who in humble voice repeated
Many a prayer and pater-noster,
    From the missal on his knee;

And, amid the tempest pealing,
Sounds of bells came faintly stealing,
Bells, that, from the neighboring kloster,
    Rang for the Nativity.

In the hall, the serf and vassal
Held, that night, their Christmas wassail;
Many a carol, old and saintly,
    Sang the minstrels and the waits.

And so loud these Saxon gleemen
Sang to slaves the songs of freemen,
That the storm was heard but faintly,
    Knocking at the castle gates.

Till at length the lays they chaunted
Reached the chamber terror-haunted,
Where the monk, with accents holy,
    Whispered at the baron's ear.

Tears upon his eyelids glistened,
As he paused awhile and listened,
And the dying baron slowly
    Turned his weary head to hear.

"Wassail for the kingly stranger
Born and cradled in a manger!
King, like David, priest, like Aaron,
    Christ is born to set us free!"

And the lightning showed the sainted
Figures on the casement painted,
And exclaimed the shuddering baron,
    "Miserere, Domine!"

In that hour of deep contrition,
He beheld, with clearer vision,
Through all outward show and fashion,
    Justice, the Avenger, rise.

All the pomp of earth had vanished,
Falsehood and deceit were banished,
Reason spake more loud than passion,
    And the truth wore no disguise.

Every vassal of his banner,
Every serf born to his manor,
All those wronged and wretched creatures,
    By his hand were freed again.

And, as on the sacred missal
He recorded their dismissal,
Death relaxed his iron features,
    And the monk replied, "Amen!"

Many centuries have been numbered
Since in death the baron slumbered
By the convent's sculptured portal,
   Mingling with the common dust:

But the good deed, through the ages
Living in historic pages,
Brighter grows and gleams immortal,
   Unconsumed by moth or rust.

RAIN IN SUMMER

How beautiful is the rain!
After the dust and heat,
In the broad and fiery street,
In the narrow lane,
How beautiful is the rain!

How it clatters along the roofs
Like the tramp of hoofs!
How it gushes and struggles out
From the throat of the overflowing spout!
Across the window pane
It pours and pours;
And swift and wide,
With a muddy tide,
Like a river down the gutter roars
The rain, the welcome rain!

The sick man from his chamber looks
At the twisted brooks;
He can feel the cool
Breath of each little pool;
His fevered brain
Grows calm again,
And he breathes a blessing on the rain.

From the neighboring school
Come the boys,
With more than their wonted noise
And commotion;
And down the wet streets
Sail their mimic fleets,

Till the treacherous pool
Engulfs them in its whirling
And turbulent ocean.

In the country, on every side,
Where far and wide,
Like a leopard's tawny and spotted hide
Stretches the plain,
To the dry grass and the drier grain
How welcome is the rain!

In the furrowed land
The toilsome and patient oxen stand;
Lifting the yoke-encumbered head,
With their dilated nostrils spread,
They silently inhale
The clover-scented gale,
And the vapors that arise
From the well-watered and smoking soil;
For this rest in the furrow after toil
Their large and lustrous eyes
Seem to thank the Lord,
More than man's spoken word.

Near at hand,
From under the sheltering trees,
The farmer sees
His pastures, and his fields of grain,
As they bend their tops
To the numberless beating drops
Of the incessant rain.
He counts it as no sin
That he sees therein
Only his own thrift and gain.

These, and far more than these,
The Poet sees!
He can behold
Aquarius old
Walking the fenceless fields of air;
And from each ample fold
Of the clouds about him rolled

Scattering everywhere
The showery rain,
As the farmer scatters his grain.

He can behold
Things manifold
That have not yet been wholly told,
Have not been wholly sung nor said.
For his thought, that never stops,
Follows the water-drops
Down to the graves of the dead,
Down through chasms and gulfs profound,
To the dreary fountain-head
Of lakes and rivers under ground;
And sees them, when the rain is done,
On the bridge of colors seven
Climbing up once more to heaven,
Opposite the setting sun.

Thus the Seer,
With vision clear,
Sees forms appear and disappear,
In the perpetual round of strange,
Mysterious change
From birth to death, from death to birth,
From earth to heaven, from heaven to earth;
Till glimpses more sublime
Of things, unseen before,
Unto his wondering eyes reveal
The Universe as an immeasurable wheel
Turning for evermore
In the rapid and rushing river of Time.

TO A CHILD

Dear child! how radiant on thy mother's knee,
With merry-making eyes and jocund smiles,
Thou gazest at the painted tiles,
Whose figures grace,
With many a grotesque form and face,

The ancient chimney of thy nursery!
The lady, with the gay macaw,
The dancing girl, the grave bashaw
With bearded lip and chin;
And, leaning idly o'er his gate,
Beneath the imperial fan of state,
The Chinese mandarin.

With what a look of proud command
Thou shakest in thy little hand
The coral rattle with its silver bells,
Making a merry tune!
Thousands of years in Indian seas
That coral grew, by slow degrees,
Until some deadly and wild monsoon
Dashed it on Coromandel's sand!
Those silver bells
Reposed of yore,
As shapeless ore,
Far down in the deep sunken wells
Of darksome mines,
In some obscure and sunless place,
Beneath huge Chimborazo's base,
Or Potosi's o'erhanging pines!

And thus for thee, O little child,
Through many a danger and escape,
The tall ships passed the stormy cape;
For thee in foreign lands remote,
Beneath the burning, tropic clime,
The Indian peasant, chasing the wild goat,
Himself as swift and wild,
In falling, clutched the frail arbute,
The fibres of whose shallow root,
Uplifted from the soil, betrayed
The silver veins beneath it laid,
The buried treasures of the pirate, Time.

But, lo, thy door is left ajar!
Thou hearest footsteps from afar!
And, at the sound,
Thou turnest round

With quick and questioning eyes,
Like one, who, in a foreign land,
Beholds on every hand
Some source of wonder and surprise
And, restlessly, impatiently,
Thou strivest, strugglest, to be free.
The four walls of thy nursery
Are now like prison walls to thee.
No more thy mother's smiles,
No more the painted tiles,
Delight thee, nor the playthings on the floor,
That won thy little, beating heart before;
Thou strugglest for the open door.

Through these once solitary halls
Thy pattering footstep falls.
The sound of thy merry voice
Makes the old walls
Jubilant, and they rejoice
With the joy of thy young heart,
O'er the light of whose gladness
No shadows of sadness
From the sombre background of memory start.

Once, ah, once, within these walls,
One whom memory oft recalls,
The Father of his Country, dwelt.
And yonder meadows broad and damp
The fires of the besieging camp
Encircled with a burning belt.
Up and down these echoing stairs,
Heavy with the weight of cares,
Sounded his majestic tread;
Yes, within this very room
Sat he in those hours of gloom,
Weary both in heart and head.

But what are these grave thoughts to thee?
Out, out! into the open air!
Thy only dream is liberty,
Thou carest little how or where.

I see thee eager at thy play,
Now shouting to the apples on the tree
With cheeks as round and red as they;
And now among the yellow stalks,
Among the flowering shrubs and plants,
As restless as the bee,
Along the garden walks,
The tracks of thy small carriage-wheels I trace;

And see at every turn how they efface
Whole villages of sand-roofed tents,
That rise like golden domes
Above the cavernous and secret homes
Of wandering and nomadic tribes of ants.
Ah, cruel little Tamerlane,
Who, with thy dreadful reign,
Dost persecute and overwhelm
These hapless Troglodytes of thy realm!

What! tired already! with those suppliant looks,
And voice more beautiful than a poet's books,
Or murmuring sound of water as it flows,
Thou comest back to parley with repose!
This rustic seat in the old apple-tree,
With its o'erhanging golden canopy
Of leaves illuminate with autumnal hues,
And shining with the argent light of dews,
Shall for a season be our place of rest.
Beneath us, like an oriole's pendent nest,
From which the laughing birds have taken wing,
By thee abandoned, hangs thy vacant swing.
Dream-like the waters of the river gleam;
A sailless vessel drops adown the stream,
And like it, to a sea as wide and deep,
Thou driftest gently down the tides of sleep.

O child! O new-born denizen
Of life's great city! on thy head
The glory of the morn is shed,
Like a celestial benison!
Here at the portal thou dost stand,
And with thy little hand

Thou openest the mysterious gate
Into the future's undiscovered land.
I see its valves expand,
As at the touch of Fate!
Into those realms of love and hate,
Into that darkness blank and drear,
By some prophetic feeling taught,
I launch the bold, adventurous thought,
Freighted with hope and fear;
As upon subterranean streams,
In caverns unexplored and dark,
Men sometimes launch a fragile bark,
Laden with flickering fire,
And watch its swift-receding beams,
Until at length they disappear,
And in the distant dark expire.

By what astrology of fear or hope
Dare I cast thy horoscope;
Like the new moon thy life appears;
A little strip of silver light,
And widening outward into night
The shadowy disk of future years;
And yet upon its outer rim,
A luminous circle, faint and dim,
And scarcely visible to us here,
Rounds and completes the perfect sphere;
A prophecy and intimation,
A pale and feeble adumbration,
Of the great world of light, that lies
Behind all human destinies.

Ah! if thy fate, with anguish fraught,
Should be to wet the dusty soil
With the hot tears and sweat of toil,—
To struggle with imperious thought,
Until the overburdened brain,
Weary with labor, faint with pain,
Like a jarred pendulum, retain
Only its motion, not its power,—
Remember, in that perilous hour,

When most afflicted and opprest,
From labor there shall come forth rest.

And if a more auspicious fate
On thy advancing steps await,
Still let it ever be thy pride
To linger by the laborer's side;
With words of sympathy or song
To cheer the dreary march along
Of the great army of the poor,
O'er desert sand, o'er dangerous moor.
Nor to thyself the task shall be
Without reward; for thou shalt learn
The wisdom early to discern
True beauty in utility;
As great Pythagoras of yore,
Standing beside the blacksmith's door,
And hearing the hammers, as they smote
The anvils with a different note,
Stole from the varying tones, that hung
Vibrant on every iron tongue,
The secret of the sounding wire,
And formed the seven-chorded lyre.

Enough! I will not play the Seer;
I will no longer strive to ope
The mystic volume, where appear
The herald Hope, forerunning Fear,
And Fear, the pursuivant of Hope.
Thy destiny remains untold;
For, like Acestes' shaft of old,
The swift thought kindles as it flies,
And burns to ashes in the skies.

THE OCCULTATION OF ORION [1]

I saw, as in a dream sublime,
The balance in the hand of Time.

[1] *The Occultation of Orion.* Astronomically speaking, this title is incorrect: as I apply to a constellation what can properly be applied to some of its stars only. But my observation is made from the hill

O'er East and West its beam impended;
And day, with all its hours of light,
Was slowly sinking out of sight,
While, opposite, the scale of night
Silently with the stars ascended.

Like the astrologers of eld,
In that bright vision I beheld
Greater and deeper mysteries.
I saw, with its celestial keys,
Its chords of air, its frets of fire,
The Samian's great Æolian lyre,
Rising through all its sevenfold bars
From earth unto the fixed stars.
And through the dewy atmosphere
Not only could I see, but hear,
Its wondrous and harmonious strings
In sweet vibration, sphere by sphere,
From Dian's circle light and near,
Onward to vaster and wider rings,
Where, chanting through his beard of snows,
Majestic, mournful, Saturn goes,
And down the sunless realms of space
Reverberates the thunder of his bass.

Beneath the sky's triumphal arch
This music sounded like a march,
And with its chorus seemed to be
Preluding some great tragedy.
Sirius was rising in the east;
And, slow ascending one by one,
The· kindling constellation shone.
Begirt with many a blazing star,
Stood the great giant Algebar.
Orion, hunter of the beast!
His sword hung gleaming by his side.
And, on his arm, the lion's hide
Scattered across the midnight air
The golden radiance of its hair.

of song, and not from that of science; and will, I trust, be found
sufficiently accurate for the present purpose.

The moon was pallid, but not faint,
And beautiful as some fair saint,
Serenely moving on her way
In hours of trial and dismay.
As if she heard the voice of God,
Unharmed with naked feet she trod
Upon the hot and burning stars,
As on the glowing coals and bars
That were to prove her strength, and try
Her holiness and her purity.
Thus moving on, with silent pace,
And triumph in her sweet, pale face,
She reached the station of Orion.
Aghast he stood in strange alarm!
And suddenly from his outstretched arm
Down fell the red skin of the lion
Into the river at his feet.
His mighty club no longer beat
The forehead of the bull; but he
Reeled as of yore beside the sea,
When, blinded by Œnopion,
He sought the blacksmith at his forge,
And, climbing up the mountain gorge,
Fixed his black eyes upon the sun.
Then, through the silence overhead,
An angel with a trumpet said,
"Forevermore, forevermore,
The reign of violence is o'er!"
And, like an instrument that flings
Its music on another's strings,
The trumpet of the angel cast
Upon the heavenly lyre its blast,
And on from sphere to sphere the words
Re-echoed down the burning chords,—
"Forevermore, forevermore,
The reign of violence is o'er!"

THE BRIDGE

I stood on the bridge at midnight,
    As the clocks were striking the hour,

And the moon rose o'er the city,
  Behind the dark church-tower.

I saw her bright reflection
  In the waters under me,
Like a golden goblet falling
  And sinking into the sea.

And far in the hazy distance
  Of that lovely night in June,
The blaze of the flaming furnace
  Gleamed redder than the moon.

Among the long, black rafters
  The waving shadows lay,
And the current that came from the ocean
  Seemed to lift and bear them away;

As, sweeping and eddying through them,
  Rose the belated tide,
And, streaming into the moonlight,
  The seaweed floated wide.

And like those waters rushing
  Among the wooden piers,
A flood of thoughts came o'er me
  That filled my eyes with tears.

How often, O, how often,
  In the days that had gone by,
I had stood on that bridge at midnight,
  And gazed on that wave and sky!

How often, O, how often,
  I had wished that the ebbing tide
Would bear me away on its bosom
  O'er the ocean wild and wide!

For my heart was hot and restless,
  And my life was full of care,
And the burden laid upon me
  Seemed greater than I could bear.

But now it has fallen from me,
    It is buried in the sea;
And only the sorrow of others
    Throws its shadow over me.

Yet whenever I cross the river
    On its bridge with wooden piers,
Like the odor of brine from the ocean
    Comes the thought of other years.

And I think how many thousands
    Of care-encumbered men,
Each bearing his burden of sorrow,
    Have crossed the bridge since then.

I see the long procession
    Still passing to and fro,
The young heart hot and restless,
    And the old subdued and slow!

And for ever and for ever,
    As long as the river flows,
As long as the heart has passions,
    As long as life has woes;

The moon and its broken reflection
    And its shadows shall appear,
As the symbol of love in heaven,
    And its wavering image here.

To the Driving Cloud

Gloomy and dark art thou, O chief of the mighty Omawhaws;
Gloomy and dark, as the driving cloud, whose name thou
    hast taken!
Wrapt in thy scarlet blanket, I see thee stalk through the
    city's
Narrow and populous streets, as once by the margin of rivers
Stalked those birds unknown, that have left us only their
    footprints.
What, in a few short years, will remain of thy race but the
    footprints?

How canst thou walk in these streets, who hast trod the green
    turf of the prairies?
How canst thou breathe in this air, who hast breathed the
    sweet air of the mountains?
Ah! 't is in vain that with lordly looks of disdain thou dost
    challenge
Looks of dislike in return, and question these walls and these
    pavements,
Claiming the soil for thy hunting-grounds, while down-
    trodden millions
Starve in the garrets of Europe, and cry from its caverns
    that they, too,
Have been created heirs of the earth, and claim its division!

Back, then, back to thy woods in the regions west of the
    Wabash!
There as a monarch thou reignest. In autumn the leaves of
    the maple
Pave the floors of thy palace-halls with gold, and in summer
Pine-trees waft through its chambers the odorous breath of
    their branches.
There thou art strong and great, a hero, a tamer of horses!
There thou chasest the stately stag on the banks of the Elk-
    horn,
Or by the roar of the Running Water, or where the
    Omawhaw
Calls thee, and leaps through the wild ravine like a brave
    of the Blackfeet!

Hark! what murmurs arise from the heart of those moun-
    tainous deserts!
Is it the cry of the Foxes and Crows, or the mighty Behe-
    moth,
Who, unharmed, on his tusks once caught the bolts of the
    thunder,
And now lurks in his lair to destroy the race of the red man?
Far more fatal to thee and thy race than the Crows and the
    Foxes,
Far more fatal to thee and thy race than the tread of Behe-
    moth,

Lo! the big thunder-canoe, that steadily breasts the Mis-
    souri's
Merciless current! and yonder, afar on the prairies, the
    camp-fires
Gleam through the night, and the cloud of dust in the gray
    of the daybreak
Marks not the buffalo's track, nor the Mandan's dexterous
    horse-race;
It is a caravan, whitening the desert where dwell the
    Camanches!
Ha! how the breath of these Saxons and Celts, like the blast
    of the east-wind,
Drifts evermore to the west the scanty smokes of thy wig-
    wams!

SONGS

SEAWEED

When descends on the Atlantic
    The gigantic
Storm-wind of the equinox,
Landward in his wrath he scourges
    The toiling surges,
Laden with seaweed from the rocks:

From Bermuda's reefs; from edges
    Of sunken ledges,
In some far-off, bright Azore;
From Bahama, and the dashing,
    Silver-flashing
Surges of San Salvador;

From the tumbling surf, that buries
    The Orkneyan skerries,
Answering the hoarse Hebrides;
And from wrecks of ships, and drifting
    Spars, uplifting
On the desolate, rainy seas;—

Ever drifting, drifting, drifting
    On the shifting

Currents of the restless main;
Till in sheltered coves, and reaches
    Of sandy beaches,
All have found repose again.

So when storms of wild emotion
    Strike the ocean
Of the poet's soul, ere long
From each cave and rocky fastness,
    In its vastness,
Floats some fragment of a song:

From the far-off isles enchanted,
    Heaven has planted
With the golden fruit of Truth;
From the flashing surf, whose vision
    Gleams Elysian
In the tropic clime of Youth;

From the strong Will, and the Endeavor
    That forever
Wrestles with the tides of Fate;
From the wreck of Hopes far scattered,
    Tempest-shattered,
Floating waste and desolate;—

Ever drifting, drifting, drifting
    On the shifting
Currents of the restless heart;
Till at length in books recorded,
    They, like hoarded
Household words, no more depart.

THE DAY IS DONE

The day is done, and the darkness
    Falls from the wings of Night,
As a feather is wafted downward
    From an eagle in his flight.

I see the lights of the village
    Gleam through the rain and the mist,
And a feeling of sadness comes o'er me,
    That my soul cannot resist:

A feeling of sadness and longing,
  That is not akin to pain,
And resembles sorrow only
  As the mist resembles the rain.

Come, read to me some poem,
  Some simple and heartfelt lay,
That shall soothe this restless feeling,
  And banish the thoughts of day.

Not from the grand old masters,
  Not from the bards sublime,
Whose distant footsteps echo
  Through the corridors of Time.

For, like strains of martial music,
  Their mighty thoughts suggest
Life's endless toil and endeavor;
  And to-night I long for rest.

Read from some humbler poet,
  Whose songs gushed from his heart,
As showers from the clouds of summer,
  Or tears from the eyelids start;

Who, through long days of labor,
  And nights devoid of ease,
Still heard in his soul the music
  Of wonderful melodies.

Such songs have power to quiet
  The restless pulse of care,
And come like the benediction
  That follows after prayer.

Then read from the treasured volume
  The poem of thy choice,
And lend to the rhyme of the poet
  The beauty of thy voice.

And the night shall be filled with music,
  And the cares that infest the day,
Shall fold their tents, like the Arabs,
  And as silently steal away.

AFTERNOON IN FEBRUARY

The day is ending,
The night is descending;
The marsh is frozen,
  The river dead.

Through clouds like ashes
The red sun flashes
On village windows
  That glimmer red.

The snow recommences;
The buried fences
Mark no longer
  The road o'er the plain;

While through the meadows,
Like fearful shadows,
Slowly passes
  A funeral train.

The bell is pealing
And every feeling
Within me responds
  To the dismal knell;

Shadows are trailing,
My heart is bewailing
And toiling within
  Like a funeral bell.

TO AN OLD DANISH SONG BOOK

Welcome, my old friend,
Welcome to a foreign fireside,
While the sullen gales of autumn
Shake the windows.

The ungrateful world
Has, it seems, dealt harshly with thee,
Since, beneath the skies of Denmark,
First I met thee.

There are marks of age,
There are thumb-marks on thy margin,
Made by hands that clasped thee rudely,
At the alehouse.

Soiled and dull thou art;
Yellow are thy time-worn pages,
As the russet, rain-molested
Leaves of autumn.

Thou art stained with wine
Scattered from hilarious goblets,
As these leaves with the libations
Of Olympus.

Yet dost thou recall
Days departed, half-forgotten,
When in dreamy youth I wandered
By the Baltic,—

When I paused to hear
The old ballad of King Christian
Shouted from suburban taverns
In the twilight.

Thou recallest bards,
Who, in solitary chambers,
And with hearts by passion wasted,
Wrote thy pages.

Thou recallest homes
Where thy songs of love and friendship
Made the gloomy Northern winter
Bright as summer.

Once some ancient Scald,
In his bleak, ancestral Iceland,
Chanted staves of these old ballads
To the Vikings.

Once in Elsinore,
At the court of old King Hamlet,
Yorick and his boon companions
Sang these ditties.

Once Prince Frederick's Guard
Sang them in their smoky barracks;
Suddenly the English cannon
Joined the chorus!

Peasants in the field,
Sailors on the roaring ocean,
Students, tradesmen, pale mechanics,
All have sung them.

Thou hast been their friend;
They, alas! have left thee friendless!
Yet at least by one warm fireside
Art thou welcome.

And, as swallows build
In these wide, old-fashioned chimneys,
So thy twittering songs shall nestle
In my bosom,—

Quiet, close, and warm,
Sheltered from all molestation,
And recalling by their voices
Youth and travel.

WALTER VON DER VOGELWEID [1]

Vogelweid the Minnesinger,
   When he left this world of ours,
Laid his body in the cloister,
   Under Würtzburg's minster towers.

And he gave the monks his treasures,
   Gave them all with this behest:
They should feed the birds at noon-tide
   Daily on his place of rest;

[1] *Walter von der Vogelweid.* Walter von der Vogelweid, or Bird-Meadow, was one of the principal Minnesingers of the thirteenth century. He triumphed over Heinrich von Ofterdingen in that poetic contest at Wartburg Castle, known in literary history as the War of Wartburg.

Saying, "From these wandering minstrels
   I have learned the art of song;
Let me now repay the lessons
   They have taught so well and long."

Thus the bard of love departed;
   And, fulfilling his desire,
On his tomb the birds were feasted
   By the children of the choir.

Day by day, o'er tower and turret,
   In foul weather and in fair,
Day by day, in vaster numbers,
   Flocked the poets of the air.

On the tree whose heavy branches
   Overshadowed all the place,
On the pavement, on the tombstone,
   On the poet's sculptured face.

On the cross-bars of each window,
   On the lintel of each door,
They renewed the War of Wartburg,
   Which the bard had fought before.

There they sang their merry carols,
   Sang their lauds on every side;
And the name their voices uttered
   Was the name of Vogelweid.

Till at length the portly abbot
   Murmured, "Why this waste of food?
Be it changed to loaves henceforward
   For our fasting brotherhood."

Then in vain o'er tower and turret,
   From the walls and woodland nests,
When the minster bells rang noontide,
   Gathered the unwelcome guests.

Then in vain, with cries discordant,
   Clamorous round the Gothic spire,
Screamed the feathered Minnesingers
   For the children of the choir.

Time has long effaced the inscriptions
  On the cloister's funeral stones,
And tradition only tells us
  Where repose the poet's bones.

But around the vast cathedral,
  By sweet echoes multiplied,
Still the birds repeat the legend,
  And the name of Vogelweid.

DRINKING SONG

INSCRIPTION FOR AN ANTIQUE PITCHER

Come, old friend! sit down and listen!
  From the pitcher, placed between us,
How the waters laugh and glisten
  In the head of old Silenus!

Old Silenus, bloated, drunken,
  Led by his inebriate Satyrs;
On his breast his head is sunken,
  Vacantly he leers and chatters.

Fauns with youthful Bacchus follow;
  Ivy crowns that brow supernal
As the forehead of Apollo,
  And possessing youth eternal.

Round about him, fair Bacchantes,
  Bearing cymbals, flutes, and thyrses,
Wild from Naxian groves, or Zante's
  Vineyards, sing delirious verses.

Thus he won, through all the nations,
  Bloodless victories, and the farmer
Bore, as trophies and oblations,
  Vines for banners, ploughs for armor.

Judged by no o'erzealous rigor,
  Much this mystic throng expresses:
Bacchus was the type of vigor,
  And Silenus of excesses.

These are ancient ethnic revels,
  Of a faith long since forsaken;
Now the Satyrs, changed to devils,
  Frighten mortals wine-o'ertaken.

Now to rivulets from the mountains
  Point the rods of fortune-tellers;
Youth perpetual dwells in fountains,—
  Not in flasks, and casks, and cellars.

Claudius, though he sang of flagons
  And huge tankards filled with Rhenish,
From that fiery blood of dragons
  Never would his own replenish.

Even Redi, though he chaunted
  Bacchus in the Tuscan valleys,
Never drank the wine he vaunted
  In his dithyrambic sallies.

Then with water fill the pitcher
  Wreathed about with classic fables;
Ne'er Falernian threw a richer
  Light upon Lucullus' tables.

Come, old friend, sit down and listen!
  As it passes thus between us,
How its wavelets laugh and glisten
  In the head of old Silenus!

THE OLD CLOCK ON THE STAIRS

L'éternité est une pendule, dont le balancier dit et redit sans cesse
ces deux mots seulement, dans le silence des tombeaux: "Toujours!
jamais! Jamais! toujours!"

                                        JACQUES BRIDAINE.

Somewhat back from the village street
Stands the old-fashioned country-seat.
Across its antique portico
Tall poplar-trees their shadows throw.
And from its station in the hall
An ancient timepiece says to all,—
        "Forever—never!
        Never—forever!"

Halfway up the stairs it stands,
And points and beckons with its hands
From its case of massive oak,
Like a monk, who, under his cloak,
Crosses himself, and sighs, alas!
With sorrowful voice to all who pass,—
    "Forever—never!
    Never—forever!"

By day its voice is low and light;
But in the silent dead of night,
Distinct as a passing footstep's fall,
It echoes along the vacant hall,
Along the ceiling, along the floor,
And seems to say, at each chamber-door,—
    "Forever—never!
    Never—forever!"

Through days of sorrow and of mirth,
Through days of death and days of birth,
Through every swift vicissitude
Of changeful time, unchanged it has stood,
And as if, like God, it all things saw,
It calmly repeats those words of awe,—
    "Forever—never!
    Never—forever!"

In that mansion used to be
Free-hearted Hospitality;
His great fires up the chimney roared;
The stranger feasted at his board;
But, like the skeleton at the feast,
That warning timepiece never ceased,—
    "Forever—never!
    Never—forever!"

There groups of merry children played,
There youth and maidens dreaming strayed;
O precious hours! O golden prime,
And affluence of love and time!

Even as a miser counts his gold,
Those hours the ancient timepiece told,—
  "Forever—never!
  Never—forever!"

From that chamber, clothed in white,
The bride came forth on her wedding night;
There, in that silent room below,
The dead lay in his shroud of snow
And in the hush that followed the prayer,
Was heard the old clock on the stair,—
  "Forever—never!
  Never—forever!"

All are scattered now and fled,
Some are married, some are dead;
And when I ask with throbs of pain,
"Ah! when shall they all meet again?"
As in the days long since gone by,
The ancient timepiece makes reply,—
  "Forever—never!
  Never—forever!"

Never here, forever there,
Where all parting, pain, and care,
And death, and time shall disappear,—
Forever there, but never here!
The horologe of Eternity
Sayeth this incessantly,—
  "Forever—never!
  Never—forever!"

THE ARROW AND THE SONG

I shot an arrow into the air,
It fell to earth, I knew not where;
For, so swiftly it flew, the sight
Could not follow it in its flight.

I breathed a song into the air,
It fell to earth, I knew not where;
For who has sight so keen and strong,
That it can follow the flight of song?

Long, long afterward, in an oak
I found the arrow, still unbroke;
And the song, from beginning to end,
I found again in the heart of a friend.

SONNETS

THE EVENING STAR

Lo! in the painted oriel of the West,
   Whose panes the sunken sun incarnadines,
   Like a fair lady at her casement, shines
The evening star, the star of love and rest!
And then anon she doth herself divest
   Of all her radiant garments, and reclines
   Behind the sombre screen of yonder pines,
With slumber and soft dreams of love opprest.
O my beloved, my sweet Hesperus!
   My morning and my evening star of love!
My best and gentlest lady! even thus,
   As that fair planet in the sky above,
Dost thou retire unto thy rest at night,
And from thy darkened window fades the light.

AUTUMN

Thou comest, Autumn, heralded by the rain,
   With banners, by great gales incessant fanned,
   Brighter than brightest silks of Samarcand,
And stately oxen harnessed to thy wain!
Thou standest, like imperial Charlemagne,
   Upon thy bridge of gold; thy royal hand
   Outstretched with benedictions o'er the land,
Blessing the farms through all thy vast domain.
Thy shield is the red harvest moon, suspended
   So long beneath the heaven's o'erhanging eaves;
Thy steps are by the farmer's prayers attended;
   Like flames upon an altar shine the sheaves;
And, following thee, in thy ovation splendid,
   Thine almoner, the wind, scatters the golden
       leaves!

DANTE

Tuscan, that wanderest through the realms of gloom,
　　With thoughtful pace, and sad, majestic eyes,
　　Stern thoughts and awful from thy soul arise,
Like Farinata from his fiery tomb.
Thy sacred song is like the trump of doom;
　　Yet in thy heart what human sympathies,
　　What soft compassion glows, as in the skies
The tender stars their clouded lamps relume!
Methinks I see thee stand, with pallid cheeks,
　　By Fra Hilario in his diocese,
As up the convent-walls, in golden streaks,
　　The ascending sunbeams mark the day's decrease;
And, as he asks what there the stranger seeks,
　　Thy voice along the cloister whispers, "Peace!"

TRANSLATIONS

THE HEMLOCK TREE

FROM THE GERMAN

O hemlock tree! O hemlock tree! how faithful are thy
　　branches!
　　Green not alone in summer time,
　　But in the winter's frost and rime!
O hemlock tree! O hemlock tree! how faithful are thy
　　branches!

O maiden fair! O maiden fair! how faithless is thy bosom!
　　To love me in prosperity,
　　And leave me in adversity!
O maiden fair! O maiden fair! how faithless is thy bosom!

The nightingale, the nightingale, thou tak'st for thine example!
　　So long as summer lasts she sings,
　　But in the autumn spreads her wings.
The nightingale, the nightingale, thou tak'st for thine example!

The meadow brook, the meadow brook, is mirror of thy false-
　　hood!

It flows so long as falls the rain,
In drought its springs soon dry again.
The meadow brook, the meadow brook, is mirror of thy false-
hood!

ANNIE OF THARAW

FROM THE LOW GERMAN OF SIMON DACH

Annie of Tharaw, my true love of old,
She is my life, and my goods, and my gold.

Annie of Tharaw, her heart once again
To me has surrendered in joy and in pain.

Annie of Tharaw, my riches, my good,
Thou, O my soul, my flesh and my blood!

Then come the wild weather, come sleet or come snow,
We will stand by each other, however it blow.

Oppression, and sickness, and sorrow, and pain,
Shall be to our true love as links to the chain.

As the palm-tree standeth so straight and so tall,
The more the hail beats, and the more the rains fall,—

So love in our hearts shall grow mighty and strong,
Through crosses, through sorrows, through manifold wrong.

Shouldst thou be torn from me to wander alone
In a desolate land where the sun is scarce known,—

Through forests I'll follow, and where the sea flows,
Through ice, and through iron, through armies of foes.

Annie of Tharaw, my light and my sun,
The threads of our two lives are woven in one.

Whate'er I have bidden thee thou hast obeyed,
Whatever forbidden thou hast not gainsaid.

How in the turmoil of life can love stand,
Where there is not one heart, and one mouth, and one hand?

Some seek for dissension, and trouble, and strife;
Like a dog and a cat live such man and wife.

Annie of Tharaw, such is not our love;
Thou art my lambkin, my chick, and my dove.

Whate'er my desire is, in thine may be seen;
I am king of the household, and thou art its queen.

It is this, O my Annie, my heart's sweetest rest,
That makes of us twain but one soul in one breast.

This turns to a heaven the hut where we dwell;
While wrangling soon changes a home to a hell.

THE STATUE OVER THE CATHEDRAL DOOR

FROM THE GERMAN OF JULIUS MOSEN

Forms of saints and kings are standing
    The cathedral door above;
Yet I saw but one among them
    Who had soothed my soul with love.

In his mantle,—wound about him,
    As their robes the sowers wind,—
Bore he swallows and their fledglings,
    Flowers and weeds of every kind.

And so stands he calm and childlike,
    High in wind and tempest wild;
O, were I like him exalted,
    I would be like him a child!

And my songs,—green leaves and blossoms,—
    To the doors of heaven would bear,
Calling, even in storm and tempest,
    Round me still these birds of air.

THE LEGEND OF THE CROSSBILL

FROM THE GERMAN OF JULIUS MOSEN

On the cross the dying Saviour
    Heavenward lifts his eyelids calm,
Feels, but scarcely feels, a trembling
    In his pierced and bleeding palm.

And by all the world forsaken,
  Sees he how with zealous care
At the ruthless nail of iron
  A little bird is striving there.

Stained with blood and never tiring,
  With its beak it doth not cease,
From the cross 't would free the Saviour,
  Its Creator's Son release.

And the Saviour speaks in mildness:
  "Blest be thou of all the good!
Bear, as token of this moment,
  Marks of blood and holy rood!"

And that bird is called the crossbill;
  Covered all with blood so clear,
In the groves of pine it singeth
  Songs, like legends, strange to hear.

THE SEA HATH ITS PEARLS

FROM THE GERMAN OF HEINRICH HEINE

The sea hath its pearls,
  The heaven hath its stars;
But my heart, my heart,
  My heart hath its love.

Great are the sea and the heaven;
  Yet greater is my heart,
And fairer than pearls and stars
  Flashes and beams my love.

Thou little, youthful maiden,
  Come unto my great heart;
My heart, and the sea, and the heaven
  Are melting away with love!

Poetic Aphorisms

FROM THE SINNGEDICHTE OF FRIEDRICH VON LOGAU. SEVENTEENTH CENTURY

Money

Whereunto is money good?
Who has it not wants hardihood,
Who has it has much trouble and care,
Who once has had it has despair.

The Best Medicine

Joy and Temperance and Repose
Slam the door in the doctor's nose.

Sin

Man-like is it to fall into sin,
Fiend-like is it to dwell therein,
Christ-like is it for sin to grieve,
God-like is it all sin to leave.

Poverty and Blindness

A blind man is a poor man, and blind a poor man is;
For the former seeth no man, and the latter no man sees.

Law of Life

Live I, so live I,
To my Lord heartily,
To my Prince faithfully,
To my Neighbor honestly
Die I, so die I.

Creeds

Lutheran, Popish, Calvinistic, all these creeds and doctrines three
Extant are; but still the doubt is, where Christianity may be.

The Restless Heart

A millstone and the human heart are driven ever round;
If they have nothing else to grind, they must themselves
be ground.

Christian Love

Whilom Love was like a fire, and warmth and comfort it
bespoke;
But, alas! it now is quenched, and only bites us, like the
smoke.

Art and Tact

Intelligence and courtesy not always are combined;
Often in a wooden house a golden room we find.

Retribution

Though the mills of God grind slowly, yet they grind exceeding small;
Though with patience he stands waiting, with exactness
grinds he all.

Truth

When by night the frogs are croaking, kindle but a torch's
fire,
Ha! how soon they all are silent. Thus Truth silences the
liar.

Rhymes

If perhaps these rhymes of mine should sound not well in
strangers' ears,
They have only to bethink them that it happens so with
theirs;
For so long as words, like mortals, call a fatherland their
own,
They will be most highly valued where they are best and
longest known.

CURFEW

I

Solemnly, mournfully,
  Dealing its dole,
The Curfew Bell
  Is beginning to toll.

Cover the embers,
  And put out the light;
Toil comes with the morning
  And rest with the night.

Dark grow the windows,
  And quenched is the fire;
Sound fades into silence,—
  All footsteps retire.

No voice in the chambers,
  No sound in the hall!
Sleep and oblivion
  Reign over all!

II

The book is completed,
  And closed, like the day;
And the hand that has written it
  Lays it away.

Dim grows its fancies;
  Forgotten they lie;
Like coals in the ashes
  They darken and die.

Song sinks into silence,
  The story is told,
The windows are darkened,
  The hearth-stone is cold.

Dark and darker
  The black shadows fall;
Sleep and oblivion
  Reign over all.

THE SEASIDE AND THE FIRESIDE

DEDICATION

As one who walking in the twilight gloom,
  Hears round about him voices as it darkens,
And seeing not the forms from which they come,
  Pauses from time to time, and turns and hearkens;

So walking here in twilight, O my friends!
  I hear your voices, softened by the distance,
And pause, and turn to listen, as each sends
  His word of friendship, comfort, and assistance.

If any thought of mine, or sung or told,
  Has ever given delight or consolation,
Ye have repaid me back a thousand fold,
  By every friendly sign and salutation.

Thanks for the sympathies that ye have shown!
  Thanks for each kindly word, each silent token,
That teaches me, when seeming most alone,
  Friends are around us, though no word be spoken.

Kind messages that pass from land to land;
  Kind letters, that betray the heart's deep history,
In which we feel the pressure of a hand,—
  One touch of fire,—and all the rest is mystery!

The pleasant books, that silently among
  Our household treasures take familiar places,
And are to us as if a living tongue
  Spake from the printed leaves or pictured faces!

Perhaps on earth I never shall behold,
  With eye of sense, your outward form and semblance;
Therefore to me ye never will grow old,
  But live forever young in my remembrance.

Never grow old, nor change, nor pass away!
  Your gentle voices will flow on forever,
When life grows bare and tarnished with decay,
  As through a leafless landscape flows a river.

Not chance of birth or place has made us friends,
  Being oftentimes of different tongues and nations,
But the endeavor for the selfsame ends,
  With the same hopes, and fears, and aspirations.

Therefore I hope to join your seaside walk,
  Saddened, and mostly silent, with emotion;
Not interrupting with intrusive talk
  The grand, majestic symphonies of ocean.

Therefore I hope, as no unwelcome guest,
  At your warm fireside, when the lamps are lighted,
To have my place reserved among the rest,
  Nor stand as one unsought and uninvited!

By the Seaside

THE BUILDING OF THE SHIP

  "Build me straight, O worthy Master!
    Staunch and strong, a goodly vessel,
  That shall laugh at all disaster,
    And with wave and whirlwind wrestle!"

The merchant's word
Delighted the Master heard;
For his heart was in his work, and the heart
Giveth grace unto every Art.
A quiet smile played round his lips,
As the eddies and dimples of the tide
Play round the bows of ships,
That steadily at anchor ride.
And with a voice that was full of glee,
He answered, "Ere long we will launch
A vessel as goodly, and strong, and staunch,
As ever weathered a wintry sea!"

And first with nicest skill and art,
Perfect and finished in every part,
A little model the Master wrought,
Which should be to the larger plan
What the child is to the man,
Its counterpart in miniature;
That with a hand more swift and sure
The greater labor might be brought
To answer to his inward thought.
And as he labored, his mind ran o'er
The various ships that were built of yore,
And above them all, and strangest of all
Towered the Great Harry, crank and tall,
Whose picture was hanging on the wall,
With bows and stern raised high in air,
And balconies hanging here and there,
And signal lanterns and flags afloat,
And eight round towers, like those that frown
From some old castle, looking down
Upon the drawbridge and the moat.
And he said with a smile, "Our ship, I wis,
Shall be of another form than this!"

It was of another form, indeed;
Built for freight, and yet for speed,
A beautiful and gallant craft;
Broad in the beam, that the stress of the blast
Pressing down upon sail and mast
Might not the sharp bows overwhelm;
Broad in the beam, but sloping aft
With graceful curve and slow degrees,
That she might be docile to the helm
And that the current of parted seas,
Closing behind, with mighty force,
Might aid and not impede her course.

In the shipyard stood the Master,
    With the model of the vessel,
That should laugh at all disaster,
    And with wave and whirlwind wrestle!

Covering many a rood of ground,
Lay the timber piled around;
Timber of chestnut and elm and oak,
And scattered here and there, with these,
The knarred and crooked cedar knees;
Brought from regions for away,
From Pascagoula's sunny bay,
And the banks of the roaring Roanoke!
Ah! what a wondrous thing it is
To note how many wheels of toil
One thought, one word, can set in motion!
There's not a ship that sails the ocean,
But every climate, every soil,
Must bring its tribute, great or small,
And help to build the wooden wall!

The sun was rising o'er the sea,
And long the level shadows lay,
As if they, too, the beams would be
Of some great, airy argosy,
Framed and launched in a single day.
That silent architect, the sun,
Had hewn and laid them every one,
Ere the work of man was yet begun.
Beside the Master, when he spoke,
A youth, against an anchor leaning,
Listened, to catch his slightest meaning.
Only the long waves, as they broke
In ripples on the pebbly beach,
Interrupted the old man's speech.
Beautiful they were, in sooth,
The old man and the fiery youth!
The old man, in whose busy brain
Many a ship that sailed the main
Was modelled o'er and o'er again;—
The fiery youth, who was to be
The heir of his dexterity,
The heir of his house, and his daughter's hand,
When he had built and launched from land
What the elder head had planned.

"Thus," said he, "will we build this ship!
Lay square the blocks upon the slip,
And follow well this plan of mine.
Choose the timbers with greatest care;
Of all that is unsound beware;
For only what is sound and strong
To this vessel shall belong.
Cedar of Maine and Georgia pine
Here together shall combine.
A goodly frame, and a goodly fame,
And the UNION be her name!
For the day that gives her to the sea
Shall give my daughter unto thee!"

The Master's word
Enraptured the young man heard;
And as he turned his face aside,
With a look of joy and a thrill of pride
Standing before
Her father's door,
He saw the form of his promised bride.
The sun shone on her golden hair,
And her cheek was glowing fresh and fair,
With the breath of morn and the soft sea air.
Like a beauteous barge was she,
Still at rest on the sandy beach,
Just beyond the billow's reach;
But he
Was the restless, seething, stormy sea!

Ah, how skilful grows the hand
That obeyeth Love's command!
It is the heart and not the brain,
That to the highest doth attain,
And he who followeth Love's behest
Far exceedeth all the rest!
Thus with the rising of the sun
Was the noble task begun,
And soon throughout the shipyard's bounds
Were heard the intermingled sounds

Of axes and of mallets, plied
With vigorous arms on every side;
Plied so deftly and so well,
That, ere the shadows of evening fell,
The keel of oak for a noble ship,
Scarfed and bolted, straight and strong,
Was lying ready, and stretched along
The blocks, well placed upon the slip.
Happy, thrice happy, every one
Who sees his labor well begun,
And not perplexed and multiplied,
By idle waiting for time and tide!

And when the hot, long day was o'er,
The young man at the Master's door
Sat with the maiden calm and still.
And within the porch, a little more
Removed beyond the evening chill,
The father sat, and told them tales
Of wrecks in the great September gales,
Of pirates upon the Spanish Main,
And ships that never came back again,
The chance and change of a sailor's life,
Want and plenty, rest and strife,
His roving fancy, like the wind,
That nothing can stay and nothing can bind,
And the magic charm of foreign lands,
With shadows of palms, and shining sands,
Where the tumbling surf,
O'er the coral reefs of Madagascar,
Washes the feet of the swarthy Lascar,
As he lies alone and asleep on the turf.
And the trembling maiden held her breath
At the tales of that awful, pitiless sea,
With all its terror and mystery,
The dim, dark sea, so like unto Death,
That divides and yet unites mankind!
And whenever the old man paused, a gleam
From the bowl of his pipe would awhile illume

The silent group in the twilight gloom,
And thoughtful faces, as in a dream;
And for a moment one might mark
What had been hidden by the dark,
That the head of the maiden lay at rest,
Tenderly, on the young man's breast!

Day by day the vessel grew,
With timbers fashioned strong and true,
Stemson and keelson and sternsonknee,
Till, framed with perfect symmetry,
A skeleton ship rose up to view!
And around the bows and along the side
The heavy hammers and mallets plied,
Till, after many a week, at length,
Wonderful for form and strength,
Sublime in its enormous bulk,
Loomed aloft the shadowy hulk!
And around it columns of smoke, upwreathing,
Rose from the boiling, bubbling, seething
Caldron, that glowed,
And overflowed
With the black tar, heated for the sheathing.
And amid the clamors
Of clattering hammers,
He who listened heard now and then
The song of the Master and his men:—

"Build me straight, O worthy Master,
    Staunch and strong, a goodly vessel,
That shall laugh at all disaster,
    And with wave and whirlwind wrestle!"

With oaken brace and copper band,
Lay the rudder on the sand,
That, like a thought, should have control
Over the movement of the whole;
And near it the anchor, whose giant hand
Would reach down and grapple with the land,
And immovable and fast
Hold the great ship against the bellowing blast!

And at the bows an image stood,
By a cunning artist carved in wood,
With robes of white, that far behind
Seemed to be fluttering in the wind.
It was not shaped in a classic mould,
Not like a Nymph or Goddess of old,
Or Naiad rising from the water,
But modelled from the Master's daughter!
On many a dreary and misty night,
'T will be seen by the rays of the signal light,
Speeding along through the rain and the dark,
Like a ghost in its snow-white sark,
The pilot of some phantom bark,
Guiding the vessel, in its flight,
By a path none other knows aright!
Behold, at last,[1]
Each tall and tapering mast
Is swung into its place;
Shrouds and stays
Holding it firm and fast!
Long ago,
In the deer-haunted forests of Maine,
When upon mountain and plain
Lay the snow
They fell,—those lordly pines!
Those grand, majestic pines!

[1] *Behold, at last,*
Each tall and tapering mast
Is swung into its place.

I wish to anticipate a criticism on this passage by stating, that sometimes, though not usually, vessels are launched fully rigged and sparred. I have availed myself of the exception, as better suited to my purposes than the general rule; but the reader will see that it is neither a blunder nor a poetic license. On this subject a friend in Portland, Me., writes me thus:—

"In this State, and also, I am told, in New York, ships are sometimes rigged upon the stocks, in order to save time, or to make a show. There was a fine, large ship launched last summer at Ellsworth, fully rigged and sparred. Some years ago a ship was launched here, with her rigging, spars, sails, and cargo aboard. She sailed the next day and—was never heard of again! I hope this will not be the fate of your poem!"

Mid shouts and cheers
The jaded steers,
Panting beneath the goad,
Dragged down the weary, winding road
Those captive kings so straight and tall.
To be shorn of their streaming hair,
And, naked and bare,
To feel the stress and the strain
Of the wind and the reeling main,
Whose roar
Would remind them for evermore
Of their native forests they should not see again.

And everywhere
The slender, graceful spars
Poise aloft in the air,
And at the mast-head,
White, blue, and red,
A flag unrolls the stripes and stars.
Ah! when the wanderer, lonely, friendless,
In foreign harbors shall behold
That flag unrolled,
'T will be as a friendly hand
Stretched out from his native land,
Filling his heart with memories sweet and endless!

All is finished! and at length
Has come the bridal day
Of beauty and of strength.
To-day the vessel shall be launched!
With fleecy clouds the sky is blanched,
And o'er the bay,
Slowly, in all his splendors dight,
The great sun rises to behold the sight.

The ocean old,
Centuries old,
Strong as youth, and as uncontrolled,
Paces restless to and fro,
Up and down the sands of gold.
His beating heart is not at rest;

And far and wide,
With ceaseless flow,
His beard of snow
Heaves with the heaving of his breast.
He waits impatient for his bride.
There she stands,
With her foot upon the sands,
Decked with flags and streamers gay
In honor of her marriage day,
Her snow-white signals fluttering, blending,
Round her like a veil descending,
Ready to be
The bride of the gray, old sea.

On the deck another bride
Is standing by her lover's side.
Shadows from the flags and shrouds,
Like the shadows cast by clouds,
Broken by many a sunny fleck,
Fall around them on the deck.

The prayer is said,
The service read,
The joyous bridegroom bows his head.
And in tears the good old Master
Shakes the brown hand of his son,
Kisses his daughter's glowing cheek
In silence, for he cannot speak,
And ever faster
Down his own the tears begin to run.
The worthy pastor—
The shepherd of that wandering flock,
That has the ocean for its wold,
That has the vessel for its fold,
Leaping ever from rock to rock—
Spake, with accents mild and clear,
Words of warning, words of cheer,
But tedious to the bridegroom's ear.
He knew the chart
Of the sailor's heart,

All its pleasures and its griefs,
All its shallows and rocky reefs,
All those secret currents, that flow
With such resistless undertow,
And lift and drift, with terrible force,
The will from its moorings and its course.
Therefore he spake, and thus said he:—
"Like unto ships far off at sea,
Outward or homeward bound, are we.
Before, behind, and all around,
Floats and swings the horizon's bound,
Seems at its distant rim to rise
And climb the crystal wall of the skies,
And then again to turn and sink,
As if we could slide from its outer brink.
Ah! it is not the sea,
It is not the sea that sinks and shelves,
But ourselves
That rock and rise
With endless and uneasy motion,
Now touching the very skies,
Now sinking into the depths of ocean.
Ah! if our souls but poise and swing
Like the compass in its brazen ring,
Ever level and ever true
To the toil and the task we have to do,
We shall sail securely, and safely reach
The Fortunate Isles, on whose shining beach
The sights we see, and the sounds we hear,
Will be those of joy and not of fear!"

Then the Master,
With a gesture of command,
Waved his hand;
And at the word,
Loud and sudden there was heard,
All around them and below,
The sound of hammers, blow on blow,
Knocking away the shores and spurs.
And see! she stirs!

She starts,—she moves,—she seems to feel
The thrill of life along her keel,
And, spurning with her foot the ground,
With one exulting, joyous bound,
She leaps into the ocean's arms!
And lo! from the assembled crowd
There rose a shout, prolonged and loud,
That to the ocean seemed to say,—
"Take her, O bridegroom, old and gray,
Take her to thy protecting arms,
With all her youth and all her charms!"
How beautiful she is! How fair
She lies within those arms, that press
Her form with many a soft caress
Of tenderness and watchful care!
Sail forth into the sea, O ship!
Through wind and wave, right onward steer!
The moistened eye, the trembling lip,
Are not the signs of doubt or fear.
Sail forth into the sea of life,
O gentle, loving, trusting wife,
And safe from all adversity
Upon the bosom of that sea
Thy comings and thy goings be!
For gentleness and love and trust
Prevail o'er angry wave and gust;
And in the wreck of noble lives
Something immortal still survives!

Thou, too, sail on, O Ship of State!
Sail on, O UNION, strong and great!
Humanity with all its fears,
With all the hopes of future years,
Is hanging breathless on thy fate!
We know what Master laid thy keel,
What Workmen wrought thy ribs of steel,
Who made each mast, and sail, and rope,
What anvils rang, what hammers beat,
In what a forge and what a heat
Were shaped the anchors of thy hope!

Fear not each sudden sound and shock,
'T is of the wave and not the rock;
'T is but the flapping of the sail,
And not a rent made by the gale!
In spite of rock and tempest's roar,
In spite of false lights on the shore,
Sail on, nor fear to breast the sea!
Our hearts, our hopes, are all with thee,
Our hearts, our hopes, our prayers, our tears,
Our faith triumphant o'er our fears,
Are all with thee,—are all with thee!

THE EVENING STAR

Just above yon sandy bar,
  As the day grows fainter and dimmer,
Lonely and lovely, a single star
  Lights the air with a dusty glimmer.

Into the ocean faint and far
  Falls the trail of its golden splendor,
And the gleam of that single star
  Is ever refulgent, soft, and tender.

Chrysaor rising out of the sea,
  Showed thus glorious and thus emulous,
Leaving the arms of Callirrhoë,
  Forever tender, soft, and tremulous.

Thus o'er the ocean faint and far
  Trailed the gleam of his falchion brightly;
Is it a God, or is it a star
  That, entranced, I gaze on nightly!

THE SECRET OF THE SEA

Ah! what pleasant visions haunt me
  As I gaze upon the sea!
All the old romantic legends,
  All my dreams, come back to me.

Sails of silk and ropes of sandal,
   Such as gleam in ancient lore;
And the singing of the sailors,
   And the answer from the shore.

Most of all, the Spanish ballad
   Haunts me oft, and tarries long,
Of the noble Count Arnaldos
   And the sailor's mystic song.

Like the long waves on a sea-beach,
   Where the sand and silver shines,
With a soft, monotonous cadence,
   Flow its unrhymed lyric lines;—

Telling how the Count Arnaldos,
   With his hawk upon his hand,
Saw a fair and stately galley,
   Steering onward to the land;—

How he heard the ancient helmsman
   Chant a song so wild and clear,
That the sailing sea-bird slowly
   Poised upon the mast to hear,

Till his soul was full of longing,
   And he cried, with impulse strong,—
"Helmsman! for the love of heaven,
   Teach me, too, that wondrous song!"

"Wouldst thou,"—so the helmsman answered,
   "Learn the secret of the sea?
Only those who brave its dangers
   Comprehend its mystery!"

In each sail that skims the horizon,
   In each landward-blowing breeze,
I behold that stately galley,
   Hear those mournful melodies;

Till my soul is full of longing
   For the secret of the sea,
And the heart of the great ocean
   Sends a thrilling pulse through me.

TWILIGHT

The twilight is sad and cloudy,
  The wind blows wild and free,
And like the wings of sea-birds
  Flash the white caps of the sea.

But in the fisherman's cottage
  There shines a ruddier light
And a little face at the window
  Peers out into the night.

Close, close it is pressed to the window,
  As if those childish eyes
Were looking into the darkness,
  To see some form arise.

And a woman's waving shadow
  Is passing to and fro,
Now rising to the ceiling,
  Now bowing and bending low.

What tale do the roaring ocean,
  And the night-wind, bleak and wild,
As they beat at the crazy casement,
  Tell to that little child?

And why do the roaring ocean,
  And the night-wind, wild and bleak,
As they beat at the heart of the mother,
  Drive the color from her cheek?

SIR HUMPHREY GILBERT [1]

Southward with fleet of ice
  Sailed the corsair Death;
Wild and fast blew the blast,
  And the east wind was his breath.

[1] *Sir Humphrey Gilbert.* "When the wind abated and the vessels were near enough, the Admiral was seen constantly sitting in the stern, with a book in his hand. On the 9th of September he was seen for the last time, and was heard by the people of the Hind to say, 'We are as near heaven by sea as by land.' In the following night,

His lordly ships of ice
 Glistened in the sun;
On each side, like pennons wide,
 Flashing crystal streamlets run.

His sails of white sea-mist
 Dripped with silver rain;
But where he passed there were cast
 Leaden shadows o'er the main.

Eastward from Campobello
 Sir Humphrey Gilbert sailed;
Three days or more seaward he bore,
 Then, alas! the land-wind failed.

Alas! the land-wind failed,
 And ice-cold grew the night;
And never more, on sea or shore,
 Should Sir Humphrey see the light.

He sat upon the deck,
 The Book was in his hand;
"Do not fear! Heaven is as near,"
 He said, "by water as by land!"

In the first watch of the night,
 Without a signal's sound,
Out of the sea, mysteriously,
 The fleet of Death rose all around.

The moon and the evening star
 Were hanging in the shrouds;
Every mast, as it passed,
 Seemed to rake the passing clouds.

They grappled with their prize,
 At midnight black and cold!
As of a rock was the shock;
 Heavily the ground-swell rolled.

the lights of the ship suddenly disappeared. The people in the other vessel kept a good look-out for him during the remainder of the voyage. On the 22d of September they arrived, through much tempest and peril, at Falmouth. But nothing more was seen or heard of the Admiral.—*Belknap's American Biography*, I. 203.

Southward through day and dark,
   They drift in close embrace.
With mist and rain, to the Spanish Main;
   Yet there seems no change of place.

Southward, forever southward,
   They drift through dark and day;
And like a dream, in the Gulf-Stream
   Sinking, vanish all away.

THE LIGHTHOUSE

The rocky ledge runs far into the sea,
   And on its outer point some miles away,
The Lighthouse lifts its massive masonry,
   A pillar of fire by night, of cloud by day.

Even at this distance I can see the tides,
   Upheaving, break unheard along its base,
A speechless wrath, that rises and subsides
   In the white lip and tremor of the face.

And as the evening darkens, lo! how bright,
   Through the deep purple of the twilight air,
Beams forth the sudden radiance of its light
   With strange, unearthly splendor in its glare!

Not one alone; from each projecting cape
   And perilous reef, along the ocean's verge,
Starts into life a dim, gigantic shape,
   Holding its lantern o'er the restless surge.

Like the great giant Christopher it stands
   Upon the brink of the tempestuous wave,
Wading far out among the rocks and sands,
   The night-o'ertaken mariner to save.

And the great ships sail outward and return,
   Bending and bowing o'er the billowy swells,
And ever joyful, as they see it burn,
   They wave their silent welcomes and farewells.

They come forth from the darkness and their sails
   Gleam for a moment only in the blaze,
And eager faces, as the light unveils,
   Gaze at the tower, and vanish while they gaze.

The mariner remembers when a child,
   On his first voyage, he saw it fade and sink;
And when, returning from adventures wild,
   He saw it rise again o'er ocean's brink.

Steadfast, serene, immovable, the same
   Year after year, through all the silent night
Burns on for evermore that quenchless flame,
   Shines on that inextinguishable light!

It sees the ocean to its bosom clasp
   The rocks and sea-sand with the kiss of peace;
It sees the wild winds lift it in their grasp,
   And hold it up, and shake it like a fleece.

The startled waves leap over it; the storm
   Smites it with all the scourges of the rain,
And steadily against its solid form
   Press the great shoulders of the hurricane.

The sea-bird wheeling round it, with the din
   Of wings and winds and solitary cries,
Blinded and maddened by the light within,
   Dashes himself against the glare, and dies.

A new Prometheus, chained upon the rock,
   Still grasping in his hand the fire of Jove,
It does not hear the cry, nor heed the shock,
   But hails the mariner with words of love.

"Sail on!" it says, "sail on, ye stately ships!
   And with your floating bridge the ocean span;
Be mine to guard this light from all eclipse,
   Be yours to bring man nearer unto man!"

THE FIRE OF DRIFT-WOOD

We sat within the farmhouse old,
   Whose windows, looking o'er the bay,
Gave to the sea-breeze, damp and cold,
   An easy entrance, night and day.

Not far away we saw the port,—
   The strange, old-fashioned, silent town,—
The lighthouse,—the dismantled fort,—
   The wooden houses, quaint and brown.

We sat and talked until the night,
   Descending, filled the little room;
Our faces faded from the sight,
   Our voices only broke the gloom.

We spake of many a vanished scene,
   Of what we once had thought and said,
Of what had been, and might have been,
   And who was changed, and who was dead.

And all that fills the hearts of friends,
   When first they feel, with secret pain,
Their lives thenceforth have separate ends,
   And never can be one again;

The first slight swerving of the heart,
   That words are powerless to express,
And leave it still unsaid in part,
   Or say it in too great excess.

The very tones in which we spake
   Had something strange, I could but mark;
The leaves of memory seemed to make
   A mournful rustling in the dark.

Oft died the words upon our lips,
   As suddenly, from out the fire
Built of the wreck of stranded ships,
   The flames would leap and then expire.

And, as their splendor flashed and failed,
  We thought of wrecks upon the main,—
Of ships dismasted, that were hailed
  And sent no answer back again.

The windows, rattling in their frames,—
  The ocean, roaring up the beach,—
The gusty blast,—the bickering flames,
  All mingled vaguely in our speech;

Until they made themselves a part
  Of fancies floating through the brain,
The long-lost ventures of the heart,
  ' That send no answers back again.

O flames that glowed! O hearts that yearned!
  They were indeed too much akin,
The drift-wood fire without that burned,
  The thoughts that burned and glowed within.

By the Fireside

RESIGNATION

There is no flock, however watched and tended,
  But one dead lamb is there!
There is no fireside, howsoe'er defended,
  But has one vacant chair!

The air is full of farewells to the dying,
  And mournings for the dead;
The heart of Rachel, for her children crying,
  Will not be comforted!

Let us be patient! These severe afflictions
  Not from the ground arise,
But oftentimes celestial benedictions
  Assume this dark disguise.

We see but dimly through the mists and vapors
  Amid these earthly damps;
What seem to us but sad, funereal tapers
  May be heaven's distant lamps.

There is no Death! What seems so is transition.
　　This life of mortal breath
Is but a suburb of the life elysian,
　　Whose portal we call Death.

She is not dead,—the child of our affection,—
　　But gone unto that school
Where she no longer needs our poor protection,
　　And Christ himself doth rule.

In that great cloister's stillness and seclusion,
　　By guardian angels led,
Safe from temptation, safe from sin's pollution,
　　She lives, whom we call dead.

Day after day we think what she is doing
　　In those bright realms of air;
Year after year, her tender steps pursuing,
　　Behold her grown more fair.

Thus do we walk with her, and keep unbroken
　　The bond which nature gives,
Thinking that our remembrance, though unspoken,
　　May reach her where she lives.

Not as a child shall we again behold her;
　　For when with raptures wild
In our embraces we again enfold her,
　　She will not be a child;

But a fair maiden, in her Father's mansion,
　　Clothed with celestial grace;
And beautiful with all the soul's expansion
　　Shall we behold her 'face.

And though at times impetuous with emotion
　　And anguish long suppressed,
The swelling heart heaves moaning like the ocean,
　　That cannot be at rest,—

We will be patient, and assuage the feeling
　　We may not wholly stay;
By silence sanctifying, not concealing,
　　The grief that must have way.

THE BUILDERS

All are architects of Fate,
  Working in these walls of Time;
Some with massive deeds and great,
  Some with ornaments of rhyme.

Nothing useless is, or low;
  Each thing in its place is best;
And what seems but idle show
  Strengthens and supports the rest.

For the structure that we raise,
  Time is with materials filled;
Our to-days and yesterdays
  Are the blocks with which we build.

Truly shape and fashion these;
  Leave no yawning gaps between;
Think not, because no man sees,
  Such things will remain unseen.

In the elder days of Art,
  Builders wrought with greatest care
Each minute and unseen part;
  For the Gods see everywhere.

Let us do our work as well,
  Both the unseen and the seen!
Make the house, where Gods may dwell,
  Beautiful, entire, and clean.

Else our lives are incomplete,
  Standing in these walls of Time,
Broken stairways, where the feet
  Stumble as they seek to climb.

Build to-day, then, strong and sure
  With a firm and ample base;
And ascending and secure
  Shall to-morrow find its place.

Thus alone can we attain
     To those turrets, where the eye
Sees the world as one vast plain,
     And one boundless reach of sky.

SAND OF THE DESERT IN AN HOUR-GLASS

A handful of red sand, from the hot clime
     Of Arab deserts brought,
Within this glass becomes the spy of Time,
     The minister of Thought.

How many weary centuries has it been
     About those deserts blown!
How many strange vicissitudes has seen,
     How many histories known!

Perhaps the camels of the Ishmaelite
     Trampled and passed it o'er,
When into Egypt from the patriarch's sight
     His favorite son they bore.

Perhaps the feet of Moses, burnt and bare,
     Crushed it beneath their tread;
Or Pharaoh's flashing wheels into the air
     Scattered it as they sped;

Or Mary, with the Christ of Nazareth
     Held close in her caress,
Whose pilgrimage of hope and love and faith
     Illumed the wilderness;

Or anchorites beneath Engaddi's palms
     Pacing the Dead Sea beach,
And singing slow their old Armenian psalms
     In half-articulate speech;

Or caravans, that from Bassora's gate
     With westward steps depart;
Or Mecca's pilgrims, confident of Fate,
     And resolute in heart!

These have passed over it, or may have passed!
  Now in this crystal tower
Imprisoned by some curious hand at last,
  It counts the passing hour.

And as I gaze, these narrow walls expand:—
  Before my dreamy eye
Stretches the desert with its shifting sand,
  Its unimpeded sky.

And borne aloft by the sustaining blast,
  This little golden thread
Dilates into a column high and vast,
  A form of fear and dread.

And onward, and across the setting sun,
  Across the boundless plain,
The column and its broader shadow run,
  Till thought pursues in vain.

The vision vanishes! These walls again
  Shut out the lurid sun,
Shut out the hot, immeasurable plain;
  The half-hour's sand is run!

BIRDS OF PASSAGE

  Black shadows fall
  From the lindens tall,
  That lift aloft their massive wall
    Against the southern sky;

  And from the realms
  Of the shadowy elms
  A tide-like darkness overwhelms
    The fields that round us lie.

  But the night is fair,
  And everywhere
  A warm, soft vapor fills the air,
    And distant sounds seem near;

And above in the light
Of the star-lit night,
Swift birds of passage wing their flight
    Through the dewy atmosphere.

I hear the beat
Of their pinions fleet,
As from the land of snow and sleet
    They seek a southern lea.

I hear the cry
Of their voices high
Falling dreamily through the sky,
    But their forms I cannot see.

O, say not so!
Those sounds that flow
In murmurs of delight and woe
    Come not from wings of birds.

They are the throngs
Of the poet's songs.
Murmurs of pleasures, and pains, and wrongs,
    The sound of wingèd words.

This is the cry
Of souls, that high
On toiling, beating pinions, fly,
    Seeking a warmer clime.

From their distant flight
Through realms of light
It falls into our world of night,
    With the murmuring sound of rhyme.

THE OPEN WINDOW

The old house by the lindens
    Stood silent in the shade,
And on the gravelled pathway
    The light and shadow played.

I saw the nursery windows
　　Wide open to the air;
But the faces of the children,
　　They were no longer there.

The large Newfoundland house-dog
　　Was standing by the door;
He looked for his little playmates,
　　Who would return no more.

They walked not under the lindens,
　　They played not in the hall;
But shadow, and silence, and sadness
　　Were hanging over all.

The birds sang in the branches,
　　With sweet, familiar tone;
But the voices of the children
　　Will be heard in dreams alone!

And the boy that walked beside me,
　　He could not understand
Why closer in mine, ah! closer,
　　I pressed his warm, soft hand!

KING WITLAF'S DRINKING HORN

Witlaf, a king of the Saxons,
　　Ere yet his last he breathed,
To the merry monks of Croyland
　　His drinking horn bequeathed,—

That, whenever they sat at their revels,
　　And drank from the golden bowl,
They might remember the donor,
　　And breathe a prayer for his soul.

So sat they once at Christmas,
　　And bade the goblet pass;
In their beards the red wine glistened
　　Like dewdrops in the grass.

They drank to the soul of Witlaf,
  They drank to Christ the Lord,
And to each of the Twelve Apostles,
  Who had preached his holy word.

They drank to the Saints and Martyrs
  Of the dismal days of yore,
And as soon as the horn was empty
  They remembered one Saint more.

And the reader droned from the pulpit,
  Like the murmur of many bees,
The legend of good Saint Guthlac,
  And Saint Basil's homilies;

Till the great bells of the convent,
  From their prison in the tower,
Guthlac and Bartholomæus,
  Proclaimed the midnight hour.

And the Yule-log cracked in the chimney,
  And the Abbot bowed his head,
And the flamelets flapped and flickered,
  But the Abbot was stark and dead.

Yet still in his pallid fingers
  He clutched the golden bowl,
In which, like a pearl dissolving,
  Had sunk and dissolved his soul.

But not for this their revels
  The jovial monks forbore,
For they cried, "Fill high the goblet!
  We must drink to one Saint more!"

GASPAR BECERRA

By his evening fire the artist
  Pondered o'er his secret shame;
Baffled, weary and disheartened,
  Still he mused, and dreamed of fame.

'T was an image of the Virgin
   That had tasked his utmost skill;
But alas! his fair ideal
   Vanished and escaped him still.

From a distant Eastern island
   Had the precious wood been brought;
Day and night the anxious master
   At his toil untiring wrought;

Till, discouraged and desponding,
   Sat he now in shadows deep,
And the day's humiliation
   Found oblivion in sleep.

Then a voice cried, "Rise, O master!
   From the burning brand of oak
Shape the thought that stirs within thee!"
   And the startled artist woke,—

Woke, and from the smoking embers
   Seized and quenched the glowing wood;
And therefrom he carved an image,
   And he saw that it was good.

O thou sculptor, painter, poet!
   Take this lesson to thy heart;
That is best which lieth nearest;
   Shape from that thy work of art.

PEGASUS IN POUND

Once into a quiet village,
   Without haste and without heed.
In the golden prime of morning,
   Strayed the poet's wingèd steed.

It was Autumn, and incessant
   Piped the quails from shocks and sheaves,
And, like living coals, the apples
   Burned among the withering leaves.

Loud the clamorous bell was ringing
   From its belfry gaunt and grim;
'T was the daily call to labor,
   Not a triumph meant for him.

Not the less he saw the landscape,
   In its gleaming vapor veiled;
Not the less he breathed the odors
   That the dying leaves exhaled.

Thus, upon the village common,
   By the school-boys he was found;
And the wise men, in their wisdom,
   Put him straightway into pound.

Then the sombre village crier,
   Ringing loud his brazen bell,
Wandered down the street proclaiming
   There was an estray to sell.

And the curious country people
   Rich and poor, and young and old,
Came in haste to see this wondrous
   Wingèd steed, with mane of gold.

Thus the day passed, and the evening
   Fell, with vapors cold and dim;
But it brought no food nor shelter,
   Brought no straw nor stall for him.

Patiently, and still expectant,
   Looked he through the wooden bars,
Saw the moon rise o'er the landscape,
   Saw the tranquil, patient stars;

Till at length the bell at midnight
   Sounded from its dark abode,
And from out a neighboring farmyard,
   Loud the cock Alectryon crowed.

Then, with nostrils wide distended,
   Breaking from his iron chain,
And unfolding far his pinions,
   To those stars he soared again.

On the morrow, when the village
  Woke to all its toil and care,
Lo! the strange steed had departed,
  And they knew not when nor where.

But they found, upon the greensward
  Where his struggling hoofs had trod,
Pure and bright, a fountain flowing
  From the hoof-marks in the sod.

From that hour, the fount unfailing
  Gladdens the whole region round,
Strengthening all who drink its waters,
  While it soothes them with its sound.

TEGNER'S DRAPA

I heard a voice, that cried,
"Balder the Beautiful
Is dead, is dead!"
And through the misty air
Passed like the mournful cry
Of sunward sailing cranes.

I saw the pallid corpse
Of the dead sun
Borne through the Northern sky.
Blasts from Niffelheim
Lifted the sheeted mists
Around him as he passed.

And the voice forever cried,
"Balder the Beautiful
Is dead, is dead!"
And died away
Through the dreary night,
In accents of despair.

Balder the Beautiful,
God of the summer sun,
Fairest of all the Gods!

Light from his forehead beamed,
Runes were upon his tongue,
As on the warrior's sword.

All things in earth and air
Bound were by magic spell
Never to do him harm;
Even the plants and stones
All save the mistletoe,
The sacred mistletoe!

Hœder, the blind old God,
Whose feet are shod with silence,
Pierced through that gentle breast
With his sharp spear, by fraud,
Made of the mistletoe!
The accursed mistletoe!

They laid him in his ship,
With horse and harness,
As on a funeral pyre.
Odin placed
A ring upon his finger,
And whispered in his ear.

They launched the burning ship!
It floated far away
Over the misty sea,
Till like the sun it seemed,
Sinking beneath the waves.
Balder returned no more!

So perish the old Gods!
But out of the sea of Time
Rises a new land of song,
Fairer than the old.
Over its meadows green
Walk the young bards and sing.

Build it again,
O ye bards,
Fairer than before;

Ye fathers of the new race,
Feed upon morning dew,
Sing the new Song of Love!

The law of force is dead!
The law of love prevails!
Thor, the thunderer,
Shall rule the earth no more,
No more, with threats,
Challenge the meek Christ.

Sing no more,
O ye bards of the North,
Of Vikings and of Jarls!
Of the days of Eld
Preserve the freedom only,
Not the deeds of blood!

SONNET

On Mrs. Kemble's Reading from Shakespeare

O precious evenings! all too swiftly sped!
Leaving us heirs to amplest heritages
Of all the best thoughts of the greatest sages,
And giving tongues unto the silent dead!
How our hearts glowed and trembled as she read,
Interpreting by tones the wondrous pages
Of the great poet who foreruns the ages,
Anticipating all that shall be said!
O happy Reader! having for thy text
The magic book, whose Sibylline leaves have caught
The rarest essence of all human thought!
O happy Poet! by no critic vext!
How must thy listening spirit now rejoice
To be interpreted by such a voice!

THE SINGERS

God sent his singers upon earth
With songs of sadness and of mirth,

That they might touch the hearts of men,
And bring them back to heaven again.

The first a youth, with soul of fire
Held in his hand a golden lyre;
Through groves he wandered, and by streams,
Playing the music of our dreams.

The second, with a bearded face,
Stood singing in the market-place,
And stirred with accents deep and loud
The hearts of all the listening crowd.

A gray, old man, the third and last,
Sang in cathedrals dim and vast,
While the majestic organ rolled
Contrition from its mouths of gold.

And those who heard the Singers three
Disputed which the best might be;
For still their music seemed to start
Discordant echoes in each heart.

But the great Master said, "I see
No best in kind, but in degree;
I gave a various gift to each,
To charm, to strengthen, and to teach.

"These are the three great chords of might,
And he whose ear is tuned aright
Will hear no discord in the three,
But the most perfect harmony."

SUSPIRIA

Take them, O Death! and bear away
  Whatever thou canst call thine own!
Thine image, stamped upon this clay,
  Doth give thee that, but that alone!

Take them, O Grave! and let them lie
  Folded upon thy narrow shelves
As garments by the soul laid by,
  And precious only to ourselves!

Take them, O great Eternity!
Our little life is but a gust,
That bends the branches of thy tree,
And trails its blossoms in the dust.

HYMN

For My Brother's Ordination

Christ to the young man said: "Yet one thing
more;
If thou wouldst perfect be,
Sell all thou hast and give it to the poor,
And come and follow me!"

Within this temple Christ again, unseen,
Those sacred words hath said,
And his invisible hands to-day have been
Laid on a young man's head.

And evermore beside him on his way
The unseen Christ shall move,
That he may lean upon his arm and say,
"Dost thou, dear Lord, approve?"

Beside him at the marriage feast shall be,
To make the scene more fair;
Beside him in the dark Gethsemane
Of pain and midnight prayer.

O holy trust! O endless sense of rest!
Like the belovèd John
To lay his head upon the Saviour's breast,
And thus to journey on!

THE BLIND GIRL OF CASTÈL-CUILLÈ, [1]

From the Gascon of Jasmin

Only the Lowland tongue of Scotland might
Rehearse this little tragedy aright;
Let me attempt it with an English quill;
And take, O Reader, for the deed the will.

I

At the foot of the mountain height
Where is perched Castèl-Cuillè.
When the apple, the plum, and the almond tree
In the plain below were growing white,
This is the song one might perceive
On a Wednesday morn of Saint Joseph's Eve:

"The roads should blossom, the roads should bloom,
So fair a bride shall leave her home!
Should blossom and bloom with garlands gay,
So fair a bride shall pass to-day!"

This old Te Deum, rustic rites attending,
Seemed from the clouds descending;
When lo! a merry company
Of rosy village girls, clean as the eye,
Each one with her attendant swain,
Came to the cliff, all singing the same strain;
Resembling there, so near unto the sky,

Rejoicing angels, that kind Heaven has sent
For their delight and our encouragement.
Together blending,
And soon descending
The narrow sweep
Of the hillside steep,

---

[1] Jasmin, the author of this beautiful poem, is to the South of France what Burns is to the South of Scotland,—the representative of the heart of the people,—one of those happy bards who are born with their mouths full of birds (*la bouco pleno d'aouzelous*). He has written his own biography in a poetic form, and the simple narrative of his poverty, his struggles, and his triumphs is very touching. He still lives at Agen, on the Garonne; and long may he live there to delight his native land with native songs!

They wind aslant
Towards Saint Amant,
Through leafy alleys
Of verdurous valleys
With merry sallies,
Singing their chant:

"The roads should blossom, the roads should bloom,
So fair a bride shall leave her home!
Should blosom and bloom with garlands gay,
So fair a bride shall pass to-day!"

It is Baptiste, and his affianced maiden,
With garlands for the bridal laden!

The sky was blue; without one cloud of gloom,
    The sun of March was shining brightly,
And to the air the freshening wind gave lightly
    Its breathings of perfume.

When one beholds the dusky hedges blossom,
A rustic bridal, ah! how sweet it is!
    To sounds of joyous melodies,
That touch with tenderness the trembling bosom,
        A band of maidens
        Gayly frolicking,
        A band of youngsters
        Wildly rollicking!
            Kissing,
            Caressing,
        With fingers pressing,
            Till in the veriest
        Madness of mirth, as they dance,
        They retreat and advance,
            Trying whose laugh shall be loudest and merriest;
        While the bride, with roguish eyes,
    Sporting with them, now escapes and cries:
        "Those who catch me
            Married verily
            This year shall be!"
        And all pursue with eager haste,
        And all attain what they pursue,
And touch her pretty apron fresh and new,

And the linen kirtle round her waist.
Meanwhile, whence comes it that among
These youthful maidens fresh and fair,
So joyous, with such laughing air,
Baptiste stands sighing, with silent tongue?
And yet the bride is fair and young!
Is it Saint Joseph would say to us all,
That love, o'er-hasty, precedeth a fall?
O, no! for a maiden frail, I trow,
Never bore so lofty a brow!
What lovers! they give not a single caress!
To see them so careless and cold to-day,
These are grand people, one would say.
What ails Baptiste? what grief doth him oppress?
It is, that, half way up the hill,
In yon cottage, by whose walls
Stand the cart-house and the stalls,
Dwelleth the blind orphan still
Daughter of a veteran old;
And you must know, one year ago,
That Margaret, the young and tender,
Was the village pride and splendor,
And Baptiste her lover bold.
Love, the deceiver, them ensnared;
For them the altar was prepared
But alas! the summer's blight,
The dread disease that none can stay,
The pestilence that walks by night,
Took the young bride's sight away.
All at the father's stern command was changed;
Their peace was gone, but not their love estranged.
Wearied at home, ere long the lover fled;
Returned but three short days ago,
The golden chain they round him throw,
He is enticed, and onward led
To marry Angela, and yet
Is thinking ever of Margaret.

Then suddenly a maiden cried,
"Anna, Theresa, Mary, Kate!

Here comes the cripple Jane!" And by a fountain's side
    A woman, bent and gray with years,
    Under the mulberry-trees appears,
    And all towards her run, as fleet,
    As had they wings upon their feet.
    It is that Jane, the cripple Jane,
    Is a soothsayer, wary and kind.
She telleth fortunes, and none complain.
    She promises one a village swain,
    Another a happy wedding-day,
    And the bride a lovely boy straightway.
    All comes to pass as she avers;
    She never deceives, she never errs.

    But for this once the village seer
    Wears a countenance severe,
And from beneath her eyebrows thin and white
    Her two eyes flash like cannons bright
    Aimed at the bridegroom in waistcoat blue,
    Who, like a statue, stands in view;
    Changing color, as well he might,
    When the beldame wrinkled and gray
    Takes the young bride by the hand,
    And, with the tip of her reedy wand
    Making the sign of the cross, doth say:—
    "Thoughtless Angela, beware!
    Lest, when thou weddest this false bridegroom,
    Thou diggest for thyself a tomb!"
And she was silent; and the maidens fair
Saw from each eye escape a swollen tear;
But on a little streamlet silver-clear,
    What are two drops of turbid rain?
    Saddened a moment, the bridal train
    Resumed the dance and song again;
The bridegroom only was pale with fear;—
    And down green alleys
    Of verdurous valleys,
    With merry sallies,
    They sang the refrain:—

"The roads should blossom, the roads should bloom,
So fair a bride shall leave her home!
Should blossom and bloom with garlands gay,
So fair a bride shall pass to-day!"

II

And by suffering worn and weary,
But beautiful as some fair angel yet,
    Thus lamented Margaret,
    In her cottage lone and dreary:—
    "He has arrived! arrived at last!
Yet Jane has named him not these three days past;
    Arrived! yet keeps aloof so far!
And knows that of my night he is the star!
Knows that long months I waited alone, benighted,
And count the moments since he went away!
Come! keep the promise of that happier day,
That I may keep the faith to thee I plighted!
What joy have I without thee? what delight?
Grief wastes my life, and makes it misery;
Day for the others ever, but for me
    Forever night! forever night!
When he is gone 't is dark! my soul is sad!
I suffer! O my God! come, make me glad.
When he is near, no thoughts of day intrude;
Day has blue heavens, but Baptiste has blue eyes!
Within them shines for me a heaven of love,
A heaven all happiness, like that above,
    No more of grief! no more of lassitude!
Earth I forget,—and heaven, and all distresses,
When seated by my side my hand he presses;
    But when alone, remember all!
Where is Baptiste? he hears not when I call!
A branch of ivy, dying on the ground,
    I need some bough to twine around!
In pity come! be to my suffering kind!
True love, they say, in grief doth more abound!
    What then—when one is blind?

"Who knows? perhaps I am forsaken!
Ah! woe is me! then bear me to my grave!
O God! what thoughts within me waken!
Away! he will return! I do but rave!
 He will return! I need not fear!
 He swore it by our Saviour dear;
 He could not come at his own will;
 Is weary, or perhaps is ill!
 Perhaps his heart, in this disguise,
 Prepares for me some sweet surprise!
But some one comes! Though blind, my heart can see!
And that deceives me not! 'tis he! 'tis he!"

 And the door ajar is set,
 And poor, confiding Margaret
Rises, with outstretched arms, but sightless eyes;
'T is only Paul, her brother, who thus cries:—
 "Angela the bride has passed!
 I saw the wedding guests go by;
Tell me, my sister, why were we not asked?
 For all are there but you and I!"

 "Angela married! and not send
 To tell her secret unto me!
 O speak! who may the bridegroom be?"
 "My sister, 't is Baptiste, thy friend!"

A cry the blind girl gave, but nothing said;
A milky whiteness spreads upon her cheeks;
 An icy hand, as heavy as lead,
 Descending, as her brother speaks,
 Upon her heart, that has ceased to beat,
 Suspends awhile its life and heat.
She stands beside the boy, now sore distressed,
A wax Madonna as a peasant dressed.

 At length, the bridal song again
 Brings her back to her sorrow and pain.
 "Hark! the joyous airs are ringing!
 Sister, dost thou hear them singing?
 How merrily they laugh and jest!
 Would we were bidden with the rest!

I would don my hose of homespun gray,
And my doublet of linen striped and gay!
Perhaps they will come; for they do not wed
Till to-morrow at seven o'clock, it is said!"
"I know it!" answered Margaret;
Whom the vision, with aspect black as jet,
Mastered again; and its hand of ice
Held her heart crushed, as in a vice!
"Paul, be not sad! 'T is a holiday;
To-morrow put on thy doublet gay!
But leave me now for a while alone."
Away, with a hop and a jump, went Paul,
And, as he whistled along the hall,
Entered Jane, the crippled crone.

"Holy Virgin! what dreadful heat!
I am faint, and weary, and out of breath;
But thou art cold,—art chill as death;
My little friend! what ails thee, sweet?"

"Nothing! I heard them singing home the bride,
And, as I listened to the song,
I thought my turn would come ere long,
Thou knowest it is at Whitsuntide.
Thy cards forsooth can never lie,
To me such joy they prophesy,
Thy skill shall be vaunted far and wide
When they behold him at my side.
And poor Baptiste, what sayest thou?
It must seem long to him;—methinks I see him now!"
Jane, shuddering, her hand doth press:
"Thy love I cannot all approve;
We must not trust too much to happiness;—
Go, pray to God, that thou mayst love him less!"
"The more I pray, the more I love!
It is no sin, for God is on my side!"
It was enough; and Jane no more replied.

Now to all hope her heart is barred and cold;
But to deceive the beldame old

She takes a sweet, contented air;
Speak of foul weather or of fair,
At every word the maiden smiles!
Thus the beguiler she beguiles;
So that, departing at the evening's close,
She says, "She may be saved! she nothing knows!"

Poor Jane, the cunning sorceress!
Now that thou wouldst, thou art no prophetess!
This morning, in the fulness of thy heart,
Thou wast so, far beyond thine art!

III

Now rings the bell, nine times reverberating,
And the white daybreak, stealing up the sky,
Sees in two cottages two maidens waiting,
How differently!
Queen of a day, by flatterers caressed,
The one puts on her cross and crown.
Decks with a huge bouquet her breast,
And flaunting, fluttering up and down,
Looks at herself, and cannot rest.

The other, blind, within her little room,
Has neither crown nor flower's perfume;
But in their stead for something gropes apart,
That in a drawer's recess doth lie,
And, 'neath her bodice of bright scarlet dye,
Convulsive clasps it to her heart.

The one, fantastic, light as air,
'Mid kisses ringing,
And joyous singing,
Forgets to say her morning prayer!
The other, with cold drops upon her brow,
Joins her two hands, and kneels upon the floor,
And whispers, as her brother opes the door,
"O God! forgive me now!"

And then the orphan, young and blind,
Conducted by her brother's hand,
Towards the church, through paths unscanned,
With tranquil air, her way doth wind.
Odors of laurel, making her faint and pale,
Round her at times exhale,
And in the sky as yet no sunny ray,
But brumal vapors gray.

Near that castle, fair to see,
Crowded with sculptures old, in every part,
Marvels of nature and of art,
And proud of its name of high degree,
A little chapel, almost bare
At the base of the rock, is builded there;
All glorious that it lifts aloof,
Above each jealous cottage roof,
Its sacred summit, swept by autumn gales,
And its blackened steeple high in air,
Round which the osprey screams and sails.

"Paul, lay thy noisy rattle by!"
Thus Margaret said, "Where are we? we ascend!"
"Yes; seest thou not our journey's end?
Hearest not the osprey from the belfry cry?
The hideous bird, that brings ill luck, we know!
Dost thou remember when our father said,
The night we watched beside his bed,
'O daughter, I am weak and low;
Take care of Paul; I feel that I am dying!'
And thou, and he, and I, all fell to crying?
Then on the roof the osprey screamed aloud;
And here they brought our father in his shroud.
There is his grave; there stands the cross we set;
Why dost thou clasp me so, dear Margaret?
Come in! The bride will be here soon:
Thou tremblest! O my God! thou art going to swoon!"
She could no more,—the blind girl, weak and weary!
A voice seemed crying from that grave so dreary,
"What wouldst thou do, my daughter?"—and she
started;

And quick recoiled, aghast, fainthearted;
But Paul, impatient, urges ever more
     Her steps towards the open door;
And when, beneath her feet, the unhappy maid
Crushes the laurel near the house immortal,
And with her head, as Paul talks on again,
     Touches the crown of filigrane
     Suspended from the low-arched portal,
     No more restrained, no more afraid,
     She walks, as for a feast arrayed,
And in the ancient chapel's sombre night
     They both are lost to sight.

          At length the bell,
          With booming sound,
          Sends forth, resounding round,
Its hymeneal peal o'er rock and down the dell.
     It is broad day, with sunshine and with rain;
          And yet the guests delay not long,
          For soon arrives the bridal train,
          And with it brings the village throng.

In sooth, deceit maketh no mortal gay,
For lo! Baptiste on this triumphant day,
Mute as an idiot, sad as yester-morning,
Thinks only of the beldame's words of warning.
And Angela thinks of her cross, I wis;
To be a bride is all! The pretty lisper
Feels her heart swell to hear all round her whisper,
"How beautiful! how beautiful she is!"
          But she must calm that giddy head,
          For already the Mass is said;
          At the holy table stands the priest;
The wedding ring is blessed; Baptiste receives it;
Ere on the finger of the bride he leaves it,
          He must pronounce one word at least!
'T is spoken; and sudden at the groomsman's side
" 'Tis he!" a well-known voice has cried.
And while the wedding guests all hold their breath,
Opes the confessional, and the blind girl, see!

"Baptiste," she said, "since thou hast wished my death,
As holy water be my blood for thee!"
And calmly in the air a knife suspended!
Doubtless her guardian angel near attended,
    For anguish did its work so well,
  That, ere the fatal stroke descended,
    Lifeless she fell!

  At eve, instead of bridal verse,
  The De Profundis filled the air;
  Decked with flowers a simple hearse
  To the churchyard forth they bear;
  Village girls in robes of snow
  Follow, weeping as they go;
  Nowhere was a smile that day
No, ah no! for each one seemed to say:—

"The roads should mourn and be veiled in gloom,
So fair a corpse shall leave its home!
Should mourn and should weep, ah well-away!
So fair a corpse shall pass to-day."

A CHRISTMAS CAROL [1]

From the Noei Bourguignon de Gui Barozal

    I hear along our street
    Pass the minstrel throngs;
    Hark! they play so sweet,
On their hautboys, Christmas songs!
    Let us by the fire
    Ever higher
Sing them till the night expire!

---

[1] "In the Glossary, the *Suche,* or Yule-log, is this defined:—
"This is a huge log, which is placed on the fire on Christmas Eve,
and which in Burgundy is called, on this account, *lai Suche de Noei.*
Then the father of the family, particularly among the middle classes,
sings solemnly Christmas carols with his wife and children, the small-
est of whom he sends into the corner to pray that the Yule-log may
bear him some sugar-plums. Meanwhile, little parcels of them are
placed under each end of the log, and the children come and pick
them up, believing, in good faith, that the great log has borne them."

In December ring
Every day the chimes;
Loud the gleemen sing
In the streets their merry rhymes.
Let us by the fire
Ever higher
Sing them till the night expire.

Shepherds at the grange,
Where the Babe was born,
Sang, with many a change,
Christmas carols until morn.
Let us by the fire
Ever higher
Sing them till the night expire.

These good people sang
Songs devout and sweet;
While the rafters rang,
There they stood with freezing feet.
Let us by the fire
Ever higher
Sing them till the night expire.

Nuns in frigid cells
At this holy tide,
For want of something else,
Christmas songs at times have tried.
Let us by the fire
Ever higher
Sing them till the night expire.

Washerwomen old,
To the sound they beat,
Sing by rivers cold,
With uncovered heads and feet.
Let us by the fire
Ever higher
Sing them till the night expire.

Who by the fireside stands
Stamps his feet and sings;
But he who blows his hands
Not so gay a carol brings.
Let us by the fire
Ever higher
Sing them till the night expire!

MISCELLANEOUS

THE VILLAGE BLACKSMITH

UNDER a spreading chestnut tree
    The village smithy stands;
The smith, a mighty man is he,
    With large and sinewy hands;
And the muscles of his brawny arms
    Are strong as iron bands.

His hair is crisp, and black, and long,
    His face is like the tan;
His brow is wet with honest sweat,
    He earns whate'er he can,
And looks the whole world in the face,
    For he owes not any man.

Week in, week out, from morn till night,
    You can hear his bellows blow;
You can hear him swing his heavy sledge,
    With measured beat and slow,
Like a sexton ringing the village bell,
    When the evening sun is low.

And children coming home from school
    Look in at the open door;
They love to see the flaming forge,
    And hear the bellows roar,
And catch the burning sparks that fly
    Like chaff from a threshing floor.

He goes on Sunday to the church,
    And sits among his boys;
He hears the parson pray and preach,
    He hears his daughter's voice,
Singing in the village choir,
    And it makes his heart rejoice.

It sounds to him like her mother's voice,
  Singing in Paradise!
He needs must think of her once more,
  How in the grave she lies;
And with his hard, rough hand he wipes
  A tear out of his eyes.

Toiling,—rejoicing,—sorrowing,
  Onward through life he goes;
Each morning sees some task begin,
  Each evening sees it close;
Something attempted, something done,
  Has earned a night's repose.

Thanks, thanks to thee, my worthy friend,
  For the lesson thou hast taught!
Thus at the flaming forge of life
  Our fortunes must be wrought;
Thus on its sounding anvil shaped
  Each burning deed and thought!

ENDYMION

The rising moon has hid the stars;
Her level rays, like golden bars,
    Lie on the landscape green,
    With shadows brown between.

And silver white the river gleams,
As if Diana, in her dreams,
    Had dropt her silver bow
    Upon the meadows low.

On such a tranquil night as this,
She woke Endymion with a kiss,
    When, sleeping in the grove,
    He dreamed not of her love.

Like Dian's kiss, unaskt, unsought,
Love gives itself, but is not bought!
    Nor voice, nor sound betrays
    Its deep, impassioned gaze.

It comes,—the beautiful, the free,
The crown of all humanity,—
 In silence and alone
 To seek the elected one.

It lifts the boughs, whose shadows deep,
Are Life's oblivion, the soul's sleep,
 And kisses the closed eyes
 Of him, who slumbering lies.

O, weary hearts! O, slumbering eyes!
O, drooping souls, whose destinies
 Are fraught with fear and pain,
 Ye shall be loved again!

No one is so accurst by fate,
No one so utterly desolate,
 But some heart, though unknown,
 Responds unto his own.

Responds,—as if with unseen wings,
An angel touched its quivering strings;
 And whispers in its song,
 "Where hast thou stayed so long!"

THE TWO LOCKS OF HAIR

FROM THE GERMAN OF PFIZER

A youth, light-hearted and content,
 I wander through the world;
Here, Arab-like, is pitched my tent
 And straight again is furled.

Yet oft I dream, that once a wife
 Close to my heart was locked,
And in the sweet repose of life
 A blessèd child I rocked.

I wake! Away that dream,—away!
 Too long did it remain!
So long, that both by night and day
 It ever comes again.

The end lies ever in my thought;
 To a grave so cold and deep
The mother beautiful was brought;
 Then dropt the child asleep.

But now the dream is wholly o'er,
 I bathe mine eyes and see;
And wander through the world once more,
 A youth so light and free.

Two locks,—and they are wondrous fair,—
 Left me that vision mild;
The brown is from the mother's hair,
 The blond is from the child.

And when I see that lock of gold,
 Pale grows the evening-red;
And when the dark lock I behold,
 I wish that I were dead.

IT IS NOT ALWAYS MAY

NO HAY PAJAROS EN LOS NIDOS DE ANTANO
Spanish Proverb

The sun is bright,—the air is clear,
 The darting swallows soar and sing,
And from the stately elms I hear
 The blue-bird prophesying Spring.

So blue yon winding river flows,
 It seems an outlet from the sky,
Where waiting till the west wind blows,
 The freighted clouds at anchor lie.

All things are new;—the buds, the leaves,
 That gild the elm-tree's nodding crest,
And even the nest beneath the eaves;—
 There are no birds in last year's nest!

All things rejoice in youth and love,
 The fulness of their first delight!
And learn from the soft heavens above
 The melting tenderness of night.

Maiden, that read'st this simple rhyme,
  Enjoy thy youth, it will not stay;
Enjoy the fragrance of thy prime,
  For O! it is not always May!

Enjoy the Spring of Love and Youth,
  To some good angel leave the rest;
For time will teach thee soon the truth,
  There are no birds in last year's nest!

THE RAINY DAY

The day is cold, and dark, and dreary;
It rains, and the wind is never weary;
The vine still clings to the mouldering wall,
But at every gust the dead leaves fall,
  And the day is dark and dreary.

My life is cold, and dark, and dreary;
It rains, and the wind is never weary;
My thoughts still cling to the mouldering Past,
But the hopes of youth fall thick in the blast,
  And the days are dark and dreary.

Be still, sad heart! and cease repining;
Behind the clouds is the sun still shining;
Thy fate is the common fate of all,
Into each life some rain must fall,
  Some days must be dark and dreary.

GOD'S-ACRE

I like that ancient Saxon phrase which calls
  The burial-ground God's-Acre! It is just;
It consecrates each grave within its walls,
  And breathes a benison o'er the sleeping dust.

God's-Acre! Yes, that blessèd name imparts
  Comfort to those who in the grave have sown
The seed, that they had garnered in their hearts,
  Their bread of life, alas! no more their own.

Into its furrows shall we all be cast,
  In the sure faith, that we shall rise again
At the great harvest, when the archangel's blast
  Shall winnow, like a fan, the chaff, and grain.

Then shall the good stand in immortal bloom,
  In the fair gardens of that second birth;
And each bright blossom mingle its perfume
  With that of flowers, which never bloomed on earth.

With thy rude ploughshare, Death, turn up the sod,
  And spread the furrow for the seed we sow;
This is the field and Acre of our God,
  This is the place where human harvests grow!

TO THE RIVER CHARLES

River! that in silence windest
  Through the meadows, bright and free,
Till at length thy rest thou findest
  In the bosom of the sea!

Four long years of mingled feeling,
  Half in rest, and half in strife,
I have seen thy waters stealing
  Onward, like the stream of life.

Thou hast taught me, Silent River!
  Many a lesson, deep and long;
Thou hast been a generous giver;
  I can give thee but a song.

Oft in sadness and in illness,
  I have watched thy current glide,
Till the beauty of its stillness
  Overflowed me, like a tide.

And in better hours and brighter,
  When I saw thy waters gleam,
I have felt my heart beat lighter,
  And leap onward with thy stream.

Not for this alone I love thee,
  Nor because thy waves of blue
From celestial seas above thee
  Take their own celestial hue.

Where yon shadowy woodlands hide thee,
  And thy waters disappear,
Friends I love have dwelt beside thee,
  And have made thy margin dear.

More than this;—thy name reminds me
  Of three friends, all true and tried;
And that name, like magic, binds me
  Closer, closer to thy side.

Friends my soul with joy remembers!
  How like quivering flames they start,
When I fan the living embers
  On the hearth-stone of my heart!

'T is for this, thou Silent River!
  That my spirit leans to thee;
Thou hast been a generous giver,
  Take this idle song from me.

BLIND BARTIMEUS

Blind Bartimeus at the gates
Of Jericho in darkness waits;
He hears the crowd;—he hears a breath
Say, "It is Christ of Nazareth!"
And calls, in tones of agony,
'Ιησοῦ, ἐλέησόν με!

The thronging multitudes increase;
Blind Bartimeus, hold thy peace!
But still, above the noisy crowd,
The beggar's cry is shrill and loud
Until they say, "He calleth thee!"
Θάρσει, ἔγειραι, φωνεῖ σε!

Then saith the Christ, as silent stands
The crowd, "What wilt thou at my hands?"
And he replies, "O give me light!"
Rabbi, restore the blind man's sight!

And Jesus answers, "Ὕπαλε,
Ἡ πίστις σου σέσωκέ σε!

Ye that have eyes, yet cannot see,
In darkness and in misery,
Recall those mighty Voices Three,
Ἰησοῦ ἐλέησόν με!
θάρσει, ἔγειραι, ὕπαγε!
Ἡ πίστις σου σέσωκε σε!

THE GOBLET OF LIFE

Filled is Life's goblet to the brim,
And though my eyes with tears are dim,
I see its sparkling bubbles swim,
And chaunt a melancholy hymn
    With solemn voice and slow.

No purple flowers,—no garlands green,
Conceal the goblet's shade or sheen,
Nor maddening draughts of Hippocrene,
Like gleams of sunshine, flash between
    Thick leaves of mistletoe.

This goblet, wrought with curious art,
Is filled with waters, that upstart,
When the deep fountains of the heart,
By strong convulsions rent apart,
    Are running all to waste.

And as it mantling passes round,
With fennel it is wreathed and crowned,
Whose seed and foliage sun-imbrowned,
Are in its waters steeped and drowned,
    And give a bitter taste.

Above the lowly plants it towers,
The fennel, with its yellow flowers,
And in an earlier age than ours
Was gifted with the wondrous powers,
    Lost vision to restore.

It gave new strength, and fearless mood;
And gladiators, fierce and rude,
Mingled it in their daily food;
And he who battled and subdued,
    A wreath of fennel wore.

Then in Life's goblet freely press,
The leaves that give it bitterness,
Nor prize the colored waters less,
For in thy darkness and distress
    New light and strength they give!

And he who has not learned to know
How false its sparkling bubbles show,
How bitter are the drops of woe,
With which its brim may overflow,
    He has not learned to live.

The prayer of Ajax was for light;
Through all that dark and desperate fight,
The blackness of that noonday night,
He asked but the return of sight,
    To see his foeman's face.

Let our unceasing, earnest prayer
Be, too, for light,—for strength to bear
Our portion of the weight of care,
That crushes into dumb despair
    One half the human race.

O suffering, sad humanity!
O ye afflicted ones, who lie
Steeped to the lips in misery,
Longing, and yet afraid to die,
    Patient, though sorely tried!

I pledge you in this cup of grief,
Where floats the fennel's bitter leaf!
The Battle of our Life is brief,
The alarm,—the struggle,—the relief,—
    Then sleep we side by side.

MAIDENHOOD

Maiden! with the meek, brown eyes,
In whose orbs a shadow lies
Like the dusk in evening skies!

Thou whose locks outshine the sun
Golden tresses, wreathed in one,
As the braided streamlets run!

Standing, with reluctant feet,
Where the brook and river meet,
Womanhood and childhood fleet!

Gazing, with a timid glance,
On the brooklet's swift advance,
On the river's broad expanse!

Deep and still, that gliding stream
Beautiful to thee must seem,
As the river of a dream.

Then why pause with indecision,
When bright angels in thy vision
Beckon thee to fields Elysian?

Seest thou shadows sailing by,
As the dove, with startled eye,
Sees the falcon's shadow fly?

Hearest thou voices on the shore,
That our ears perceive no more,
Deafened by the cataract's roar?

O. thou child of many prayers!
Life hath quicksands,—Life hath snares!
Care and age come unawares!

Like the swell of some sweet tune,
Morning rises into noon,
May glides onward into June.

Childhood is the bough, where slumbered
Birds and blossoms many-numbered;—
Age, that bough with snows encumbered.

Gather, then, each flower that grows,
When the young heart overflows,
To embalm that tent of snows.

Bear a lily in thy hand;
Gates of brass cannot withstand
The touch of that magic wand.

Bear through sorrow, wrong, and ruth,
In thy heart the dew of youth,
On thy lips the smile of truth.

O, that dew, like balm, shall steal
Into wounds, that cannot heal,
Even as sleep our eyes doth seal;

And that smile, like sunshine, dart
Into many a sunless heart,
For a smile of God thou art.

EXCELSIOR

The shades of night were falling fast,
As through an Alpine village passed
A youth, who bore, 'mid snow and ice,
A banner with the strange device,
        Excelsior!

His brow was sad; his eye beneath,
Flashed like a falchion from its sheath,
And like a silver clarion rung
The accents of that unknown tongue,
        Excelsior!

In happy homes he saw the light
Of household fires gleam warm and bright;
Above, the spectral glaciers shone,
And from his lips escaped a groan,
        Excelsior!

"Try not the Pass!" the old man said;
"Dark lowers the tempest overhead,
The roaring torrent is deep and wide!"
And loud that clarion voice replied
        Excelsior!

"O stay," the maiden said, "and rest
Thy weary head upon this breast!"
A tear stood in his bright blue eye,
But still he answered, with a sigh,
      Excelsior!

"Beware the pine-tree's withered branch!
Beware the awful avalanche!"
This was the peasant's last Good-night,
A voice replied, far up the height,
      Excelsior!

At break of day, as heavenward
The pious monks of Saint Bernard
Uttered the oft-repeated prayer,
A voice cried through the startled air,
      Excelsior!

A traveller, by the faithful hound,
Half-buried in the snow was found,
Still grasping in his hand of ice
That banner with the strange device,
      Excelsior!

There in the twilight cold and gray,
Lifeless, but beautiful, he lay,
And from the sky, serene and far,
A voice fell, like a falling star,
      Excelsior!

PROMETHEUS

OR THE POET'S FORETHOUGHT

Of Prometheus, how undaunted
   On Olympus' shining bastions
His audacious foot he planted,
Myths are told and songs are chaunted,
   Full of promptings and suggestions.

Beautiful is the tradition
  Of that flight through heavenly portals,
The old classic superstition
Of the theft and the transmission
  Of the fire of the Immortals!

First the deed of noble daring,
  Born of heavenward aspiration,
Then the fire with mortals sharing,
Then the vulture,—the despairing
  Cry of pain on crags Caucasian.

All is but a symbol painted
  Of the Poet, Prophet, Seer;
Only those are crowned and sainted
Who with grief have been acquainted,
  Making nations nobler, freer.

In their feverish exultations,
  In their triumph and their yearning,
In their passionate pulsations,
In their words among the nations,
  The promethean fire is burning.

Shall it, then, be unavailing,
  All this toil for human culture?
Through the cloud-rack, dark and trailing,
Must they see above them sailing
  O'er life's barren crags the vulture?

Such a fate as this was Dante's,
  By defeat and exile maddened;
Thus were Milton and Cervantes,
Nature's priests and Corybantes,
  By affliction touched and saddened.

But the glories so transcendent
  That around their memories cluster,
And, on all their steps attendant,
Make their darkened lives resplendent
  With such gleams of inward lustre!

All the melodies mysterious,
  Through the dreary darkness chaunted;
Thoughts in attitudes imperious,
Voices soft, and deep, and serious,
  Words that whispered, songs that haunted!

All the soul in rapt suspension,
  All the quivering, palpitating
Chords of life in utmost tension,
With the fervor of invention,
  With the rapture of creating!

Ah, Prometheus! heaven-scaling!
  In such hours of exultation
Even the faintest heart, unquailing,
Might behold the vulture sailing
  Round the cloudy crags Caucasian!

Though to all there is not given
  Strength for such sublime endeavor,
Thus to scale the walls of heaven,
And to leaven with fiery leaven
  All the hearts of men for ever;

Yet all bards, whose hearts unblighted
  Honor and believe the presage,
Hold aloft their torches lighted,
Gleaming through the realms benighted,
  As they onward bear the message!

THE LADDER OF ST. AUGUSTINE

Saint Augustine! well hast thou said,
  That of our vices we can frame
A ladder,[1] if we will but tread
  Beneath our feet each deed of shame!

All common things, each day's events,
  That with the hour begin and end,
Our pleasures and our discontents,
  Are rounds by which we may ascend.

[1] The words of St. Augustine are, "De vitiis nostris scalam nobis facimus, si vitia ipsa calcamus." Sermon III. *De Ascensione.*

The low desire, the base design,
   That makes another's virtues less;
The revel of the ruddy wine,
   And all occasions of excess;

The longing for ignoble things;
   The strife for triumph more than truth;
The hardening of the heart, that brings
   Irreverence for the dreams of youth;

All thoughts of ill; all evil deeds,
   That have their root in thoughts of ill;
Whatever hinders or impedes
   The action of the nobler will;—

All these must first be trampled down
   Beneath our feet, if we would gain
In the bright fields of fair renown
   The right of eminent domain.

We have not wings, we cannot soar;
   But we have feet to scale and climb
By slow degrees, by more and more,
   The cloudy summits of our time.

The mighty pyramids of stone
   That wedge-like cleave the desert airs,
When nearer seen, and better known,
   Are but gigantic flights of stairs.

The distant mountains, that uprear
   Their solid bastions to the skies,
Are crossed by pathways, that appear
   As we to higher levels rise.

The heights by great men reached and kept
   Were not attained by sudden flight,
But they, while their companions slept,
   Were toiling upward in the night.

Standing on what too long we bore
   With shoulders bent and downcast eyes,
We may discern—unseen before—
   A path to higher destinies.

Nor deem the irrevocable Past,
  As wholly wasted, wholly vain
If, rising on its wrecks, at last
  To something nobler we attain.

THE PHANTOM SHIP [1]

In Mather's Magnalia Christi,
  Of the old colonial time,
May be found in prose the legend
  That is here set down in rhyme.

A ship sailed from New Haven,
  And the keen and frosty airs,
That filled her sails at parting,
  Were heavy with good men's prayers.

"O Lord! if it be thy pleasure"—
  Thus prayed the old divine—
"To bury our friends in the ocean,
  Take them, for they are thine!"

But Master Lamberton muttered,
  And under his breath said he,
"This ship is so crank and walty
  I fear our grave she will be!"

And the ships that came from England,
  When the winter months were gone,
Brought no tidings of this vessel
  Nor of Master Lamberton.

This put the people to praying
  That the Lord would let them hear
What in his greater wisdom
  He had done with friends so dear.

[1] A detailed account of this "apparition of a Ship in the Air" is given by Cotton Mather in his Magnalia Christi, Book I, Ch. VI. It is contained in a letter from the Rev. James Pierpont, Pastor of New Haven. To this account Mather adds these words:—
  "Reader, there being yet living so many credible gentlemen, that were eye-witnesses of this wonderful thing, I venture to publish it for a thing as undoubted as 't is wonderful."

And at last their prayers were answered:—
    It was in the month of June,
An hour before the sunset
    Of a windy afternoon,

When, steadily steering landward,
    A ship was seen below,
And they knew it was Lamberton, Master,
    Who sailed so long ago.

On she came, with a cloud of canvas,
    Right against the wind that blew,
Until the eye could distinguish
    The faces of the crew.

Then fell her straining topmasts,
    Hanging tangled in the shrouds,
And her sails were loosened and lifted,
    And blown away like clouds.

And the masts, with all their rigging,
    Fell slowly, one by one,
And the hulk dilated and vanished,
    As a sea-mist in the sun!

And the people who saw this marvel
    Each said unto his friend,
That this was the mould of their vessel,
    And thus her tragic end.

And the pastor of the village
    Gave thanks to God in prayer,
That, to quiet their troubled spirits,
    He had sent this Ship of Air.

THE WARDEN OF THE CINQUE PORTS

A mist was driving down the British Channel,
    The day was just begun,
And through the window-panes, on floor and panel,
    Streamed the red autumn sun.

It glanced on flowing flag and rippling pennon,
    And the white sails of ships;
And, from the frowning rampart, the black cannon
    Hailed it with feverish lips.

Sandwich and Romney, Hastings, Hythe, and Dover
    Were all alert that day,
To see the French war-steamers speeding over,
    When the fog cleared away.

Sullen and silent, and like couchant lions,
    Their cannon, through the night,
Holding their breath, had watched, in grim defiance,
    The sea-coast opposite.

And now they roared at drum-beat from their stations
    On every citadel;
Each answering each, with morning salutations,
    That all was well.

And down the coast, all taking up the burden,
    Replied the distant forts,
As if to summon from his sleep the Warden
    And Lord of the Cinque Ports.

Him shall no sunshine from the fields of azure,
    No drum-beat from the wall,
No morning gun from the black fort's embrasure,
    Awaken with its call!

No more, surveying with an eye impartial
    The long line of the coast,
Shall the gaunt figure of the old Field Marshal
    Be seen upon his post!

For in the night, unseen, a single warrior,
    In sombre harness mailed,
Dreaded of man, and surnamed the Destroyer,
    The rampart wall has scaled.

He passed into the chamber of the sleeper,
    The dark and silent room,
And as he entered, darker grew, and deeper,
    The silence and the gloom.

He did not pause to parley or dissemble,
    But smote the Warden hoar;
Ah! what a blow! that made all England tremble
    And groan from shore to shore.

Meanwhile, without, the surly cannon waited,
    The sun rose bright o'erhead;
Nothing in Nature's aspect intimated
    That a great man was dead.

HAUNTED HOUSES

All houses wherein men have lived and died
    Are haunted houses. Through the open doors
The harmless phantoms on their errands glide,
    With feet that make no sound upon the floors.

We meet them at the door-way, on the stair,
    Along the passages they come and go,
Impalpable impressions on the air,
    A sense of something moving to and fro.

There are more guests at table than the hosts
    Invited; the illuminated hall
Is thronged with quiet, inoffensive ghosts,
    As silent as the pictures on the wall.

The stranger at my fireside cannot see
    The forms I see, nor hear the sounds I hear;
He but perceives what is; while unto me
    All that has been is visible and clear.

We have no title-deeds to house or lands;
    Owners and occupants of earlier dates
From graves forgotten stretch their dusty hands,
    And hold in mortmain still their old estates.

The spirit-world around this world of sense
    Floats like an atmosphere, and everywhere
Wafts through these earthly mists and vapors dense
    A vital breath of more ethereal air.

Our little lives are kept in equipoise
By opposite attractions and desires;
The struggle of the instinct that enjoys,
And the more noble instinct that aspires.

These perturbations, this perpetual jar
Of earthly wants and aspirations high,
Come from the influence of an unseen star,
An undiscovered planet in our sky.

And as the moon from some dark gate of cloud
Throws o'er the sea a floating bridge of light,
Across whose trembling planks our fancies crowd
Into the realm of mystery and night,—

So from the world of spirits there descends
A bridge of light, connecting it with this,
O'er whose unsteady floor, that sways and bends,
Wander our thoughts above the dark abyss.

IN THE CHURCHYARD AT CAMBRIDGE

In the village churchyard she lies,
Dust is in her beautiful eyes,
  No more she breathes, nor feels, nor stirs;
At her feet and at her head
Lies a slave to attend the dead,
  But their dust is white as hers.

Was she a lady of high degree,
So much in love with the vanity
  And foolish pomp of this world of ours?
Or was it Christian charity,
And lowliness and humility,
  The richest and rarest of all dowers?

Who shall tell us? No one speaks;
No color shoots into those cheeks,
  Either of anger or of pride,
At the rude question we have asked;
Nor will the mystery be unmasked
  By those who are sleeping at her side.

Hereafter?—And do you think to look
On the terrible pages of that Book
   To find her failings, faults, and errors?
Ah, you will then have other cares,
In your own short-comings and despairs,
   In your own secret sins and terrors!

THE EMPEROR'S BIRD'S-NEST

Once the Emperor Charles of Spain,
   With his swarthy, grave commanders,
I forget in what campaign,
Long besieged, in mud and rain,
   Some old frontier town of Flanders.

Up and down the dreary camp,
   In great boots of Spanish leather,
Striding with a measured tramp,
These Hidalgos, dull and damp,
   Cursed the Frenchmen, cursed the weather.

Thus as to and fro they went
   Over upland and through hollow,
Giving their impatience vent,
Perched upon the Emperor's tent,
   In her nest, they spied a swallow.

Yes, it was a swallow's nest,
   Built of clay and hair of horses,
Mane, or tail, or dragoon's crest,
Found on hedgerows east and west,
   After skirmish of the forces.

Then an old Hildalgo said,
   As he twirled his gray mustachio,
"Sure this swallow overhead
Thinks the Emperor's tent a shed,
   And the Emperor but a Macho!" [1]

---

[1] *Macho*, in Spanish, signifies a mule. *Golondrina* is the feminine form of *Golondrino*, a swallow, and also a cant name for a deserter.

Hearing his imperial name
　Coupled with those words of malice,
Half in anger, half in shame,
Forth the great campaigner came
　Slowly from his canvas palace.

"Let no hand the bird molest,"
　Said he solemnly, "nor hurt her!"
Adding then, by way of jest,
"Golondrina is my guest,
　'T is the wife of some deserter!"

Swift as bowstring speeds a shaft,
　Through the camp was spread the rumor,
And the soldiers, as they quaffed
Flemish beer at dinner, laughed
　At the Emperor's pleasant humor.

So unharmed and unafraid
　Sat the swallow still and brooded,
Till the constant cannonade
Through the walls a breach had made,
　And the siege was thus concluded.

Then the army, elsewhere bent,
　Struck its tents as if disbanding,
Only not the emperor's tent,
For he ordered, ere he went,
　Very curtly, "Leave it standing!"

So it stood there all alone,
　Loosely flapping, torn and tattered,
Till the brood was fledged and flown,
Singing o'er those walls of stone
　Which the cannon-shot had shattered.

The Two Angels

Two angels, one of Life and one of Death,
　Passed o'er our village as the morning broke;
The dawn was on their faces, and beneath,
　The sombre houses hearsed with plumes of smoke.

Their attitude and aspect were the same,
    Alike their features and their robes of white;
But one was crowned with amaranth, as with flame,
    And one with asphodels, like flakes of light.

I saw them pause on their celestial way;
    Then said I, with deep fear and doubt oppressed,
"Beat not so loud, my heart, lest thou betray
    The place where thy beloved are at rest!"

And he who wore the crown of asphodels,
    Descending, at my door began to knock,
And my soul sank within me, as in wells
    The waters sink before an earthquake's shock.

I recognized the nameless agony,
    The terror and the tremor and the pain,
That oft before had filled or haunted me,
    And now returned with threefold strength again.

The door I opened to my heavenly guest,
    And listened, for I thought I heard God's voice;
And, knowing whatsoe'er he sent was best,
    Dared neither to lament nor to rejoice.

Then with a smile, that filled the house with light,
    "My errand is not Death, but Life," he said;
And ere I answered, passing out of sight,
    On his celestial embassy he sped.

'T was at thy door, O friend! and not at mine,
    The angel with the amaranthine wreath,
Pausing, descended, and with voice divine,
    Whispered a word that had a sound like Death.

Then fell upon the house a sudden gloom,
    A shadow on those features fair and thin;
And softly, from that hushed and darkened room,
    Two angels issued, where but one went in.

All is of God! If he but wave his hand,
    The mists collect, the rain falls thick and loud,
Till, with a smile of light on sea and land,
    Lo! he looks back from the departing cloud.

Angels of Life and Death alike are his;
  Without his leave they pass no threshold o'er;
Who, then, would wish or dare, believing this,
  Against his messengers to shut the door?

DAYLIGHT AND MOONLIGHT

In broad daylight, and at noon,
Yesterday I saw the moon
Sailing high, but faint and white
As a school-boy's paper kite.

In broad daylight, yesterday,
I read a Poet's mystic lay;
And it seemed to me at most
As a phantom, or a ghost.

But at length the feverish day
Like a passion died away,
And the night, serene and still,
Fell on village, vale, and hill.

Then the moon, in all her pride,
Like a spirit glorified,
Filled and overflowed the night
With revelations of her light.

And the Poet's song again
Passed like music through my brain,
Night interpreted to me
All its grace and mystery.

THE JEWISH CEMETERY AT NEWPORT

How strange it seems! These Hebrews in their graves,
  Close by the street of this fair seaport town,
Silent beside the never-silent waves,
  At rest in all this moving up and down!

The trees are white with dust, that o'er their sleep
  Wave their broad curtains in the south-wind's breath,
While underneath such leafy tents they keep
  The long, mysterious Exodus of Death.

And these sepulchral stones, so old and brown,
  That pave with level flags their burial-place,
Seem like the tablets of the Law, thrown down
  And broken by Moses at the mountain's base.

The very names recorded here are strange,
  Of foreign accent, and of different climes;
. Alvares and Rivera interchange
  With Abraham and Jacob of old times.

"Blessed be God! for he created Death!"
  The mourners said, "and Death is rest and peace;"
Then added, in the certainty of faith,
  "And giveth Life that never more shall cease."

Closed are the portals of their Synagogue,
  No Psalms of David now the silence break,
No Rabbi reads the ancient Decalogue
  In the grand dialect the Prophets spake.

Gone are the living, but the dead remain,
  And not neglected; for a hand unseen,
Scattering its bounty, like a summer rain,
  Still keeps their graves and their remembrance green.

How came they here? What burst of Christian hate,
  What persecution, merciless and blind,
Drove o'er the sea—that desert desolate—
  These Ishmaels and Hagars of mankind?

They lived in narrow streets and lanes obscure,
  Ghetto and Judenstrass, in mirk and mire;
Taught in the school of patience to endure
  The life of anguish and the death of fire.

All their lives long, with the unleavened bread
  And bitter herbs of exile and its fears,
The wasting famine of the heart they fed,
  And slaked its thirst with marah of their tears.

Anathema maranatha! was the cry
  That ran from town to town, from street to street;
At every gate the accursed Mordecai
  Was mocked and jeered, and spurned by Christian
    feet.

Pride and humiliation hand in hand
  Walked with them through the world where'er they
    went;
Trampled and beaten were they as the sand,
  And yet unshaken as the continent.

For in the background figures vague and vast
  Of patriarchs and of prophets rose sublime,
And all the great traditions of the Past
  They saw reflected in the coming time.

And thus forever with reverted look
  The mystic volume of the world they read,
Spelling it backward, like a Hebrew book,
  Till life became a Legend of the Dead.

But ah! what once has been shall be no more!
  The groaning earth in travail and in pain
Brings forth its races, but does not restore,
  And the dead nations never rise again.

OLIVER BASSELIN [1]

In the Valley of the Vire
  Still is seen an ancient mill,
With its gables quaint and queer,
  And beneath the window-sill,
      On the stone,
      These words alone:
"Oliver Basselin lived here."

Far above it, on the steep,
  Ruined stands the old Château;
Nothing but the donjon-keep
  Left for shelter or for show.
      Its vacant eyes
      Stare at the skies,
Stare at the valley green and deep.

[1] Oliver Basselin, the *"Père joyeux du Vaudeville,"* flourished in the fifteenth century, and gave to his convivial songs the name of his native valleys, in which he sang them, Vaux-de-Vire. This name was afterwards corrupted into the modern *Vaudeville.*

Once a convent, old and brown,
   Looked, but ah! it looks no more,
From the neighboring hillside down
   On the rushing and the roar
      On the stream
      Whose sunny gleam
Cheers the little Norman town.

In that darksome mill of stone,
   To the water's dash and din,
Careless, humble, and unknown,
   Sang the poet Basselin
      Songs that fill
      That ancient mill
With a splendor of its own.

Never feeling of unrest
   Broke the pleasant dream he dreamed;
Only made to be his nest,
   All the lovely valley seemed;
      No desire
      Of soaring higher
Stirred or fluttered in his breast.

True, his songs were not divine;
   Were not songs of that high art,
Which, as winds do in the pine,
   Find an answer in each heart;
      But the Mirth
      Of this green earth
Laughed and revelled in his line.

From the alehouse and the inn,
   Opening on the narrow street,
Came the loud, convivial din,
   Singing and applause of feet,
      The laughing lays
      That in those days
Sang the poet Basselin.

In the castle, cased in steel,
   Knights, who fought at Agincourt,
Watched and waited, spur on heel;

But the poet sang for sport
    Another clang,
    Songs that rang
Songs that lowlier hearts could feel.

In the convent, clad in gray,
    Sat the monks in lonely cells,
Paced the cloisters, knelt to pray,
    And the poet heard their bells;
        But his rhymes
        Found other chimes,
Nearer to the earth than they.

Gone are all the barons bold,
    Gone are all the knights and squires,
Gone the abbot stern and cold,
    And the brotherhood of friars;
        Not a name
        Remains to fame,
From those mouldering days of old!

But the poet's memory here
    Of the landscape makes a part;
Like the river, swift and clear,
    Flows his song through many a heart;
        Haunting still
        That ancient mill,
In the Valley of the Vire.

VICTOR GALRBAITH [1]

Under the walls of Monterey
At daybreak the bugles began to play,
    Victor Galbraith!
In the mist of the morning damp and gray,
These were the words they seemed to say:
    "Come forth to thy death,
    Victor Galbraith!"

---

[1] This poem is founded on fact. Victor Galbraith was a bugler in a company of volunteer cavalry; and was shot in Mexico for some breach of discipline. It is a common superstition among soldiers, that no balls will kill them unless their names are written on them. The old proverb says, "Every bullet has its billet."

Forth he came, with a martial tread;
Firm was his step, erect his head;
  Victor Galbraith,
He who so well the bugle played,
Could not mistake the words it said;
   "Come forth to thy death,
   Victor Galbraith!"

He looked at the earth, he looked at the sky,
He looked at the files of musketry,
  Victor Galbraith!
And he said, with a steady voice and eye,
"Take good aim; I am ready to die!"
   Thus challenges death
   Victor Galbraith.

Twelve fiery tongues flashed straight and red,
Six leaden balls on their errand sped;
  Victor Galbraith
Falls to the ground, but he is not dead;
His name was not stamped on those balls of lead,
   And they only scath
   Victor Galbraith.

Three balls are in his breast and brain,
But he rises out of the dust again,
  Victor Galbraith!
The water he drinks has a bloody stain;
"O kill me, and put me out of my pain!"
   In his agony prayeth
   Victor Galbraith.

Forth dart once more those tongues of flame,
And the bugler has died a death of shame,
  Victor Galbraith!
His soul has gone back to whence it came,
And no one answers to the name,
   When the Sergeant saith,
   "Victor Galbraith!"

Under the walls of Monterey
By night a bugle is heard to play,
  Victor Galbraith!

Through the mist of the valley damp and gray
The sentinels hear the sound and say,
    "That is the wraith
    Of Victor Galbraith!"

MY LOST YOUTH

Often I think of the beautiful town
    That is seated by the sea;
Often in thought go up and down
The pleasant streets of that dear old town,
    And my youth comes back to me.
        And a verse of a Lapland song
        Is haunting my memory still:
    "A boy's will is the wind's will,
And the thoughts of youth are long, long thoughts."

I can see the shadowy lines of its trees,
    And catch, in sudden gleams,
The sheen of the far-surrounding seas,
And islands that were the Hesperides
    Of all my boyish dreams.
        And the burden of that old song,
        It murmurs and whispers still:
    "A boy's will is the wind's will,
And the thoughts of youth are long, long thoughts."

I remember the black wharves and the slips,
    And the sea-tides tossing free:
And Spanish sailors with bearded lips,
And the beauty and mystery of the ships,
    And the magic of the sea.
        And the voice of that wayward song
        Is singing and saying still:
    "A boy's will is the wind's will,
And the thoughts of youth are long, long thoughts."

I remember the bulwarks by the shore,
    And the fort upon the hill;
The sunrise gun, with its hollow roar,
The drum-beat repeated o'er and o'er,

And the bugle wild and shrill. ·
   And the music of that old song
   Throbs in my memory still:
"A boy's will is the wind's will,
And the thoughts of youth are long, long thoughts."

I remember the sea-fight far away,[1]
   How it thundered o'er the tide!
And the dead captains, as they lay
In their graves, o'erlooking the tranquil bay,
   Where they in battle died.
   And the sound of that mournful song
   Goes through me with a thrill:
"A boy's will is the wind's will,
And the thoughts of youth are long, long thoughts."

I can see the breezy dome of groves,
   The shadows of Deering's Woods;
And the friendships old and the early loves
Come back with a Sabbath sound, as of doves
   In quiet neighborhoods.
   And the verse of that sweet old song,
   It flutters and murmurs still:
"A boy's will is the wind's will,
And the thoughts of youth are long, long thoughts."

I remember the gleams and glooms that dart
   Across the schoolboy's brain;
The song and the silence in the heart,
That in part are prophecies, and in part
   Are longings wild and vain.
   And the voice of that fitful song
   Sings on, and is never still:
"A boy's will is the wind's will,
And the thoughts of youth are long, long thoughts."

There are things of which I may not speak;
   There are dreams that cannot die;
There are thoughts that make the strong heart weak,
And bring a pallor into the cheek,

[1] This was the engagement between the Enterprise and Boxer, off the harbor of Portland, in which both captains were slain. They were buried side by side, in the cemetery on Mountjoy.

And a mist before the eye.
  And the words of that fatal song
  Come over me like a chill:
"A boy's will is the wind's will,
And the thoughts of youth are long, long thoughts."

Strange to me now are the forms I meet
  When I visit the dear old town;
But the native air is pure and sweet,
And the trees that o'ershadow each well-known street,
  As they balance up and down,
    Are singing the beautiful song,
    Are sighing and whispering still:
"A boy's will is the wind's will,
And the thoughts of youth are long, long thoughts."

And Deering's Woods are fresh and fair,
  And with joy that is almost pain
My heart goes back to wander there,
And among the dreams of the days that were,
  I find my lost youth again.
    And the strange and beautiful song,
    The groves are repeating it still:
"A boy's will is the wind's will,
And the thoughts of youth are long, long thoughts."

THE ROPEWALK

In that building, long and low,
With its windows all a-row,
  Like the port-holes of a hulk,
Human spiders spin and spin,
Backward down their threads so thin
  Dropping, each a hempen bulk.

At the end, an open door;
Squares of sunshine on the floor
  Light the long and dusky lane;
And the whirring of a wheel,
Dull and drowsy, makes me feel
  All its spokes are in my brain.

As the spinners to the end
Downward go and reascend,
    Gleam the long threads in the sun;
While within this brain of mine
Cobwebs brighter and more fine
    By the busy wheel are spun.

Two fair maidens in a swing,
Like white doves upon the wing,
    First before my vision pass;
Laughing, as their gentle hands
Closely clasp the twisted strands,
    At their shadow on the grass.

Then a booth of mountebanks,
With its smell of tan and planks,
    And a girl poised high in air
On a cord, in spangled dress,
With a faded loveliness,
    And a weary look of care.

Then a homestead among farms,
And a woman with bare arms
    Drawing water from a well;
As the bucket mounts apace,
With it mounts her own fair face,
    As at some magician's spell.

Then an old man in a tower,
Ringing loud the noontide hour,
    While the rope coils round and round
Like a serpent at his feet,
And again, in swift retreat,
    Nearly lifts him from the ground.

Then within a prison-yard,
Faces fixed, and stern, and hard,
    Laughter and indecent mirth;
Ah! it is the gallows-tree!
Breath of Christian charity,
    Blow, and sweep it from the earth!

Then a schoolboy, with his kite
Gleaming in a sky of light,
    And an eager, upward look;
Steeds pursued through lane and field;
Fowlers with their snares concealed
    And an angler by a brook.

Ships rejoicing in the breeze,
Wrecks that float o'er unknown seas,
    Anchors dragged through faithless sand;
Sea-fog drifting overhead,
And, with lessening line and lead,
    Sailors feeling for the land.

All these scenes do I behold,
These, and many left untold,
    In that building long and low;
While the wheel goes round and round,
With a drowsy, dreamy sound,
    And the spinners backward go.

The Golden Mile-Stone

Leafless are the trees; their purple branches
    Spread themselves abroad, like reefs of coral,
        Rising silent
In the Red Sea of the Winter sunset.

From the hundred chimneys of the village,
Like the Afreet in the Arabian story,
        Smoky columns
Tower aloft into the air of amber.

At the window winks the flickering fire-light;
Here and there the lamps of evening glimmer,
        Social watch-fires
Answering one another through the darkness.

On the hearth the lighted logs are glowing,
And like Ariel in the cloven pine tree
        For its freedom
Groans and sighs the air imprisoned in them.

By the fireside there are old men seated,
Seeing ruined cities in the ashes,
    Asking sadly
Of the Past what it can ne'er restore them.

By the fireside there are youthful dreamers,
Building castles fair, with stately stairways,
    Asking blindly
Of the Future what it cannot give them.

By the fireside tragedies are acted
In whose scenes appear two actors only,
    Wife and husband,
And above them God the sole spectator.

By the fireside there are peace and comfort,
Wives and children, with fair, thoughtful faces,
    Waiting, watching
For a well-known footstep in the passage.

Each man's chimney is his Golden Mile-stone;
Is the central point, from which he measures
    Every distance
Through the gateways of the world around him.

In his farthest wanderings still he sees it;
Hears the talking flame, the answering night-wind,
    As he heard them
When he sat with those who were, but are not.

Happy he whom neither wealth nor fashion,
Nor the march of the encroaching city,
    Drives an exile
From the hearth of his ancestral homestead.

We may build more splendid habitations,
Fill our rooms with paintings and with sculptures,
    But we cannot
Buy with gold the old associations!

CATAWBA WINE

This song of mine
Is a Song of the Vine,
To be sung by the glowing embers
Of wayside inns,
When the rain begins
To darken the drear Novembers.

It is not a song
Of the Scuppernong,
From warm Carolinian valleys,
Nor the Isabel
And the Muscadel
That bask in our garden alleys.

Nor the red Mustang,
Whose clusters hang
O'er the waves of the Colorado,
And the fiery flood
Of whose purple blood
Has a dash of Spanish bravado.

For richest and best
Is the wine of the West,
That grows by the Beautiful River;
Whose sweet perfume
Fills all the room
With a benison on the giver.

And as hollow trees
Are the haunts of bees,
For ever going and coming;
So this crystal hive
Is all alive
With a swarming and buzzing and humming.

Very good in its way
Is the Verzenay,
Or the Sillery soft and creamy;
But Catawba wine
Has a taste more divine,
More dulcet, delicious, and dreamy.

There grows no vine
By the haunted Rhine,
By Danube or Guadalquivir,
Nor an island or cape,
That bears such a grape
As grows by the Beautiful River.

Drugged is their juice
For foreign use,
When shipped o'er the reeling Atlantic,
To rack our brains
With the fever pains,
That have driven the Old World frantic.

To the sewers and sinks
With all such drinks,
And after them tumble the mixer;
For a poison malign
Is such Borgia wine,
Or at best but a Devil's Elixir.

While pure as a spring
Is the wine I sing,
And to praise it, one needs but name it;
For Catawba wine
Has need of no sign,
No tavern-bush to proclaim it.

And this Song of the Vine,
This greeting of mine,
The winds and the birds shall deliver
To the Queen of the West,
In her garlands dressed,
On the banks of the Beautiful River.

Santa Filomena [1]

Whene'er a noble deed is wrought,
Whene'er is spoken a noble thought,
Our hearts, in glad surprise,
To higher levels rise.

[1] "At Pisa the church of San Francisco contains a chapel dedicated
lately to Santa Filomena; over the altar is a picture, by Sabatelli,

The tidal wave of deeper souls
Into our inmost being rolls,
    And lifts us unawares
    Out of all meaner cares.

Honor to those whose words or deeds
Thus help us in our daily needs,
    And by their overflow
    Raise us from what is low!

Thus thought I, as by night I read
Of the great army of the dead,
    The trenches cold and damp,
    The starved and frozen camp,—

The wounded from the battle-plain
In dreary hospitals of pain,
    The cheerless corridors,
    The cold and stony floors.

Lo! in that house of misery
A lady with a lamp I see
    Pass through the glimmering gloom,
    And flit from room to room.

And slow, as in a dream of bliss,
The speechless sufferer turns to kiss
    Her shadow, as it falls
    Upon the darkening walls.

As if a door in heaven should be
Opened and then closed suddenly,
    The vision came and went,
    The light shone and was spent.

On England's annals, through the long
Hereafter of her speech and song,
    That light its rays shall cast
    From portals of the past.

representing the Saint as a beautiful, nymph-like figure, floating down
from heaven, attended by two angels bearing the lily, palm, and
javelin, and beneath, in the foreground, the sick and maimed, who are
healed by her intercession."—MRS. JAMESON, *Sacred and Legendary
Art,* II. 298.

A Lady with a Lamp shall stand
In the great history of the land,
    A noble type of good,
    Heroic womanhood.

Nor even shall be wanting here
The palm, the lily, and the spear,
    The symbols that of yore
    Saint Filomena bore.

THE DISCOVERER OF THE NORTH CAPE

A LEAF FROM KING ALFRED'S OROSIUS

Othere, the old sea-captain,
    Who dwelt in Helgoland,
To King Alfred, the Lover of Truth,
Brought a snow-white walrus-tooth,
    Which he held in his brown right hand.

His figure was tall and stately,
    Like a boy's his eye appeared;
His hair was yellow as hay,
But threads of a silvery gray
    Gleamed in his tawny beard.

Hearty and hale was Othere,
    His cheek had the color of oak;
With a kind of laugh in his speech,
Like the sea-tide on a beach,
    As unto the King he spoke.

And Alfred, King of the Saxons,
    Had a book upon his knees,
And wrote down the wondrous tale
Of him who was first to sail
    Into the Arctic seas.

"So far I live to the northward,
    No man lives north of me;
To the east are wild mountain-chains,
And beyond them meres and plains;
    To the westward all is sea.

"So far I live to the northward,
    From the harbor of Skeringes-hale,
If you only sailed by day,
With a fair wind all the way,
    More than a month would you sail.

"I own six hundred reindeer,
    With sheep and swine beside;
I have tribute from the Finns,
Whalebone and reindeer-skins,
    And ropes of walrus-hide.

"I ploughed the land with horses,
    But my heart was ill at ease,
For the old seafaring men
Came to me now and then,
    With their sagas of the seas;—

"Of Iceland and of Greenland,
    And the stormy Hebrides,
And the undiscovered deep;—
I could not eat nor sleep
    For thinking of those seas.

"To the northward stretched the desert,
    How far I fain would know;
So at last I sallied forth,
And three days sailed due north,
    As far as the whale-ships go.

"To the west of me was the ocean,
    To the right the desolate shore,
But I did not slacken sail
For the walrus or the whale,
    Till after three days more.

"The days grew longer and longer,
    Till they became as one,
And southward through the haze
I saw the sullen blaze
    Of the red midnight sun.

"And then uprose before me,
  Upon the water's edge,
The huge and haggard shape
Of that unknown North Cape,
  Whose form is like a wedge.

"The sea was rough and stormy,
  The tempest howled and wailed,
And the sea-fog, like a ghost,
Haunted that dreary coast,
  But onward still I sailed.

"Four days I steered to eastward,
  Four days without a night:
Round in a fiery ring
  Went the great sun, O King,
  With red and lurid light."

Here Alfred, King of the Saxons,
  Ceased writing for a while;
And raised his eyes from his book,
With a strange and puzzled look,
  And an incredulous smile.

But Othere, the old sea-captain,
  He neither paused nor stirred,
Till the King listened, and then
Once more took up his pen,
  And wrote down every word.

"And now the land," said Othere,
  "Bent southward suddenly,
And I followed the curving shore
And ever southward bore
  Into a nameless sea.

"And there we hunted the walrus,
  The narwhale, and the seal;
Ha! 't was a noble game!
And like the lightning's flame
  Flew our harpoons of steel.

"There were six of us all together,
  Norsemen of Helgoland;
In two days and no more
We killed of them threescore,
  And dragged them to the strand!"

Here Alfred the Truth-Teller
  Suddenly closed his book,
And lifted his blue eyes,
With doubt and strange surmise
  Depicted in their look.

And Othere the old sea-captain
  Stared at him wild and weird,
Then smiled, till his shining teeth
Gleamed white from underneath
  His tawny, quivering beard.

And to the King of the Saxons,
  In witness of the truth,
Raising his noble head,
He stretched his brown hand, and said,
  "Behold this walrus-tooth!"

DAYBREAK

A wind came up out of the sea,
And said, "O mists, make room for me."

It hailed the ships, and cried, "Sail on,
Ye mariners, the night is gone."

And hurried landward far away,
Crying, "Awake! it is the day."

It said unto the forest, "Shout!
Hang all your leafy banners out!"

It touched the wood-bird's folded wing,
And said, "O bird, awake and sing."

And o'er the farms, "O chanticleer,
Your clarion blow; the day is near."

It whispered to the fields of corn,
"Bow down, and hail the coming morn."

It shouted through the belfry-tower,
"Awake, O bell! proclaim the hour."

It crossed the churchyard with a sigh,
And said, "Not yet! in quiet lie."

THE FIFTIETH BIRTHDAY OF AGASSIZ

MAY 28, 1857

It was fifty years ago
  In the pleasant month of May,
In the beautiful Pays de Vaud,
  A child in its cradle lay.

And Nature, the old nurse, took
  The child upon her knee,
Saying: "Here is a story-book
  Thy Father has written for thee.

"Come, wander with me," she said,
  "Into regions yet untrod;
And read what is still unread
  In the manuscripts of God."

And he wandered away and away
  With Nature, the dear old nurse,
Who sang to him night and day
  The rhymes of the universe.

And whenever the way seemed long,
  Or his heart began to fail,
She would sing a more wonderful song,
  Or tell a more marvellous tale.

So she keeps him still a child,
  And will not let him go,
Though at times his heart beats wild
  For the beautiful Pays de Vaud;

Though at times he hears in his dreams
  The Ranz des Vaches of old,
And the rush of mountain streams
  From glaciers clear and cold;

And the mother at home says, "Hark!
   For his voice I listen and yearn;
It is growing late and dark,
   And my boy does not return!"

CHILDREN

Come to me, O ye children!
   For I hear you at your play,
And the questions that perplexed me
   Have vanished quite away.

Ye open the eastern windows,
   That look towards the sun,
Where thoughts are singing swallows
   And the brooks of morning run.

In your hearts are the birds and the sunshine,
   In your thoughts the brooklet's flow,
But in mine is the wind of Autumn
   And the first fall of the snow.

Ah! what would the world be to us
   If the children were no more?
We should dread the desert behind us
   Worse than the dark before.

What the leaves are to the forest,
   With light and air for food,
Ere their sweet and tender juices
   Have been hardened into wood,—

That to the world are children;
   Through them it feels the glow
Of a brighter and sunnier climate
   Than reaches the trunks below.

Come to me, O ye children!
   And whisper in my ear
What the birds and the winds are singing
   In your sunny atmosphere.

For what are all our contrivings,
  And the wisdom of our books,
When compared with your caresses,
  And the gladness of your looks?

Ye are better than all the ballads
  That ever were sung or said;
For ye are living poems,
  And all the rest are dead.

SANDALPHON

Have you read in the Talmud of old,
In the Legends the Rabbins have told
  Of the limitless realms of the air,—
Have you read it,—the marvellous story
Of Sandalphon, the Angel of Glory,
  Sandalphon, the Angel of Prayer?

How, erect, at the outermost gates
Of the City Celestial he waits,
  With his feet on the ladder of light,
That, crowded with angels unnumbered,
By Jacob was seen, as he slumbered
  Alone in the desert at night?

The Angels of Wind and of Fire
Chaunt only one hymn, and expire
  With the song's irresistible stress;
Expire in their rapture and wonder,
As harp-strings are broken asunder
  By music they throb to express.

But serene in the rapturous throng,
Unmoved by the rush of the song,
  With eyes unimpassioned and slow,
Among the dead angels, the deathless
Sandalphon stands listening breathless
  To sounds that ascend from below;—

From the spirits on earth that adore,
From the souls that entreat and implore
  In the fervor and passion of prayer;

From the hearts that are broken with losses,
And weary with dragging the crosses
   Too heavy for mortals to bear.

And he gathers the prayers as he stands,
And they change into flowers in his hands,
   Into garlands of purple and red;
And beneath the great arch of the portal,
Through the streets of the City Immortal
   Is wafted the fragrance they shed.

It is but a legend, I know,—
A fable, a phantom, a show,
   Of the ancient Rabbinical lore;
Yet the old mediæval tradition,
The beautiful, strange superstition,
   But haunts me and holds me the more.

When I look from my window at night,
And the welkin above is all white,
   All throbbing and panting with stars,
Among them majestic is standing
Sandalphon the angel, expanding
   His pinions in nebulous bars.

And the legend, I feel, is a part
Of the hunger and thirst of the heart,
   The frenzy and fire of the brain,
That grasps at the fruitage forbidden,
The golden pomegranates of Eden,
   To quiet its fever and pain.

EPIMETHEUS

OR THE POET'S AFTERTHOUGHT

Have I dreamed? or was it real,
   What I saw as in a vision,
When to marches hymeneal
In the land of the Ideal
   Moved my thought o'er Fields Elysian?

What! are these the guests whose glances
  Seemed like sunshine gleaming round me?
These the wild, bewildering fancies,
That with dithyrambic dances
  As with magic circles bound me!

Ah! how cold are their caresses!
  Pallid cheeks, and haggard bosoms!
Spectral gleam their snow-white dresses,
And from loose, dishevelled tresses
  Fall the hyacinthine blossoms!

O my songs! whose winsome measures
  Filled my heart with secret rapture!
Children of my golden leisures!
Must even your delights and pleasures
  Fade and perish with the capture?

Fair they seemed, those songs sonorous,
  When they came to me unbidden;
Voices single, and in chorus,
Like the wild birds singing o'er us
  In the dark of branches hidden.

Disenchantment! Disillusion!
  Must each noble aspiration
Come at last to this conclusion,
Jarring discord, wild confusion,
  Lassitude, renunciation?

Not with steeper fall nor faster,
  From the sun's serene dominions,
Not through brighter realms nor vaster,
In swift ruin and disaster,
  Icarus fell with shattered pinions!

Sweet Pandora! dear Pandora!
  Why did mighty Jove create thee
Coy as Thetis, fair as Flora,
Beautiful as young Aurora,
  If to win thee is to hate thee?

No, not hate thee! for this feeling
    Of unrest and long resistance
Is but passionate appealing,
A prophetic whisper stealing
    O'er the chords of our existence.

Him whom thou dost once enamor,
    Thou, beloved, never leavest;
In life's discord, strife, and clamor,
Still he feels thy spell of glamour;
    Him of Hope thou ne'er bereavest.

Weary hearts by thee are lifted,
    Struggling souls by thee are strengthened,
Clouds of fear asunder rifted,
Truth from falsehood cleansed and sifted,
    Lives, like days in summer, lengthened!

Therefore art thou ever dearer,
    O my Sibyl, my deceiver!
For thou makest each mystery clearer,
And the unattained seems nearer,
    When thou fillest my heart with fever!

Muse of all the Gifts and Graces!
    Though the fields around us wither,
There are ampler realms and spaces,
Where no foot has left its traces:
    Let us turn and wander thither!

THE CHILDREN'S HOUR

Between the dark and the daylight,
    When the night is beginning to lower,
Comes a pause in the day's occupations,
    That is known as the Children's Hour.

I hear in the chamber above me
    The patter of little feet,
The sound of a door that is opened
    And voices soft and sweet.

From my study I see in the lamplight,
    Descending the broad hall stair,
Grave Alice, and laughing Allegra
    And Edith with golden hair.

A whisper, and then a silence:
    Yet I know by their merry eyes
They are plotting and planning together
    To take me by surprise.

A sudden rush from the stairway,
    A sudden raid from the hall!
By three doors left unguarded
    They enter my castle wall!

They climb up into my turret
    O'er the arms and back of my chair;
If I try to escape, they surround me;
    They seem to be everywhere.

They almost devour me with kisses,
    Their arms about me entwine,
Till I think of the Bishop of Bingen
    In his Mouse-Tower on the Rhine!

Do you think, O blue-eyed banditti,
    Because you have scaled the wall,
Such an old moustache as I am
    Is not a match for you all!

I have you fast in my fortress,
    And will not let you depart,
But put you down into the dungeon
    In the round-tower of my heart.

And there will I keep you forever,
    Yes, forever and a day,
Till the walls shall crumble to ruin,
    And moulder in dust away!

ENCELADUS

Under Mount Etna he lies,
   It is slumber, it is not death;
For he struggles at times to arise,
And above him the lurid skies
   Are hot with his fiery breath.

The crags are piled on his breast,
   The earth is heaped on his head;
But the groans of his wild unrest,
Though smothered and half suppressed,
   Are heard, and he is not dead.

And the nations far away
   Are watching with eager eyes;
They talk together and say,
"To-morrow, perhaps to-day,
   Enceladus will arise!"

And the old gods, the austere
   Oppressors in their strength,
Stand aghast and white with fear
At the ominous sounds they hear,
   And tremble, and mutter, "At length!"

Ah me! for the land that is sown
   With the harvest of despair!
Where the burning cinders, blown
From the lips of the overthrown
   Enceladus, fill the air.

Where ashes are heaped in drifts
   Over vineyard and field and town,
Whenever he starts and lifts
His head through the blackened rifts
   Of the crags that keep him down.

See, see! the red light shines!
   'T is the glare of his awful eyes!
And the storm-wind shouts through the pines
Of Alps and of Apennines,
   "Enceladus, arise!"

THE CUMBERLAND

At anchor in Hampton Roads we lay,
   On board of the Cumberland, sloop-of-war;
And at times from the fortress across the bay
    The alarum of drums swept past,
     Or a bugle blast
   From the camp on the shore.

Then far away to the south uprose
   A little feather of snow-white smoke,
And we knew that the iron ship of our foes
    Was steadily steering its course
     To try the force
   Of our ribs of oak.

Down upon us heavily runs,
   Silent and sullen, the floating fort;
Then comes a puff of smoke from her guns,
    And leaps the terrible death,
     With fiery breath,
   From each open port.

We are not idle, but send her straight
   Defiance back in a full broadside!
As hail rebounds from a roof of slate,
    Rebounds our heavier hail
     From each iron scale
   Of the monster's hide.

"Strike your flag!" the rebel cries,
In his arrogant old plantation strain.
"Never!" our gallant Morris replies;
    "It is better to sink than to yield!"
     And the whole air pealed
   With the cheers of our men.

Then, like a kraken huge and black,
   She crushed our ribs in her iron grasp!
Down went the Cumberland all a wrack,
    With a sudden shudder of death,
     And the cannon's breath
   For her dying gasp.

Next morn, as the sun rose over the bay,
   Still floated our flag at the main mast-head.
Lord, how beautiful was Thy day!
     Every waft of the air
     Was a whisper of prayer,
   Or a dirge for the dead.

Ho! brave hearts that went down in the seas!
   Ye are at peace in the troubled stream,
Ho! brave land! with hearts like these,
     Thy flag, that is rent in twain,
     Shall be one again,
   And without a seam!

SNOW-FLAKES

Out of the bosom of the Air,
   Out of the cloud-folds of her garments shaken,
Over the woodlands brown and bare,
   Over the harvest-fields forsaken,
     Silent, and soft, and slow
     Descends the snow.

Even as our cloudy fancies take
   Suddenly shape in some divine expression,
Even as the troubled heart doth make
   In the white countenance confession,
     The troubled sky reveals
     The grief it feels.

This is the poem of the air,
   Slowly in silent syllables recorded;
This is the secret of despair,
   Long in its cloudy bosom hoarded,
     Now whispered and revealed
     To wood and field.

A DAY OF SUNSHINE

O gift of God! O perfect day:
Whereon shall no man work, but play;
Whereon it is enough for me,
Not to be doing, but to be!

Through every fibre of my brain,
Through every nerve, through every vein,
I feel the electric thrill, the touch
Of life, that seems almost too much.

I hear the wind among the trees
Playing celestial symphonies:
I see the branches downward bent,
Like keys of some great instrument.

And over me unrolls on high
The splendid scenery of the sky,
Where through the sapphire sea the sun
Sails like a golden galleon,

Towards yonder cloud-land in the West,
Towards yonder Islands of the Blest,
Whose steep sierra far uplifts
Its craggy summits white with drifts.

Blow, winds! and waft through all the rooms
The snow-flakes of the cherry-blooms!
Blow, winds! and bend within my reach
The fiery blossoms of the peach!

O Life and Love! O happy throng
Of thoughts, whose only speech is song!
O heart of man! canst thou not be
Blithe as the air is, and as free?

SOMETHING LEFT UNDONE

Labor with what zeal we will,
    Something still remains undone,
Something uncompleted still
    Waits the rising of the sun.

By the bedside, on the stair,
    At the threshold, near the gates,
With its menace or its prayer,
    Like a mendicant it waits;

Waits, and will not go away;
　　Waits, and will not be gainsaid;
By the cares of yesterday
　　Each to-day is heavier made;

Till at length the burden seems
　　Greater than our strength can bear,
Heavy as the weight of dreams,
　　Pressing on us everywhere.

And we stand from day to day,
　　Like the dwarfs of times gone by,
Who, as Northern legends say,
　　On their shoulders held the sky.

WEARINESS

O little feet! that such long years
Must wander on through hopes and fears,
　　Must ache and bleed beneath your load;
I, nearer to the wayside inn
Where toil shall cease and rest begin,
　　Am weary, thinking of your road!

O little hands! that, weak or strong,
Have still to serve or rule so long,
　　Have still so long to give or ask;
I, who so much with book and pen
Have toiled among my fellow-men,
　　Am weary, thinking of your task.

O little hearts! that throb and beat
With such impatient, feverish heat,
　　Such limitless and strong desires;
Mine that so long has glowed and burned,
With passions into ashes turned,
　　Now covers and conceals its fires.

O little souls! as pure and white
And crystalline as rays of light
　　Direct from heaven, their source divine;

Refracted through the mist of years,
How red my setting sun appears,
How lurid looks this soul of mine!

NUREMBERG

In the valley of the Pegnitz, where across broad meadow-lands
Rise the blue Franconian mountains, Nuremberg, the ancient,
    stands.

Quaint old town of toil and traffic, quaint old town of art
    and song,
Memories haunt thy pointed gables, like the rooks that round
    them throng:

Memories of the Middle Ages, when the emperors, rough and
    bold,
Had their dwelling in thy castle, time-defying, centuries old;

And thy brave and thrifty burghers boasted, in their uncouth
    rhyme,
That their great imperial city stretched its hand through every
    clime.[1]

In the courtyard of the castle, bound with many an iron band
Stands the mighty linden planted by Queen Cunigunde's hand;

On the square the oriel window, where in old heroic days
Sat the poet Melchior singing Kaiser Maximilian's praise.[2]

Everywhere I see around me rise the wondrous world of Art:
Fountains wrought with richest sculpture standing in the com-
    mon mart;

[1] *That their great imperial city stretched its hand through every
clime.* An old popular proverb of the town runs thus:—

> *"Nürnberg's Hand*
>   *Geht durch alle Land."*
>
> Nuremberg's hand
>   Goes through every land.

[2] *Sat the poet Melchior singing Kaiser Maximilian's praise.* Melchior
Pfinzing was one of the most celebrated German poets of the sixteenth
century. The hero of his *Teuerdank* was the reigning emperor, Maximilian; and the poem was to the Germans of that day what the
Orlando Furioso was to the Italians. Maximilian is mentioned before
in the *Belfry of Bruges.*

And above cathedral doorways saints and bishops carved in
    stone,
By a former age commissioned as apostles to our own.

In the church of sainted Sebald sleeps enshrined his holy
    dust,[1]
And in bronze the Twelve Apostles guard from age to age
    their trust;

In the church of sainted Lawrence stands a pix of sculpture
    rare,[2]
Like the foamy sheaf of fountains, rising through the painted
    air.

Here, when Art was still religion, with a simple, reverent heart,
Lived and labored Albrecht Dürer, the Evangelist of Art;

Hence in silence and in sorrow, toiling still with busy hand,
Like an emigrant he wandered, seeking for the Better Land.

Emigravit is the inscription on the tombstone where he lies;
Dead he is not,—but departed,—for the artist never dies.

Fairer seems the ancient city, and the sunshine seems more
    fair,
That he once has trod its pavement, that he once has breathed
    its air!

Through these streets so broad and stately, these obscure and
    dismal lanes,
Walked of yore the Mastersingers, chanting rude poetic
    strains.

[1] *In the church of sainted Sebald sleeps enshrined his holy dust.*
The tomb of Saint Sebald, in the church which bears his name, is one
of the richest works of art in Nuremberg. It is of bronze, and was
cast by Peter Vischer and his sons, who labored upon it thirteen
years. It is adorned with nearly one hundred figures, among which
those of the Twelve Apostles are conspicuous for size and beauty.

[2] *In the church of sainted Lawrence stands a pix of sculpture rare.*
This pix, or tabernacle for the vessels of the sacrament, is by the
hand of Adam Kraft. It is an exquisite piece of sculpture in white
stone, and rises to the height of sixty-four feet. It stands in the choir,
whose richly-painted windows cover it with varied colors.

From remote and sunless suburbs, came they to the friendly
    guild,
Building nests in Fame's great temple, as in spouts the swal-
    lows build.

As the weaver plied the shuttle, wove he too the mystic rhyme,
And the smith his iron measures hammered to the anvil's
    chime;

Thanking God, whose boundless wisdom makes the flowers
    of poesy bloom
In the forge's dust and cinders, in the tissues of the loom.
Here Hans Sachs, the cobbler-poet, laureate of the gentle
    craft,
Wisest of the Twelve Wise Masters,[1] in huge folios sang and
    laughed.

But his house is now an ale-house, with a nicely sanded floor
And a garland in the window, and his face above the door;

Painted by some humble artist, as in Adam Puschman's song,[2]
As the old man gray and dove-like, with his great beard white
    and long.

And at night the swart mechanic comes to drown his cark and
    care,
Quaffing ale from pewter tankards, in the master's antique
    chair.

---

[1] *Wisest of the Twelve Wise Masters.* The Twelve Wise Masters
was the title of the original corporation of the Mastersingers. Hans
Sachs, the cobbler of Nuremberg, though not one of the original
Twelve, was the most renowned of the Mastersingers, as well as the
most voluminous. He flourished in the sixteenth century; and left behind him thirty-four folio volumes of manuscript, containing two
hundred and eight plays, one thousand and seven hundred comic
tales, and between four and five thousand lyric poems.

[2] *As in Adam Puschman's song.* Adam Puschman, in his poem on
the death of Hans Sachs, describes him as he appeared in a vision:—

        "An old man,
    Gray and white, and dove-like,
    Who had, in sooth, a great beard,
    And read in a fair, great book,
    Beautiful, with golden clasps."

Vanished is the ancient splendor, and before my dreamy eye
Wave these mingling shapes and figures, like a faded tapestry.

Not thy Councils, not thy Kaisers, win for thee the world's regard;
But thy painter, Albrecht Dürer, and Hans Sachs, thy cobbler-
bard.

Thus, O Nuremberg, a wanderer from a region far away,
As he paced thy streets and court-yards, sang in thought his
careless lay:

Gathering from the pavement's crevice, as a floweret of the
soil,
The nobility of labor,—the long pedigree of toil.

Modern Library of the World's Best Books

COMPLETE LIST OF TITLES IN

THE MODERN LIBRARY

*For convenience in ordering
please use number at right of title*